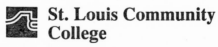 **St. Louis Community College**

Forest Park
Florissant Valley
Meramec

Instructional Resources
St. Louis, Missouri

# IMAGES OF SAVAGES

In recent times major efforts have been made to eliminate racial prejudice, but there is plenty of evidence that it still survives. Gustav Jahoda demonstrates how deeply rooted western perceptions going back more than a thousand years are still feeding racial prejudice today. In *Images of Savages* he explains how beliefs about monstrous humanoid man-eaters in classical antiquity and 'wild men of the woods' in the Middle Ages influenced the manner in which early explorers such as Columbus viewed the 'savages' they encountered.

Another early tradition was the 'ape-likeness' of savages, and especially blacks, coupled with notions about their unbridled sexuality. This persisted through the ages, reaching its culmination during the nineteenth century, when it gained scientific respectability. Lasting well into the twentieth century, its remnants are far from being extinct in popular culture.

This highly original socio-historical contextualization will be invaluable to scholars of psychology, sociology and anthropology, and to all those interested in the sources of racial prejudice.

**Gustav Jahoda** is Emeritus Professor of Psychology at the University of Strathclyde. A pioneer of cross-cultural fieldwork, his previous publications include *Psychology and Anthropology* (1982), *Acquiring Culture* (1988) and *Crossroads between Culture and Mind* (1992).

# IMAGES OF SAVAGES

Ancients roots of modern prejudice
in western culture

*Gustav Jahoda*

London and New York

First published 1999
by Routledge
11 New Fetter Lane, London EC4P 4EE

Simultaneously published in the USA and Canada
by Routledge
29 West 35th Street, New York, NY 10001

© 1999 Gustav Jahoda

Typeset in Baskerville by
Keystroke, Jacaranda Lodge, Wolverhampton
Printed and bound in Great Britain by
Biddles Ltd, Guildford and King's Lynn

*British Library Cataloguing in Publication Data*
A catalogue record for this book is available from the British Library

*Library of Congress Cataloging in Publication Data*
Jahoda, Gustav.
Images of savages : ancient roots of modern prejudice in western
culture / Gustav Jahoda.
Includes bibliographical references and index.
1. Ethnocentricism. 2. Prejudices. 3. Racism. I. Title.
GN495.8.J34     1998
305.8–dc21     98–11795

ISBN 0–415–17952–1 (hbk)
ISBN 0–415–18855–5 (pbk)

FOR
FIONA, JEAN, ROBERT, STEPHEN, AND . . . ?

# CONTENTS

*List of illustrations*                                    ix
*Preface*                                                  xi
*Acknowledgements*                                         xx

1  Introduction                                            1

**PART I**
**From Renaissance to Enlightenment**                      **13**

2  The savage Americans                                    15

3  The savage Africans                                     26

4  The puzzle of apes and men                              36

**PART II**
**Animality and beastly man-eating**                       **51**

5  The 'Negro' and the ape                                 53

6  Towards scientific racism                               63

7  On the animality of savages                             75

8  Cannibalism at issue                                    97

9  The fascinating horror                                  113

**PART III**

## The image of the savage as child-like    **129**

10  From ancestor to child                                           131

11  Rescuing the 'benighted savage': missionaries and colonial
    administrators                                                   141

12  Why savages are child-like: 'arrested development' and the
    'biogenetic law'                                                 152

13  Heads I win, tails you lose: from 'recapitulation' to
    'neoteny'                                                        164

14  How child-likeness lingered in 20th-century psychology           178

**PART IV**

## Perspectives and interpretations    **195**

15  Images mirrored at the popular level                             197

16  The relativity of images                                        214

17  The continuity of images                                        229

    Postscript: The images as symptoms and supports of
    racism                                                          243

    *Notes*                                                         249
    *References and further reading*                                258
    *Author index*                                                  281
    *Subject index*                                                 288

# ILLUSTRATIONS

## Figures

| | | |
|---|---|---|
| 1.1 | Representations dating from the thirteenth century of some of the 'monstrous races' | 3 |
| 1.2 | Fifteenth-century representation of a 'Wild Man' and a 'Wild Woman' | 6 |
| 2.1 | Disgusting African food habits: eating raw intestines | 17 |
| 2.2 | A typical representation of 'cruel Indians' | 21 |
| 4.1 | Rape of a black woman by an ape | 37 |
| 4.2 | Eighteenth-century representation of aquatic humanoids | 39 |
| 4.3 | Examples of Linnean types: a Troglodyte and a Pygmy | 40 |
| 6.1 | A classical Greek profile juxtaposed by Virey with those of a 'Negro' and an ape | 71 |
| 6.2 | Camper's illustration of 'facial angles' | 72 |
| 7.1 | The 'Hottentot Venus' as an object of curiosity | 80 |
| 7.2 | Vogt's attempted demonstration of the similarity between the skulls of 'Negroes' and European 'idiots' | 84 |
| 7.3 | Illustration from a racist American book published early in the present century | 91 |
| 8.1 | Sixteenth-century engraving of a Tupinamba cannibal feast | 103 |
| 9.1 | Posed photograph dating from about 1890, purporting to show 'Fijian cannibals' | 113 |
| 9.2 | Drawing of an old woman by Schweinfurth | 119 |
| 9.3 | Schweinfurth's nasty caricatures of African women | 119 |
| 9.4 | 'Cannibal' joke | 124 |
| 11.1 | 'Fetish worship' in Ashanti and the Belgian Congo | 144 |
| 15.1 | A stuffed Bechuana tribesman | 209 |
| 15.2 | Members of Parliament on the terrace of the House of Commons with a pathetic group of Pygmies | 212 |
| P.1 | *Punch* cartoon depicting Africans 'aping' Europeans | 246 |

## Tables

8.1  Frequencies of various themes in 16th-century German literature
     on the 'New World'                                              101
12.1 Developmental phases according to Romanes                        163

# PREFACE

Many years ago I was on a boat travelling to West Africa, where I was due to take up a post as the first psychologist at what was then the University College of the Gold Coast (now the University of Ghana). I was joining a department headed by a distinguished African scholar, the late Kofi Busia. My fellow passengers ranged from novices like myself to a number of 'Old Coasters' who had spent a considerable part of their lives in West Africa. Among the latter were commercial agents and artisans, who generally seemed content to get back to a setting where their social status was considerably higher than it would have been back in Britain. Beneath the outward bonhomie, however, there was an unease about the changes then taking place: the Gold Coast had been granted internal self-government, which meant that Africans would move into more responsible positions.

What many among them appeared to dread, though seldom giving voice to it explicitly, was having to serve under an African superior. Instead, they exchanged numerous anecdotes about the ineptitude and childishness of their African subordinates, to whom they sometimes referred as 'black monkeys' or 'baboons'. One evening, well tanked up, they discussed sex, and even after all this time I distinctly recall the precise words of one of the group: 'I wouldn't touch any of them black bitches with a barge-pole.' I was then naive enough to be astonished on subsequently seeing that same man one night in Accra with a beautiful African girl, in a posture suggestive of intimacy.

Although this was not the first, and certainly not the last occasion when I heard these offensive labels bandied about, they were seldom expressed with such strength of feeling, and that is why I recall the event so vividly. However, at the time I saw all this as simply a manifestation of intense prejudice, and gave it little further thought.

My experience in West Africa brought home to me the powerful effects of cultural influences, and shook my faith in the conventional natural science model for psychology. I began to do what was to become known as 'cross-cultural psychology', and later moved even further away towards 'cultural psychology' (cf. Cole 1996; Shweder 1990). In the course of preparing a study of the historical precursors of this distinctive alternative approach (Jahoda 1993), I immersed myself in late 18th- and 19th-century writings on psychological topics. It was intriguing to come across numerous descriptions of savages, strikingly reminiscent of those used by my fellow-travellers on the boat in relation to Africans; and similar not merely as regards the derogatory terms applied, but also in the emotional tone in which they were voiced. Certain characterizations, notably those of savages as ape-like or child-like, recurred quite regularly. This led me to the realization that there must be a deeper social and psychological significance to such labelling, which I wanted to understand. I began by looking for studies that might enlighten me, with only limited success. It became clear that if I wanted to learn more about the ideas and feelings which generated such images, and the functions they served, I would have to pursue the matter myself; and this I determined to do.

There exists of course a vast body of modern anthropological and historical literature more or less relevant to my theme. It concerns relationships between Europeans and those non-Europeans originally known as 'savages', later in slightly less uncomplimentary terms as 'primitives'. However, as far as I have been able to ascertain, few of the authors looked at the issues from the particular perspective adopted here. Hence it is difficult for me to comply with the usual practice of indicating other books covering similar ground. For some aspects of the present work it would be an enormous list, and those from whom I have borrowed are of course acknowledged in the text. As already mentioned, I have not come across any that share exactly the same objectives. One which may appear to do so is Sinclair's (1977) *The savage: a history of misunderstanding*. Although its descriptive content overlaps to some extent with that of the present work, the sub-title indicates that its conceptual orientation is very different. Attributing the ways Europeans perceived savages to 'misunderstanding' is a little like calling a miscarriage of justice a 'clerical error' – failing to appreciate the great complexity of the processes involved.

There are also some books whose titles are liable to suggest that they might be germane to the present theme, for instance, Kuklick's (1991) *The savage within*; but it actually deals with the history of anthropological ideas, the title being metaphorical. By contrast, *The wild man within*, edited by Dudley and Novak (1972), contains several fine essays that are highly pertinent. In particular, the introductory piece by Hayden White is a penetrating discussion of the concept of 'wildness'. Two other books which provided me with inspiration were Tinland's (1968) *L'homme sauvage*, and another edited by Poliakov (1975) entitled *Hommes et bêtes: entretiens sur le racisme*. None of these, however, was informed by the psychological orientation that guided my efforts.

The work involved the collection of a mass of material, much of it at second hand, but a good deal was also taken from original sources. The dual strategy employed in seeking to organize all this into meaningful patterns should be at least briefly outlined. One approach was to consider the manner in which, from antiquity onwards, reports of encounters between Europeans and savages were received by theologians, philosophers, and later scientists; their interpretations of such reports; the speculations and theories about the nature of savages to which the reports gave rise, and the forms in which these ideas filtered down to the public at large. The complementary approach, integrated as far as possible with the first, examines how pre-existing myths, doctrines or theories influenced the perceptions of first-hand observers and subsequent secondary interpretations. Some of these themes have been extensively studied by historians of ideas, to whom I am of course greatly indebted. As will become apparent, I drew freely on their work, though not necessarily agreeing with their interpretations. This is because, with few exceptions, historians' purposes did not coincide with mine; and often my use of their work was confined to extracting relevant bits of information from the broader context in which they were embedded.

As regards anthropology, modern theories are discussed only in relation to the specific issue of cannibalism. Otherwise the concern is chiefly with its pre-decessors, namely 19th-century physical anthropology, 'craniology' and early ethnography. There is no clear borderline between the latter and reports by explorers, travellers, missionaries and colonial administrators down the centuries, all of which yielded important information on how savages were viewed.

Since the orientation of the work is, at least in a broad sense, psychological, I should state my position in this respect, which differs somewhat from that of the mainstream. As already mentioned, I attribute greater weight than the majority of my colleagues to cultural and socio-historical influences on psychological functioning, though such a stance is currently gaining ground. Moreover, like some anthropologists and historians, and unlike most academic psychologists, I am sympathetic to some psychoanalytic tenets. This does not refer to attempts to 'psychoanalyse' historical figures, which usually seem to me quite unconvincing. But I agree with the anthropologist Clyde Kluckhohn, who maintained that psychoanalysis, unlike most academic psychology, has something useful to say about human nature in the raw. In my opinion the postulation of such general psychic processes as 'projection' is entirely defensible, as is the importance attributed to the sexual sphere. It would be difficult to account otherwise for the heavy emphasis on sexuality that stands out in European images of savages. This aspect is also the salient theme of Robert Young's (1995) *Colonial desire*, though he erred in thinking that 'no one bothered too much about the differences between races' (p. 92) before the end of the 18th century. By contrast, Anne McClintock (1995), whose orientation is feminist as well as neo-psychoanalytic, does not make this mistake. She shows that already since the Renaissance, America and Africa had become (in her felicitous phrase) 'porno-tropics for the European imagination' (p. 22). There is no doubt that profound emotions were involved in relations to 'the Other', which are insufficiently considered in most psychological accounts of race relations.

Yet there is a further question concerning ways in which current psychological theories of a more orthodox kind might contribute to an understanding of the images. Psychologists usually frame such problems in terms of the concept of 'prejudice', as I once did myself. However, what constitutes a prejudice is historically and culturally contingent, and as such the concept is not helpful when one is concerned with trans-historical continuity of images.

At this point an unavoidable one-sidedness should be noted: the project is trans-historical but not trans-cultural, since the images considered are Western. These constitute of course merely one side of a coin, the other being non-western peoples' images of Europeans – an issue only briefly touched upon in the text. Both in turn are sub-sets of a wider category, variously named 'ethnocentricity' or 'ethnocentrism', and rightly said by the anthropologist Ioan Lewis (1985, p. 15) to be 'the natural condition of mankind'. In an important sense the images are a consequence of this universal tendency to differentiate between one's own kind and what have come to be known as generic 'Others'. While anthropologists base their view on extensive observations, social psychologists have arrived at the same conclusion as a result of experimentation with small groups. One of those most prominent in this field was the late Henri Tajfel, whose main collaborator has recently summarized the implications of this work:

> [Tajfel] suggested that there was a psychological requirement that groups provide their members with a positive social identity and that the positive aspects of social identity were inherently comparative in nature, deriving from evaluative comparisons between groups. It followed that to provide positive social identity, groups needed to distinguish themselves positively from other groups and that intergroup comparisons were focused on the maintenance and establishment of positively valued distinctiveness for one's ingroup.
>
> (Turner 1996, p. 16)

Such an analysis provides a rationale for the psychological tendencies towards ethnocentrism, and the emphasis on group identity is also highly pertinent. It further indicates that 'Otherness' is a matter of degree, which in principle can range from Others just outside the immediate circle to the totally strange and alien.

LeVine and Campbell (1972) have surveyed theories of ethnocentrism and proposed a series of factors likely to affect the content and degree of accuracy of stereotyped images. Factors making for low accuracy are likely to include great spatial distance between the groups, and little interaction. This clearly applied to relations between Europeans and savages during most of past history. They further argued (p. 161), 'Those conditions leading to low accuracy of stereotypes will produce images or stereotypes most reflecting ingroup motives, wishes, guilts, fears and frustrations.' In other words, the content of images will often be primarily a function of the psychological make-up and needs of the perceivers rather than of the actual characteristics of those perceived.

As mentioned above, psychologists active in this general area usually see themselves as dealing with 'prejudice', which in turn results in the 'sterotyping' of out-groups. A 'stereotype' was defined by Allport (1954, p. 191) in his classical book on prejudice as 'an exaggerated belief associated with a category'.[1]

Psychologists seeking to isolate the causes of prejudice and stereotyping usually tend to focus on individual development and character, as influenced by prevailing socio-economic and cultural circumstances. Without questioning the relevance of such factors, it is the thesis of this book that important aspects of the problem can only be understood by a recognition of its historical origins. Most social psychological approaches either ignore history altogether, or at best pay lip-service to it. For instance, a recent comprehensive text confines itself to the following statement:

> History is important because it is this which bequeathes us our language, our cultural traditions and norms, and our social institutions. All these play a significant part in how we come to construe our world in terms of different social categories, the first and indispensable precursor to all forms of prejudice.
>
> (Brown 1995, p. 11)

One might question the latter claim, since in the more remote past the problem was often how the Others should be categorized. There was, for instance, much debate as to whether they were fully rational humans.

In spite of the fact that characterizations of the Other remained astonishingly uniform through the ages, I prefer not to call them 'stereotypes', since that is a rather narrowly cognitive concept. The term 'images' has the advantage of conveying a far richer range of meanings, encompassing not only perceptions and mental representations but also, importantly, feelings.

It was necessary to limit the scope of the inquiry, concentrating on the most salient images used in the representation of savages. These comprise 'animality', notably 'apishness', and cannibalism, which are the most ancient, most enduring, and carry the heaviest emotional load; they are at the exotic extreme of 'Otherness'. Next in salience was 'child-likeness', widespread from the mid-19th century to the first three decades of the 20th century. Furthermore, during the second half of the 19th century a whole network of images developed, linked at least tenuously to that of the savage. It included the lower classes, criminals, the mentally ill and even women. This cluster was generated by several biological theories then in vogue. What all these people were believed to have in common with the savage was that they were less evolved or 'degenerate'. This shows that during that period the images of savages were but one element, albeit a critical one, in efforts on the part of European middle-class males to define themselves in relation to Others. Moreover, in a wider perspective, ideas about human nature, and the place of humans in nature, were in the melting pot from the 18th century onwards; and the complex struggle to grapple with these issues is by no means over. This general topic is brilliantly illuminated with regard to 19th-century thought by Stocking's (1987) *Victorian anthropology*.

Since the overall stress is on the predominant pejorative images, something should be said about the 'noble savage'. This was an idealized image which flourished during the Enlightenment and coexisted with that of the 'ignoble' savage. The image of the 'noble' savage will only be considered in passing, since it served ideological rather than psychological functions. With the passing of the Enlightenment all savages, deprived of their nobility, came to be generally viewed as close to animality.

## Some caveats

Two major caveats are in order. First, the emphasis is on the most salient images listed above; these, to put it mildly, were unflattering. As a consequence, the overall picture of climates of opinion is somewhat biased. This is because scant attention is given to minorities who held relatively more positive images of savages, or at least repudiated the extreme negative ones. Second, although the ideas expressed by a number of key figures will be discussed in representative detail, the basic level of analysis still concerned images rather than the individuals holding them. Hence the impression conveyed of the attitudes of particular individuals may be misleading, since it was not feasible to always present a faithful portrayal of the range of views held by a person. The problem may be illustrated by taking the case of Voltaire. In his *Traité de métaphysique* ([1734][2] 1937) he begins by taking the perspective of a visitor from space looking at the various species (espèces) of man in a seemingly neutral fashion, concluding that they could not have descended from the same ancestor. Later in the same work he states: 'I see men who seem to me superior to these negroes, as the negroes are to the apes, and as the apes are to oysters' (p. 33). After some twenty years, in the *Essai sur les moeurs* (1756), he continues to argue in the same vein, seeking to show that climate could not account for race differences, since 'Negroes and Negresses, transported to colder countries, still produce there *animals* of their species' (p. 6; my emphasis). Yet in a subsequent section on 'savages' he asks the rhetorical question whether this refers to (French) rustics living in poor huts with their animals, speaking a dialect unintelligible to townspeople, having to pay heavy taxes, being press-ganged into armies and so on. Voltaire then contrasts these European savages with those others one calls savages who 'can produce for themselves all they need' and 'are infinitely superior to our own. . . . The peoples of America and Africa are free, and our savages do not even have the idea of liberty' (p. 23). One could of course interpret these divergent statements in terms of context and type of comparison, but for my purposes it would often be sufficient to note in such a case that Voltaire attributed animality to blacks.

For the period prior to the 18th century it is difficult to know the extent to which the images were held among various sections of the population. Increasingly ample evidence becomes available thereafter, though it was not possible to attempt a statistical study; this would be a major research enterprise in itself, one for which I am not equipped.

There is one further question requiring at least brief mention, and that concerns the 'truth' or otherwise of the images to be reviewed. There is no simple answer to this. In the 19th century it was believed to be a 'scientific truth' that savages, but not Europeans, are biologically close to apes; today we know that to be false. Or again, take the issue of sexuality, long thought to have been 'excessive' or even totally unrestrained among savages. If one takes as a standard the sexual behaviour prescribed by the church over the centuries, or Victorian official morality, then clearly many pre-literate peoples, though by no means all of them, enjoyed greater sexual freedom. But in comparison with the contemporary West, this would not be true. The only general statement one can reasonably make is that the image of the savage has long been grossly distorted, even though it was sometimes no more than a caricature, in the sense of a gross exaggeration of characteristic traits.

In sum, it will be apparent that this book cannot be claimed to constitute a piece of historical scholarship in the strict sense; nor, on the other hand, is it a mere excavation of quaint bits and pieces. It is perhaps best viewed as a kind of web, whose strands are drawn variously from the history of ideas, from 'psychohistory', from anthropology and from psychology. At the same time I have sought to avoid technical jargon, so that the general argument should be accessible to the non-specialized reader.

It has been rightly said that 'history is written for the consumption of contemporaries, and therefore carries with it judgements of the time in which it is written' (Rosa 1996, p. 355). In addition, as already noted, the standpoint from which the past is viewed here is that of a cultural psychologist, and others with a different background might have told a somewhat different story. However, it seems to me highly unlikely that the broad picture would be very dissimilar, or would challenge my conclusion that some historical images remain far from negligible influences in race relations at the close of the 20th century.

## The structure of the book

The organization is partly topical and partly chronological, since a purely chronological one would have been unwieldy and confusing. Throughout, an effort is made to interpret the phenomena described, and to indicate possible causal influences. Following an introduction dealing with early origins and some psychological aspects, the main body of the work consists of four parts. The first of these describes early images of American Indians and blacks, including an account of the doctrine of the 'Great Chain of Being' which dominated thought about the Others until at least the end of the 18th century. The onset of the Enlightenment also saw a flurry of speculation about the then uncertain boundary between humans and apes. The second and third parts are topic-oriented, with a roughly chronological sequence within each topic. The first two chapters of Part II document the shift from a 'philosophical' concern with the relationship between humans and apes towards the 'scientific' notion of savages, and especially blacks, as near-apes. In Chapter 3, 19th-century 'race' theories, being well known, are only touched upon, the emphasis being on their manifestations in terms of images of 'animality'. The persistence of these images, even in science, until well into the 20th century, is described. The remaining chapters of Part II are concerned with the image of cannibalism, including widespread beliefs about cannibals with tails. The modern debate as to the reality of cannibalism is reviewed, and it is shown that the image still has profound psychological significance.

Part III focuses on various aspects of the child image, beginning with the Enlightenment, which had conceived savagery as 'the childhood of humanity'. This subsequently underwent a radical transformation, when the savage as an individual came to be seen as child-like. The wide-ranging attributions of childish traits by various categories of Europeans, above all those connected with the colonies, are detailed. Subsequent chapters examine the several theories put forward to account for savage child-likeness, the so-called 'biogenetic law' being the most prominent and influential. The two final chapters of Part III analyse the reverberations of such ideas in the child psychologies of the 1920s and 1930s, and as such constitute a footnote to the history of child psychology.

Part IV is devoted to more general issues. Since much of the preceding material had been drawn from scholarly writings, or those of explorers or missionaries, it was necessary to show that the images were more widely diffused. Hence a survey is provided of the ways in which, from the 18th century onwards, the images came to be reflected and propagated at the popular level in literature, the press, exhibitions of savages and other forms of entertainment.

Chapter 16 covers a range of related themes, starting with a comparison of the different images. It is pointed out that the disparaging images did not necessarily result in corresponding behaviour: this was only possible when the Europeans were in positions of power over the savages, which was by no means invariably the case. The effects of secular changes are considered, which comprised two main types: initially the attribution of savagery remained relatively independent of skin pigmentation, so that more remote European peoples were thus regarded. This changed with the progressive transformations of western societies, which led to an increasingly sharp divergence between European and savage cultures.

Yet in spite of such radical changes the images remained remarkably constant. This is illustrated in the final chapter of Part IV, which critically reviews various theories seeking to account for the continuity. It also suggests that in the light of our knowledge of the close kinship between ourselves and apes, the continuity now takes a different form at the scientific level.

Finally, a short postscript spells out some implications of the broad thesis, especially as regards race relations.

## A note on style

It will have been observed from the above that I have not continued to place what are now offensive terms like 'savage' in inverted commas; doing so throughout would have been exceedingly cumbersome. More generally, the text abounds with politically incorrect designations. This is because it follows the usage current in the past, and changing such terms into more polite forms would be anachronistic.

Where the bibliographic references are to an original source in French or German, the translations are my own.

# ACKNOWLEDGEMENTS

Not for the first time I am indebted to Ioan Lewis, who commented on an early draft of the manuscript from an anthropological perspective. Among others who have helped with critical and constructive comments were Peter Collett, Albert Pepitone, and an anonymous reviewer. I am particularly grateful to Bernd Krewer who, as ever, went to great trouble in tracking down obscure German publications. Others who made useful suggestions, or drew my attention to relevant materials, include Gabriel Bertrand, Charles Romain Mbele, Graham Richards, Geneviève Vermes, Maurice McCullough and Fernando Vidal. Pierre Dasen not only provided generous hospitality in Geneva, but gave me the opportunity of trying out some of my ideas on his colleagues and students.

I should also like to acknowledge the invaluable assistance provided by the staff of several libraries, notably the British Library, the Bibliothèque Nationale in Paris, the Bibliothèque Publique et Universitaire in Geneva, the Staatsbibliotheken in Munich and Vienna, Cambridge and Glasgow University libraries, and last but certainly not least, that of my own university, notably Dr Cargill Thompson and Mr Allan, who dealt patiently and efficiently with my numerous requests.

Several of the study visits abroad were made possible by a grant from the Nuffield Foundation, for which I am grateful.

Finally, I am more than grateful to Andrea: during the years of struggle with the project, her moral support helped to sustain me.

# 1

# INTRODUCTION

Images of the Other, that strange, exotic, incomprehensible creature, feared, abhorred, and yet in some ways also envied, have run as a constant thread through the European past. The remote ancestry of the images dates back mainly to Greco-Roman and later Judaeo-Christian traditions. These were influential until the early modern period and, as will be shown in due course, there are writers who maintain that they remain so even at present. A psychological process will also be examined that helps to throw light on the manner in which these images affected the perception of savages.

## The 'monstrous' or 'Plinian' races

A conspectus of these strange races was provided by Pliny the Elder in the first century AD. Drawn in the main from Greek sources, it listed a bewildering array of humanoid creatures, far richer in their variety than the rather stereotyped modern representations of 'aliens' in science fiction. They included people without mouths who lived on smells, headless ones with eyes in their shoulders, others with the heads of dogs, and a race with only one foot, so large that it was used as a sunshade. Some of them probably had a realistic basis, such as the 'Bragmanni', wise men who lived in caves, whose name is likely to be a corruption of 'Brahman'. Similarly, 'Pygmies' had been reported in travel accounts by Herodotus. Of particular interest in the present context are the 'anthropophagi' or 'man-eaters', who in due course became known as 'cannibals'. As will be shown in detail later (Chapter 8), 'cannibalism' always remained a key symbol of savagery.

The 'monstrous races' were invariably said to live in remote places, but remoteness in the psychological as much as in the geographical sense. While some sources referred them to Asia or 'Ethiopia' (a term then applied to Africa), others located them in more distant parts of what we now know as 'Europe'. Thus in the 11th century a bishop, Adam of Bremen (?–1075), wrote an account of the inhabitants in his region and beyond (Adam of Bremen, trans. Tschan 1959). His characterizations of neighbouring peoples, although fanciful in parts, seem on the whole to be realistically based. Those living in the more northerly regions, however, were represented by Adam as 'monstrous races' (pp. 200–1):

In this sea there are also very many other islands, all infested by ferocious barbarians. . . . Likewise, round about the shore of the Baltic Sea, it is said, live the Amazons in what is now called the land of women. Some declare that these women conceive by sipping water. Some, too, assert that they are made pregnant by the merchants who pass that way, or by the men they hold captive in their midst, or by various monsters, which are not rare there. . . . And when these women come to give birth, if the offspring be of the male sex, they become Cynocephali; if of the feminine kind, they become most beautiful women. Living by themselves, the latter spurn consort with men and, if men come near, even drive them manfully away. The Cynocephali are men who have their heads on their breasts. They are often seen in Russia as captives and they voice their words in barks. . . . Palefaced, green, and macrobiotic, that is, long-lived men, called Husi, also live in those parts. Finally, there are those who are given the name of Anthropophagi and they feed on human flesh.

At that period there was as yet nothing like a 'European' identity, even in the weakest sense. The larger unit of which people felt themselves to be part was 'Christendom', as distinct from the infidel Muslims and the pagans; the latter included Scandinavians, Slavs, Magyars, and also the Celtic fringe of Welsh, Irish and Scots.

The following two centuries saw the beginnings of long-distance explorations, and the weird and wonderful beings allegedly encountered were described in terms of the Plinian races (see Figure 1.1). Among the travel reports which drew on that tradition, the best known was that of Sir John Mandeville.[1] It appeared around the middle of the 14th century, was translated into several languages and went through numerous editions. The flavour of its content may be exemplified by the following extract:

And in those isles are many manners of folk of divers conditions. In one of them is a manner of folk of great stature, as they were giants, horrible and foul to the sight; and they have but one eye, and that is in the midst of the forehead. They eat raw flesh and raw fish. In another isle are foul men of figure without heads, and they have eyes in either shoulder one, and their mouths are round shaped like a horseshoe, y-midst their breasts. In another isle are men without heads; and their eyes and their mouths are behind in their shoulders.

(Letts [1346?] 1953, Vol. 1, pp. 141/2)

It is believed that the above passage referred to the Andaman Islands, but the geography often remained somewhat nebulous. For instance, 'Aethiopes' (or 'burnt faces') were often indifferently located either in India or Africa.

2

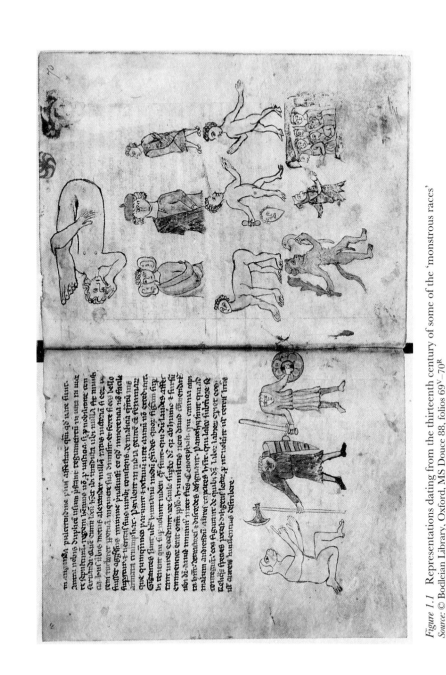

*Figure 1.1*  Representations dating from the thirteenth century of some of the 'monstrous races'
*Source:* © Bodleian Library, Oxford, MS Douce 88, folios 69ᵛ–70ᴿ

The records of such early explorations underwent a series of transformations. The perceptions of the travellers themselves were bound to be selective, and they interpreted much of what they saw in terms of their preconceptions. Nonetheless, realities are likely to have imposed some constraints, even though that left plenty of room for fanciful embroidery. Pigafetta, who had sailed with Magellan's first circumnavigation of the globe in the 15th century, returned from the Philippines after Magellan's death there and wrote an account of their adventures. In it he mentioned East Indians who were some eighteen inches high and had ears so long that at night one was used as a mattress and the other as a blanket.

When it came to the chroniclers who collected travellers' tales at second- or nth-hand, freedom to invent was extensive. As demonstrated in classical experiments by Bartlett (1932), culturally alien material comes to be assimilated in the process of transmission to the culturally familiar; and what was familiar at the time was the notion of 'monstrous races'. This is a point that will be further expanded below.

Let me now briefly turn to another aspect of the Greek tradition, which concerns such beings as satyrs, fauns, nymphs and sileni (wood gods). These were characterized by their unrestrained licentiousness – White (1978, p. 170) described them graphically as 'little more than ambulatory genitalia'. In the present context it is worth noting that there are strong indications of past confusions between the mythological satyr and a large monkey or gibbon, known to Pliny as 'satyrus'. This was probably the species which gave rise to the following description by Pliny:

> [T]he Choromandae are a savage and wild people; distinct voice and speech have they none, but in steed thereof, they keepe an horrible gnashing and hideous noise: rough they are and hairie all over their bodies, eies they have red like the houlets [owls] and toothed they be like dogs.
> (Plinius Secundus [AD 77] 1601, p. 156, cited in Dickason 1984, p. 73)

In 1699 Edward Tyson published his pioneering account of the dissection of a creature subsequently identified as a chimpanzee under the lengthy title: *Orang-Outang, sive Homo Sylvestris: or: the* ANATOMY *of a* PYGMIE *compared with that of a Monkey, an Ape and a Man. To which is added A Philological Essay Concerning the Pygmies, the Cynocephali, the Satyrs and Sphinges of the Ancients. Wherein it will appear that they are all either Apes or Monkeys, and not Men, as formerly pretended.* This was a significant event, to which I shall return below. Here it is necessary to note Tyson's argument that beliefs in the monstrous races, satyrs and other hybrid monsters had in fact all been the result of misconstruing monkeys or apes; the same, he maintained, was true of *homo sylvestris*, the 'Wild Man of the Woods', whose rather different antecedents will now be outlined.

## The 'Wild Man of the Woods'

The Greeks in their myths conceived of indiscriminate interbreedings between gods, humans and animals, so that any resulting abnormal species would not have seemed upsetting or even unduly astonishing; nor did they necessarily ascribe any moral deficiencies to such imagined creatures. The opposite was true of the ancient Hebrews, for whom interbreeding of different natural kinds was abhorrent, since they believed that it produced a wild and evil race of giants. The manner in which these ideas became, fatefully, linked with the name of Ham has been described by White (1978, p. 161):

> After the flood . . . evil and (therefore) wildness returned to the world, especially in the descendants of Noah's youngest son, Ham, who was cursed for revealing his father's nakedness. From Ham was descended . . . that breed of 'wild men' who combined Cain's rebelliousness with the size of the primal giants. They must also have been black, since, through etymological conflation, the Hebrews ran together word roots used to indicate the color black, the land of Egypt (i.e of bondage), the land of Canaan (i.e of pagan idolatry), the condition of accursedness (and, ironically, apparently the notion of fertility), with the proper name of Ham and its adjectival variations.

Gervase of Tilbury wrote around 1212: 'It is said that the "Aethiopians" descend from Cush, son of Ham, because the Hebraic word Cush is translated as "Aethiops" (cited in Medeiros 1985, p. 129). Much later the legend of Ham was seized upon as providing a biblical justification for the oppression of blacks. In early Christianity it led, probably through fusion with pre-Christian mythology, to the image of the 'Wild Man of the Woods' (see Figure 1.2). Saint Augustine identified Nimrod as a descendant of Ham and as responsible for the building of the tower of Babel and the subsequent fragmentation of humanity. Nimrod thus seems to have been one of the main sources of the myth of the Wild Man. This figure, also known as that of the 'Hairy Wild Man', gradually emerged in the literature and art of the Middle Ages and became common in European folklore by the end of the period. A savage creature of the woods, he was usually pictured with a body covered in hair excepting only his face, knees and elbows (the same applied to pictures of wild women, whose usually pendant breasts were also devoid of hair). The Wild Man was typically shown wielding a large stick or even a tree trunk, indicative of his brute strength (for descriptions of illustrations cf. Mason 1990). Living a solitary life apart from the company of bears and devils, he was devoid of speech and the use of reason. Knowing neither God nor morality he was a slave to his passions, and carried off women whom he not only raped but, according to Edmund Spenser's *Faerie Queene*, subsequently ate. The females were said to have an irrepressible desire to copulate with ordinary men. Both sexes were conceived as being acquainted with nature's secrets, close to but not quite animals.

*Figure 1.2*  Fifteenth-century representation of a 'Wild Man' and a 'Wild Woman'
*Source:* Copyright © Fitzwilliam Museum, University of Cambridge.

These figures embodied some of the features of the Plinian races, but in other respects resembled the satyr of antiquity with its horned forehead, goat-like lower body and a disproportionately large phallus. The satyr shared with the Wild Man its semi-animality and, above all, an unrestrained sexual appetite. Bernheimer (1952), who wrote an authoritative account of the image of the Wild Man, suggested that it constituted a Freudian projection of prohibited libidinal impulses; the erotic colouring is certainly pronounced. Accordingly, during the Middle Ages the myth, frowned upon by the ecclesiastical authorities, remained largely an oral tradition at the popular level. A change occurred during the Renaissance with its return to classical values, when wildness was sometimes perceived as a release from the fetters of civilization, a duality one encounters again in the Enlightenment dichotomy of the 'noble' versus 'ignoble' savage. It was also during the Enlightenment that serious philosophical and scientific discussions began concerning the relationship between animals, notably apes, and humans. In view of the crucial role played by the concept of 'animality' from the initial contacts with savages onwards, a preliminary outline of the background will be useful.

## 'Animality' and the symbolism of ape and child

Europeans, taking their own physical appearance and mode of life as the criteria of full humanity, found the savages wanting. Their different pigmentation, their nakedness, the kinds of foods they consumed (often thought to include human flesh) and other negatively regarded characteristics attributed to them were taken as indications of their *animality*. Over the centuries, one of the most common epithets applied to them was that of the 'beastly' savage. This was not merely a matter of casual labelling, for profound issues of the nature of humanity came to be raised, and in the early 19th century the great naturalist Cuvier was to provide scientific arguments for the greater animality of savages.

While savages were sometimes compared to several kinds of wild animals, for obvious reasons monkeys and apes greatly predominated. It should be mentioned at this point that long prevailing European ideas and feelings about animals are by no means universal. In many cultures, notably hunting-and-gathering ones, animals are believed to have souls and to be in close partnership with humans. Nor is this confined to non-literate cultures: in Japan it is precisely the monkey that is used 'as a metaphor for humans in relation to animals and as a metaphor for the Japanese in relation to foreigners' (Ohnuki-Tierny 1987, p. 7). In both European and Japanese cultures the monkey was situated at the borderline between humans and non-humans but was evaluated very differently, probably owing to contrasting religious traditions. In Japan the monkey was viewed historically as a shaman mediating between the Mountain Deity and humans, endowed with healing powers. In the Greco-Christian tradition the monkey was something of an anomaly, as will be documented later in more detail. Here it will be sufficient to mention that monkeys and apes resemble humans in many respects, yet are not humans, thereby occupying a marginal position between the two categories of humanity and animality.[2] Anthropologists have shown that such anomalies are apt to evoke strong feelings. For instance, Leach (1964, p. 39), who discussed the kind of verbal abuse where humans are called animal names, stated that 'it is the ambiguous categories that attract the maximum interest and the most intense feeling of taboo. The general theory is that taboo applies to categories which are anomalous with respect to clear-cut category oppositions'.

It may also be noted that there was support for the comparison of savages with monkeys and apes from popular folklore. In medieval illustrations the Wild Man of the Woods often looks very ape-like, and there is considerable overlap between the characteristics attributed to wild men and apes. The notions associated with the latter have been extensively documented by Janson (1952). From antiquity onwards, the similarity between humans and apes had not merely been recognized, but in the case of Aristotle and Galen even exaggerated.

Aristotle's description of intra-uterine development in *De Animalibus* referred to a progression 'from sperm, to a fungus-like shape, to that of an unshaped animal, to the shape of an ape, and finally – one stage before the fully human configuration of the fetus – to the shape of a Pygmy' (cited in Friedman 1981, p. 191). The Greeks, and subsequently the Romans, implicitly assumed the human-like nature of apes by attributing to them negative moral features (trickster, sycophant, hypocrite) and regarding them as physically repulsive and ugly – perhaps with a view to stressing the distinction between apes and humans in a context where they perceived close similarities. At any rate, given this image, and the uncertain categorization in classical literature of different species, it is not surprising that apes came to be associated with some of the mythical races, notably satyrs and cynocephali ('dog-heads'). It is clear that already at that stage the image of the ape carried a heavy if somewhat variable symbolic baggage.

With the spread of Christianity in Europe the ape came to be linked symbolically first with the devil, and later with sin. From the 14th century onwards the sin connected with the ape became more and more frequently that of carnal desire. This referred to some extent to female looseness, but primarily concerned males. Apes were supposed to have extraordinary potency, and by the 16th century the ape had become the emblem of unbridled sexuality. There were numerous tales of apes raping women, and here is an example dating back to the beginning of the 17th century. A woman shipwrecked on an island populated by apes was repeatedly raped by one of them; she had two children from this ape, and was eventually rescued by Portuguese sailors. The story was repeated by de Maillet in the 18th century, and many later ones were located either in Asia or the interior of Africa. Thomas Jefferson, the enlightened third president of the United States, not merely subscribed to this belief, but thought one could draw some lessons from it about a wish to mate with one's superiors: just as the orang-utan prefers black women to females of his own species, so blacks prefer whites. Cases of apes raping women were still occasionally reported as late as the 19th century.

While predatory sexuality was the main theme, there were other subsidiary ones. The ape also represented the image of the fool, and a prominent feature of that, stressed since antiquity, was a propensity to imitate slavishly. Such imitation was taken as indicating a lack of reason which was also supposed to characterize savages. As a rather extreme 19th-century example a French 'litterateur' may be cited, who maintained that his novel was not imaginary but faithfully based on travellers' accounts. Michiels (1853) described in full anatomical detail the supposedly close physical resemblances between Africans and anthropoid apes. In a footnote he cited a report of African women who picked the fleas from the head of a black chief and took pleasure in eating them. He commented: 'It is . . . not the ape that imitates man in Africa, but man who imitates the ape' (p. 114).[3]

This example illustrates the continuity of images, but, as will be shown below, this does not mean that they performed precisely the same psychological functions in every period. As far as the later Middle Ages were concerned, apes and such legendary creatures as the monstrous races, satyrs and the wild men of the woods were, in the Lévi-Straussian phrase, 'good to think'. They provided familiar categories and attributes with which to incorporate the strange Other into one's world view. As has been pointed out, notably by Mason (1990), the Other was to a large extent constructed rather than merely perceived. And in contrast to Lévi-Strauss, whose phrase referred mainly to cognition, the images were imbued with powerful feelings, usually though not invariably negative.

The trope of the 'child-likeness' of the savages to which I now turn had a somewhat different history. It does not seem to have been linked to medieval folk-lore, and was largely absent as long as contacts between Europeans and savages remained relatively transitory. Although applied occasionally from the conquests in the New World onwards, it did not really become widespread until the 19th-century colonial expansion.

The meaning of the trope of the child can be dealt with more briefly, since it did not carry quite such heavy symbolic baggage. Ever since Greco-Roman antiquity certain key attributes of childhood have remained relatively constant, though others have undergone significant variations. Prominent among the constants is the child's inability to handle its own affairs and consequent dependence. This is a function of its lack of understanding and reason – the child is still ignorant. Connected with this is a natural tendency to imitate others. The ancients also believed the child to be innocent, but this is a view that was denied by some Christian doctrines.

There is, it may be noted, a certain overlap between the images of apes and children. Both were viewed as being closer to nature than adult Europeans, imitative and lacking reason and morality. All these features have, either singly or more usually in combination, at various times formed part of the image of the savage. By the 19th century both the images of ape-likeness and child-likeness of savages had achieved roughly equal prominence. Moreover, they were often applied jointly to savages, regardless of the inherent contradictions that this entailed.

## The principle of 'familiarity'

How was it possible to identify newly encountered peoples with the 'monstrous races' or the equally mythical wild men of the woods or to compare them with animals and children? This is hard for us to understand nowadays, and calls for some explanation. The issue is of course a complex one, to which I shall return, but one interesting approach to the problem will be considered at this point.

It has long been noted that when people are faced with something strange they seek to make sense of it by relating it to something more familiar. Thus as early as the 18th century Vico's second axiom ran as follows: 'Whenever men can form no idea of distant and unknown things, they judge them by what is familiar and at hand' (cited in Lilla 1993, p. 133). In his theory of social representation, influenced by Bartlett, Moscovici has called this 'anchoring' and defined it as 'a process which draws something foreign and disturbing that intrigues us into our particular system of categories and compares it to the paradigm of a category which we think to be suitable' (Moscovici 1984, p. 29). A somewhat similar notion was subsequently put forward by Pagden (1993) in a context directly related to the present theme, namely the encounter between Europeans and Amerindians. Referring to it as 'the principle of attachment', he credited the great German explorer Alexander von Humboldt with its original formulation. Pagden's concept, judging from his examples, is broader than Moscovici's, extending to unwarranted inferences based on similarities of particular traits. For instance, he cites the reasoning of Ovideo, a 16th-century historiographer of the 'American Indies'. Ovideo noted that Thracians practised polygamy and sacrificed foreign visitors; the Amerindian Taino also practised polygamy, which led him to conclude (in the absence of any direct evidence) that the Taino must also be addicted to human sacrifice. Nonetheless, in its fundamentals the overlap between Moscovici's and Pagden's concepts is extensive, as may be gathered from the latter's summary:

> From Columbus to Humboldt the principle of attachment served to make the incommensurable seem commensurable. . . . Attachment allowed for the creation of an initial (if sometimes troubling) familiarity. It also allowed the discoverer to make some measure of classification. Above all, it allowed him to name, and by naming to take cognitive possession of what he had 'laid eyes on'.
>
> (Pagden 1993, p. 36)

Faced with the exotic and imcomprehensible, Europeans tended to interpret the Others in terms of familiar categories, such as the Plinian races or the wild men.

If the principle is general it should apply not just to Europeans, and it is not difficult to show that this was the case. When the Spanish conquistadores arrived at the court of the Mexican emperor Montezuma, he ordered human sacrifices to be made for them because he believed the strangers to be gods – a tragic misconception (Bitterli 1971, p. 91).[4] The Bakongo, who lived in what is now Zaire, called Europeans during the 19th century *ndundu*, their term for albinos. Moreover, they believed that Europeans are not born like themselves but emerged from water, where they went back to sleep at night; and sometimes they were regarded as ancestors who had come back (MacGaffey 1972).

These are examples of responses by people who have come into contact with Others who are radically different from themselves in physical appearance, language, customs and manners. They fell back on their cosmology in order to find a meaningful place for the strange Europeans who had penetrated their world.

There was, however, an asymmetry stemming from the fact that the Europeans usually arrived as explorers or conquerors. In both roles they almost invariably saw themselves as superior – as indeed they usually were, at least technically – and often came to be perceived as such by the Others. This enhanced the probability that Europeans would view them as less than fully human, more like animals or children, and accordingly treat them as such.

What I have called 'the principle of familiarity' has a seductive clarity and simplicity which is somewhat misleading. The simplicity is largely confined to cases like the one mentioned by Humboldt, where exotic plants were named by travellers after familiar ones to which they bore some resemblance, however slight. When it comes to European encounters with hitherto unknown peoples, there were always multiple ways in which they could be potentially categorized according to familiar templates. The kind of image of the Others that came to be constructed, on the basis of real or alleged 'facts' about them, will have been dependent on the prior background of ideas and values of the perceivers; and if these varied, so did the result of assimilation to the 'familiar'. It is only after images have become culturally conventionalized that more uniformity can be expected.

This may be illustrated in relation to a relatively minor episode that took place around the middle of the 14th century, and has been described by Fernandez-Armesto (1987). In the course of early Atlantic exploration, the Canary Islands were rediscovered (having been known in antiquity). The hitherto unknown savages found there aroused a great deal of speculative debate, with two groups adopting radically conflicting positions as a consequence of selectively empha-sizing different aspects of reports on the islanders. Prominent humanistic scholars focused on the nakedness, lack of interest in gold and silver and generally simple and seemingly idyllic way of life of the islanders. This led them to the belief that theirs was the innocence of the mythical 'Golden Age'. Others connected with the church and the temporal powers took a less rosy view. They were motivated to justify the conquest and subsequent conversion of the islanders. Accordingly, they stressed the seemingly repulsive aspects of the lives of the islanders which, it should be noted, were largely the obverse of the same coin. They were said to have flat faces like monkeys, to howl like dogs, to eat raw food and to observe bestial customs; among these was public sexual intercourse and the sharing of women, who allegedly gave birth like animals. This description embodied most of the features that were in due course to typify the image of the ape-like savage, with the single major exception of cannibalism. It is also worth noting that the generic term for Canarians later became *sylvestris fere homines*, or some similar version of wild men.

Generally speaking, the context of prevailing ideas and ideologies, including the state of scientific knowledge, powerfully affected varying interpretations of the nature of the savage. For instance, during the Enlightenment the idealized 'noble savage' represented a picture of closeness to nature, simplicity, freedom and robust health as a counterpoint to what were felt by some to be the evils of a corrupt civilization and lack of liberty. Others took a much less sanguine view of savage life, as will be shown in due course. In between there were mixed notions, like those of the cynical Voltaire. Having received a copy of Rousseau's *Discourse on the origin of inequality*, he acknowledged this in a typically caustic manner:

I have received your new book against the human race, and thank you for it. Never was such a cleverness used in the design to make us all stupid. One longs, on reading your book, to walk on all fours. But as I have lost that habit for more than sixty years, I feel unhappily the impossibility of resuming it. Nor can I embark on the search of the savages of Canada, because the maladies to which I am condemned render a European surgeon necessary to me; because war is going on in these regions; and because the example of our actions has made the savages as bad as ourselves.

(Cited in Russell 1946, p. 715)

In sum, the image of the savage was always refracted through lenses consisting of particular ideas, interests and values. These led sometimes to a favourable picture, but most of the time and for most Europeans it was one epitomized by such deprecatory images as that of ape-likeness. The story of all this will now be told in more detail, beginning with the American Indians.

# Part I

# FROM RENAISSANCE TO ENLIGHTENMENT

# 2

# THE SAVAGE AMERICANS

Compared with the repercussions of the voyages of Columbus and the Spanish conquest of America, the incident of the Canarians was insignificant. There is a vast literature on the topic, and only some aspects relevant to the present theme will be singled out here.

When Columbus embarked on his first voyage, belief in the Plinian races was still firm, and it is likely that he had read Mandeville's famous book of travels. At any rate, on reaching what he took to be the East Indies, Columbus confidently expected to come across specimens of monstrous races. In the course of this and subsequent voyages he took every opportunity of enquiring about them, and was rewarded with reports of anthropophagi, men with one eye, men with tails, amazons, giants and creatures with dogs' heads. Given the fact that communication with the Indians was difficult and largely conducted by means of gestures, it is evident that Columbus must have heard what he wanted to hear. Personally he recorded only having seen three sirens (who turned out not to be particularly beautiful), and later he admitted, with apparent regret, not having been able to establish the presence of several of the monstrous races; anthropophagy (man-eating), however, was regarded by Columbus and most of his successors as being widespread.

Although not regarded as monsters except for their alleged cannibalism, American Indians initially tended to be classed as 'wild men' and sometimes described as *homines sylvestres*. For the Bishop of Santa Marta in Columbia the Indians were 'not men with rational souls but wild men of the woods, for which reason they could retain no Christian doctrine, nor virtue nor any kind of learning' (cited in Pagden 1982, p. 23). This identification as 'wild men' resulted in Indians being commonly described and pictorially represented as 'hairy', in spite of protestations by first-hand observers such as Léry ([1578]1990), who had noted precisely the opposite. It was no coincidence that the 'hairy' Indians tended to be accused of extreme sexual licence; while much later, when it became generally known that they depilated themselves and the men had no beards, they came to be regarded as sadly lacking in libido. That these changes went in parallel is unlikely to have been just coincidence, since the sexual symbolism of hair has been well established in both European and non-European cultures.[1]

Regarding the Indians as 'wild men', sub-human and irrational and therefore incapable of being converted to Christianity suited those Spaniards who conquered vast areas of the New World. It meant an absence of constraints concerning the manner in which Indians could be treated. However, in 1537 Pope Paul III issued a famous Bull which condemned as heretical the opinion that the Indians were irrational and incapable of receiving the faith. This had little effect on the behaviour of the conquistadores, who had settled in the new lands and wanted to extend their domains. Their spokesmen in the homeland were pitted against critics who questioned the legitimacy of waging war against the Amerindians, of treating them cruelly and reducing them to slavery. The issues were widely and passionately debated in a manner not seen again until the Abolitionist Movement from the end of the 18th century. This is probably one of the reasons why American Indians became relatively more salient in European consciousness than Africans, remaining the prototypical savages until the 18th century.

Here it would not be relevant – nor would I be competent – to discuss the debate in general. The focus will be on the use of the tropes of animality and child-likeness, which means that the views cited will be in the main those of defenders of the colonists. Hence little will be said about Bartolomé de Las Casas and other champions of the Indians.

As previously mentioned, the actual word used was not 'savages' but 'barbarians' – until the 16th century the term 'savage' referred only to wild woodland. Much of the debate turned on the interpretations of the writings of Aristotle, who had seemed to equate *barbaroi* with 'natural' (i.e. innately determined) slaves. The views of a Scottish theologian, John Mair, were adduced by those who wanted to prove the natural inferiority of the Indians:

> These people [the inhabitants of the Antilles] live like beasts on either side of the equator . . . wherefore the first person to conquer them, justly rules over them because they are by nature slaves.
>
> (Cited in Pagden 1982, p. 38)

Mair's pronouncement carried weight because of his reputation as a theologian, and not because he had any special knowledge of the inhabitants of the New World. As has already been shown in relation to the Canarians, a more or less stereotypical image of savages was crystallizing around that period. It is reflected in the writings of the Dominican Tomas Ortiz, who sought to justify the ill-treatment of the Indians by listing their faults, deficiencies and sins. His list is so comprehensive that it will usefully serve as a kind of summary:

> On the mainland they eat human flesh. They are more licentious than any other people. Justice does not exist for them. They go entirely naked, have no respect of true love and virginity, and are stupid and thoughtless. . . . They are violent and thereby worsen their innate faults.

. . . They eat lice, spiders and worms which they eat raw wherever they find them.

(Cited in Todorov 1985, p. 182)

It was a portrait one finds repeated with minor variations over subsequent centuries, in relation not merely to American Indians, but to African blacks and savages in other parts of the world. The negative aspects of most of this litany are self-evident, but the broader implications of the reference to eating habits needs some explanation.

In the writings of European moralists about the deadly sins of the flesh, lechery and gluttony have usually been coupled. Nutrition is an even more fundamental biological need than sex, and both have always been socially regulated and heavily endowed with symbolic meaning. This applies particularly to the opposition of 'raw versus cooked', which constituted the topic of the first volume of Lévi-Strauss' *Mythologiques* (1964). Put very crudely, it corresponds roughly to the opposition of 'nature versus culture'. It was an ancient notion, subsequently taken up by Christian theology, that those who eat raw food are not civilized: according to Albertus Magnus (1200–80) all potential food, with the exception of milk, must be transformed before it becomes edible.

*Figure 2.1* Disgusting African food habits: tearing apart intestines and eating them raw
*Source:* Dapper (1670).

17

This image in medieval Europe of raw food as unsuitable for civilized people can be illustrated by Le Goff's (1985) analysis of the 12th-century story of a knight who, as a result of traumatic experiences, regressed to a state of savagery: he roamed the forests naked, nourishing himself from raw food. The English sailor Martin Frobisher (*c.* 1535–94) had this to say about the north-east American Indians whom he had encountered on his second voyage:

> If they for necessities sake stand in need of the premises, such grass as the Countrey yeeldeth they plucke up and eate, not deintily, or salletwise to allure their stomacks to appetite: but for necessities sake without salt, oyles or washing, like brute beasts devouring the same.
>
> (Cited in Pearce 1953, p. 5)

The fact that Indians ate raw insects aroused the suspicion that they had connections with the devil, who was also believed to have such filthy habits. It will be recalled that apes were symbolically linked with the devil as well as with lasciviousness; so there existed a complex of associations in European thought of the period, suggesting evil and animality. A great deal of this survived into the modern period. For instance, an article about food habits in a serious French journal in the mid-19th century contained the following passages:

> The Eskimo, the Fuegians and, more rarely, the Hottentots, eat raw meat with an altogether bestial gluttony.... The Fuegian devours anything he finds, rotten fish, great molluscs and octopuses that are entirely decomposed. The Australian eats reptiles raw.... These singular deviations from the habitual practices of civilization indicate that these nations have fallen to the last degree of mindlessness.
>
> (Anon 1854, p. 224)

The phrases 'bestial' and 'mindlessness' are of course strongly suggestive of mere animality attributed to these peoples.

Returning to the 16th-century Spanish detractors of the Indians, it is noteworthy that animality was one of the most common tropes. Domingo de Betanzos, a prominent Dominican missionary, literally regarded the Indians as animals possessing neither soul nor reason, though he retracted on his deathbed (Parry 1940). Gil Gregorio referred to Indians as 'talking animals', and Garcia de Loaysa regarded them as 'soulless parrots in human guise' (Pagden 1982, p. 93). Other prominent figures also held the opinion that the Indians 'are not truly humans, with a rational mind, but rather a third species of animal between human and ape' (O'Gorman 1941, p. 305). Hinojosa compared Indian languages to the cries of baboons (Pagden 1982, p. 183).[2]

Among the comparisons with children, Vitoria's was particularly scathing, and the reference to their diet is worth noting:

> Although these barbarians are not entirely lacking in judgement, they are little different from the feebleminded. . . . It would seem that for these barbarians the same applies as to the feebleminded, for they cannot govern themselves better than simple-minded idiots. They are not even better than beasts and wild animals, because they take neither more dainty nor better food than these. Their stupidity is much greater than that of the children or feebleminded of other peoples.
>
> (Cited in Todorov 1985, p. 181)

Another comment of a similar kind is particularly instructive, for it illustrates once again the role of far-fetched analogical reasoning in arriving at opinions about the Indians. Ovideo told a story about Queen Isabella, patroness of Columbus. On hearing from him that trees in the Indies had shallow roots because of heavy rainfall, she concluded that such a land must also produce shallow people, untruthful and inconstant. Ovideo praised Isabella's shrewdness, endorsing her inference by stating that 'these people of the Indies are very untruthful and of little firmness, like children of six or seven years old, or not even as reliable as them' (cited in Gerbi 1973, p. 40).

The most extensive set of negative characterizations of the Indians was put forward by Juan de Sepulveda, Las Casas' opponent in their great dispute. These were cast by Todorov (1985, p. 185) into a series of binary oppositions, among them the following:

Indians:Spaniards = children:adults = apes:humans

In view of the common use of animal tropes by detractors of the Indians, it may be noted that their defender, Las Casas, frequently employed them himself. Drawing on biblical imagery, he inverted the attributions. Thus he likened the Indians to ewes or gentle lambs, towards whom, he said, the Spaniards behaved like wild wolves, tigers or lions (Pelletier 1994).

Las Casas had employed such images to condemn Spanish attitudes and actions, while portraying the Indians as innocent victims. Similarly, for the conquistadores and their intellectual protagonists, likening Indians to children, apes or other animals was essentially a way of drawing attention to their alleged sub-humanity or at least inferiority, held to justify their treatment.

## The subsequent debate about the phenomenon of the New World

It was not only the inhabitants of the New World whom Europeans found puzzling, but the whole character of the continent, its flora and fauna being so vastly different from that of Europe. One explanation for this was suggested in the 16th century by Francis Bacon: America is a *young* continent where the flood happened later, drowning most of the people; that is why the population is so small, naked and barbarous. It accounts, too, for the wetness and humidity found in much of the continent, which Ovideo had stressed. Montaigne, who also regarded the New World as young, viewed it positively as closer to nature; this also applied to the savages, whom he compared favourably with Europeans.

In the middle of the 18th century the great naturalist Buffon took up the problem, starting from his realization that animals in America are not merely very different, but also generally weaker than those of the Old World. As a scientist who had abandoned simple creationism, Buffon advanced the hypothesis that America was young because it had more recently emerged from the ocean. This also accounted for the humidity and general unfavourableness of the climate, which in turn meant that larger animals could not develop, while 'colder' ones, notably insects, multiplied. This was supported by what he believed to be the fact that animals imported to America became, without exception, smaller there.

The bulk of Buffon's elaborate arguments were concerned with zoology, but he wanted to show that his general principles applied equally to the human inhabitants:

> For although the savage of the New World is of almost the same stature as the men of our world, that does not suffice for him to be an exception to the general rule of the reduction of living nature in the whole continent. The savage is feeble and small in his organs of generation; he has neither body hair nor beard, and no ardour for the female of his kind. Although lighter than the European, on account of his running more, he is nevertheless much less strong in body: he is also much less sensitive, and yet more fearful and more cowardly; he lacks vivacity, and is lifeless in his soul; the activity of his body is less an exercise or voluntary movement than an automatic reaction to his needs; take from him hunger and thirst, and you will destroy at the same time the active cause of all his movements; he will remain either standing there stupidly or recumbent for days at a time.
>
> (Cited in Gerbi 1973, p. 6)

Being few in number, and leading an 'animal-like existence', the Indians have made little or no impact on nature which remains in its wild state. In some passages Buffon took a more generous view, pointing out the special status of humans so that – unlike animals – the inhabitants of the New and Old Worlds were at least commensurable. He vacillated between several interpretations of the state of the humans, describing them variously as being degenerate or immature. Yet the burden of his thesis remained: humans in the New World are handicapped, in the same way and for the same reasons as animals.

The view that Americans were immature was categorically denied by the abbé Cornelius de Pauw, whose *Recherches philosophiques sur les Américains* was published in 1768, two years after Buffon's essay had appeared. For de Pauw the case of the

*Figure 2.2* A typical representation of 'cruel Indians'
Source: Don George Juan and Don Antoine de Ulloa, *Voyage Historique de l'Amerique Meridionale* (1792).

American Indians, whom he regarded as degenerates, was hopeless: 'they are like idiot children, incurably lazy and incapable of any mental progress whatsover' (Gerbi 1973, p. 55). De Pauw was very dogmatic, unwilling to let any inconvenient facts stand in the way of his arguments. Thus when a critic pointed to the high culture of the Incas, to which their remarkable architecture testified, he simply denied this, declaring that they only had crude little huts.

In spite of the many absurdities of de Pauw's harsh anti-Indian judgements, his writings set off a lengthy series of debates that reverberated well into the 19th century. Buffon, appalled by de Pauw's misuse of his ideas, changed his position towards a more positive stance on the Indians: they were certainly not degenerate, only immature. Writers with first-hand experience, including Thomas Jefferson, sought to refute de Pauw. Others, on the contrary, were persuaded. For instance, Kant, who had originally regarded the Indians as 'noble savages', described them as a 'semi-degenerate race' after having read de Pauw. Another 18th-century German scholar, Meiners (of whom more below), had this to say about them:

> The Americans are unquestionably the most depraved among all human, or human-like creatures of the whole earth, and they are not only much weaker than the Negroes, but also much more inflexible, harder, and lacking in feelings. Despite the fact that this communication

21

contains only a few traits of the terrible portrait of the bodily and moral nature of the Americans, one will nonetheless feel, and be astonished, that the inhabitants of a whole continent are so closely related to dumb animals.

(Meiners 1787, p. 230)

The debates about the nature of the Americans were pursued with intensity and passion by just about every prominent thinker of the period. They have been described in detail and penetratingly analysed in the fascinating work of Gerbi (1973). Here my modest purpose is merely to show how the views of de Pauw and his followers created a climate of opinion in which the American Indians came to be regarded as barely human. Obviously, after the creation of the United States, they were no longer referred to simply as 'the Americans'. Moreover, the detractors tended to focus more on the South American Indians, though this did not mean that North American Indians were held in much higher esteem.[3]

At the beginning of the 19th century the King of Bavaria sent an expedition to Brazil, which produced a lengthy report (von Spix and von Martius 1823, Vol. 1, pp. 377–8) in which they expressed regret at the *immaturity* of the Indians. They also presented a character sketch:

> The temperament of the Indians is as yet undeveloped and manifests itself as phlegm. All mental processes [Seelenkräfte], yes even the higher sensibility, appear as if in a state of paralysis. They live without reflection on the whole of creation, on the causes and inner connections of things, their senses directed only at self-preservation. . . . Cold and lazy even in family relationships, he follows animal instinct more than tender inclination, and his love for woman takes only the form of cruel jealousy; besides a thirst for revenge, this is the only passion whereby his atrophied soul can be torn from its dull indifference . . . he sleeps part of the day, plays when not hunting with his domestic animals, or gazes thoughtlessly in front of him.

They also commented on their small genitalia and, as appears from the above, implied scant interest in sex. The passage bears a striking resemblance to that previously cited from Buffon. One might have supposed that first-hand observers would explode some of the old myths; but in reality their accounts are no more accurate than those of writers like Buffon or de Pauw who had obtained all their information at second hand. As often happens they saw mainly what they had expected to see, and the reputation of the South American Indians as animal-like savages underwent little change. For example, as part of his first venture into *Völkerpsychologie*, Wilhelm Wundt gave examples of peoples at various stages of development of their morals and customs [sittliches Leben]. Among the lowest of the low were, for him, South Sea Islanders and South American Indians. This was his comment on the latter:

The forest Indians of South America, who are *sittlich* [in morality and customs] equally low, are at the same time so undeveloped in intellectual talent that one can hardly compare them with the other primitives [Naturvölker] considered here. One might well say of some of these hordes that they are not much more than apes endowed with language.
(Wundt 1863, Vol. 2, p. 452).[4]

North American Indians fared little better, being treated almost as vermin unless they happened to be useful as allies in the wars either against other Indian tribes or between whites. A 17th-century account of Indians as enemies described them as being 'like wolves, continually yelling and gaping for their prey'; they were called 'bloody and deceitful monsters' and 'perfect children of the devil' (cited in Marshall and Williams 1982, p. 189). An American writer at the end of the 18th century referred to them as 'the animals, vulgarly called Indians' (Brackenridge 1782, cited in Pearce 1953, p. 54). During the 19th century they were seen as an obstacle to the grand westward movement, driven from their territories, decimated in numerous battles, and the remainder progressively herded into reservations. The Indians were regarded as a dying race, having inevitably to be sacrificed to the advance of civilization. The great geologist Sir Charles Lyell wrote: 'few future events are more certain than the speedy extermination of the Indians of N. America and the savages of New Holland' (Lyell 1830–3, Vol. II, p. 56). Few seem to have disputed this, and there was nothing like the passionate debate that had divided the Spaniards. Hence there was no need to argue the inferiority of the Indians, which was largely taken for granted. Even though they were not overtly classed as 'animals' during the 19th century, they were certainly deprived of any civil rights and literally 'non-persons'. When in 1879 lawyers issued a writ of *habeas corpus* on behalf of some Indians, the United States attorney objected on the grounds that they were 'not persons within the meaning of the law of the United States' (Campbell 1989, p. 247). In the event the judge granted the writ, but the fact that the argument could be used is significant. It was not until the Indian Citizenship Act of 1924 that the worst aspects of their legal disabilities were removed.[5]

By the turn of the 20th century the 'child' label began to be applied again more frequently, but not specifically to the Indians: psychological theories had appeared which stressed similarities between children and all kinds of savages.

## Indians and other savages

The case of the American Indians was an outstanding example of European encounters with hitherto unknown peoples, showing how difficult it was for Europeans to fit them into their pre-existing world view. For at least two centuries the discourse about the Indians, and their pictorial representations, was laden with traditional images often grossly at variance with the physical reality of the Indians and their actual ways of life. The manner in which they came to be perceived, whether as irremediably sub-human or potentially improvable, was also to a considerable extent a function of the conflicting aims of different categories of Europeans; notably conquest and exploitation versus missionary efforts.

The present discussion focused mainly on the use of the child and animal/ape tropes to American Indians. Before leaving this topic I should therefore mention that several important studies have dealt, from differing standpoints, with the general problem of European images of Amerindians. I have already referred to Pagden (1993), who had named the 'principle of attachment', and who provided an insightful account of the interactions between Europeans and the people of the New World. Bucher (1981), basing herself on the illustrations accompanying an early book of voyages, undertook an intriguing Lévi-Straussian analysis of underlying European structures of thought. Among other things it explored, in much greater depth, the conceptual ramifications of diet, which I have briefly touched upon above. Most radical is the work of Mason (1990, p. 8), whose thesis is that '"America" is not seen through European eyes: it is constructed from European images of Europe's own repressed and outward projected Others'; and the task is therefore one of 'deconstruction' along the lines of Derrida. His discussion is frequently most illuminating, especially concerning the part played by the monstrous races in shaping early representations of the inhabitants of the New World, and the idea complexes that influenced debates about their nature. In the course of the 20th century the old image of the cruel and worthless savage has gradually become inverted and romanticized into that of the 'Native American'. They are now seen as having been brave, clean-living peoples whose practices were a model of environmental preservation. While these new images have been extensively exploited commercially,[6] there is little indication that they have led to a greater understanding of, or respect for, Indian cultures.

Returning to the present more limited theme, it should be noted that the early Spanish debates were not without reverberations in other parts of Europe. Sixteenth-century works in English, which included translation from Spanish and Portuguese, conveyed an image of peoples who are 'bestial, cannibalistic, sexually abandoned, and, in general, moved entirely by passion rather than reason' (Nash 1972, p. 57). These reports also influenced the ideas of Europeans concerned with African savages. In this connection I shall quote an English traveller, whose rather extreme views about the inhabitants of the Cape of Good Hope clearly owed something to the arguments of Sepulveda and other Spanish opponents of the Indians:

> Their language is rather apishly than articulately sounded, with whom [i.e. the apes] 'tis thought they have unnatural mixture, so as what the comentator [sic] . . . observed long since [saying] they have a voice 'twixt humane and beast, makes that supposition to be of more credit, that they have a beastly copulation or conjuncture. So as considering the resemblance they bear with Baboons, which I could observe kept

frequent company with the Women, their speech . . . rather agreeing
with beasts then men.

Now what philosophers alleadge concerning the function of the soul,
may be made applicable to these Animals, saying, that the soul of Man
gradually rather then specifically differenced from the souls of Beasts . . .
Upon which account, the *Spaniard* of late years made it the Subject of
their dispute. Whether the *Indians* were of discent from *Adam*, or no? or
whither they were not rather a middle species of *Men* and *Apes*.

(Herbert 1665, p. 19; emphases in original)

This passage is of particular interest for several reasons. It contains speculation
about the origins of certain savages through miscegenation between humans and
apes that later gained wider currency: 'It is not unlikely' wrote Voltaire ([1756]
1963, p. 8) 'that in the hot countries apes subjugated girls.' The passage also calls
into question the orthodox Christian doctrine that all humans are descended from
Adam and Eve, known as 'monogenism'. While it was still generally accepted
during the 17th century, there had been a few prior dissident thinkers, one of
whom was Paracelsus (1493–1541), who had proposed that the children of Adam
did not inhabit the whole world, and that some 'hidden countries' had been
populated through another creation. Later a French Huguenot, Isaac de La
Peyrère (1594–1676), suggested that there had been a 'pre-Adamite' creation of
animals together with savages. These views about multiple creations or (as framed
once theological supremacy had crumbled), about diverse biological origins, is
called 'polygenism'. Herbert must have been familiar with the earlier discussions
when he doubted the Hottentots' descent from Adam. Finally, there is his
reference to 'a middle species' which rests on the assumptions of the biological
doctrine of 'The Great Chain of Being' that held sway from antiquity to the
19th century, and was the focus of intense 18th-century debates. It was connected
initially with the question of the relationship between humans and apes, where-
after the focus shifted towards that between apes and blacks. Before considering
these issues, it will be necessary first to retrace our steps and look at early images
of blacks.

# 3

# THE SAVAGE AFRICANS

## The ambiguity of medieval images of blacks

The shock of the European encounter with the savages of the New World, the initial European response and the subsequent course of European speculations and images have been exhaustively documented. By contrast, blacks had been known in Europe since antiquity, but information as to how they were regarded during the Middle Ages remains largely fragmentary and often seemingly contradictory. There has been a tendency to make overly simple generalizations about what is an exceedingly complex issue. What seems certain is that in Greco-Roman antiquity there was little or no prejudice against blacks as such (Snowden 1970). Like the light-skinned Scythians (nomadic people from north of the Black Sea) they were often slaves, but were also employed as mercenaries or travelled to Greece or Rome for commercial or diplomatic reasons; intermarriage occurred and was accepted. The Greeks knew about savages further in the interior of Africa (Baldry 1965), but this did not affect their attitude to the blacks among them. Moreover, until the latter part of the Roman period, blacks were not linked to any of the monstrous races. Black soldiers fought in the Roman armies, and in 149 BC, after the Carthagenian wars, North Africa became part of the Roman Empire as '*provincia Africa*'. The Romans must have had some contacts with the African interior, since the mosaics in Pompeii contain pictures of pygmies.

The change towards more unfavourable views of blacks seems to have begun during the early Christian period. For several of the church fathers in the West the colour black was associated with darkness, the devil and evil, and this has been suggested as a causal factor (Pieterse 1992, p. 24). However, the symbolism of black and white had already been prevalent in Greece and Rome, black having been the colour of evil demons (de Medeiros 1985, p. 227), and this does not appear to have had any bearing on attitudes towards blacks. On the other hand there is evidence that it did have such an effect already at the beginning of the 5th century. The monk John Cassian wrote a series of spiritual *Conferences*, some of which depicted the devil 'in the shape of a hideous Negro', or a demon 'like a Negro woman, ill-smelling and ugly'. Since Cassian's admirer, St Benedict, ordered the *Conferences* to be read in the monasteries, they probably had a wide circulation (Dunstan 1964/5).

After the rise of Islam and the Arab conquest of North Africa, Muslims became the arch-enemy of Christendom, cutting off Europe from any possibility of direct contact with the 'land of the blacks' south of the Sahara. The notion of 'Muslims' and 'blacks' was conflated in the term 'Moors', and only later a distinction came to be drawn between 'white Moors' and 'Blackamoors'. From this, one author, Elfasi (1988, p. 19) has concluded that

> the presumed identification of black Africans with Muslims fashioned the European image of black Africans as the impersonation of sin, evil and inferiority. It was in those early medieval times that European negative attitudes, prejudices and hostility to peoples of black skin emerged.

However, as we have seen, the images pre-dated Islam. Furthermore, black Ethiopians were welcomed by European rulers as potential allies against the Muslims, and Ethiopian ambassadors were at European courts. In the 13th century the German emperor Frederick II of Hohenstaufen had blacks guarding his treasures. There were, it is true, black slaves in all the regions bordering the Mediterranean, but they were only one group among many others, including Greeks, Bulgarians, Turks and so on. While blacks were usually in inferior positions there were exceptions, such as the 'Aethiops' who was a high officer in Venice. Or again, a Toulousian noble was reported to have an African wife at the beginning of the 15th century (Debrunner 1979). It is also noteworthy that in numerous medieval sculptures and paintings such figures as the Queen of Sheba, or saints like St Gregorius and the mythical 'Prester John' were represented as blacks.

There was, however, another side. During the period from the 13th to the 15th centuries 'Aethiopians' (then a general term denoting African blacks) were characterized by a number of scholastics and others in a manner strikingly reminiscent of some of the stereotypes that echoed down the centuries. Marco Polo wrote that the blacks are naked and horribly ugly, like devils; Mathieu Paris, Brunetto Latini and Roger Bacon referred to their 'debauchery'; John Mandeville described them as black, ugly giants with huge sexual organs; and Ludolph de Suchem mentioned a region peopled by black men and women with the bodies of monkeys (de Medeiros 1985).

All this shows the co-existence of quite different images during that period. Some individual blacks, whether real people or mythical figures, were accepted and sometimes enjoyed considerable esteem. Yet in the background lurked lurid images of the horrible inhabitants of distant 'Aethiopia' influenced, as detailed later, by the survival of stories about the 'monstrous races'. Particular events were liable to colour attitudes. For instance, there was a phase when Mansa Musa, the ruler of Mali – a black African kingdom – became celebrated in the mediterranean world. This was because of his spectacular pilgrimage to Mecca, in the course of which he held splendid court and liberally distributed gold:

> In the Catalan Atlas of 1375, the ruler of Mali is portrayed like a Latin monarch, save only for his black face . . . bearded, crowned and throned, with panoply of orb and sceptre, he is perceived as a sophisticate, not a savage: a sovereign equal in standing to any Christian prince. This resplendent impression did not last. By the mid-fifteenth century, when direct contact with the outposts of Mali was briefly opened up by Portuguese penetration of Gambia, Mali was in decline. Familiarity bred contempt and the heirs of the Mansa came to be seen as stage niggers – crude racial stereotypes dangling simian sexual organs.
>
> (Fernandez-Armesto 1987, p. 147)

What I have presented are of course mere snippets, but they do show that the evidence points in different directions. Any overall judgement of medieval perceptions of blacks is therefore hazardous. It would seem that these varied with time, place and specific circumstances. However, as indicated at the end of the above quotation, a secular change to more uniformly unfavourable views does appear to have taken place, beginning with the European push southwards.

At one time Cape Bojador, some way south of what is now Morocco, had been regarded as the extreme limit of navigable seas, due to the belief that beyond it the heat was such that no one could survive. On orders of Prince Henry the Navigator, a Portuguese captain first sailed along the African coast south of Cape Bojador in 1433. It was a turning point, leading to a series of explorations further and further along the coast of West Africa, and the beginning of the exploitation of the newly discovered territories: the first gold and slaves from Rio d'Oura were brought back to Portugal in 1442, a trade that went on at an increasing scale. Efforts at Christianization went hand in hand with the trade, and there was never any suggestion at that time – as there had been in the case of the American Indians – that Africans were so irrational that they could not be converted. The Portuguese ruling classes, recognizing that Africans had structures of authority, entered into compacts with African chiefs. But such an open-minded view was not generally shared, as shown by a well-known episode.

A papal Bull had granted the Portuguese kings the title of 'Lord of Guinea', giving them suzerainty over the local rulers. One of these, a Wolof king from Senegal known as Bemoim, sought the help of his overlord, the Portuguese king, John II, in a dispute with other chiefs. In 1488 he travelled to Portugal and was received by John II with all the honours then regarded as due to a person of high rank. When the Wolof king converted to Christianity he was royally feted and told that he would be treated just like any other Christian prince. A fleet of twenty caravels, commanded by a certain general Pero Vaz da Cunha, then took him back towards home. When the expedition had reached Senegal, Pero Vaz murdered Bemoim with his sword. The reasons are obscure – da Cunha claimed there had been treachery. King John II, though reported to have been very angry, did not punish Pero Vaz after his return to Portugal. Russell (1986), who examined this case in considerable depth, was led to conclude that the idealistic egalitarianism implicit in the doctrine of the community of the faithful was unacceptable to John's subjects, and that he dared not execute a Portuguese noble for the murder of a black African. Portugal had by then become a society where blacks were perceived as base slave material, irrespective of their rank in their own country, and whatever their religious affiliation. Moreover, stories about the depravity of Africans had began to circulate.

The slaves who landed in Lagos (in Portugal) during the reign of Henry the Navigator were cruelly divided up and allocated to masters irrespective of family relationships. But once sold they seem to have been treated more humanely; they were baptized and became servants, or were sometimes taught crafts. A witness of the period, D'Azurara, pitied them when they disembarked, but felt that a kinder fate was awaiting them:

> Thus, having left the country in which they were dwelling to the perdition of their souls and bodies, they had now all things to the contrary. I say perdition of souls because they were pagans without the light or flame of the Holy Faith; and perdition of many of their bodies because they lived like beasts without any of the customs of rational creatures, since they did not even know what were bread and wine, nor garments of cloth, nor life in the shelter of a house; and worse still was their ignorance, which deprived them of all knowledge of good and permitted them only a life of brutish idleness.
>
> (Cited in Debrunner 1979, p. 37)

This kind of argument, namely that the slave trade did the Africans a favour, continued to be voiced over the centuries.

For instance, a work by the noted 19th-century historian James Froude contains the following passage:

> On the continent of Africa were another race, savage in their natural state, which would domesticate like animals . . .
>
> The black races varied like other animals: some were gentle and timid, some were ferocious as wolves. The strong tyrannized over the weak, made slaves of their prisoners, occasionally ate them, and those they did not eat were sacrificed at what they called their *customs* – offered them up and cut their throats at the altars of their idols . . . [the customs] were suspended while the slave trade gave the prisoners a value. They revived when the slave trade was abolished.
>
> (Froude 1895, pp. 49–50)

Going back to the 15th-century trade in slaves, this had begun by the Portuguese capturing the slaves themselves. They penetrated far into the interior – partly for this purpose, and partly in the then usual search for gold. However, after having initially been taken by surprise, the Africans soon grew wise to the threat and fought back vigorously. Hence the Portuguese, and later the many other nations who followed them into the trade, mainly confined themselves to establishing forts on the coast and purchased slaves from the local chiefs. From then on the interior of Africa became the mysterious 'dark continent'.

At that period new information was provided by a pioneer whose writings remained a major source of knowledge about Africa for almost three centuries. Alhassan Ibn Mohammed Alwazzan (*c.* 1492–1552), known as Leo Africanus, was a Cordovan Moor who wrote the *History and description of Africa*. A remarkably able and versatile man, he travelled extensively not merely in North Africa, but also south of the Sahara. Leo gave accounts of several 'kingdoms of the Negroes', and was greatly impressed by some of the towns, notably Kano and Timbuktu with their wealthy merchants and learned men. But he also visited more remote pagan parts which, to an educated Muslim, appeared appallingly primitive. This led him to observe that

> The Negroes leade a beastly kinde of life, being utterly destitute of the use of reason, dexteritie or wit, and of all artes. Yea they so behave themselves as if they had continually lived in a forest among wilde beasts. They have great swarmes of harlots among them; whereupon a man might easily conjecture their manner of living.
>
> (Cited in Hallett 1965, p. 58)

Subsequent European commentators tended to conveniently overlook what Leo had said about the rich culture of African cities, focusing on his harsh judgement of the 'beastly Negroes'. What had happened, in the cases of Leo Africanus, the Portuguese, and soon other European trading nations, was that they became aware of the cultural gulf that divided them from Africans in their homelands. That gulf was to widen much further in the following centuries, leading to a progressively greater disparagement of Africans and others regarded as savages.

## The tradition of the 'monstrous races' and other influences

Among the numerous Plinian or 'monstrous' races three were particularly significant in the present context, namely the anthropophagi, Garamantes and pygmies. Their initial geographical locations tended to be vague, since India was often confused with Africa – presumably it was sometimes just a shorthand for 'far away'. Later they came to be more firmly assigned to 'Aethiopia', the Garamantes and anthropophagi originally being seen as neighbouring peoples, and later conflated.

The Garamantes, mentioned by Strabo (*c.* 60 BC to AD 20), were supposed to have been living in the interior of Africa south of Libya (Strabo 1932). Solinus, a 3rd-century Roman geographer, described them as follows:

The Ethiopian Garamantes have no knowledge of marriage: it is the custom of the country to have the women in common. Hence only the mothers recognize their sons; the honorable title of father cannot be applied to anyone. Who could, in effect, distinguish a father in the midst of such moral licence? So the Ethiopian Garamantes are rightly regarded as a degenerate people since, as a consequence of that promiscuity, the family name is sadly lost.

(Solin [?] 1847, p. 231)

About neighbouring peoples Solinus wrote that some were enormously tall and others anthropophagi or man-eaters, characteristics subsequently associated with the Garamantes. The reason why the Garamantes are important is that stories such as those of their depraved sexual mores came to be passed down the centuries. For instance, the 13th-century friar Bartholomew the English described a variety of 'Ethiopians' in the manner of the 'monstrous races' – creatures with no heads, satyrs and so on: 'Others there be which like beasts live without wedding, and dwell with women without law, and such be called Garamantes' (Steele 1905, p. 89).

The mores attributed to the Garamantes came increasingly to be applied to Africans at large. The lecherous Negro was a stock figure in Elizabethan drama, and Duval (1685) retold the description by Solinus almost verbatim. Of other peoples in that region he said that 'They have so much of the Beast, that they are born blind, and do not see until five dayes and . . . they . . . have large members'. Moreover, 'their shape makes them resemble apes' (Duval 1685, pp. 406–7). There was thus a continuous thread from some of the 'monstrous races' to the image of African savages.

The pygmies are among the most ancient of the monstrous races. Homer referred to them, and Herodotus told a story about a group of travellers to the interior of Africa who had been attacked by small black men. A later edition of Pliny's works contained the following commentary on Pliny's account of them, drawn from a writer called Ctesias:

He [i.e. Ctesias] reports that in the centre of India there are black men called Pygmies. They speak the same language as other Indians. They are very small: the tallest among them are two cubits [about a metre] high, but the majority measure one-and-a half cubits. Their hair is very long; it reaches down to their knees, and their beard is longer than in any other human species. . . . Their male member is so long that it hangs down to their ankles; it is thick; they themselves are snub-nosed and ugly.

(André and Filliozat 1980, Book IV, p. 101)

The description of their grotesquely large penises was a forerunner of another characteristic later stereotypically attributed to blacks. It is a notion that has survived through the ages, and even nowadays attempts are made to give it once again scientific respectability (cf. Chapter 7).

Although pygmies did not figure prominently in the popular travel literature, the question of their position within the hierarchical cosmological order of the Great Chain of Being constituted an intriguing philosophical puzzle for medieval scholastics. The doctrine of the Great Chain dominated European thought over the greater part of its history. It consisted of a broad framework that left the boundaries of species uncertain, thereby giving rise to much debate. Since it played an important role during the transitional period of the 18th century it is necessary to outline its history.[1]

## The Great Chain of Being

The concept of a comprehensive ordering principle of nature, called in antiquity *scala naturae*, was taken over from neo-Platonism, mainly through Saint Augustine, and incorporated in modified form into Christian philosophy. The doctrine of 'the Great Chain of Being' dominated thinking about humanity's place in nature until its demise was brought about by the rise of the new biology at the turn of the 19th century. Even later, some great figures such as Goethe, or the race theorist Robert Knox (1791–1862), continued to believe in it (cf. Rehbock 1983). The 'Great Chain of Being' was conceived as a comprehensive hierarchical order, instituted by the Creator, in which the varieties of objects of creation are arranged in infinitely small gradations, from minerals via plants, animals and humans right up to the angels, in increasing degrees of perfection. It embodied the 'principle of continuity' which emphasized the inter-connectedness of all things: humans are linked with angels in as much as both have intelligence; they have sensibility in common with animals, and vegetable life with plants; even with stones there is the basic joint property of just being.

In addition to the principle of continuity referring to an infinity of intermediate positions on the scale, it also embodied that of 'plenitude', implying that there is no specifiable limit to the varieties of creation. Humans were regarded as occupying a middle position between the lower animals and the angels and other higher beings. It was seen as the task of scholars, and later also science, to discover the right slot into which any particular organism was to be inserted.

A classical example of the manner in which this task was tackled, which also happens to be highly relevant to the present theme, concerns the status of the 'pygmy', extensively debated during the later Middle Ages. An outstanding contribution to this debate was made by Albertus Magnus (*c.* 1200–80), generally regarded as the foremost philosopher of nature of his time. Like Saint Augustine, he believed in the 'monstrous races', including creatures who were supposed to be half-human and half-goat, or apes with the head of a dog. A marginal case for him was that of the pygmy, and his information about that type was derived largely, though not exclusively, from Aristotle. While there are some imaginary aspects of his account, it does seem to be mainly based on valid information about an African ethnic group. Before dealing with this key issue in more detail it is worth noting that, unlike Saint Augustine, Albertus did not categorize beings with a partly human form as humans. He did, however, follow Saint Augustine in adopting mortality and the possession of 'reason' as the crucial criteria of humanity.

Interestingly, Albertus took for granted a correlation between physical and mental similarity, with greater anatomical complexity implying more sophis-ticated mental functioning; and this correlation served him as an organizing principle in his classification of the animal world. This foreshadowed some of the ideas put forward by Cuvier some five centuries later.

Prior to Albertus there had been the simple dichotomy of man, the most perfect of the animal creation, and the beasts in a descending scale. He inserted what he called the 'man-like beasts', namely the pygmy and the ape. As pointed out by Janson (1952, p. 85), this

> must be regarded as an advance of major significance; after all, the intermediate category of *similitudines hominis*, which Albertus was the first to establish, provides the earliest conception of the 'missing link', the earliest attempt to bridge the chasm between mankind and the rest of the animal world.

This is of course not to say that he anticipated evolutionary theories, since, for him as for the rest of the medieval world, species remained permanently fixed.

The status of the pygmy presented Albertus with a problem, since that creature appeared to approximate 'ordinary humans' most closely. Thus he noted that the face of the pygmy is more similar to a man's than it is to the face of an ape. When describing common elements he made the seemingly bizarre observation that man, pygmy and ape are the only animals that cannot waggle their ears. Curiously enough, echoes of this kind of quaint notion seem to have persisted over the centuries. For instance, the prominent French psychologist Henri Piéron (1909, p. 125) regarded it as a distinguishing mark between 'civilized' and 'primitives' that few of the former but all of the latter *can* voluntarily move their ears!

Comparative physical characteristics, however, play only a secondary role in Albertus Magnus' discussion, the major emphasis being on modes of psycho-logical functioning. Here Albertus developed a scale spanning the whole of the animal world. All animals are capable of receiving sensory impressions, and those confined to such impressions constitute the lowest level. Next there are those that are able to store such impressions in memory, and a further step is the combination of memory and what we might call elementary cognitive skills (still below *ratio* or 'reason'). Such a capacity, he argued, enables bees to accumulate provisions. The next higher levels are distinguished by the ability to profit from experience, but this does not mean that organisms at those levels can form concepts. Yet there are animals that can attain *imitatio artis*, something at least roughly approximating art and science: these are the apes and pygmies, though they are not on the same level. The ape has memory and the faculty of imitation, but is indiscriminate as to what is imitated – it is mere playfulness. This belief in the ape's propensity to slavishly imitate remained a persistent one, not merely in folklore but on the part of scholars and scientists. Since it will be encountered again repeatedly, it should be noted that modern primatological studies have failed to confirm it (Byrne 1995). Returning to Albertus Magnus, he took the view that the pygmy is quite different:

> he has first of all *memory*, and the ability to *compare* memory images with each other. Yet while man advances from this to general concepts, the pygmy remains with images; but he can differentiate between that which is *useful* or *damaging* to him, and therefore does not immediately imitate anything one shows him. The second difference from the ape is the possession of *language*. When one reads this one thinks that Albertus thereby disposes of any difference between man and pygmy. But that is not the case. . . . While other animals can express their feelings through sounds, the pygmy can speak and is capable of expressing particular representations by means of articulate sounds. Such representations, however, are of an entirely particularistic and sensory character; thereby pygmy language differs from that of men, which can deal with concepts.
>
> (Koch 1931, p. 204; emphases in original)

Albertus likened the pygmies to the feebleminded, possessing only the shadow of reason. Hence they are incapable of what we would call 'culture': they form no regular communities, have neither proper art nor science, and lack morality and shame. In some remarkable respects these ideas anticipate those of the 19th-century scientist Carl Vogt, discussed in Chapter 7, who from a Darwinian evolutionary position viewed idiots as intermediate between Negroes and apes. In so far as Albertus credited pygmies with language, he was also more generous than some of his successors, who were unwilling to concede a capacity for articulate speech to some savages. There were some other scholars during that period spanning the 12th and 13th centuries who were concerned with that same topic of the status of pygmies, notably Petrus de Alvernia. Their arguments, while lacking the incisiveness and coherence of Albertus Magnus, ran along similar lines.

Albertus Magnus in *de Animalibus* also followed Galen and Arab authors in seeking to interpret the characteristics of 'Aethiopians' (i.e. African blacks) as consequences of a hot climate. These are the black colour, curly hair and prognathism, the supposed forward projection of the jaw. The early reference to prognathism is interesting, since this concept was to play a significant part in subsequent 'apishness' theories. It was accepted even by those, like Bryan Edwards (1743–1880), who did not regard this supposedly ape-like trait as denoting African inferiority. In his *History of the British West Indies* (1793) he wrote:

34

I cannot help observing, too, that the conformation of the face, in a great majority of them, very much resembles that of a baboon. I believe indeed that there is, in most of the nations of Africa, a greater elongation of the lower jaw, than among the people of Europe.

(Cited in Jordan 1968, p. 237)

Although Albertus treated the Aethiopians separately from the pygmies, he was clearly aware that pygmies had traditionally been described as being black. Hence his intense preoccupation with the relative status of men, pygmies and apes seems inconsistent with Jordan's suggestion that the association between blacks and apes resulted from the fact that 'European explorers had stumbled across Negroes and the most man-like of apes simultaneously' (Jordan 1968, p. 229). While the exact date of the European discovery of anthropoid apes is disputed, scattered reports during the Renaissance aroused hardly any interest. Precise knowledge of them was not recorded until the 17th century, and blacks had of course been known in Europe long before that time. In any case, as Janson (1952) rightly noted, the discovery of the great apes had initially little effect on European thought.[2]

My reason for dwelling at some length on the ideas of Albertus Magnus is not only that they were penetrating and in some respects astonishingly modern, but they anticipated an intensive 18th-century debate dealing with essentially the same issues.

# 4

# THE PUZZLE OF APES AND MEN

Four centuries after Albertus Magnus, the scientific revolution transformed the approach to natural phenomena away from scholastic debate towards empirical studies. Yet the doctrine of 'the Great Chain' continued to hold sway, so that the task of science was conceived as that of documenting it in more detail and thereby progressively disclosing the universal plan. Thomas Sprat, historian of the Royal Society, wrote in 1667 that one of its main objectives was to discover ever more facts of nature and to insert them in their proper place in the Chain. This was precisely the aim of Edward Tyson (1651–1708), whose important monograph published in 1699 has already been mentioned (p. 4). He carried out a careful and thorough dissection of what he called a 'pygmie', but has in fact been shown to have been a chimpanzee, one of the first types of anthropoid apes introduced into Europe. His report meticulously described this first systematic empirical study comparing the anatomy of apes and humans. Tyson concluded that despite its name and many structural similarities the 'pygmie' was not a man, but an intermediate animal between man and monkey. Although Tyson decided that his 'pygmie' was not a human being, this does not mean that he was free from the conceptions characterizing his period. He found it puzzling that in spite of the anatomical similarity to humans, with a perfect larynx, the 'pygmie' did not speak. He concluded that the difference must be accounted for by a metaphysical principle lacking in apes. The plausibility of such speculation was enhanced by the fact that, in terms of the Great Chain, humans are positioned on the borderline between the visible and the invisible. The question of why the higher apes do not speak was also discussed later by Buffon, who had been much impressed by Tyson's work, and came to similar conclusions. It is also noteworthy that Tyson humanized the 'pygmie' by depicting him standing upright, supported by a stick, which is significant since bipedalism had long been one of the criteria of humanity. In this he was not alone – the representations of apes during that period were often strikingly anthropomorphic. In other respects Tyson also shared contemporary beliefs. Thus in one of his writings he cited at length the story first published in Milan in 1608, mentioned in Chapter 3, about the woman who was raped by apes (see Figure 4.1).

*The Orang-Outang carrying off a Negro Girl.*

Published as the Act directs May 1.st 1795.

*Figure 4.1* A belief in sexual relations between black women and apes was not uncommon during the 18th century, and persisted into the 19th. This example is British.

As was already indicated in his title, Tyson concluded that the various monstrous races and satyrs of antiquity had in fact been apes. His inclusion of pygmies in these categories resulted in a widespread belief during the 18th century that these were also just fabulous creatures. His general assessment of the nature of humans reflected his faith in the Great Chain: 'Man is part *Brute*, part an *Angel*; and it is that *Link* in the *Creation*, that joyns them both together' (Tyson 1699, p. 55; emphasis in original).

In his *Essay concerning human understanding* (1690), Tyson's contemporary John Locke went so far as to assert the impossibility of defining what 'man' is. According to Locke, one cannot say that man results from the sexual union of two human beings, it being 'well known', according to him, that man and ape can procreate together (Book III, Chapter VI, Section 23). Consequently Locke regarded divisions into *genus* and *species* as essentially arbitrary, a view initially shared by Buffon and based on the Great Chain: given continuity, rigid de-marcations make no sense. Buffon later came to abandon this position and adopted the criterion of fertility in the second generation as defining the limits of species. Charles Etienne Bonnet (1720–93), a Swiss naturalist and philosopher, and Jean Baptiste Robinet (1735–1820) reformulated the doctrine of the Great Chain, stripping it of some of its theological trappings. Moreover, in the phrase coined by Lovejoy (1936) they 'temporalized' it, moving away from the conception of a creation static from the beginning of time. While Bonnet felt able to divide the scale into four large orders (inorganic; organic but inanimate; organic and animate, but without reason; organic, animate and rational), Robinet argued that this violated the principle of continuity. All classifications are bound to be arbitrary: an intelligence superior to ours would see that there are as many steps as there are individuals.

As I have already indicated, The Great Chain was not so much a theory as a rather vague doctrine, and as such not falsifiable. This left the door open to a whole range of beliefs about all sorts of creatures, none of which could be regarded as being 'unnatural'. So it is not surprising that the existence of all kinds of hybrids, some based on ancient traditions, continued to be accepted by many Enlightenment thinkers.[1] For instance, the early evolutionist Benoit de Maillet (1656–1738) had a theory that terrestrial animals, including humans, came originally from the sea; and differences between human populations were explained by their descent from different aquatic creatures (see Figure 4.2). His evidence for this theory consisted of what he and others then regarded as the numerous well-authenticated cases of mermaids and mermen. This was not unusual at the time: Robinet produced a long list of such alleged cases. De Maillet also believed in the existence of peoples with tails. He reported an interview with an Italian courtesan who told how she had spent the night with a man whose face was white, with a black beard and a body as hairy as a bear. Moreover, he had a tail half a foot long and smelled so strongly of 'savage' that she nearly fainted (Tinland 1968, pp. 49–51). De Maillet's conviction was shared by the eccentric Scottish judge James Burnet, better known as Lord Monboddo (1714–99), who

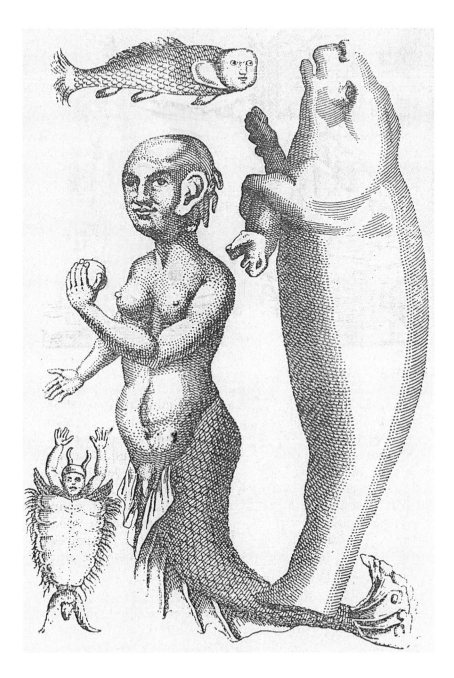

*Figure 4.2* Eighteenth-century representation of humanoids. According to de Maillet, humans descended from such aquatic creatures
*Source:* Robinet (1768)

cited the supposedly watertight case of a teacher of mathematics at Inverness who had a tail, also half a foot long – that seems to have been the standard length (Bryson 1945, p. 71). Although this may seem absurd, I will later show that the belief in humans with tails persisted until the middle of the 19th century.

Throughout the Age of Reason the doctrine of the 'Great Chain' remained for most an unassailable article of faith, radically criticized only by such unorthodox spirits as Dr Johnson and Voltaire. Within that same theoretical framework the relationship between humans and the great apes became a burning issue for much of the 18th century. As Buffon put it, the existence of the apes constituted a challenge to humans to define their true identity.

## Attempts at classifying humans

The doubts then surrounding the question of the relationship between humans and anthropoids are reflected in the work of Carl Linnaeus (1707–78), the founder of modern biological taxonomy. Primarily a botanist, he reduced the

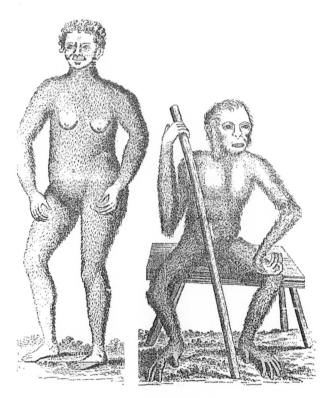

*Figure 4.3*  Examples of Linnean types: on the left a Troglodyte, on the right a Pygmy; note the latter's ape-like fur and prehensile feet
*Source:* From C. Linnaeus, *Amoenitates academicae* (1749).

immense descriptive material on the flora amassed by his predecessors to an orderly system. Subsequently he extended his classifications to cover the 'animal kingdom', and when it came to humans he was evidently very unsure. Thus in the first edition of his *System of nature* (1735) he classed man as a quadruped animal, together with the ape and the sloth. When a critic raised objections, Linnaeus replied that he would be quite willing to change this classification if someone would show him 'a generic character by which to distinguish man from the ape' (cited in Bynum 1974, p. 24).

Sub-divisions of 'man' included both the 'tailed man' and, as an anomaly, *Homo sylvestris*. The latter term is a direct translation of the Indonesian name for the orang-utan; there long remained a considerable terminological confusion over the different kinds of anthropoid apes, usually all labelled orang-utan. After several further changes, the final edition of 1758 introduced the general order of *Primates*, sub-divided by genus into *homo*, *simia*, *lemurs* and so on. *Homo* was dichotomized into two species: *Sapiens*, diurnal, and *Sylvestris* or *Troglodytes*, nocturnal (see Figure 4.3). The latter pair of terms referred to a strange mixture of mythical beings, apes, albinos and mutes. *Homo sapiens* had six sub-categories, four of them familiar to us: Americans, Europeans, Asians and Africans. The first of the two others was *Homo ferus*, the 'Wild Man', based on stories of children or adults found to live among animals in the woods, whose status gave rise to much discussion.[2] Finally, *Homo monstruosus* referred, on the one hand, to natural abnormalities such as giants or dwarfs, and on the other to artificial ones like eunuchs or those with compressed or elongated heads. The whole effort was monstrously confused, the outcome of having tried to incorporate a mixture of real and imaginary beings into a unitary scheme. The bracketing of humans and apes, shocking to some, was defended by one of the disciples of Linnaeus who expanded the master's treatment of *Simiae*:

> Their habits, and ingenuity in practising tricks and jokes, besides their imitation of others (that is, their readiness in following the fashion of the age), make them so like ourselves, that it is difficult to draw any natural distinction between man and his imitator – the ape.
>
> (Hoppe 1760, cited in Slotkin 1965, p. 181)

While there was at that time no dispute about the close anatomical similarity of apes to humans, including apparently the organs of speech, and also some similarities in behaviour, the interpretations of such resemblances were widely divergent. Buffon was one of those fascinated by the problem. In 1740 he saw a young chimpanzee in Paris which had been trained to eat at table, musing that the animal had the same brain as humans and yet had no language and, he supposed, could not think, so that the performance was quasi-mechanical. Buffon and other 18th-century naturalists followed Tyson in adopting a Cartesian interpretation: God had endowed humans with a rational soul, as manifest by language, which was denied to apes as to other animals.

41

This standpoint was attacked from two opposite directions. The sensationalist Etienne Condillac (1715–80) in his *Traité des animaux* (1755) rejected such a sharp disjunction which represented animals, including apes, as mere automata. He argued that animals also have mental processes including feelings and thoughts, as shown by their communications and purposive actions.[3] The radical materialist Julien La Mettrie (1709–51) maintained in his *L'histoire naturelle de l'ame* (1746) and *L'homme machine* (1748) that neither men nor animals have souls. He made the shrewd point that it was absurd to take language as evidence of an immortal soul since mutes, classified wrongly by Linnaeus as a separate species, were still humans; therefore language as such was not a necessary criterion of humanity. He adduced the fact that mutes could be taught sign language and the deaf trained to produce speech, which he thought might perhaps also be done with apes, who would then become indistinguishable from ordinary humans.

Yet there was another side to this rational and tough-minded materialist. In a section of his *Oeuvres philosophiques* headed 'On savage men, called Satyrs', he wrote that savage men were fairly common in India and Africa. In a footnote he mentioned that two years previously there had appeared at the fair of St Laurent a great ape resembling a satyr, and then gave the following description of the species:

> they run fast and have unbelievable strength. In front of the body they have nowhere any hair; but on the back one gets the impression of a forest of black bristling hair, the whole back being covered with it. The face of these animals resembles a human face.
>
> Nothing is more lascivious, more shameless, and more disposed to fornication, than these animals . . . they . . . make love with as little restraint as dogs.
>
> (La Mettrie 1751, Histoire VI, p. 200)

The accompanying confused discussion refers to ancient authors like Pliny and Plutarch, as well as to some contemporary naturalists. It is not clear whether he regarded the creature as a savage or a peculiar kind of ape with a human face – the contradictions in his account indicate that he himself could not make up his mind. The hairy aspect no doubt harks back to the wild men of medieval folklore. The fact that La Mettrie was so completely taken in by a fairground exhibit, and made statements about that mythical creature which could have been made a thousand years earlier, demonstrates the persistence of the satyr/ape/savage–lechery complex of ideas.

## Is language uniquely human?

Let me return to the question of language, which was clearly a key issue in the debate concerning the relationship between apes and humans. Jean Jacques Rousseau (1712–78), in his *Discours sur l'Inégalité* (1750), challenged the assumption by Buffon and others that possession of language in its current form had been a ready-made gift to humanity. On the contrary, he argued, it was a product of gradual development over a long time-span in various sets of what we would call socio-cultural conditions, and there might well have been a time when there was little difference between the modes of communication of men and apes. In a footnote he went even further, suggesting that apes might just be underdeveloped humans:

> All these observations on the varieties that may be produced by a thousand causes, and have in fact been produced in the human species, make me doubt if diverse animals similar to humans, taken to be beasts by travellers without much examination, or because of some differences they noted in their external appearance, or only because these animals did not speak, might not in fact be veritable savage men.
>
> (Rousseau [1750] 1964, p. 208)

Having been dispersed in the woods, they might have failed to develop their potential faculties and thus remained in a state of nature. In response to Buffon, who had declared that the uniquely superior status of humans was evidenced by the impossibility of a fertile union between men and beasts, Rousseau argued that this remained unproven; and he proposed an experiment that might be attempted by 'the crudest observers' to put the matter to the test. According to Zimmermann (1777, cited by Tinland 1968), such an experiment had actually been carried out in London, when a male orang-utan was offered a prostitute. While the result was negative, the test was said to have been inconclusive, since it should have been done between a man and a female orang who had known each other for some time.

Monboddo, a follower of Rousseau, went much further in affirming that humans and orang-utans are one and the same species. Why should humans and apes have been designed on exactly the same plan, he asked, but the latter equipped with supposedly superfluous vocal organs? Should we treat them as a separate species just because they have not yet reached the stage of making use of these organs? No doubt it was because it fitted in so well with his thesis that Monboddo readily credited the stories of men with tails.

Although often ridiculed for his views, Monboddo was certainly not a fool. He drew a distinction between potential and realized capacities that is reminiscent of our competence–performance dichotomy. Rejecting the possession of articulate language as a necessary criterion of humanity, he contended that intelligence could be expressed by actions without the intermediary of the arbitrary conventions we call 'words', a position later also espoused by Piaget.[4] Many of his observations were perceptive and in advance of his time, but he went too far when he claimed in his book *On the origins and progress of language* (Burnet 1773, p. 175) the existence of simian 'nations':

not only solitary savages, but a whole nation, have been found without the use of speech. This is the case of the Ouran Outangs, that are found in the kingdom of Angola in Africa, and in several parts of Asia. They are exactly of the human form, walking erect, not upon all fours, like the savages that have been found in Europe; they use sticks for weapons; they live in society; they make huts of branches of trees and they carry off negro girls, whom they make slaves of, and use both for work and pleasure. These facts are related of them by Mr. Buffon in his natural history . . . they are of our species, and though they have made some progress in the arts of life they have not come the length of language.

In seeking to invoke the authority of Buffon, Monboddo was less than candid. For while it is correct that Buffon reported such tales,[5] he also voiced considerable scepticism regarding their truth.

While greatly interested in the radical differences between ethnic groups, Buffon nevertheless remained a firm monogenist. He was probably the first to employ the term 'race' in something approaching its modern sense. He defined races as varieties of the species whose characters have become hereditary as a result of the continuous actions of the same causes that produce individual differences; but he was not very consistent in his usage.

While making a clear distinction between humans and apes, Buffon saw the 'lowest savages' as rather close to the brutes. He described 'American man' and blacks at some length, in contrasting but equally unflattering terms. He drew a particularly repulsive portrait of what were then regarded as the lowest of the savages and thus closest to the anthropoid apes, namely the Hottentots:[6] animal-like eyes, thick and protruding lips, flat nose, a stupid and fierce look; the females with long slack breasts, the skin of their belly hanging down to the knees; everybody hideous, covered with encrusted dirt. Yet as far as categorization was concerned, all these externals were unimportant to Buffon, because the Hottentots had the divine gift of thought and language, and were thus part of humankind.

It has been suggested by Todorov (1993) that 'the racialist theory in its entirety is found in Buffon's writings' (p. 103). While it is true that he put forward a number of ideas which later became part of racialist theories, it seems to me that this claim goes too far, for two main reasons: one is Buffon's frequent emphasis on environmental causes and, more importantly, his acknowledgement that races shade into each other.

## Literal or metaphorical usage of 'apishness'?

While Buffon drew a clear line between humans, however 'low', and apes, this had not always been the case. In order to consider this issue, I shall refer again to some earlier accounts. The general legacy of classical ethnology, with its various forms of monstrous hybrids, was no doubt instrumental in promoting the circulation of

44

numerous colourful tales that were still being given credence early in the 17th century. For instance, Samuel Purchas (1577–1626), a compiler of chronicles, accepted the report by a Roman writer to the effect that there were people in Africa who, swinging from branch to branch with great agility, fed on the tops of trees. It is an image still sometimes evoked by racists who wish to insult blacks.

There were also many instances of stories regarding the 'beastly conjunctions' between blacks and apes mentioned by Herbert (Chapter 2, p. 24). These tales have been documented by Jordan (1968), who saw in them a major source of the ascription of 'apishness' to blacks. Of particular interest in this connection is his account of the section on apes in Edward Topsell's *Histories of fourefootted beastes* (1607). This emphasizes the 'venerousness' of apes, who ravish women with their outsize 'virile member'.[7] Topsell also drew physiognomic lessons: 'Men that have low and flat nostrils are libidinous as Apes that attempt women, and having thicke lippes the upper hanging over the neather, they are deemed fooles, like the lips of Asses and Apes' (cited in Jordan 1968, p. 30). In addition, Topsell related apes to devils and satyrs, and thereby to blackness and evil – all associations rooted in medieval symbolism. Moreover, the notion of gradation among living beings made the linkage between the lowest savages and the most human-like animals a plausible one – as has been shown, it was a notion that persisted for centuries.

Another writer who produced a detailed and incisive study of attitudes to blacks during that period was Barker (1978). While accepting the general case made out by Jordan regarding the influence of the classical tradition and the reports of ape–human copulation, he accused Jordan of selective use of sources. Barker put forward two main criticisms: he pointed out that by the 17th century a great deal of factual information about Africa had been published, and within that body of writings the 'apishness' theme was a rather minor one; furthermore, he contended that belief in hybrid monsters had weakened already during the 17th century, and had disappeared altogether by the 18th century.

As regards the first point, even my less exhaustive perusal of the relevant literature confirms Barker's contention of relative rarity. Nonetheless, most of the accounts are very unflattering, especially concerning sexual mores; and animal comparisons are extremely common, even though apes are not so often specifically mentioned.

As for the second point, namely the alleged rejection of the possibility of hybrid monsters in the 18th century, Barker was mistaken. Even as late as the first quarter of the 19th century Jules Virey (1775–1847), a naturalist and professor of pharmacy (about whom more later) was able to pen the following lurid diatribe:

> One could presume that hairy savages are half-breeds of apes and women . . . how many negresses, surprised by a libertine troop of satyrs, in the African forests, could have begotten half-breeds? How many even of female Jockos [chimpanzees], wild Messalinas, have voluntarily prostituted themselves to the ardour of Africans? One knows nothing

about what kind of love goes on in these ancient forests, where the heat of the climate, the brutal life of the inhabitants, the solitude and the delirium of passion, without law, religion, morals, can lead to daring everything; and these degraded beings, these monsters half-way between humans and apes . . . will long remain unknown to us.

(Virey 1826, Vol. 2, pp. 400–1)

The frequent application of animal epithets to savages raises the question of whether this could have been meant literally. Historians appear to be unanimous in rejecting this possibility. Tinland (1968, p. 48) cited an early voyager to Lapland who affirmed never to have seen an animal as similar to humans as the Laplander; he added at once that in fact the voyager had no real doubts about the nature of this 'animal'. This was also the view of Jordan (1968, p. 116):

> English observers in West Africa were sometimes so profoundly impressed by the Negro's deviant behavior that they resorted to a powerful metaphor with which to express their own sense of difference from them. They knew perfectly well that Negroes were men, yet they frequently described the Africans as 'brutish' or 'bestial' or 'beastly'.

Or again, Curtin (1965, p. 35) commented that 'The travellers often condemned individual Africans as bad men – or all Africans as savage men – but they left the clear impression that Africans *were* men'. Barker was equally confident that epithets like 'brutish' or 'beastly' are not to be taken literally: 'The censure universally bestowed on savages was, it cannot be overemphasised, a product of an equally universal certainty that the dividing line between man and animal was clear cut' (Barker 1978, p. 95).

In the face of such consensus it is probably rash to raise some doubt, even if only tentatively. Yet one might wonder whether these mid-20th-century writers might not have been influenced by their feeling that no one could possibly have been unsure about the humanity of savages. Barker especially, who was so categorical about the 'clear-cut dividing line', ignored the fact that before Tyson the boundary between humans and apes had remained very uncertain; and even after him the great Linnaeus, as has been shown above, remained far from confident about the dividing lines between various kinds of real or mythical humans and non-humans.

Moreover, at that period the human-like qualities of apes were commonly overestimated, thereby decreasing the distance separating them from humans. For instance, in an early geography book one finds the statement that 'The BABOONS in *Guiny* do the Natives very great pieces of service, for they fetch Water, turn the Spit, and wait at table, etc. ' (Morden 1700, p. 508). As will be shown below, similar notions could still be found at the beginning of the 19th century. Such overlaps in conceptions of the behavioural characteristics of humans and apes also make it more plausible that early travellers were at least unsure about how to categorize savages, and their accounts sometimes seemed to indicate some doubts. This was particularly true of first encounters, which must have been quite traumatic. Here is how Johann Christian Hoffmann, a German who visited the Cape in 1671, recorded his reactions:

> Here everything appeared to me strange, and strangest of all the wild mode of life of these peoples, which I viewed at the outset more as monstrous apes than as righteous humans, and certainly! because of their brutishness they have almost nothing that resembles a human, and therefore they are in truth the most miserable men I have ever seen.
>
> (Cited in Jahn 1964, pp. 36–7)

He went on to refer to their incomprehensible clucking as being more like the noise of fowl than a human language, which was an oft-repeated comparison.[8] They were also said to be naked, ugly and stinking, the women having 'horribly long breasts' which he likened to sacks of leather. Their food also disgusted him, and for these and a variety of other reasons he concluded that 'in truth one can count them more as stupid beasts than sensible humans' (p. 39).

Hoffman's first impression, it will have been noted, was that of being faced with 'monstrous apes'. What could have given rise to such a response? One answer might be that Hoffman had read or heard about the conventional wisdom regarding 'ape-likeness', and was therefore primed by his prior expectations. Yet there is another possibility, readily overlooked if one views things through 20th-century spectacles; and it requires an effort of imagination to put oneself into the shoes of these early travellers. The following passage provides some relevant clues:

> Just imagine taking some normal people, stripping off their clothes, taking away all their other possessions, depriving them of the power of speech, and reducing them to grunting, without changing their anatomy at all. Put them in a cage in the zoo next to the chimp cages, and let the rest of us clothed and talking people visit the zoo. Those speechless caged people would be seen for what we all really are: a chimp that has little hair and walks upright.
>
> (Diamond 1991, pp. 1–2)

The picture presented by Hoffman's savages corresponded rather closely to the above description. They were almost completely naked, had very few possessions, seemed to lack articulate speech and ate food appearing to Europeans as unfit for human consumption; if their pigmentation was dark,[9] then this also made them appear to resemble anthropoids more than Europeans.

Another consideration is that not all African peoples were rated as being on the same low level by the better informed. In particular, there was a belief in a kind of gradient of increasing degrees of savagery the further south one moved in Africa. As one traveller, John Matthews ([1788]1966, p. 159) put it: 'trace the manners of the natives, the whole extent from Cape Cantin to the Cape of Good Hope, and you find a constant and almost regular gradation in the scale of understanding, till the wretched Cafre sinks nearly below the Ouran Outang.'[10] It does sound as though Matthews did not regard the 'Cafres' as fully human.

As far as the planters and their slaves were concerned, none of this would of course apply. But as Barker himself stated, 'British people, especially in the West Indies, had treated Negroes as if they were animals rather than human beings' (1978, p. 59), and such behaviour was liable to lead to corresponding ideas – not perhaps that blacks were literally dumb animals, but that in a real sense they were less than human. There is also the fact that as late as 1776 African slaves were officially classified together with 'all Manner of Goods and Merchandise whatsoever' (Walvin 1973, p. 40); this must have reflected widely held views and seems hardly compatible with an acceptance of the ordinary humanity of Africans. In fact Samuel Estwick, an agent in London for West Indian planters, published a pamphlet in 1772 in which he argued that Negro slaves, being property, could not be human beings in the same way as Englishmen. Estwick's pamphlet provided the (unacknowledged) basis for Edward Long's notorious work that will be considered below.

Apart from first-hand observers, it is not difficult to find commentators with similar opinions. For instance, Rousselot de Surgy, a French *philosophe*, wrote in the mid-18th century that 'Nature seems to ascend from oran-outangs to Pongos (an ethnic group in the Congo) to man' (cited in Cohen 1980, p. 87), thereby explicitly excluding the Pongos from the category of humans. Even Granville Sharp, one of the major figures in the fight against slavery in England, was less than firm in asserting the humanity of blacks:

> I am far from having any particular esteem for the Negroes; but as I think myself obliged to consider them as *men*, I am certainly obliged also to use my best endeavours to prevent their being treated as *beasts* by our unchristian countrymen.
>
> (Cited in Curtin 1965, p. 53)

In sum, I would suggest that there is considerable evidence against the claims made by most historians that there were never any doubts about the real humanity of savages.

Another question that is also debatable concerns the extent to which the ape image was to be found at the popular level. There are some indications that it may have been fairly widespread. The powerful symbolic links between apes and blacks, which have been shown to go back centuries, are likely to have endured in the popular mind – indeed, their effects still remain discernible. In the 18th century they were reinforced by numerous freak shows and similar entertainments featuring savages and/or apes:

The familiar hypothesis of the 'missing link' – the as yet unidentified occupant of the twilight zone between human beings and the rest of the animal world – was recurrently invoked when creatures suitable for the role turned up. There was, for example, the 'Man Teger, lately brought from the East Indies, a most strange and wonderful creature, the like never before seen in England . . . from the Head downwards resembling a man, its fore parts clear, and its hinder parts all Hairy . . . taking a glass of Ale in his hand like a Christian, Drinks it, also plays at Quarter Staff.

(Altick 1978, p. 38)

The promoters of such entertainments probably neither knew nor cared about the distinction between human and ape established by Tyson. The posters and newspaper advertisements for such shows tended to stress in a sensational manner the apishness of savages or the human-likeness of apes. Barker (1978), who discussed this in some detail, warned against overestimating the effects of such influences since at that period the London public 'had daily experience of the human attributes of Negroes' (1978, p. 58). Such a view assumes that contact *ipso facto* serves as a corrective; but the history of such contacts does not bear this out. The presence of Jews in Germany did not prevent the Nazis from persuading many Germans of their sub-humanity. But in the absence of solid evidence of the kind found in contemporary writings, the conclusion must remain speculative.

## The savage as ancestor and the 'noble savage'

In spite of the initial warning in the preface, my emphasis on the ape image, which is one of the central themes of this book, risks creating a wrong impression of the climate of 18th-century opinion. At least a brief correction of the perspective is therefore desirable.

Until the latter part of the century, Enlightenment thinkers took a largely benevolently tolerant view of savages. The philosophy of progress, to which many adhered, saw savagery as merely a stage through which humankind generally passed before achieving civilization. As Degérando, one of the *Observateurs de l'homme* put it, by travelling to distant places one also travels backwards in time, seeing one's own roots. The Scottish philosopher Adam Ferguson (1723–1816) drew a sympathetic portrait of 'our species in its rude state', which clearly shows that the travellers and explorers on whose reports he relied had provided fair descriptions of the savages they had encountered.

There were also those who heaped extravagant praise upon savages, holding them up as models for a civilization that had become corrupted. Sterling qualities were attributed to peoples all over the world: American Indians were said (notably by French writers) to be free and independent, in contrast to the lack of political freedom at home; the inhabitants of the South Sea Islands were seen to lead a voluptuous life, happily free from sexual restraints. As regards Africans, I shall give a more detailed example summarized from a mission report:

The Africans combine honesty and frankness with a generosity which one might almost regard as too far-reaching. They practice the teaching of the Scriptures literally, and do not care for the morrow. They never imagine that they would ever be lacking in food or clothing. They are always ready to share the little they have with those who had suffered misfortune. . . . This is contrasted with Europeans, who give nothing for nothing.

(Abbé Proyarts 1776, cited in Krauss 1978, p. 44)

It is readily seen that such a panegyric is the obverse of the more usual stereotypes of the lazy and happy-go-lucky African who does not observe any property rights. At any rate, it will be evident even from these brief comments that the ape image was only one element, albeit an important one, in a complex set of representations. The debate during the earlier part of the century had been about the relationship between humans at large and apes; subsequently it became focused on the relative closeness to apes of particular ethnic groups, especially blacks.

# Part II

# ANIMALITY AND BEASTLY MAN-EATING

# 5

# THE 'NEGRO' AND THE APE

## Preliminary sketch of some background factors

The shift in perspective away from the question of the relationship between humans and apes, and towards an ordering of human races according to their supposed degree of proximity to apes, was indicative of a shift from Enlightenment values towards racial intolerance. It is difficult to be certain about the chronology of this transition. There is some evidence that, contrary to what is often believed, it may already have been under way by the mid-18th century, well before the rise of the anti-slavery movement. An African from the Guinea Coast, Anthony William Amo, was brought to Holland as a child in about 1707. His intellectual talents having been recognized, he was educated there and went on first to the University of Halle in 1729 and then to Wittenberg. After publishing a treatise, he moved to Jena in 1740 where he taught philosophy. A few years later he became subjected to what we would call racist attacks and was forced to return to Africa in 1747 (Martin-Luther Universität 1968).

The nature of these changes constitutes a historical problem that seems to have been insufficiently explored, and several of the interpretations that have been put forward appear questionable. For instance, Wokler's (1980) discussion of the background to the earlier 'ape debate' concluded that the change was 'no doubt closely linked to the slow demise of conjectural history in the same period, to the growth of craniology, phrenology and studies of the brain as alternatives to earlier philosophies of the human mind, and, in linguistics, to the development of philology' (p. 1174). Some of these developments, such as craniology and phrenology, did not take place until after the 'ape debate' was already well under way, and thus could hardly have contributed to initiating it. Moreover, such an interpretation locates the sources of change entirely within the intellectual domain, without regard to the wider socio-political context. The period under consideration witnessed some cataclysmic events, and it would be surprising if these had nothing to do with the intellectual changes.

The most obvious factor was of course the anti-slavery movement in Britain, whose supporters had some favourable, albeit condescending things to say about blacks and their human rights. The defenders of the vested interests in slavery, in order to counter this, sought to show that blacks are less than human, and their prominent mouthpiece was Edward Long.

Another of the the great events that influenced the image of savages was the French Revolution and its aftermath. The fall of despotism removed the need for the noble savage as a model of free men. For a while the savage became endowed with solid republican virtues: simple in his needs and wants, courageous and of great endurance. He was compared with the ancient Celts who rose from primitivism to high civilization, the implication being that all savages were capable of it.

All this changed when the reaction set in, though the romantic 'child of nature' lingered on in literature. The evolutionary progressivism that had characterized the Enlightenment, and provided the rationale for its relative tolerance, fell into desuetude. The call was for a return to faith and obedience rather than reliance on reason. A prominent exponent of this counter-revolutionary ideology was Joseph de Maistre (1753–1821), whose view of savages was based on a strange version of human history. According to him, savages were peoples who had in the past committed heinous sins, and as a punishment had been reduced to the sorry state prevalent in every continent except Europe. The radical shift in attitudes was not confined to political doctrinaires like de Maistre, or to the quasi-scientific writings of Virey. It was also reflected in the theoretical stances of that great innovator in biology, Georges Cuvier.

Although the German states had not taken part in the slave trade, nor themselves been involved in the Revolution, the resulting intellectual ferment affected them powerfully. The discussions about the status of savages in general, and blacks in particular, were at least as lively in Germany as in Britain and France. The active interchanges among scholars in these countries meant that they were generally familiar with each other's work.

The outcome of all this was a definite trend towards more negative views of savages in general. This applied even to the inhabitants of the South Sea Islands, who had for a time been idealized. In France their reputation suffered a blow when in 1785 twelve members of an expedition led by La Pérouse were killed in Samoa. In England also a change of opinion came about through the religious revival which created the London Missionary Society. Its members, far from seeing the free and easy way of life and sexual mores of the South Sea Islanders as paradisical, regarded it as evidence of the ignoble savagery of people who existed in an animal-like state (cf. Jaspers 1972).

The curious fact has also been noted that the developments which led to what might be called the 'racialization' of the Great Chain, and the subsequent burgeoning of race theories, coincided with the abolition of the slave trade. It has been suggested that the paradox was only apparent, and that race theories had the latent function of countering the threat posed by blacks becoming equals. It is a view that will be further discussed in a later chapter.

## Long's obloquy on the apishness of blacks

Edward Long's *History of Jamaica* (1774) was a watershed. In it he developed the thesis that blacks not only constitute a species intermediate between humans and apes, but are closer to the latter. His theoretical ideas were not original; neither was his account of the characteristics of blacks, which drew together in more colourful form a great deal that had often been written about them earlier. But his radical thesis had not previously been formulated in such explicit and passionate terms. Historians have argued about the extent of his influence, which is surprising, since they rarely fail to devote many pages to his work. Barker (1978) has extensively examined his ideas in the context of the socio-political and intellectual background. I owe a great deal to his discussion, though disagreeing with some of his judgements. My own presentation will be mainly confined to the central 'ape' theme.

Edward Long (1734–1813) was a planter and judge in Jamaica, a complicated person who did not simply identify with the planters. While relegating blacks to the status of animality, he was by no means uncritical of the numerous abuses of which his fellow-planters had been guilty.[1] This had the curious consequence that his arguments were widely though of course selectively quoted by abolitionists as well as their opponents. The theoretical foundation of his argument rested on a somewhat idiosyncratic version of the Great Chain. The account of Long's views that follows is based chiefly on the extensive chapter devoted to 'Negroes' in the second volume of his *History*. I must say that my previous encounters with what several authors had said about Long's work did not really prepare me for the shock of reading his distasteful rantings.

Long's arguments, spelled out at great length, were designed to prove the close resemblances between blacks and orang-utans. Needless to say, he had no high opinion of the intellectual capacities of the blacks, which he compared to those of simians:

> Their genius (if it can be so called) consists alone in trick and cunning, enabling them, like monkeys and apes, to be thievish and mischievous, with a peculiar dexterity. They seem unable to combine ideas, or pursue a chain of reasoning.
>
> (Long 1774, Vol. 2, p. 377)

Long had much to say about the animality of their physical features, said to have 'a covering of wool, like the bestial fleece, instead of hair'; their smell is 'bestial or fetid'; the women's nipples are large 'as if adapted by nature to the peculiar conformation of their children's mouths'; 'the women are delivered with little or no labour; they have therefore no more occasion for midwives than the female orang-outang, or any other wild animal'. It is hinted that they are cannibals: 'Why should we doubt that the same ravenous savage, who can feast on the roasted quarters of an ape (that *mock-man*), would be no less delighted with the sight of a loin or buttock of human flesh, prepared in the same manner?'

Presumably mindful of the widely held opinion that the possession of language is a key criterion for distinguishing humans and animals, Long sought to overcome this objection by trying to show that it is invalid; in this he was probably influenced by Monboddo, though his line of argument was somewhat different. He suggested that orang-utans probably have some rudimentary language for the communication of meaning, 'whether it resembles the gabbling of turkeys, like that of the Hottentots, or the hissing of serpents'. He proposed an experiment whereby orang-utans were to be trained in human language, and expected it to succeed.

In an earlier anonymous anti-abolitionist pamphlet (['A Planter'] Long, 1772, pp. 48–9) he had merely touched upon sexual aspects:

> The lower class of women in *England*, are remarkably fond of blacks, for reasons too brutal to mention; they would connect themselves with horses and asses, if the laws permitted them.

Later in the same piece he held out the spectre of the mongrelization of England, which would spread from the lower classes right up to the aristocracy and make the English as bad as the Portuguese 'in complexion of skin and baseness of mind'.

In his book on Jamaica Long went even further in suggesting sexual relationships between blacks and apes:

> I do not think that an orang-outang husband would be a dishonour to an Hottentot female; for what are the Hottentots? They are . . . a people certainly very stupid, and very brutal. In many respects they are more like beasts than men.
>
> (1774, Vol. 2, p. 364)

> [Orang-utans do not] seem at all inferior in their intellectual faculties to many of the Negro race; with some of whom, it is credible that they have the most intimate connexion and consanguinity. The amorous intercourse between them may be frequent; the negroes themselves bear testimony that such intercourses actually happen; and it is certain, that both races agree perfectly well in lasciviousness of disposition.
>
> (Ibid., p. 370)

In this connection it is worth mentioning Barker's (1978, p. 42) comment to the effect that Long 'may have been a humane man rationalizing his acquiescence in an inhumane system. . . . His extreme reaction against interracial sex was justifiable on his own terms'. But when it came to Creoles there was no further sign of Long's distaste for 'lascivious amours'. He evidently approved and even admired the skills of Creole women in negotiating and conducting sexual affairs:

[The Creole women's] notions of love are, that it is free and transitory. This is well known to their white gallants, for even the authority of a master must bend to the more absolute empire of Cupid.

(Long 1774, Vol. 2, p. 415)

One is inclined to suspect that Long himself was to be counted among the 'gallants'. Whether writing negatively about the blacks, or positively about Creoles, this part of his writings is suffused by a cloying sexuality that throws more light on the writer than on his subject. Long protests too much, and his account is suggestive of obsessive sexual fantasies.

In my view there can be little doubt that Long's influence must have been considerable, even if (as Barker (1978, p. 51) claimed) his application of the notion of the Great Chain to race 'left him in a position of precarious intellectual isolation'. The *History* was widely read and reprinted in New York in 1788. Long had some prominent followers, and others seem to have appropriated the gist of his thesis without explicitly acknowledging him. Stripped of some of its crudities, Long's key contention of the closeness of blacks to apes was to become the leitmotif of 19th-century thought on race.

While the connection with abolitionism is unquestionable, it cannot be the whole story; for it fails to account for the fact that most later writers on race adhered to Long's central thesis of greater animality, while at the same time proclaiming their opposition to slavery.[2] The issue appears to have acquired its own momentum as a philosophical-scientific puzzle, though other factors later came into play. The puzzle was, essentially, whether the psychological distance separating the lowly savage from European genius was compatible with a unitary human nature. No doubt largely as a result of Long's influence, a negative answer like that of Smellie became more common:

How many gradations may be traced between a stupid Huron, or a Hottentot, and a profound philosopher? Here the distance is immense, but Nature has occupied the whole by almost infinite shades of gradation.

In descending the scale of animation, the next step, it is humiliating to remark, is very short. Man, in his lowest condition, is evidently linked, both in the form of his body and the capacity of his mind, to the large and small orang-outang. These again, by another slight gradation, are connected to the apes, who, like the former, have no tails.

(Smellie 1790, pp. 552–3, cited in Bynum 1974)

It is interesting to compare the above passage with a similar one written some eighty years later by Darwin ([1871] 1901, p. 99), who addressed essentially the same issue when he referred to the difference

in intellect, between a savage who uses hardly any abstract terms, and a Newton or Shakespeare. Differences of this kind between the highest men of the highest races and the lowest savages, are connected by the finest gradations. Therefore it is possible that they might pass and be developed into each other.

The similarity between the passages is striking, and casual scanning might well lead one to suppose that they are saying much the same thing. In fact, they reflect a radical transformation of ideas over the period. Smellie was expounding the doctrine of the Great Chain, with its gradations permanently fixed, while Darwin was arguing that however great the apparent gap, it could have been bridged by evolutionary processes. The former, unlike the latter, implied that race differences have been ordained by nature and are unchangeable. However, as will become apparent in due course, this does not mean that all evolutionists were monogenists, like Darwin.

## Soemmering and White: first attempts at scientific proof

By the latter part of the 18th century Long's thesis had become widely known, and a German anatomist, Samuel Thomas Soemmering (1755–1830), took up the issue. A convinced believer in the Great Chain, he was concerned with the question as to where blacks belong: are they fully human, descended from the same original pair as whites, or located midway between animals and humans? His aim was to throw light on the problem through comparative anatomical studies.

Soemmering's account, mainly based on an examination of three skulls in his possession, and the dissection of four corpses, was published in a book entitled *On the bodily difference between Moor and European* (1784). In the introduction he explained that judgements about the lowly status of the 'Moor' in the Great Chain rested largely on prejudice, and he wanted to investigate the matter objectively. His fundamental assumption was that the main distinction between animals and men lies in the 'organ of intellect', and therefore he concentrated on the brain. But what features of the brain would constitute an adequate basis for comparison? Soemmering eliminated several possibilities, such as simple weight (much greater in elephants), or even the ratio of total body- to brain-weight (since it is more favourable among birds). Eventually he came up with 'the thickness of nerves', clearly very pleased with his discovery. His reasoning was that the nerves, especially those in the brain, subserve merely the 'vital functions'; hence given the same cranial capacity, thicker nerves entail a lesser quantity of cerebral matter available for the higher cognitive functions.

Soemmering claimed to have found not merely that total cranial capacity is somewhat less among blacks, but more importantly their nerves, and especially the sensory nerves, are much thicker. Singling out the sensory nerves was connected with the widespread belief that savages have exceedingly acute sense organs; there is also the notion of the 'mobile ears' of savages, which harks back to

Albertus Magnus: 'As is well known, savages have mobile outstanding ears, and therefore far sharper and far-reaching hearing than we have' (Soemmering 1784, p. 14).

Soemmering adduced some other, relatively minor arguments (for example, blacks have almost ape-like fingers and toes) to reinforce his conclusion that the 'Moor' is rather closer to the apes than Europeans. Yet in spite of this, he declared, they are still humans – leaving things rather in the air by facing both ways. The book was generally well received, with the major exception of his friend Blumenbach (about whom more in Chapter 6), one of the great figures of the period, who had serious reservations.

Soemmering attributed some of the critical responses to his work to misunderstandings, and brought out a revised and enlarged edition in 1785, substituting 'Negro' for 'Moor' in the title. He attempted to show the validity of the doctrine of the Great Chain by listing other adherents, and his actual arguments in this respect were largely borrowed from Long. Little further empirical evidence was put forward, but extensive quotations were used in an effort to bolster his case. Thus he cited a French missionary according to whom Negroes have limited mental ability, many being completely stupid. Soemmering even adduced the fact of living in the same climate as an indication that blacks and apes have something in common. However, he stated that his findings did not provide any justification for the institution of slavery – presumably because Blumenbach had referred to this. In spite of such efforts to please, Blumenbach himself took a poor view of Soemmering's general thesis, as shown by this ironic passage in which he did not mention his friend:

> What has been asserted about the Ethiopians, namely that they are closer to apes than other peoples, I readily admit in the sense that one could, for instance, say that the breed of domestic pigs with hooves . . . is closer to horses than other pigs. But such a relative comparison in general [carries] no weight.
>
> (Cited in Lilienthal 1990, p. 43)

A Manchester surgeon, Charles White (1728–1813), came across extracts from the work of Soemmering that were translated for him by a colleague at Manchester Royal Infirmary. These anatomical disquisitions were more radical in tone than Soemmering's eventual conclusions (Lilienthal 1990), but they partly inspired him to write *An account of the regular gradation in man* (White 1799). This opens with a purple passage about the Great Chain of Being (p. 1):

> Every one who has made Natural History an object of study, must have been led occasionally to contemplate the beautiful gradation that subsists amongst created beings, from the highest to the lowest. From man down to the smallest reptile, whose existence can be discovered only by the microscope, Nature exhibits to our view an immense chain of beings,

endued with various degrees of intelligence and active powers, suited to their stations in the general system.

His aim was to demonstrate that the African is 'nearer to the brute creation than any other human species' (p. 42). In contrast to many other speculative writers on this theme, he must at least be credited with an attempt to provide evidence for his position. For this reason the quaint empirical study on which he embarked is worth outlining.

Casting around for ways of establishing the lowly status of blacks, he hit upon the notion that the length of their lower arms would, as with the higher apes, be relatively greater than in whites. He had a skeleton of a Negro in his museum, proceeded to measure it, and it seemed to confirm his hunch. Aware that this was not enough, he went on to measure all the skeletons available in Manchester; these consisted of nine Europeans, one more Negro, and some unspecified others. Comparing the two Negroes with the European skeletons, he found their lower arms to be longer in proportion to the upper arm and the height of the body.

Thereafter he continued to measure living subjects in order to strengthen his case. It is interesting that he displayed an awareness of possible methodological pitfalls. This led him to compare 'the first 12 negroes I met with, and also . . . the first 12 Europeans, of nearly corresponding stature that I measured . . . so that no selection was made in either case for the purpose of serving an hypothesis' (p. 52). His supposedly random sample of Europeans consisted mainly of his own family and servants. It is also clear that there were considerable technical problems in carrying out the measurements with live subjects, problems which White mentioned, only to dismiss them. He then claimed that his predictions were supported in every one of twelve (inadequately specified) pairings.

Apart from this one more fully documented aspect, White listed an extensive series of features which, he claimed, supported his thesis. For instance: 'the lower part of the [Africans'] chin, instead of projecting outward, retreats, or falls back, as in the ape' (p. 43). This is of course the direct opposite of the prognathism then more usually attributed to blacks. The same approximation to the ape, he suggested, applies to skull, eye sockets, nose, jaws, feet, thigh and so on; the single exception were the lips, which are thinner in the ape – a fact he tried hard to explain away.

It is a litany that was to be frequently repeated by others in the course of the 19th century. Several of his assertions were directly taken from Long, for example, 'Negresses have larger nipples than Europeans – Brutes have still larger nipples' (p. 63). While discussing breast shapes, White burst into the following panegyric (p. 137):

> In what other quarter of the globe shall we find the blush that overspreads the soft features of the beautiful women of Europe. . . . Where, except on the bosom of the European woman, two such plump and snowy white hemispheres, tipt with vermillion?

The perennial refrain about the size of the male sex organ is duly recorded (p. 61):

> that the PENIS of an African is larger than that of an European, has, I believe, been shewn in every anatomical school in London. Preparations of them are preserved in most anatomical museums; and I have one in mine. I have examined several living Negroes, and found it invariably to be the case.

White also seemed pleased to learn from Long that the lice of Negroes are darker than those of Europeans, which he regarded as proof of a fundamental difference; this was because he believed that animal parasites had been especially assigned to particular species of hosts. Even modes of functioning were grist to his mill (p. 85):

> in comparing the classes of mankind with each other and with the brute creation . . . there is a gradation also discernible in the senses of *seeing, hearing* and *smelling*, in *memory* and in the powers of *mastication*, but in a contrary order . . . the European being least perfect, the African more so, and the brutes most perfect of all, in these particulars.

White must have felt some qualms about his position, for in concluding he posed the question whether such harping on black animality was appropriate at a time of anti-slavery sentiment. His answer was to the effect that he was simply conducting scientific investigations, though he declared himself opposed to slavery and was willing to concede that blacks have souls. Such a defence of scientific rigour and detachment was often used thereafter, and is not unknown even today.

Not everyone accepted the claims of Soemmering and White. A physician to the colony of Sierra Leone, Thomas Winterbottom (1803), refuted them on the basis of first-hand observations. He cited Soemmering as a bad example of a naturalist who is always anxious to detect every alleged link in the Great Chain. As far as White's account is concerned, he stated that he had noticed neither intellectual inferiority nor sensory superiority among Africans, commenting on the latter as follows:

> Mr. White has not favoured us with any instances of the superiority of Africans in the above points, and I am persuaded that his remarks on the subject are perfectly unfounded . . . I have never heard such circumstances noticed, either by the Africans themselves, or by Europeans residing in Africa. . . .
>
> I observed in them, indeed, a superior quickness of discovering game in a forest; but this faculty is acquired by practice.
>
> (Winterbottom 1803, Vol. II, p. 273)

A man of sturdy common sense, untroubled by speculations about the Great Chain, Winterbottom relied on his personal experience. He had a high regard for the qualities of Africans, and went so far as to compare their behaviour favourably with the 'baseness and depravity of manners' to be found among Europeans in West Africa. He was, however, in a minority in his time, compared with the vociferousness of those in Britain and other parts of Europe who proclaimed the near-animality of non-Europeans. The alleged superior sensory acuity of savages, implying their greater animality, was constantly referred to and remained unquestioned until the end of the 19th century, when it was challenged in the pages of *Nature*. Rivers (1901) was the first to demonstrate the falsity of the notion experimentally.

Although Germany had not been involved in the slave trade, Soemmering was not alone in his interest in the status of blacks and other races. The broader theoretical issues concerning the origins of the diversity of peoples on earth were being actively discussed. Academic communication was well established, and the writings of Long and others were widely known. These debates, and a notorious contribution from France, will be considered in the next chapter.

# 6

# TOWARDS SCIENTIFIC RACISM

The debate in Germany reflected the changing climate of opinion, progressively tilting against the Enlightenment view of savagery as a stage in the evolution of humanity. The debate was wide-ranging, including Herder and Kant, but I shall concentrate on a small group of key figures in close contact, the most outstanding of whom was Blumenbach, whose views were diametrically opposed to those of Meiners, his colleague at the University of Göttingen. Meiners was a polygenist who wrote in defence of slavery, Blumenbach a monogenist who stressed the unity of the human species. Their personal styles were equally contrasting: Meiners a speculative philosopher with a heavy ideological commitment, Blumenbach a sober scientist concerned with empirical evidence.

There was also Soemmering, discussed in Chapter 5, who had been a close friend of Blumenbach while they were undergraduates. Another friend of Soemmering's was Johann Georg Forster (1754–94), who while still in his teens had accompanied his father on Cook's second voyage. Blumenbach, it will be recalled, had been critical of Soemmering's book; but Soemmering's other friend, Forster, was much more ambiguous in his response, seemingly not wishing to offend. He declared that, not being an anatomist himself, he was not qualified to judge, but he suggested to Soemmering that he should mention the decisive argument for the humanity of the Negroes, namely their capacity for speech. Forster's views are set out most clearly in his critique of two essays by Kant on the subject of race. Accusing Kant of applying philosophical categories without reference to empirical reality, he warmly recommended Soemmering's book. Forster's adherence to the Great Chain is indicated by his reference to 'the fruitful thought, that everything in creation is linked by small steps [Nüancen]' (Forster [1786] 1969, Vol. 2, p. 85). In a lengthy and rather convoluted passage he discussed the relationship between whites, blacks and apes in the series of animals on earth. It boils down to the statement that, though among the various human types blacks most closely resemble the apes, there remains a critical gap: 'Thus an ape-like human is no ape' (p. 86). Forster was unable to make up his mind as regards monogeny or polygeny, but while uncertain about some issues he clearly abhorred slavery, making an emotional appeal against the animalization entailed by its practice.

As will already have become apparent, the major figure who stressed the full humanity of blacks was Johann Friedrich Blumenbach (1752–1840), professor of medicine and natural history, who is generally regarded as the founder of physical anthropology. He had become inspired by his teacher Büttner, who possessed a fine collection of naturalia and frequently displayed at his lectures travel books with illustrations of exotic peoples. Blumenbach later assembled a famous collection of skulls, and throughout his life remained an avid reader of travel reports; but unlike many others, notably his colleague Meiners, Blumenbach was a critical reader. He went so far as to arrange the reports about particular peoples in chronological order, and compared them. He found quite striking contradictions and incon-sistencies, noting also that if a work was regarded as a *locus classicus*, the tendency was merely to copy it (cf. Plischke 1937). Blumenbach had scant regard for the doctrine of the Great Chain, certainly treating it as inapplicable within the human species. Moreover, he was rather sceptical about a number of then current beliefs, such as the supposed 'fact' that savage women give birth as easily as animals.

Blumenbach's major work was his *De generis humani varietate nativa* ([1795] 1865), which pioneered an empirical approach to the classification of races by the shape of the skull. He refuted some of Linnaeus' more extravagant notions, showing, for instance, that albinos are not a separate species but people who suffer from an infirmity that affects both skin and eyes. He also went to great trouble to investigate and disprove some of the stories used by Linnaeus to support his contentions.[1] Blumenbach did not devise any system of measurement but proposed a method of comparison whereby skulls, with the lower jaws removed, are placed on a surface and viewed from above, the so-called *norma verticalis*. In practice he made little use of his method and did not base his classification on it. The reason why it is important is that it led in the 19th century to the elaboration of the 'cephalic index' (i.e. the ratio of the breadth of the skull to its length expressed as a percentage) by Anders Retzius (1796–1860), which subsequently became one of the main tools of craniology.

Of chief concern here are Blumenbach's views about racial differences, based on the study of both his extensive collection of skulls and of the contemporary travel literature. In his view, skull shapes suggest a division into five major races, namely Caucasian, Mongolian, Ethiopian, American and Malaysian. He enthused about the beauty and symmetry of a young female Georgian skull, which probably accounts for his view that the Caucasian is the highest type and also the original race from which others were subsequently derived by a process he called 'degeneration'. For him this term had no negative connotations, and he meant by it a diversification resulting from the influence of climatic and other factors that came to be transmitted by heredity. At the same time Blumenbach rejected any sharp dividing lines between such races, emphasizing the unity of humankind as a species:

> No variety of mankind exists, whether of colour, countenance, or stature,
> etc. , so singular as not to be connected with others of the same kind by

such an imperceptible transition, that it is very clear that all are related, and only differ from each other in degree.

([1795]1865, pp. 98–9)

It must be admitted that in his earlier writings Blumenbach had painted a rather unflattering portrait of the physical characteristics of 'Ethiopians', as he had initially termed Africans; he described them variously as having a 'knotty forehead', 'puffy lips' and being often 'bandy-legged'. Later he radically shifted his position, possibly as a result of a personal encounter.[2] Certainly in his later years he made a point of getting to know Africans, reading the literature about them, and collecting and measuring African skulls. As a result, he criticized others who depicted blacks as inferior or even as a separate species, stressing that Africans have the same mental abilities and potential as the rest of humanity. He referred to 'the good disposition and faculties of our black brethren' and devoted several pages to citing examples of black ability, concluding as follows:

> there is no so-called savage nation known under the sun which has so much distinguished itself by such examples of perfectibility and original capacity for scientific culture, and thereby attached itself so closely to the most civilized nations of the earth, *as the Negro*.
> (Blumenbach [1795] 1865, p. 312; emphasis in original)

Blumenbach was later extensively cited by writers such as the anatomist Tiedemann (1837), who were concerned to show that blacks are full members of the human family rather than intermediate between humans and apes. Blumenbach was strongly opposed to the teachings of Meiners, a defender of slavery, whom Soemmering had called 'the beloved philosopher of our fatherland' (1784, p. xiii). The views propagated by Meiners were distasteful to Blumenbach, though as a colleague in Göttingen he attacked him only obliquely.

Christoph Meiners (1747–1816) described himself as 'a teacher of wordly wisdom' [Weltweisheit], in other words a philosopher. He was a man of immense erudition who exerted considerable influence in his time. Like Vico, the ambitious Meiners wanted to found a 'new science' dealing with the nature of man, his past and his future. Unlike Vico's, his teachings were fundamentally based on ideas of racial and sexual inequality and did not endure, though they were temporarily resurrected by Nazi race theorists. The wide range of his writings, and their reception, have been surveyed by Rupp-Eisenreich (1983), and I shall merely present some selected aspects relevant to my theme.

Nowadays Meiners usually rates only a cursory mention in histories of anthropology, focused on his idiosyncratic criteria for the classification of races. In his *Sketch of the history of mankind* (Meiners 1785) he proposed that 'One of the most important characteristics of tribes and peoples is beauty or ugliness' (p. 43), claiming that only people of Caucasian stock (but excepting Slavs) deserve the epithet of beauty. While in this early work it was only one, albeit an important criterion for the classification of peoples, it later became for him *the* major one. In

65

a subsequent lengthy article Meiners (1788) sought to document in detail the characteristics of the 'ugly peoples'. Those of mongoloid descent, he alleged, resemble 'the feeble-minded or lunatics of our continent inasmuch as they have much thicker skulls and much larger heads' (p. 280). In American savages the hair grows almost down to their eyebrows; in China women are preferred whose eyes are as piggish [schweinsartig] as possible; the faces of Negroes have an apish appearance, and so on.

In other writings Meiners (1787) put forward a theory concerning what may be roughly translated as the 'adaptability' of different peoples, with a strong accent on the animality of the 'ugly races'. Meiners started with the observation that humans have settled in the most diverse climatic conditions and utilize a wide range of foodstuffs, unlike animals confined to a narrow ecological range and limited to certain kinds of nourishment. Yet paradoxically humans are more sensitive to pain and adverse weather, suffer more illnesses and recover more slowly from injuries, and cannot cope with raw or indigestible foods.

While this is true of humans in general, there are substantial variations in adaptability among the different races of man:

> The more intelligent and noble people are by nature, the more adaptable, sensitive, delicate and soft is their body; on the other hand, the less they possess the capacity and disposition towards virtue, the more they lack adaptability; and not only that, but the less sensitive are their bodies, the more can they tolerate extreme pain or the rapid alteration of heat and cold; the less they are exposed to illnesses, the more rapidly their recovery from wounds that would be fatal for more sensitive peoples, and the more they can partake of the worst and most indigestible foods . . . without noticeable ill effects.
>
> (Meiners 1787, pp. 211/2)

Belief in such hardiness of the backward races formed at that time part of the conventional wisdom, pushed by Meiners to greater extremes. For him the noblest race were the Celts, and he points out that they were able to conquer various parts of the world. Yet they are more sensitive to heat and cold, fall more easily prey to sickness, and their delicacy is shown by the fact that they are fussy about what they eat.

The Slavs are clearly an inferior race, less sensitive and more resistant to disease. This is illustrated by a series of anecdotes: for instance, Russians are content with rough food and can eat poisonous fungi without coming to any harm; other Slavs bake sick people in an oven and then make them roll in the snow – saunas were not fashionable in Meiners' Germany. Below the Slavs are the peoples of the Middle East and Asia, all limited in intelligence and of an evil disposition, which goes together with lack of adaptability and insensitivity.

Meiners went on to discuss the Negroes and Americans who 'approach animals most closely'. With regard to the Negroes, he referred to the anatomical studies of

Soemmering, expressing his conviction that it is not only their colour but their whole bodily structure that governs their capacities, dispositions and tempera-ment. Thus in the Negroes the parts of the head concerned with the mastication of food, i.e. jaw muscles and bones, and teeth, are much bigger and stronger than those of Europeans. Their heads are larger, but the brain is smaller and the nerves coarser. They can eat practically anything, such as raw and stinking rotten meat. Their females give birth as easily as wild beasts. They are seldom ill, even in the West Indies where they are maltreated, and can endure any amount of pain 'as if they had no human, barely animal, feeling'. Meiners tells the story of a Negro, condemned to death by slow-burning fire; when his back was already half cooked, he asked for a pipe and smoked it placidly. Lest this evoke some admiration in the reader, Meiners added: 'If one wanted to attribute this quiet endurance of [suffering] not to the lack of feeling of the thick-skinned and coarse-nerved Negro, but to his steadfastness, then one would have to rate [the lowest kinds of animals] more highly than the greatest heroes of antiquity and modern times' (1787, p. 230).

If the Negroes are bad, according to Meiners, the Americans are even worse, as he proclaimed in a passage already cited (p. 21). Other confabulations abound: American skulls are so thick that, as the Spanish conquerors found, the best blades shatter on them. Their skin is thicker than that of an ox. They can walk naked in the hottest sun as well as the coldest winter. The Americas harbour the most gluttonous monsters – they can feed on all kinds of foul offal, drink the most polluted water and consume without ill effect vast quantities of alcohol that would kill the strongest beast. They live to a ripe old age, without diminution of their strength: one can see 100-year-old men jumping on to their horses as easily as the fittest youngsters. They seldom suffer illness, and make miraculous recoveries from the severest wounds. There is a lengthy account of the self-inflicted wounds of their endurance tests and their unbelievable cruelty to their enemies, described in lovingly grisly detail over several pages.

At the same time, the Americans are not only the most unfeeling of peoples, they are also the least adaptable: they cannot get used to other climates, food or modes of life. When the Jesuits brought Indians to their mission, they began to die in large numbers. They were, Meiners argued, quite unable to adapt to their changed circumstances, lapsing into a deadly melancholy. Examples of this kind abound, without any suggestion that European diseases might have been the cause. Here again Meiners seemed anxious lest the reader be led to draw the wrong conclusion, namely that the Americans are so happy in their way of life that depriving them of it kills them:

one can only conclude from this that the unfeeling Americans are . . . so lacking in adaptability that they are almost as little able as wild beasts to get used to another climate, and even more so to other kinds of food and modes of life.

(Meiners 1787, p. 246)

Meiners greatly expanded on these and other themes in a large work entitled *Researches on the variations in human nature* (1815). It contains more alleged anatomical details of various races, and their supposed sexual peculiarities are examined in prurient detail. For instance, men in north-east Asia are said to have very small genitals and their women, by contrast, very large ones; owing to this misfit, the women disdain their own men, preferring Russians and Cossacks. In addition, American (Indian) women and Negresses are said to have always shown a decided preference for Europeans; this was a stereotypical theme in the (male-authored) literature on blacks. Meiners failed to explain why black women should be so keen on white men, given the fact that he dwelt in some detail on the extraordinarily large and 'animal-like' penis of Negro males. Generally he maintained that unduly weak (as among American Indians) and unduly strong sexual drives (as among Africans, Chinese, Japanese and peoples of the South Sea Islands) were equally bad – only Europeans have it just right.

I should make it clear once again that the above is certainly not a balanced account of Meiners' approach. His writings contain many sensible and perceptive passages; for instance, some of his comments on the abilities and shortcomings of various peoples foreshadow topics of study by 20th-century cross-cultural psychologists.[3] Nonetheless, the notion of the permanent inferiority and animal-likeness of the 'ugly races' runs as a constant thread through most of his writings. His reading was wide but quite uncritical; furthermore, he was apt to select from the mass of material which he perused those aspects that fitted in with his thesis.

I have dealt with Meiners at some length, since his ideas were the subject of lively, often critical discussions. He was read by the young Hegel, and probably contributed to Hegel's demonic image of Africa, which he described as a place where one can find the most terrible manifestations of human nature (Hegel [1832] 1992, Vol. 12, pp. 120–9).

## Reaction in France: Virey and the human-likeness of apes

The writings of Meiners, with their strident ideological message, were widely understood as applying the lessons of history to the contemporary situation. In a French translation of one of his works the preface refers to the decadence of Rome with its 'multitudes of slaves and foreigners . . . in such a corrupting atmosphere they degraded by their admixture the entire mass of the people' (cited in Rupp-Eisenreich 1983, p. 135). A similar line was taken by the Nazi historian von Eickstedt who wrote in praise of Meiners, coupling his name with that of Virey and others like him. There is in fact evidence that Virey was familiar with the writings of Meiners (Rupp-Eisenreich 1985). However, apart from the denigration of savages, their approaches to the issue did not have much in common. Unlike Meiners, Virey was a believer in the Great Chain and argued most vigorously in the style of Long and White. Moreover, in order to render his often bizarre arguments of the close relation between blacks and apes more plausible, he took over some old notions about the supposedly remarkable accomplishments of apes.

Jules Virey (1775–1847) was a naturalist and professor of pharmacy, a follower of Rousseau and a fervent admirer of Buffon.[4] Nonetheless he was, unlike Buffon, a polygenist who believed that humans consist of separate species. His *Histoire naturelle du genre humain* was essentially a work of popularization that achieved a wide circulation. In the first edition, published in 1801, he, rather like Meiners, dichotomized humans into fair and dark; in later ones he used Camper's 'facial angle' to categorize races, a notion to which I shall return. In the earlier editions there are passages indicating that his imagination ran along much the same lines as Long's, as, for instance, in the passage already quoted (pp. 45–6) about the sexual congress in darkest Africa between Negresses and satyrs. That passage was left out in later editions, which abandoned the poetry of dark passions and assumed a somewhat more detached tone. Nonetheless, Virey voiced some quaint ideas, such as his belief that colours influence the character of everything in organic nature. Thus he said that white animals are mostly innocent and guileless, while black ones are violent and nasty; this, he suggested, applied even to flowers: white ones are harmless, and dark ones are often poisonous. This comes oddly from someone who practised pharmacy!

According to Virey, Negroes are deficient in 'morality', a term used by him in a very broad sense to include thought and knowledge, political and religious ideas. While lacking in moral relationships with each other, they have relatively more physical ones:

> negresses abandon themselves to love with transports unknown any-where else: they have large sexual organs, and those of the negroes are proportionately voluminous; for generally, as the organs of generation acquire great activity among humans, so the intellectual faculties suffer a loss of energy.
>
> (Virey 1824, Vol. II. pp. 45–6)

This 'energy theory', as I will show in due course, gained further prominence later in the 19th century. Elsewhere Virey contended that Negro intelligence is less active because of 'the narrowness of the cerebral organs'. For the same reason the heads of their infants are smaller, which accounts for the ease with which savage women give birth.

Virey constantly harped on the 'animality' of blacks:

> Moreover, the negro brutally abandons himself to the most villainous excesses; his soul is, so to say, more steeped in the material, more encrusted in animality, more driven by purely physical appetites. . . .
>
> If man consists mainly of his spiritual faculties, it is incontestable that the negro is less human in this respect; he is closer to the life of brutes,

because we see him obeying his stomach, his sexual parts, in sum his senses, rather than reason.

(Virey 1834, Vol. 2, p. 117)

The most extreme degradation, according to Virey, is to be found among the Hottentots, whose physique he characterized as being similar to that of the great apes. Their rudimentary speech, almost like the clucking of guinea-fowl, is close to the muffled cluckings of orang-utans. They, together with Papuans, display 'extreme resemblances' to apes. Actually the Negroes themselves, averred Virey, recognize their parentage with the apes, whom they regard as savage and lazy Negroes.

The counterpoint to this tirade is a chapter on orang-utans, spelling out in detail their human-like behaviour as supposedly noted by observers. They easily learn things like eating at table using cutlery and a tooth-pick, making their beds, and even playing the flute. They can be taught to dress themselves, tie their shoe-laces, and the females have a well-developed sense of modesty. As regards modesty, if this were true, then by Virey's own logic female apes would be closer to white women than black ones! At any rate, for him all this proved the family resemblance between the higher apes and what for him was the lowest form of humanity. Virey conceded at one point that he did not pretend blacks and apes were of the same species, but on the very same page also commented:

> when one notes how much the orang-outan shows the signs of intelligence, how much his morals [moeurs], his actions, his habits are analogous to those of negroes, how much he is susceptible to education, it seems to me that one cannot disagree that the least perfect of blacks is very close to the first of the apes.
>
> (Virey 1834, Vol. 2, p. 118)

Virey's strategy was to humanize the anthropoid apes and dehumanize the blacks (see Figure 6.1). As might have been expected, Virey's views, like those of Long,[5] were well received and extensively borrowed across the Atlantic, since they provided ammunition for defenders of slavery. For example, Gwenebault (1837), who acknowledged his debt to Virey, referred to the 'extreme lasciviousnes of negro women . . . their simple and animal mode of living' (p. 94). He conveyed the impression that practically everything they do is animal-like, including even their manner of resting: 'Europeans sit on chairs, Asiatics cross-legged on earth or carpets, but the *Negro* either in Africa or New Guinea . . . remains squatting on his haunches, like the monkey' (p. 106). Apart from his success in America, Virey was also for a time widely read in France, and his work went through several editions. But many of his views were so patently absurd that it was difficult to take him seriously, and his writings later fell into well-deserved oblivion.

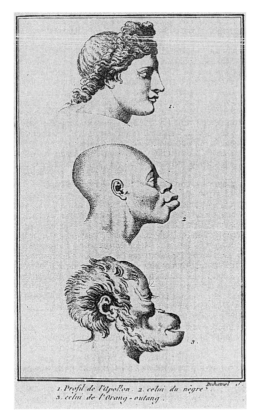

1. Profil de l'Apollon. 2. celui du nègre. 3. celui de l'Orang-outang.

*Figure 6.1* A classical Greek profile juxtaposed with those of a 'Negro' and an ape. Note the incipient 'muzzle' of the 'Negro', approximating to that of the ape (i.e. progressively lower 'facial angle').
*Source:* Virey (1824).

## Camper's 'facial angle'

The mode of classification that came to be adopted by Virey, and subsequently many others, had been devised by Camper. Previous classifications of human types had been based on criteria that were largely arbitrary, and there had been no clear way of deciding between them. The work of Camper from the 1760s onwards seemed to offer the promise of an objective criterion which involved measurement, the hallmark of science. Camper is often still only remembered as the man who first introduced quantification,[6] thereby paving the way for the craniological measures (see Figure 6.2) that became ever more elaborate as the 19th century progressed (e. g. Baker 1974; Curtin 1965).

While the 'facial angle' as such has often been mentioned and explained, and will therefore be only summarily described in a footnote,[7] an important aspect of the story is less well known, namely the fact that the method introduced by

71

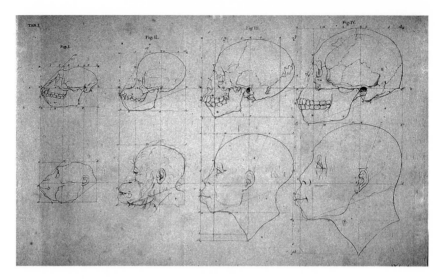

*Figure 6.2* Camper's illustration of 'facial angles'
*Source:* Camper (1794).

Camper came to be interpreted in a manner he had never intended, and that was quite contrary to his own views (Visser 1990). In effect, it was hijacked by those who believed in, and wished to prove, the existence of a racial hierarchy from the noble European to the lowest savage.

Petrus Camper (1722–89), a versatile Dutchman, was not only an outstanding comparative anatomist but also an artist and sculptor of great skill. A staunch monogenist, he emphasized in his lectures the unity of mankind, and the relative superficiality of differences he attributed to environmental causes. This did not mean a lack of interest in the varieties of forms encountered in nature. On the contrary, in his posthumously published *Works* (1794) he recounted his fascination, from an early age, with differences between animals and human races. He also studied theories of art from the Greeks onwards, noting that most European artists painted Negroes with the faces of Europeans.

Camper looked for some principle according to which the appearances of various human groups could be captured, which would also serve as a guide for their correct artistic representation. At the same time he was concerned with the concept of beauty, whose most perfect expression he saw in classical Greek sculpture. Convinced that the artists of antiquity must have worked to some abstract rules which enabled them to achieve the perfect harmony of their creations, he wanted to rediscover them. Concentrating on heads, he collected skulls of people of different ages, sexes and races. Comparing their various features, he arrived at a structural characteristic that seemed to provide the key. Accordingly, he devised a method for the quantitative assessment of the structure of the skull, whose rationale was both aesthetic and scientific.[8]

Camper identified 'facial angle' as a major source of error in the representation of different races, an idea he presented to the Academy of Drawing in 1770. He also noted that facial angles displayed a regular decline from Greek and Roman busts (90–95°) to European (80°), Negro (70°), and orang-utan (58°) heads. Thus the angle could be said to correspond to a scale from ape via savage to civilized, and Camper was of course well aware of that. In discussing some of his comparative illustrations he commented:

> The assemblage of cranium, and profiles of two apes, a negro and a Calmuck, in the first place, may perhaps excite some surprise: the striking resemblance between the race of Monkies and of Blacks, particularly upon a superficial view, has induced some philosophers to conjecture that a race of blacks originated from the commerce of the whites with ourangs and pongos; or that these monsters, by gradual improvements, finally became man.
>
> (Camper 1794, p. 32)

In writing this, Camper was merely mentioning speculations that were widespread in his time, and went on to refute them forcefully. He denied that the range of facial angles corresponds to a scale of superiority–inferiority, and never linked it to the Great Chain. Camper specifically stated that the resemblance between Negro and ape as regards a projecting jaw is merely superficial, and that there is an unbridgeable gulf between them, while there is no significant difference between whites and blacks. He also stated that everybody was descended from a single pair, it being immaterial whether that pair was black or fair. Subsequent changes, he suggested, were brought about by environmental factors such as climate, nutrition, manners, customs and education. Camper's work, originally published in 1792, received much acclaim and was soon translated into French, German and English. The only critical voice was that of Blumenbach who had two reservations: first, he objected to the facial angle being treated as the only criterion for racial classification, which Camper in fact had never claimed; second, he questioned the validity of the method because of the arbitrariness of the baseline, a critique that was justified.

The subsequent fate of Camper's ideas was an unfortunate one, since in spite of his explicit disclaimers, the regular gradient from Greek perfection to apes was later taken by many of his successors to reflect a fundamental biological feature. Visser (1990) suggests a number of reasons why this occurred. Well before publication, Camper's work had become known through informal channels, and he himself described it personally to Blumenbach and Soemmering among others. One important source of distortion was a summary of his 1770 address prepared by the then director of the Academy of Drawing. In this summary facial angles were directly linked to the doctrine of the Great Chain, and as the summary was widely circulated, also in translation, its misrepresentation gained broad currency. Moreover, it appealed to those who believed in the affinity between blacks and apes. This was true for Soemmering, White and Virey, who used this distorted version to bolster their own views. Opponents of the ape-connection theory, such as James Cowles Prichard (1786–1848), mistakenly criticized Camper on the same basis. But it was the adoption and elaboration of that version by the great Cuvier that had the most fateful consequences. The importance of Camper's 'facial angle' is evident from the fact that it was applied by craniologists for most of the 19th century, and Broca (1874) devised a so-called 'goniometer' for its more accurate measurement. It was not until a Congress of the German Anthropological Society in 1882 that a revised eye–ear plane came to be substituted for Camper's 'facial angle' (Hoyme 1953).

Hence, paradoxically, a measure devised by a convinced monogenist for the purpose of analysing aesthetic principles became a prime tool in the hands of 19th-century race theorists for demonstrating the proximity between blacks and apes. The manner in which this occurred will be the topic of the next chapter.

# 7

# ON THE ANIMALITY OF SAVAGES

From the mid-19th century onwards, interpretations of human differences were predominantly in terms of 'race'. Since there is an extensive literature on the theories of that period (e.g. Banton 1987; Stepan 1982), there is no need to cover this well-trodden ground again, except in so far as it has some bearing on the present theme. One such issue is that of monogenism versus polygenism, since it is easier and more plausible to compare certain ethnic groups to apes if it is held that their origin was separate from that of Europeans. In fact, a large majority of those who argued for the closeness of blacks to apes were polygenists.

For much of the 18th century the influence of orthodox Christianity had been powerful enough to ensure general adherence to monogenism. Buffon, for instance, was much concerned with race differences, but attributed these to historical and environmental factors, notably climate. There were some, like Lord Kames, who cautiously ventured to put forward the case for polygenism. Towards the end of the 18th century polygenism gained ground: Long in England, Meiners in Germany and Virey in France supported it. Largely due to the influence of Pritchard, there were few adherents to polygenism in Britain during the first part of the 19th century but more in America, Samuel Morton being an early example. The intellectual debate which opened the door to polygenism was based on increasing geological evidence, raising doubts about the literal interpretation of the biblical account of origins (cf. Gillispie 1951). Until the end of the 18th century the modal estimate of the age of the earth was around 6,000 years. Delisle de Sales (1741–1816) thought the earth would have taken 40,062 years to cool, and ridiculed the figure of several million suggested by tradition in India. Thereafter, in the face of much theological opposition, the time-scale expanded to an extent irreconcilable with biblical chronology. A major turning point was the publication in 1830 of Sir Charles Lyell's *Principles of geology*, which summarized the available evidence about the formation of strata and the origin of fossils. If the Bible could not be taken as a safe guide for the age of the earth, it could also be wrong about the descent of all races from Adam and Eve. Polygenism was also attractive to some philologists who were unable to reduce the diversity of languages to unity. Confusing language with race, they were looking for a biological basis to underpin their theories (Simar 1922).

In Britain, the polygenists were mainly armchair theorists such as Robert Knox, or Hamilton Smith (1848) who postulated three separate creations of Europeans, Mongols and Negroes respectively, since he found it inconceivable that races with such diverse characteristics could have a common origin. In France and Germany most writers based their views on craniological and general anatomical studies; even the great Broca was a polygenist. The advent of Darwinian evolutionism made little difference; although Darwin himself was a monogenist, as already mentioned, his theory as such was quite compatible with polygenism.

It must not be thought, however, that monogenists were necessarily egalitarian, not even in the restricted sense of a willingness to grant other ethnic groups the same potential. A case in point is Cuvier, a versatile genius who made fundamental contributions to geology and palaeontology as well as to biology. In geology he put forward the 'catastrophe theory' to account for changes, which fitted in with the biblical account of the flood but was later superseded by the work of Lyell. His radical innovations in biology provided ammunition for those who regarded the 'savage races' as innately inferior.

## Cuvier and the measure of 'animalism'

Georges Cuvier (1769–1832) first studied for the ministry, but became interested in zoology, an interest that intensified when he became tutor to the son of a nobleman in Normandy. During that period he exchanged letters with a friend, in which they discussed scientific and topical issues. One of these, dated 31 December 1790, dealt at some length with the abilities of Negroes, and Cuvier was answering his friend (Behn 1845, p. 195):

> Are you ready to credit the notion of some foolish travellers that Orang-Outans and Negroes are mutually fertile? – Your comments about Negro anatomy are good and correct. . . . Admittedly, the differences in brain and nerves are curious, but the attempt to explain thereby their mental ability seems to me ridiculous.

The following passage refers to an excerpt from Meiners, translated from a German literary journal:

> I would never have believed that a German professor would be capable of writing in such a simplistic manner. The reasoning basically amounts to this: this person is more stupid and weaker than I am, therefore I can give him a beating. . . . But what if one can prove that most of these facts are wrong or exaggerated, that the simplemindedness of the Negro stems from their uncivilized state, and that all their burdens come from us?

Cuvier then went on to cite the case of his black servant, brought to Europe from Guinea at the age of 7, and well educated by a good master. He sang the praises of this man, saying that in terms of his behaviour and accomplishments he was better than many a European. Again with reference to this servant he refuted some of the absurd statements by Meiners, such as the claim that dogs have an aversion to Negroes. At that period of his youth, Cuvier displayed a remarkably liberal and tolerant outlook, but it did not last. Unlike Blumenbach, Cuvier within a few years forgot all about his capable, virtuous and faithful servant. While I cannot explain exactly how the change came about,[1] it is clear that Cuvier developed a theory that was incompatible with his earlier views.

On the initiative of Geoffroy St Hilaire, in 1795 he was appointed assistant professor of comparative anatomy at the Jardin des Plantes, and elected a member of the prestigious Institut. In the same year Cuvier published, jointly with St Hilaire, an *Histoire naturelle des orang-outangs*, which constituted the first formulation of his theory, marking a radical transformation of his stance on human differences.

The relevant section starts with a discussion of similarities and differences in various kinds of apes, the forward extension of the snout being singled out as of special importance in terms of functioning. This is because, according to Cuvier, it indicates the relative proportion of the volume of the skull and the size of the face. A large and convex skull is a sign of 'sensibility', while the forward projection and thickness of the snout denotes brutality. There follows an immediate jump to humanity:

> In the various races of man one observes the same series of relationships as in the various species of animals, between the projection of the skull and the degree of intelligence or of that exquisite sensibility . . . which constitutes perhaps the principal basis of the differences which exist between man and man . . . none of the peoples with a depressed forehead and prominent jaws have ever furnished subjects generally equal to Europeans in the faculties of the soul; and we are so well used to this link between the proportions of the head and the quality of the mind, that the rules of physiognomy, which are based thereon, have become a commonplace notion.
>
> (Geoffroy St Hilaire and Cuvier 1795, pp. 6–7)

A few years later Cuvier was asked to write a note of research advice for the members of the Baudin expedition to Australasia. Cuvier began by stating that it had once been believed that race differences were merely superficial and confined to such aspects as skin and hair colour. But Camper's method for measuring facial angles had shown intra-racial homogeneity and substantial variations between races. These diverse structures influence the intellectual and moral faculties, so that there is 'a relationship between the perfection of the spirit and beauty of the face'. Systematic comparative research on the anatomical structures of different races is needed 'to which observations about the moral and intellectual character of each race can then be related' (Cuvier n.d., cited in Copans and Jamin 1978, pp. 173–4).

It is important to understand how radical the change introduced by Cuvier really was. Those 18th-century writers who had stressed the physical similarity of blacks and other non-European peoples to the anthropoid apes had simply taken it for granted that such similarity was the outward sign of what they saw as the ape-like psychological features of such peoples. But Cuvier advanced a theory to explain the general connection between physical and mental characteristics.

Before examining this theory in more detail, a brief glance at the emergence of biology as an autonomous science is necessary. It became transformed from being merely taxonomic, in the manner of Linnaeus and Buffon, to an 'organic-historical' approach. As shown by Figlio (1976), the concept of 'organization' of the nervous system in particular became key to understanding animal as well as human functioning. This entailed multiplex comparisons of anatomical and physiological features with the object of arriving at an index of '*animality*'. Here Cuvier played a crucial role in the transformation of ideas. For him, the more highly organized the nervous system the more advanced the 'higher faculties', and the more developed the sense of selfhood. These aspects, he believed, could be inferred from the nature of the anatomical structures. The larger the facial area with a low forehead and protruding snout (corresponding to a low facial angle), the more the organism remains tied to mere sensory functioning governed by external sensations; this provides only for the necessary adaptation to the environment to ensure survival. By contrast, a relatively small facial area (indicated by a high facial angle) signals a greater degree of internal autonomy. Similarly, the greater the cranial area, the more the organism has become liberated from purely external constraints and capable of acting under internal control, through intelligence and will, with a highly developed individuality.

The notion of prognathism as a sign of animality remained a pervasive one in anthropology throughout the 19th century, particularly in France: St Hilaire, Broca and Topinard all shared this idea; Topinard (1876) declared that women are more prognathic than men! Prognathism is of course indicated by facial angle, and in his *Lecons d'Anatomie Comparée* (1800–5) Cuvier presented details of his own measurements of facial angles. The value for Europeans was the same as that arrived at by Camper,[2] but those for Negroes (70°) and orang-utans (67°) had become almost identical. He stated: 'The nature of each animal depends largely on the relative energy of each of its functions; it is, so to speak, carried along and mastered by those of its sensations that are the strongest' (Cuvier 1800–5, Vol. II, p. 3).

This formulation was very close to that put forward later by Herbert Spencer (1820–1903), the social evolutionist. In Spencer's view savages expend so much energy on perception that they have little if any left for deliberate thought.[3] This idea was subsequently taken over by Rivers (1901): 'If too much energy is expended on the sensory foundations, it is natural that the intellectual superstructure should suffer' (p. 45). This is just one example of the way in which Cuvier's conceptions of the nature of savages (deficient intelligence, inadequate impulse control and lack of personal autonomy) continued to prevail throughout the 19th century and beyond. The beliefs themselves were on the whole not new; what *was* new was the claim that they were solidly founded on the discoveries of the new biology. Thus Cuvier contributed to laying the foundations of a racial determinism that was to increasingly dominate much of 19th-century thinking about humankind.

## The apishness of the 'Hottentot Venus'

Much has been written about that unfortunate woman, one of the best accounts being that by Gould (1982). I shall therefore not consider her case in detail here, but concentrate on an aspect central to the present theme that has not usually been emphasized: namely the extent to which Cuvier and others kept harping on her supposedly simian characteristics. Cuvier's changed attitude towards blacks, amounting to acute distaste, and his conviction of their close kinship with apes, found its most graphic expression in his memoir on the so-called 'Hottentot Venus' ([1817]1864). Her case is also important since she figured prominently in later debates.

The 'Venus' was a Sanid (Bushman)[4] woman who was taken to Europe and was exhibited in London in a cage (in fairness it must be added that she had agreed to this). Later she was taken to Paris where an animal showman displayed her for over a year under the misleading banner of 'La Vénus Hottentotte' (see Figure 7.1). There, as in England, her enlarged posterior, typical of Khoisanid women, constituted a sensational attraction. This was in 1814, when she was about 26 years old. At Cuvier's request she made herself available to him to be examined. In the memoir he described her appearance as 'brutal' and said that: 'her movements were marked by a quickness and capriciousness which reminded one of those of the monkey tribe. She had moreover a habit of pushing out her lips in the manner of the orang-outang' (Cuvier [1817] 1864, p. 214).

Calling her face 'disgusting', he said that her ears were similar to those of monkeys due to their smallness and commented in detail on the most outstanding part of her anatomy: . . . 'the enormous masses of fat which the Bushwomen carry on their buttocks . . . offer a striking resemblance to those which characterize female Mandrils [and other apes] and which take on at certain periods a truly monstrous enlargement' (1864, p. 218).

Cuvier also referred to her 'protruding snout' and flat nose, remarking that he had never seen a human head so closely resembling those of apes. Towards the end of this unpleasant litany Cuvier expressed his conviction that, given their achievements, the ancient Egyptians must have been of the same race as the Europeans, and could not have had any relation to blacks. This view was to be subsequently expounded at length by the American anatomist and race theorist S. G. Morton (1844).

The 'Hottentot Venus' died of an unspecified illness not long after Cuvier had examined her, and he obtained her body for dissection. He was particularly interested in the unusual hypertrophy of the labia minora typical of Khoisanid

*Figure 7.1* The 'Hottentot Venus' as an object of curiosity. Although the caricature is French (early 19th century) the intrusive inspections are attributed to Britons; thus what appears to be a Scottish soldier on the left is made to exclaim 'God damn, what roast beef!'

women, first noted during the 18th century. This had been an accurate observation, but many of the numerous later writings about the genitalia of blacks were absurd. This applied even to so eminent a person as Paul Broca (1824–80), who was much concerned with the effects of hybridity (inter-racial mixture), an issue that continued to be hotly debated well into the 20th century (cf. Davenport and Steggerda 1929). In his book on the topic Broca (1864, p. 28) cited with approval a passage from another French anatomist, Serres:

> One of the characters of the Ethiopian race consists in the length of the penis compared with that of the Caucasian race. This dimension coincides with the length of the uterine canal in the Ethiopian female, and both have their cause in the form of the pelvis in the Negro race. There results from this physical disposition, that the union of the Caucasian man with the Ethiopian woman is easy and without any inconvenience for the latter. The case is different in the union of the Ethiopian with a Caucasian woman, who suffers in the act, the neck of the uterus is pressed against the sacrum, so that the act of reproduction is not only painful, but frequently non-productive.

How very fortunate that supposed physiological factors served to reinforce prevailing social attitudes! In fact, as I have already mentioned, several 18th-century writers had been more realistic when they commented on the preference of 'low' women for blacks. A few years later Broca reported to the Anthropological Society of Paris the findings of some investigators who alleged that 'the penises of black men had cartilage structures like those of monkeys and that black women did not have hymens at the entrance of the vagina' (cited in Cohen 1980, p. 241).

But let me return for a moment to the 'Hottentot Venus', for this was not the end of the story of this wretched woman. Her brain was preserved for posterity, and some forty years later the prominent neurologist Gratiolet examined what he described as 'one of the most precious pieces in our cabinet'. Comparing it with the brains of Europeans, he found it much less convoluted and having 'the regularity, the symmetry of the brain folds in the inferior species'. Subsequently, he declared with delight, he had studied the brain of an idiot which 'absolutely reproduced the forms we have reported in the Hottentot Venus' (Gratiolet 1854, p. 65ff.). He mentioned in passing that he was not suggesting the 'Venus' was actually an idiot, but the implications of the resemblance were clear enough.

In Britain, Cuvier had some prominent followers, notably the anatomist Sir William Lawrence (1783–1867):

> In all the particulars just enumerated, the Negro structure approximates unequivocally to that of the monkey. It not only differs from the Caucasian model, but is distinguished from it in two respects; the intellectual characters are reduced, the animal features enlarged and exaggerated. This inferiority of organisation is attended with corresponding inferiority

of faculties; which may be proved, not so much by the unfortunate beings who are degraded by slavery, as by every fact in the past history and the present condition of Africa.

(Lawrence 1819, p. 363)

Two points are worth noting in the above passage: the reference to 'organization', which indicates the change away from the purely taxonomic approach of 18th-century biology; and the implied condemnation of slavery which may well have been genuine in Lawrence's case; but it was often a mere ritual formula, a sop to public opinion on the part of those who may be described, in modern terminology, as virulent racists.

## Empirical studies of the 'simian' character of blacks

There is no indication that Lawrence himself ever undertook any systematic comparative studies, and the passage cited above merely illustrates what was then a common view. Three German scientists later carried out investigations directly concerned with the problem of the relationship between blacks and anthropoid apes. One was the anatomist Friedrich Tiedemann (1781–1861) who compared the brains of Europeans, Negroes and orang-utans. He was unable to detect any difference between blacks and whites in the thickness of nerves of the kind postulated by Soemmering. Moreover, according to him the brains of Negroes were almost exactly the same as those of Europeans, and both differed sharply from the brains of apes (Tiedemann 1837). A more general survey was undertaken by Franz Pruner (1808–82), a doctor who spent much of his life in Egypt as professor of anatomy in Cairo. In 1839 he became personal physician to the Viceroy and acquired the title Pruner-Bey by which he became subsequently known. An early book of his on the racial composition of Egypt (1846) already gives some inkling of his attitudes: the admixture of Negro blood, he maintained, had a negative influence on the Egyptian moral character. After retiring to Paris he published a monograph on Negroes (1861), in which he sought to cover physical and, to a lesser extent, psychological aspects. Admitting that his studies had been confined to Negroes living in Egypt, this did not prevent him from making wide-ranging generalizations. The most constant feature of the Negro skeleton, he noted, is prognathism, which he interpreted as a probable return towards animality. There is the usual mention of the extraordinary size of the male member, and without referring to Tiedemann he confirmed Soemmering's claims about the thickness of the nerves; and, albeit somewhat cautiously, he cited a comment on the similarity between Negro and ape brains. Elsewhere such reservations are omitted: 'In the same way the shortening of the big toe . . . has been noted in the Negro, in some Malaysian races, and in the Hottentots, as a constant character which brings these peoples close to the apes' (Pruner-Bey 1861, p. 316).

It is interesting that the same idea was later propounded on the basis of evolutionary theory (which had not yet reached Pruner-Bey) by Ernest Haeckel (1834–1919). Haeckel's version of the theory was that humans developed from an extinct species of Old World catarrhine apes whom he called 'four-handed'. From this he inferred that peoples who used their toes were lower in the scale of evolution:

> there are wild tribes of men who can oppose the first or large toe to the other four, just as if it were a thumb. They can therefore use their 'grasping foot' like the so-called 'hinder hand', as do Apes. The Chinese boatman rows with his hinder hand, the Bengal workmen weave with it. The Negro, in whom the big toe is especially strong and freely moveable, when climbing seizes hold of the branches of the tree with it, just like the 'four-handed' Apes.
>
> (Haeckel [1876] 1906, Vol. 2, p. 368)

Haeckel included the Chinese among the less evolved peoples, which was not unusual at the time.

Returning to Pruner-Bey, he also quoted another author on the Negroes' ugliness in old age, when their face becomes rather ape-like. Although this theme crops up quite often throughout the monograph, its general tenor is relatively mild when compared with the outpourings of one of Pruner-Bey's fellow-countrymen.

Carl Vogt (1817–95) was a famous German-Swiss naturalist who in his *Lectures on man* (1864) propounded a theory about a missing link between the Negro and the ape, which he saw in microcephalous idiots. He presented illustrations of Negro, idiot and chimpanzee skulls, commenting that they form a clear series (see Figure 7.2). Vogt's work contains one of the most extensive and systematic expositions of the alleged resemblances between Negroes and apes, and was highly influential.

Vogt was an unusual man. Born in Giessen, in Germany, he studied in Switzerland under Aggasiz, who was later to emigrate to America where he became one of a group of polygenist scientists concerned to demonstrate Negro inferiority. In 1847 Vogt was appointed professor of zoology at Giessen. His political views were extremely radical, and he had to leave Giessen because of his active participation in the 1848 Revolution. He moved to a chair in natural history at Geneva, where he continued to propound his rather corrosive radical and anti-religious views.

His ideas on the present topic are most fully expressed in Chapter VII of his *Lectures on man* (1864), where he set out to compare Negroes and Germans whom he described as 'two extreme human types'. The differences between them, he claimed, are greater than those between two species of apes; and this proves that the Negro is a separate species from the European. This of course means that he was a polygenist.

Fig. 68. Negro skull, side view.

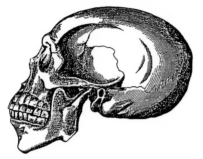

Fig. 69. Idiot skull, side view.

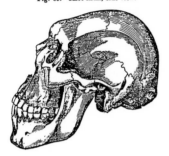

*Figure 7.2* Vogt's attempted demonstration of the similarity between the skulls of 'Negroes' and European 'idiots'
*Source:* Vogt (1864).

The remainder of the chapter is devoted to detailed comparisons of nearly all parts of the anatomy, intended to demonstrate the similarities between Negroes and apes. Thus the neck of the Negro is said to resemble that of the gorilla and, like a ram, he uses his skull in a fight. Together with other features 'all this affords a glimmer of the ape beneath the human envelope' (p. 173). Special attention is of course paid to the skull, the focus of 19th-century craniology. When discussing prognathism, Vogt refers to the Negro's 'muzzle'; and the illustrations in his book, like those in many others, seemed to bear this out. Such a mode of representation began, in scientific treatises, with Camper's diagrams of 'facial angles'. The exaggeration became gradually more pronounced, reaching their culmination in Victorian caricatures of blacks as well as other 'inferior races' such as the Irish (Curtis 1971).

Every part of the head receives detailed attention, including the teeth whose nature 'reminds us of the American monkeys in particular' (p. 176). The ratio between 'cerebral skull' and 'facial skull', a critical sign for Cuvier, is said to exhibit 'typical simiousness'; and even the hand supposedly 'has a decidedly simious character'.

While confessing that he did not possess a Negro brain, this did not prevent Vogt from discoursing at length on this topic; by now it will come as no surprise that he declares 'I find a remarkable resemblance between the ape and the lower human type' (p. 183). There is no mention of Tiedemann.

It would serve little purpose to continue this catalogue of supposed resemblances, where in accounts of the whole anatomy from head to foot the expression 'decidedly simious' recurs with monotonous regularity. Let me add that, as usual, it is stated that 'The penis is always disproportionately large' (p. 185).

Vogt confined himself largely to comparisons of males, which he claimed to be a conservative procedure. The reason was that, according to him, the female is always nearer to the animal type, so that black women would have been even more 'simious'. Lest it be thought that this was merely an idiosyncratic notion of Vogt's, I should explain that it was widespread during the 19th century. Among its most extreme expressions was that by Gustave LeBon, a disciple of Broca, whose *Psychologie des foules* (1895) is one of the classics of social psychology. LeBon declared that 'All the psychologists who have studied the intelligence of women . . . recognize today that they represent the most inferior forms of human evolution and are much closer to children and savages than to adult civilised man' (LeBon 1881, Vol. II, p. 157). He went on to say that women's emotional nature brings them close to monkeys, or even to more inferior mammals.[5]

The impact of Vogt's thesis, whose message was in tune with the dominant ethos, was reinforced by its cool tone of scientific objectivity – not for him the rantings of a Long. The book is replete with the trappings of science – pictures of skulls and brains, tables of cranial capacity and anatomical measurements. Even superficial scrutiny of some of the tables reveals their questionable character. For instance, one listing the cranial capacities of different races, arranged in rank order, is full of inconsistencies: measures of Parisians by different authors range in rank from 20 to 30; Malaysians from 11 to 25; and Greenlanders (plural) are assigned the rank 13 on the basis of a single individual!

When discussing bodily proportions Vogt, following the line previously adoped by Charles White, stated that:

> the humerus of the Negro is proportionally shorter, the forearm proportionately longer than in the German.
> This proportion is apparent at once in the table below and, as has long been observed, this is a decided approach to the animal type.
>
> (Vogt 1864, p. 179)

There are in fact two tables, based on measurements by two different authors, neither of which shows any consistent trend in the raw data. I have computed ratios of upper arm to forearm based on the relative percentage of total body length for adult males, and these are shown below:

| Author | Europeans | Negroes |
|---|---|---|
| Burmeister | 0.84 | 0.81 |
| Pruner-Bey | 0.75 | 0.78 |

The differences are not merely negligible, but go in opposite directions. Presumably because of this, Vogt embarked on a set of transformations whose rationale remains obscure to me; even so, the outcome is no more convincing. Broca (1862), who carried out similar measurements on a number of different ethnic groups, obtained equally inconsistent results. Unlike Vogt, he conceded that relative size of forearm could not be regarded as a measure of resemblance to apes.

## Other contemporary views

Some other commentators on Vogt's thesis, such as Schumann (1868), also demonstrated the flaws in his measures, but in other respects they were only critical of his claims regarding the intermediate status of idiots. This was also true of Gleisberg (1868, p. 33), who emphatically endorsed Vogt's views regarding the status of blacks:

> Yet the Negro is much more sharply separated from the white man than from the ape. For presently a Negro tribe with tails has become known in Abyssinia, whose cranial capacity has not yet been investigated. But owing to their animal-like voice, small size [etc.] they resemble apes so closely that only language, type of teeth and form of foot differentiate them from apes.

The astonishing story of the tribe with tails probably relates to the report by Ducouret, later unmasked as a fraudulent adventurer, about the 'Niam-Niams'. It says a lot about prevailing attitudes and ideas that the report, far from being cursorily dismissed, stirred up great controversy in august circles, and that a German academic should have trotted out such a tale long after it had been discredited. This was such a remarkable episode that I will describe it later in more detail.

Presenting this material from a late 20th-century perspective, as I have done, is liable to create the impression that Vogt and others sharing his beliefs were just incompetent 'racists' – a term, incidentally, that did not exist then. It is necessary to understand that Vogt, far from having been a maverick, was a highly respected scientist: a Boulevard is still named after him in Geneva. He was one of the first converts to Darwinism, and Darwin himself frequently quoted Vogt in his writings. Even Thomas Henry Huxley, Darwin's close ally and protagonist, provided ammunition for race theorists. In his book on *Man's place in nature* (1863) he opposed those who saw in Africans, Australians and other savages the 'missing links'. Yet he referred to evidence indicating that primitives are closer to chimpanzees and gorillas, and told a story about an African tribe whose tradition had it that they were once near kin to the great apes.

Lyell, the famous geologist mainly responsible for the demise of biblical chronology, became converted to Darwinism. His musings on evolution, set out in his *Scientific journals* (Wilson 1970), reveal that he also shared these notions as exemplified by the two entries cited below:

(February 5, 1859)
The inferiority of the skull of the Baboon to the Chimpanzee and Gorilla, with superior intelligence in the latter, favours the idea that the negro is next in the scale with many lost links.

(April 25, 1860)
The difference of brain is so great between the European & the Bushman as to show in this, as well as in mental capacity, a wide range. The difference in the brain of a Bushman & a gorilla is, says Prof. Huxley, less than between an Orang & a Lemur.

The notion of the similarity of (notably black) savages and apes was at the time accepted even by those who vigorously opposed the race theorists and sought to counter their arguments (cf. Jahoda 1992). One of the most prominent, Theodor Waitz (1863), felt forced to concede that their comparisons were not wholly without foundation: 'The truth is limited to the known fact, that the negro most resembles the ape' (p. 92).

Thus Vogt was in essence only elaborating a more extreme version of what in his time constituted the conventional wisdom. His book enjoyed a great vogue and went through several editions and translations. Although Vogt became an early convert to Darwinism, as was true of other race theorists, this did not mean that he adopted Darwin's monogenism or changed his views on race. The same was true of another prominent Darwinist, namely Ernest Haeckel, who suggested that the most savage tribes of Asia and Africa 'by their mode of life resemble more troops of apes than civilized human societies' (Haeckel 1877, p. 647). As mentioned above, Darwinian evolutionism, far from excluding prevalent ideas about race, could be and often was interpreted as lending support to them.

## The impact of colonialism on the animal/ape motif

Scientific doctrines about the greater 'animality' of savages continued unabated for the remainder of the 19th century and beyond. For instance, a prominent American naturalist took it for granted that 'We all accept the existence of higher and lower races, the latter being those which we now find to present greater or lesser approximations to the apes' (Cope 1887, p. 147). In American science the existence and later the heritage of slavery had, as has been shown, fostered such views even before they had become common in Europe.

The colonial expansion of the European powers during the latter part of the 19th century was accompanied by a growing interest in 'primitive psychology'. Such interest was not primarily motivated by scientific concerns, but partly by the need of administrators to understand the peoples ruled by them, and partly by a wish to inform the educated public. This was reflected in a surge of publications on this topic, notably in France. By the turn of the century savages were more frequently compared with children than with animals, an issue to be examined more fully in Chapter 11. Others harked back to notions prevalent at the end of the 18th century, one of the most unusual being Eli Reclus (1830–1905). Unlike the others, he had no academic training and was a political radical, an anarchist who was imprisoned for his convictions. Yet here one can see again the lack of any association between such views and sympathy for the colonial underdog. Far from being an anticolonialist, he saw in colonization the opening up of new horizons for humanity, a partial reversion to Enlightenment ideals. His opinions about colonial peoples followed the hoary stereotypes:

> According to physiologists, the blood of Blacks is supposed to be thicker, less red than that of the Whites; it coagulates more quickly and beats more slowly. The Black, like the Yellows of Asia, has a duller sensibility than the European; he suffers less from surgical operations and runs less risk of acute fevers; his nervous disposition is less intensive, he is not vibrant like the White.
>
> If Africa is the continent of the great anthropomorphic apes, the gorilla and the chimpanzee, it is also that of the most simian humans [the Pygmies].
>
> (Reclus 1876–94, cited in Liauzu 1992, p. 124)

In Germany, the acquisition of a colonial empire greatly stimulated the pursuit of comparative ethnological studies (cf. Probst 1991), expected to be of practical value in the administration of the colonies. This was the avowed aim of Schultze in what purported to be an authoritative work on the 'psychology of primitives'. It is worth describing his assertions in some detail, since they illustrate the persistence of crude ideas at the turn of the 20th century.

Fritz Schultze (1846–?) was a professor of philosophy and pedagogy at Dresden, who published a book on what he also, and significantly, called 'colonial psychology' (Schultze 1900, p. iii). There is no indication that he himself had any personal experience of contact with non-European peoples, except what he saw in the then popular travelling exhibits – more about this later.

He set out to provide an account, following evolutionary principles, of the psychological characteristics of primitive peoples. The introduction offers a 'classification of humanity' derived from another writer of the period (Sutherland 1898), ranging from 'savages' via 'barbarians' and 'civilized peoples' to *Kulturvölker*, the highest grade; each of these types was in turn sub-divided into 'lower', 'middle' and 'higher' sub-categories. Schultze stated that he was concerned only with savages and barbarians. The classification is thus, at least ostensibly, in terms of levels of culture rather than race. In practice, as will be seen below, the distinction is irrelevant in as much as both were taken to be closely associated. Unlike much of the earlier writing of this kind that concentrated largely on 'Negroes', the coverage was world-wide.

The first section dealing with physiological and physical-anthropological topics begins with the old issue of brain capacity, conceding that the difference between Australian Aborigines and Europeans is smaller than that between the former and the higher apes. Although passing lip-service is paid to the unity of humankind, the same paragraph states that primitives have a less well-developed brain and therefore a lesser capacity for thought (p. 19). He attributed this to environmental monotony and lack of stimulation – a view to be understood in terms of the then current belief that intellectual activity fosters the growth of the brain.

Once again the stories about the remarkable sensory acuity of primitives are rehearsed, and only the extravagant comments about the sense of smell are worth mentioning because of their strong implications of animality. The inhabitants of desert regions in Africa and Australia, he states, can scent water from a great distance; American Indians are as sensitive as bloodhounds; savages, like dogs, live in a world of smells, and their like or dislike of another person depends on their odour. This was then a common notion, mentioned also by Henri Piéron (1909): 'The olfactory sense is highly developed in most savages, especially when their life remains very brutish; it is only disgust that is lacking' (p. 121).

Returning to Schultze, he maintained that the thinking of primitives remains largely at the associative level that can also be found in animals, and that they are mainly governed by their senses [Sinnesmensch] – an echo of Cuvier. They are to some extent capable of apperception, as evidenced by the fact that they have language and myths. While they have passed the threshold of apperception, it remains rudimentary and childish, as shown by their fantasy and lack of logic. The primitives' thinking, like their will and action, are still at a concrete level. So the primitive is human and no longer an animal, but he is not yet a reflective being [Geistesmensch]. Like children, savages are readily influenced by their sensory representations [sinnlichen Vorstellungen]. Hence they are liable to rapid mood swings and apt to be led impulsively into doing foolish things. They are also highly imitative, and Schultze cited the following example from an explorer's report (1900, p. 39):

> I wanted to learn a few of their words, pointed to the sun and said 'Tupan!' (What is this?). Then I held out my hand to them in the tone of questioner. In this way I wanted to invite the thinking people [among them] to tell me what they call 'hand' in their language. Instead, I encountered a good-natured ape. [One of them] pointed to the sun, exactly as I had done myself, held out his hand to me with the same expression of questioning I had used myself, and then looked at me with great satisfaction. And whatever I tried I succeeded only in making them play orang-outang.

If Schultze had read the advice by Degérando to explorers, published a century earlier, he would perhaps have realized the absurdity of such an approach; and the fact that, if the roles had been reversed, a European might well have acted in the same 'ape-like' manner in such a situation.

Schultze credited primitives with a photographic memory, but claimed that they are barely capable of any abstraction. He maintained that primitives, whose minds are not cluttered with abstract thought, are therefore capable of remarkably detailed factual observations, an argument possibly derived from Herbert Spencer.[6]

In a section on the languages of primitives Schultze, evidently unaware of the work of Wilhelm von Humboldt and others, dilated on their childishness. Their languages do not have so many means of expression, and why not? Simply because they do not have much to express. Savages have no words for abstract concepts because they lack such concepts, and so on.

Another whole section deals with 'laziness and its consequences', which includes an absence of cleanliness – the phrase 'stink lazy' is apt, wrote Schultze; also lack of endurance, unreliabilty and just living for the day without a care. Next there is a section on gluttony and carnality, which together are the main sources of happiness of the *Naturvölker*. The savage eats practically everything, however disgusting.

A further section is significantly entitled 'Savages resemble children and animals'. Savages, with their wild swings of mood, their irresponsibility and irritability, their curiosity coupled with weakness of thought, are just like children; but perhaps they are childish more than child-like. The seemingly child-like naivety is apt to change suddenly to the blind fury of a wild animal. Civilized children learn to control their impulses and desires, but the savage remains a lifelong child. One can never trust him and has always to be on one's guard.

The section on 'The moral distance between the primitive and the civilized' contains the only passage I have been able to find that is based on first-hand observation; this occurred in the course of a visit to the zoological garden in Dresden, where a group of Ashanti from the Gold Coast was being exhibited. There he witnessed a family quarrel whose exact nature he could hardly have known since he did not understand their language, *Twi*. This did not prevent him from characterizing it as typical of the low morality of primitives, which he contrasted with what he believed to have been a similar case which he saw in Italy; there the behaviour displayed was supposed to have been noble, thereby typifying the 'ethical distance' separating a barbarian tribe from a civilized community.

The rest of the book consists of similar, and exceedingly repetitive, diatribes. I have dwelt on it in some detail, since it was published at a time when a large amount of solid ethnographic material was already available. Schultze relied almost entirely on older sources, often selectively quoted, that represented 'primitives' as an undifferentiated mass of unsavoury near-humans who largely shared the less attractive traits of children and animals. This tendency was not confined to German writers, nor to those who lacked first-hand knowledge of Africans. Thus a French colonial governor wrote about 'the Negro': 'Like the

FIG. 4.—NEGRO BOY AND APES.

On the left side of the figure there is a young Chimpanzee.
and on the right a young Orang-utan. This is a wonderfully
interesting comparison.

*Figure 7.3* This illustration featured in a racist American book published early in the
present century. The implication of the comment 'This is a wonderfully
interesting comparison' is obvious
*Source:* Shufeldt (1915) *America's Greatest Problem.*

animal, he deals with the needs of his life when the necessity for it makes itself
felt, or when it takes his fancy, or when circumstances allow it' (Cureau 1912,
p. 201).

In the early years of the 20th century some of the crassest equations with apes,
purportedly on scientific grounds, can be found in the American anti-black
literature of the period (see Figure 7.3). Although the statements made were often
said to be based on personal investigation, their resemblance to 19th-century
material is so close as to make it unlikely that it was mere coincidence:

> the hand of the typical negro, although human, often has much about it
> to remind us of the manus in the gorilla . . . I met with very black negroes
> in the South, both men, in whom the ears were conspicuously pointed at
> their upper margins as in many *Quadrumana* [the primates other than

91

humans]. . . . Many years ago I dissected an old negro man. . . . As a subject he was particularly simian in his organization, and one thing I noticed about him more than anything else, in addition to his immense copulatory organ, was the structure of his toe nails. These were . . . marvellously thickened and curved, reminding one at once of the claws on certain animals.

(Shufeldt 1907, p. 34)

This notorious writer was not merely concerned to project the simian image, but clutched at any straw that might suggest animality. Such extreme cases were, however, becoming exceptional as the ape image had largely given way to that of the grown-up child. This does not mean that it had disappeared from serious discourse, but was apt to be used more casually and descriptively, sometimes confined to particular groups:

Summing up the experiences of many African travellers, together with my own observations, I should venture to say that there is a prognathous beetling-browed, short-legged, long-armed – 'ape-like' – type of Negro dwelling in pariah tribes or cropping up as reversionary individuals in a better-looking people, to be met with all down Central Africa.

(Johnston 1902, Vol. 2, p. 510)

The term 'reversionary' is significant in this context, still implying closer evolutionary similarity.

The image of ape-likeness continued to feature during the inter-war years, even in some prestigious texts. The French Nobel Prize-winning physiologist Charles Richet, in his *La sélection humaine* (1919), likened blacks physically to apes, and intellectually to children and imbeciles. Similarly, Bauer, Fischer and Lenz, three distinguished German scientists, published a volume on *Human heredity* in 1927 that went to three editions and in 1931 appeared in English translation. It has a chapter on 'racial psychology' in which Australian Aborigines and other 'primitives' are likened to apes and the feebleminded, and is only slightly less disparaging about 'childish' Negroes.

Nevertheless, some change was under way. The features that had rendered savages so strangely exotic and even animal-like had become less prominent. Increasing numbers among colonial peoples dressed in western style could speak in intelligible (i.e. European) languages, and often had some schooling. Gradually during the 1930s it became less acceptable in educated circles to dub them 'ape-like', but that was far from true at the popular level.

Even among scientists there were some exceptions, notably the rather maverick physical anthropologist Earnest Albert Hooton, who published a book signifi-cantly entitled *Apes, men, and morons* (Hooton 1938). In it he wrote that 'Negroids' have 'a somewhat generalized foot structure with certain ape-like characters' (p. 281). Whatever this might mean, it is a clear echo of Vogt (cf. pp. 84–5).

92

Among the 'Negroids' he singled out the 'pygmy Negritos', commenting on their 'thin chimpanzee-like lips' (p. 282). This is rather curious, given the fact that blacks were usually caricatured with very thick lips, so that it is the whites, together with pygmies, who are more 'chimpanzee-like' in this respect.

Hooton was certainly atypical among anthropologists of the time, except of course for the Nazi ones, some of whom went to bizarre extremes, restricting true humanity to Aryans. A certain Dr Gauch maintained that 'Non-Nordic Man occupies an intermediate position between Nordic Man and the animal kingdom, in particular the great apes' (cited in Müller-Hill 1988, p. 81).

Anthropology in general had undergone fundamental changes in the aftermath of the First World War, prior to which the contacts between anthropologists and the people they were studying had been in the main very superficial. After the war, following Malinowski's model of fieldwork (cf. Stocking 1992), the practice became that of living among the people for a considerable time. When one shares other people's lives, rather than observing them from the outside like – or as – visitors to a zoo, the absurdity of comparing them to apes became evident.

Although it had become officially taboo to say so overtly, some anthropologists may well have privately continued to regard their hosts as inferior. A revealing example is that of Malinowski himself, who in his notorious diary relates how he was watching a beautiful girl walking ahead of him: 'Probably even with my wife I'll never have the opportunity to observe the play of back muscles for as long as with this *little animal*. At moments I was sorry I was not a savage and could not possess this pretty girl' (Malinowski 1989, p. 255; my emphasis). While 'ape-likeness' dropped out of academic publications, 'savage' was still very much in use. Throughout the inter-war years anthropologists, and notably Malinowski, published books whose titles contained the term 'savage'. One of his pupils, Audrey Richards (1932), published a work entitled *Hunger and work in a savage tribe*. It is ironic that after the Second World War she had a member of the ethnic group she had studied (the southern Bantu) in her seminar at the London School of Economics.

This brings me to the period after the Second World War, when ape-likeness ceased to be tolerable and almost completely disappeared from serious discussion. I say 'almost', since one of the most infamous Nazi authorities on what was euphemistically known as 'racial hygiene' was allowed to publish a preposterous article (Fischer 1955) about the ape-like genital features of Khosanoids. This was the only example in a purportedly scientific journal that I was able to find.

## Modern survivals

Although crude ape images are no longer respectable, there are still debates about race differences, and some highly controversial evolutionary theories are being put forward. These generally do not simply contrast 'Negroids' with the rest, but instead a hierarchy is proposed with Mongoloids at the top, Negroids at the bottom, and Caucasoids in between. In practice, however, the Mongoloid–Caucasian differences tend to be minimized: 'average Mongoloid intelligence levels are a little higher than those of Caucasoids, but the difference is relatively small as compared with other racial differences' (Lynn 1991, p. 284). The same applies to the more ambitious approach of Rushton (1995), who seeks to apply to humans a biological theory concerning the so-called $r$-$K$ scale of reproductive strategies. At one extreme ($r$) the stress is on high reproduction rates, while at the other ($K$) it is on parental care. An evolutionary continuum, illustrating the development from $r$ to $K$ as one goes from oysters to apes, is shown in his Figure 10. 2 (p. 202). Rushton also states that 'African populations . . . are least $K$-selected, and Mongoloids . . . are most $K$-selected, with Caucasoids falling intermediately' (p. xiii). Putting these two things together the obvious inference (not spelled out by Rushton in so many words) is that blacks are closest to apes. There are also extensive discussions of the genital organs (larger) and brains (smaller) of 'Negroids', all highly reminiscent of the kind of 19th-century scientific discourse that is now discredited by the majority of biologists. Rushton himself, like White or Vogt before him, seems convinced that he is merely pursuing scientific research wherever it leads. This is not the place to examine his thesis in detail.[7] However, it is relevant to comment on Rushton's account of the historical background, which raises some doubts regarding his professed impartiality. He draws heavily on the work of Baker (1974), a writer who sought to make out the case for a racial hierarchy. From this questionable source Rushton sketches a dismal picture of 19th-century Africans that is heavily biased, as demonstrated in an appendix to this chapter.

Such a preoccupation with genetic race differences was until recently fairly unusual, but appears to be once more on the increase. Rushton's position is rather extreme, since he postulates the inferiority of certain ethnic groups almost in 19th-century fashion, implying without directly stating their greater animality. Nowadays, arguments about relative degrees of animality rather lose their point in the light of our present knowledge that all of us humans are equally ape-like.

The preceding account of 19th-century discourse about the animality of savages, and its decline after the turn of the century, has been largely confined to scholarly writings. This discourse also had reverberations at the popular level where, as will be shown in later chapters, it served to give added weight to existing images.

The alleged animality of savages has long been closely connected with their supposed predilection for cannibalism, to be considered in Chapter 8. During the entire 19th century it had been taken for granted that cannibalism was widespread among savages, but today the question as to what exactly is meant by this term, and whether it ever really existed in its crass 'man-eating' form, has become a topic of intense debate.

## APPENDIX

### Rushton's selectivity in his portrait of 19th century Africans

At the outset Rushton correctly states that J.R. Baker (1974) claimed to have chosen explorers whose reports could be trusted to be reliable. It is a claim that is open to challenge, since among the writers quoted were several who could hardly be regarded as free from violent prejudice. For instance, an earlier (Samuel) Baker (1821–93) had compared the Nuer unfavourably with his pet monkey or the noble character of a dog; or John Speke, who said about the African that 'He works his wife, sells his children, enslaves all he can lay hands upon, and, unless when fighting for the property of others, contents himself with drinking, singing, and dancing like a baboon' (cited in McLynn 1992, p. 312).

In a later chapter there will be occasion to discuss in some detail the work of one of those also cited, namely Schweinfurth; and from that it will become clear that J.R. Baker's assessment of Schweinfurth's reports as 'eminently accurate' (1974, p. 349) is hardly appropriate. Generally, the account given by Baker tends to give more weight to the negative, to the low level of culture observed; but it is nonetheless far more balanced than the picture extracted therefrom by Rushton.

It is not my intention to deny those aspects which, from a 19th-century and often also 20th-century (for example, cruelty) standpoint, seem 'savage'. What I wish to show is that, by drawing from the same sources, it is possible to present a far more favourable portrait. For this purpose extracts summarized from Rushton (R) will be juxtaposed with others chosen by myself (J), all drawn from Baker (1974).

R: Naked or near naked appearance.
J: The men were wearing robes of bark cloth arranged like the Roman toga. The women also were neatly dressed.

R: Poorly developed toilet and sanitary habits.
J: The sanitary laws of Buganda required every man to build for himself something corresponding to a lavatory; [the Zulu] were accustomed to wash daily in the rivers;

R: Absence of adminstration and law;
J: [citing R himself about the Zulu] creating a military empire from Zululand through Tanzania to the Congo;

R: Simple canoes excavated from large trees with no joining parts is all they can make;
J: The Monbuttu had boats up to 38' long and 5' wide, capable of transporting cattle;

R: In some places cannibalism was practiced.

J: Over a very large part of the . . . area there is no evidence that human flesh was ever eaten, and no first-hand account of it is recorded . . . .

R: Nowhere did there appear to exist . . . ethical codes with sentiments of mercy.

J: I came to the conclusion that they are just such a strange mixture of good and evil, as men are everywhere else . . . by a selection of cases of either kind, it would not be difficult to make these people appear excessively good or uncommonly bad; Du Chaillu relates that on one occasion he and his party, nearing starvation, came unexpectedly upon some Negroes . . . These people, to whom his party were total strangers, at once provided them with food;

R: The explorers found Africans to be of low intelligence.

J: The explorers appear to have encountered very few Negrids of markedly low intelligence. . . . Particular intelligence is attributed by the explorers to members of certain tribes (p. 397).

R: The Negro . . . prefers to spend the day as lazily as possible.

J: The examples that have been given . . . all point to the success of the Negrids . . . in agriculture.

Let me say once again that the flattering image conveyed by my quotes is no more accurate than Rushton's unflattering one; both are the products of biased selection.

# 8

# CANNIBALISM AT ISSUE

[N]ever man had a more faithful, loving, sincere servant, than
Friday was to me; without passions, sullenness, or designs, perfectly
obliged and engaged; his very affections were ty'd to me, like those
of a child to a father.

(Defoe [1719] 1972, p. 198)

Thus the superior European waxes sentimental over 'his man Friday', who is
utterly dependent on his 'master'. Friday, however, had not always been such a
model servant: before meeting Crusoe, he had been a cannibal; and Crusoe had
had to wean him off a 'hankering [after human flesh] stomach' and teach him
civilized ways. *Robinson Crusoe* has been rightly described as 'a colonial romance',[1]
since it portrays the way in which the man-eating savage becomes tamed and
dominated by the superior European.

Through the ages cannibalism has been attributed to the Other, and still
remains probably the most powerful symbol of savagery. The first part of this
chapter will outline the history until the early 19th century of European ideas
about cannibalism, and some of the ways in which these have been interpreted.
Underlying such interpretations are assumptions about the nature of cannibalism.
While it had been taken for granted until quite recently that many savage peoples
did actually consume human flesh, this has now been called into question. Several
writers maintain that cannibalism is probably little more than a myth, and that the
reports about it cannot be taken as veridical.

In order to bring out the implications of such a view, it is necessary to return for
a moment to the two images of animality and child-likeness. These involve the
belief that savages are humans or semi-humans who have certain characteristics
that render them inferior to civilized Europeans. These characteristics were commonly conceived as stemming from their innate disposition or 'race'. Although the
animality or child-likeness was postulated on the basis of their real or imagined
behaviours, these were regarded merely as manifestations of an underlying
and inferior nature. When this doctrine came to be undermined by the scientific advances of the second half of the 20th century,[2] it became clear that the

97

old images of savages had been in the main a function of European modes of perception and imagining, rather than genuine attributes of peoples.

The position regarding 'cannibalism' is not so straightforward, since 'cannibalism' is both a concept closely linked to that of savagery and a form of behaviour. One vexed problem that should be mentioned at this point, and will be further pursued below, is that of deciding what kinds of behaviour should be qualified as 'cannibalism'; having noted this problem, I shall now dispense with the inverted commas around the word.

Animality and child-likeness have a somewhat different epistemological status from that of cannibalism. Once the *perceptions* of the former two have been shown to be mistaken, this at least in principle disposes of the matter. By contrast, in the case of cannibalism, the question remains whether or not such a form of behaviour has existed and perhaps continues to exist. Those concerned to rescue the reputation of savages in accordance with the egalitarian spirit of our age want to be able to show that cannibalism has probably never existed, and therefore belongs to the same 'mythical' category as animality and child-likeness. In order to examine this question, some of the relevant evidence concerning the 'reality' or otherwise of cannibalism will have to be reviewed. Whatever the answer, one thing is certain: in a climate where savagery and cannibalism were closely linked in European minds, a large proportion of allegations of cannibalism were groundless; this will be the main theme of Chapter 9.

## From Ancient Greece to the Spanish conquest of the New World

In classical Greece there were numerous myths dealing with cannibalism (cf. Kirk 1974). A common theme was that of taking revenge on someone by getting them to partake of a meal without knowing that they were eating their own child cooked. Or there was the Theban Sphinx who, like a praying mantis, ate her men after the act of love. Social evolutionists of the late 19th century treated such myths as 'savage survivals', i.e. remnants of what at one time had been actual practices. As Kirk shows, the manner in which we look at myths now is very different, viewing them essentially as symbolic, and of course Lévi-Strauss' contribution has been a key factor. Detienne (1982) provides a challenging structural analysis of Greek myths dealing with cannibalism, relating them to Greek ideas about the differences between men and animals. Among them were rules about eating, the most important one being, in the words of Porphyry, that 'Man is not an animal that eats raw flesh'. Hence the the notion of 'bestiality' was closely linked with eating uncooked food. Curiously, the Greeks, like the social evolutionists, thought that men once lived like animals, consuming raw food and each other. Such behaviour was seen as utterly incompatible with life in the polity, paralleling the later opposition between the civilized and savages. There was a gradation, both moral and geographical, from the polis to some more remote parts of Greece where people indulged in the bestiality of consuming raw food (though short of cannibalism), to distant peoples like the Scythians who were among the Anthropophagi. Thus one finds here the early roots of modes of thought that have remained pervasive in the West.

During the subsequent millennium, before Europeans had come into direct contact with savages, it was not unusual for accusations of cannibalism to be directed against minority groups of various kinds, usually religious or political opponents (Cohn 1975). Throughout this period, belief in the Plinian races (discussed in Chapter 1) remained unquestioned. By the 14th century doubts began to creep in about the existence of fabulous races in Asia, but they merely came to be displaced into the as yet unknown parts of Africa; it was not until the 17th century that the 'monstrous races' were finally relegated to the realm of fiction, though they continued for some time in pseudo-science and especially in popular imagery (Wittkower 1942).

As already mentioned, when Columbus landed he fully expected to come across members of the monstrous races. In the event he was only able to claim with certainty to have found cannibals and Amazons. He used the name 'Caniba' for an island believed to be inhabited by man-eaters, whence 'canibales', from which the current term stems. His information was second-hand, obtained from Indians who responded to his enquiries by denying cannibalism on their part, but referring to some other peoples who were supposed to practise it – a pattern that recurred over the centuries.

Subsequently cannibalism came to be attributed to a majority of Amerindians. This may well be connected to an order issued in 1503 by Queen Isabella, who had sponsored the voyage of Columbus. She commanded that Indians were not to be treated cruelly, with the exception of cannibals. In practice, of course, this gave the Conquistadores a free hand. The reputation of South American Indians for cannibalism became well established. When Charles-Marie de la Condamine set out in 1735 to lead an expedition on the Amazon, disease and slavers had cowed the Indians, who were far less menacing than he had feared. He described them as 'Voracious gluttons . . . pusillanimous and timid in the extreme, unless transported by drunkenness'; yet he added: 'notwithstanding there are at present no man-eaters along the banks of the Maranon, there yet exist inland tribes of Americans who eat their prisoners' (Keay 1991, p. 185).

During the early period of the conquest one of the Spaniards who sought to justify the ill-treatment of the Amerindians by listing their faults, deficiencies and sins was the Dominican Tomas Ortiz, already mentioned (pp. 16–17). It is significant that his list begins with the statement that they ate human flesh, evidently for him the most salient fact; he also mentioned that they ate all kinds of unsuitable foods raw, such as insects.

The Spanish writings on the Indians were translated and circulated widely in Europe, and when, during the 16th century, trade relations came to be established with the New World, other European nationals travelled there and subsequently published their experiences. In order to convey something of the nature of such reports, I will give an example drawn from the writings of the distinguished anthropologist Alfred Métraux. It refers to the anthropophagy of the Tupinamba, a South American people long notorious for its 'man-eating', and is based mainly on classical 16th-century sources such as de Léry and André Thevet. It was originally written in 1928 and later republished (Métraux 1967). 'The ancient authors took an evident delight in describing for us the horrific scenes that followed the execution' Métraux noted (p. 64), but he did not hesitate to reproduce them in gruesome detail, as a brief summary will indicate.

When prisoners had been massacred, children were encouraged to dip their hands in the blood of the dead, and even infants tasted the blood which mothers smeared on their breasts. Arms and legs were cut off close to the body, and each taken by a woman who would display them before they were cooked. The stomach of the cadaver was slashed open and children encouraged to plunge in their hands and pull out the entrails. Old women, who did the cooking, licked the fat from the sticks saying 'this is good!', some of them smearing the fat over their faces. Old women generally were said to have been particularly cruel: for instance, when the child of an enemy had been killed, one of them cut off the head and sucked out the brains through the hole at the base of the skull. There is a lot more, equally unsavoury, but this should be enough to convey the repellent picture of a 'typical' cannibal meal.

Among the authors who portrayed such scenes was Hans Staden, a German who had been captured by the Tupinamba and allegedly witnessed their anthropophagy, an experience he described in his *Wahrhaftige Historia* (1557). Although relatively few Germans were directly involved in travel to the New World, Germany was then the leading country as far as book printing was concerned, and more than a quarter of all European publications originated there. Hence the content analysis undertaken by Sixel (1966) of all the Americana that came out in German-speaking countries during the first half of the 16th century is of considerable interest. From among the extensive material he collected, only a few of the most relevant aspects can be outlined here.

Sixel discovered that the features most commonly mentioned were, in descending order of frequency, nakedness, cannibalism, religion and 'public order'.[3] 'Nakedness' tended to be associated with both 'animality' and the absence of shame, the latter often being connected with sexual promiscuity. Cannibalism was sometimes linked with the practice of human sacrifice, and it was often claimed that for some peoples human flesh was the main source of subsistence; in this connection all kinds of elaborations were proffered; for example, prisoners were said to be kept in stables like cattle, to be slaughtered when needed; sex-related themes included the castration of boy prisoners for the alleged purpose of increasing the yield of flesh; or a wife was given to a prisoner, whose child could then be eaten. As far as religion is concerned, the belief was that cannibals had none, except for devil worship. Similarly, it was almost uniformly denied that cannibals exercised any form of public order.

Sixel prepared a table, listing the frequency (in terms of number of editions out of a total of 109) by which different sets of themes figured (see Table 8.1); in it he

*Table 8.1* Frequencies of various themes in 16th-century German literature on the 'New World'

| Cultural feature | Cannibals | Non-cannibals | Mexicans |
|---|---|---|---|
| External appearance | 60 | 20 | 13 |
| Sexual life | 55 | 25 | 13 |
| Habitations | 40 | 22 | 21 |
| Subsistence | 44 | 23 | 17 |

compared peoples described respectively as cannibals, non-cannibals and Mexicans. The latter were generally recognized as being at a higher level of culture. The salience of cannibals, and the interest in their nakedness and sexual life emerge clearly from the table. Sixel himself commented that 'the cannibal was doubtlessly the most exciting figure of the American continent' (p. 183).

## Cannibalism is good to think

What Lévi-Strauss said about animals in the context of the relationship of humans to nature could perhaps also be said about cannibals: the idea of cannibalism does much to illuminate the relationship between Europeans and savages. In recent years this topic has been extensively discussed from several different theoretical standpoints, focusing on European visions of the Amerindians of the New World.

The significance of European perceptions has been extensively discussed by Anthony Pagden (1982), who also noted that by the end of the 15th century 'the anthropophagi had become a regular part of the topography of exotic lands' (p. 81); he went so far as to suggest that the European preoccupation with man-eating was something of an obsession. Spanish theologians and scholars of the period were greatly concerned about it, and Pagden provides a lucid account of the manner in which they viewed cannibalism. Apparently they had two main explanations for it, the first being the universal motive for revenge against enemies. In this connection Pagden points out that although cases of alleged cannibalism were not unknown in Europe it had hardly been seen as an everyday event, whereas for the Tupinamba it was perceived as a key feature of their culture.

The second explanation adduced was scarcity of animal meat, since Indians did not keep livestock. This belief[4] led to the fantasy of human butcher shops, frequently depicted in works on the New World, and later Africa. However, presumably since Indians engaged in hunting and fishing, some Spaniards took the view that Indians simply preferred human flesh to other kinds of food, a sure sign of their bestiality.

The various reasons why cannibalism is 'abominable to all nations which live civilized and not inhuman lives' (Pagden 1982, p. 85) were listed in detail by Francisco de Vitoria. It was not merely the sin of killing people, but failing to distinguish what is or is not proper food – what Pagden (ibid.) calls a 'radical category mistake'. Eating raw insects and worms entails the same kind of error. Moreover, as Pagden shows (p. 86), this conception also extended to sexual behaviour:

> Like the two sexual crimes – sodomy and bestiality – of which the Indians were also accused . . . their cannibalism demonstrated that they could not clearly distinguish between the rigid and self-defining categories into which the natural world was divided. The Indian could not see that other human beings were not, for him, a natural food any more than he could see that animals or creatures of the same sex were not his natural mates.

This is an interesting comment in view of the frequent conjunction of cannibalism and sexual deviance in the image of the savage. Yet it is doubtful whether such a scholastic formulation can be taken at face value – it is more likely to constitute a rationalization of deeper antagonisms. At any rate, the Spaniards' belief that Indians were unable to make what for them seemed 'obvious' discriminations contributed to their view of the Indians as intellectually inadequate.

This theme of a link between cannibalism and sexuality is also prominent in the work of Bucher (1981). She undertook a Lévi-Straussian structural analysis, tinged with some psychoanalytic elements, of the illustrations in de Bry's *Great Voyages*, published in the 16th century (see Figure 8.1). Bucher sought to infer from these engravings 'the manner in which cannibalism, this major taboo for our culture, may have been conceived, perceived and portrayed at that period' (p. 48) by Protestant artists. Bucher's analysis is highly ingenious, but bound to remain speculative. I shall therefore confine myself to briefly quoting her description of how the Tupinamba were represented, which is striking enough (p. 50):

> These three vices [gluttony, hate and lust] clearly combine in the portrayal of cannibal rituals: the combative and hostile atmosphere of a large number of scenes depicting daily life in the Tupinamba village; the aggressive gestures of the men, even more pronounced among the women, biting their nails with envy at the sight of the prisoner, whom they force to shout 'I am your food'. To this must be added the vaguely erotic gestures made by two figures of women: one caresses her companion's sexual parts during a ritual dance they perform around their victim . . . another does the same thing to herself, during a cannibal meal, while biting the nails of her other hand, at the sight of the intestines the women and children share.

It will be evident that this description of the pictures is fused with interpretations, though they seem quite plausible. At any rate, there can be no doubt that strong sexual elements entered into the portrayal of cannibal feasts, which is how the engravers must have imagined them. There is even some connection with the ape

*Figure 8.1* One of the engravings of Tupinamba cannibal feasts discussed by Bucher
*Source:* Theodor de Bry (1593) *America, Part III.* Frankfurt. Courtesy of the British Library.

image, since pictures of monkeys suggested to Bucher (1982) that the sexual perversities of the cannibal women were imitations of, or imitated by, monkeys.

Pagden's cool historical account contrasts with Bucher's more adventurous structural analysis; and a further step takes us to the post-structuralist and semiotic approach of Mason (1990), which consists of a 'deconstruction' of texts. His general thesis, if I understand it correctly, is that European writings about the New World are more a distorted mirror image[5] of Europe itself than accounts of American reality. Before Columbus it was the internal European Others, the Plinian races, Wild Men and Women of the Woods, witches and suchlike, 'which functioned as negative images by which European culture defined itself as a culture at all'; and he suggested that 'the imagery of these exotic races, projected onto the inhabitants of the New World, came to supplant the more traditional images of the Wild Man . . . Europe's inner Indians came to be replaced by its outer Indians' (Mason 1990, p. 97). Mason discusses in fascinating detail the parallelism between the attributes of intra-European Others and those of American Indians; for instance, he shows how closely the images of European witches with their sagging breasts correspond to de Bry's illustrations of cannibalistic hags. These snippets utterly fail to do justice to the range and subtlety of Mason's arguments.

What Mason and Bucher appear to have in common is their contention that European ideas about cannibalism are constructions, based on what Cohn (1975) called 'Europe's inner demons'; Bucher referred to 'myths', while Mason's preference for 'alterity' indicates his post-structuralist stance. In a later work Bucher (1982) drew a distinction – one which would probably not commend itself to Mason – between two main European conceptions of cannibalism: namely cannibalism as savagery, and cannibalism as monstrosity. The former stresses the contrast between savages and civilized nations; in the latter the excluded nations of cannibals 'are brought nearer to other excluded or abnormal persons of sixteenth century society', notably 'witches who indulge in foul and heinous deeds . . . mixed with a kind of diabolical eroticism' (Bucher 1982, p. 75).

All these highly sophisticated discussions amount in essence to thinking about what 16th-century Europeans thought about cannibalism; and doing so, inevitably, from a late 20th-century perspective. The question concerning the extent to which those thoughts of 16th-century Europeans corresponded to any 'reality' is regarded at best as secondary. Pagden (1982) does express his view that 'except for survival cannibalism and extreme revenge' (p. 83) Amerindians did *not* eat men, and Bucher appears to share this opinion; for Mason the question would be simply irrelevant.

But it is a question that has to be asked if one wants to know whether or not European ideas about cannibals were pure fantasy or myth, and it is a question to which I will shortly return.

During the 17th and 18th centuries the European preoccupation with cannibalism appears to have declined. This is of course not to say that routine attributions of cannibalism to savages ceased, but theological and philosophical speculation became less frequent. It was not until the second half of the 19th century that cannibalism was to become a burning topic once again.

## Myth or fact?

As will be shown later in more detail, before the Second World War no one seems to have questioned the existence of man-eating as a simple fact. Thereafter its reality began to be called into question by several writers, but was reaffirmed by others. For instance, at the beginning of his lectures on cannibalism, Lévi-Strauss commented on the lack of interest in the topic on the part of modern anthropologists 'to the point that some of them have come to question the former existence of cannibalism in regions of the world for which nevertheless numerous and concordant testimonies exist' (1984, p. 141). The onset of such scepticism, it may be noted, coincided with the end of colonialism and the effort on the part of social scientists to present non-Europeans in a more favourable light. This in itself, of course, does not prove anything either way.

In order to examine the issue, some distinctions (omitting only individual pathology) have to be drawn that are largely of quite recent origin. One aspect is the long recognized difference between cannibalism as a social practice, and the eating of human flesh in extreme famine situations, now usually called 'crisis cannibalism'. Cases of this kind have been reported since ancient times, and one of the earliest is to be found in the Old Testament; it refers to a woman eating her son during a famine (II Kings 6, v. 28). Sometimes, as in 13th-century Spain, permission was even formally given under certain circumstances:

> according to the true law of Spain a father who is besieged in a castle he holds from his lord, may, if so beset with hunger that he has nothing to eat, eat his child with impunity rather than surrender the castle without permission of the lord.
>
> (Cited in Boswell 1991, p. 329)

One of the most recent instances was that of the air crash in the Andes, when survivors were forced to eat the passengers who had died (Read 1974). There is no problem with this kind of event, and no one has ever questioned its occurrence.

At the end of the 19th century a distinction came to be drawn between 'endo- ' and 'exo-cannibalism', i.e. eating people either within or from outside one's community; both of course could coexist. During the early part of the 20th century cannibalism as a social practice was further dichotomized into 'ceremonial' or now more commonly known as 'ritual' cannibalism on the one hand, and 'real' cannibalism on the other. An early delineation of the difference runs as follows:

> we have drawn a distinction between the cases in which the object is the material one of making a meal, and that in which it is purely ceremonial, as is proved by the fact that only a small portion of the body is eaten as a mark of affection and sympathy.
>
> (Hobhouse *et al.* 1930, p. 240)

While the above distinction marked a historical phase it is problematic, since some of the accounts suggest they were describing a ritual cannibal meal of the bodies of enemies. Although this would fall under the above category of 'making a meal', and therefore 'real' cannibalism in their sense, it is not the same as what Forde (1963) called 'a perverted desire for human flesh', and others 'ferocious' cannibalism.

All this may seem like so much hair-splitting, but it is very relevant to the arguments in the debate. The best known protagonist of the thesis that canni-balism is probably only a myth is William Arens (1979), who sought to show that nearly all accounts of it are questionable. His views have been subjected to an incisive critique by Lewis (1986), whose discussion of the whole topic is illuminating. Here I shall consider some of the arguments of another author, Erwin Frank (1987), who shares Arens' broad stance but takes a somewhat different line; and since his contribution is in German and has not to my knowledge been translated, it is less widely known.

## Frank's critique and the question of its validity

At the outset Frank draws attention to the polysemy of the term 'cannibal' noted above: is it appropriate, he asks, to use the term when peoples mix the powdered remains of the deceaseds' bones into a beverage and drink it in their honour? Would it be cannibalistic to suck the blood from one's own or another person's wound? And what about the Eucharist? This might appear ridiculous, but that is merely because our conventional wisdom always locates cannibals in remotest Africa or Brazil. Such a spontaneous assocation between cannibalism and temporal/spatial distance is perfectly justified; careful study of witnesses and testimonies confirms that cannibals are a 'beyond-the-border' phenomenon:

> They exist only *there* where, and *as long as*, there is a boundary between the world of the reporter and that quite different world; an unknown world which strengthens the hypothesis of the possible existence of the totally different, even of the unthinkable.
>
> (Frank 1987, p. 200; emphasis in the original)

As long as a territory remained blank on the map, it was claimed that it contained cannibals; once explored, the cannibals are moved further away into the as yet unknown parts. Moreover, why is it that cannibalism was often supposed to have been given up without resistance immediately after European colonization, or even earlier, when many other 'perverse' institutions like polygamy, genital mutilation, fetishism and so on continued unchanged?

Frank also cites a series of historical examples such as those of Jews and heretics who had also been accused of cannibalism. We do not believe now that these ever were really cannibals, but we are prepared to believe it of indigenous Africans and Americans. It would be easy to add more recent examples to those cited by Frank. As late as the 17th century, 'cannibalism' was attributed even to such alleged savages as the Irish (Carlin 1984) and the Highland Scots, both then marginal peoples in relation to Europe.

Frank also uses Arens' argument, demolished by Lewis, that witchcraft and cannibalism have the same epistemological status. He also correctly states that many peoples accuse their neighbours of cannibalism, suggesting that all such slurs are equally unfounded: 'we do not lack cannibals . . . but we badly lack unquestionable sources and credible eye-witnesses (1987, p. 205). Like Arens, he suggests that most of the evidence about cannibalism is unreliable. Thus in relation to what he calls the 'typical Tupinamba-ritual of imprisonment, ritual killing and subsequent consumption' (p. 212), he argues that it is precisely the close agreement among different reports that is suspicious, indicative of plagiarism. Hence, he concludes, it is a waste of time to elaborate classifications or consider the functions of cannibalism, when we do not know if it was ever really practised; and the same applies to speculations by archaeologists about pre-historic cannibalism (cf. e.g. Helmuth 1968).[6]

Frank then raises the question of why we believe almost anything about savages. He cites the example of Alexander von Humboldt, an intelligent and enlightened man, yet who was ready to credit a story about a chief who kept a harem not merely for his sexual pleasure, but also as a mobile food store. The answer proposed by Frank is a psychological one: when we receive such information we have already been primed with preconceptions about the awful deeds of which savages are capable, and there is a historically conditioned powerful association between savagery and cannibalism. This also means that if someone is labelled a cannibal, then one tends to believe that person to be capable of any act, however abhorrent. While this is a shrewd observation, no doubt applicable in numerous cases, it does not exclude the correctness of some reports.

Frank's arguments are illustrated with much richer and more colourful material than my bare summary indicates. However, the general line will be clear: like Arens, he set out reasons why we should not trust the reports, making some interesting points that cannot be found in Arens. Although he does not actually state his position explicitly, he obviously regards 'beastly' cannibalism as mere fantasy, rooted in psychological dispositions.

Similar passion is displayed by others who appear to see their role as that of defending the Other from what they regard as slurs. Thus Hulme (1986, p. 81) accuses even those falling back on the formula 'not proven' of acquiescing 'to the implicit violence of colonial discourse'. It seems to me that this is an indefensible stance. There is conclusive evidence that relatively mild forms of 'ritual' cannibalism do exist, and were probably more widespread in the past before missionaries and colonial administrators prohibited it (Sanday 1986). Among the best documented cases are those of the Trobrianders studied by Malinowski (described by Lewis 1986, p. 73), and of the Bimin-Kuskusmin of Papua New Guinea, which was also witnessed by an anthropologist (Poole 1983). He observed 'female agnates of a lineage eating small morsels of their dead kinsman's lower belly fat, a practice designed to "recycle" his procreative and ritual strength within his patrilineage' (Poole 1983, p. 16); similarly, he saw male kinsmen eat fragments of a dead woman's bone marrow. While this is hardly the kind of ferocious and disgusting behaviour usually associated with the word 'cannibalism', their reported eating of 'female' parts of their dead enemies' bodies in order to deprive them of full ancestor status comes closer to it.

This last example – eating parts of enemy corpses – was not actually witnessed by an observer: should one therefore discount it? Judging from Frank's examples, he probably would not regard the 'milder' behaviours as falling within the category of 'cannibalism' at all. His critique seems mainly directed at 'ferocious' cannibalism of the Tupinamba kind, which Frank regards as European fantasies. But even these allegations cannot be summarily dismissed, and not only because of the recent reappraisals of the documentary evidence cited by Lewis (1986, p. 75). Before going any further, let me say that I do *not* believe that there ever was cannibalism prompted merely by a special liking for human flesh.

As will have become evident by now, the whole notion of 'cannibalism' is a difficult and controversial one, influenced almost as much by sentiment as by evidence, and bedevilled by semantic issues. It is usually hard to decide whether a particular form of behaviour really exists; and if it does, whether or not it really constitutes anthropophagy; and if so, whether or not it is a sanctioned social practice. The issue may be illustrated by my attempt to follow up a statement by Cohn (1975, p. 7) to the effect that 'It is certain that in our own century, in Sierra Leone, the secret society of "human leopards" killed and ate young people'. A footnote refers as a source to Beatty's (1915) account of the trials concerning the 'leopard society'. The Preface to this work was by one of the judges involved in the trials. On p. v he wrote, 'The question as to cannibalism it is not possible to answer with any degree of certainty', explaining at some length that the legal issue before the court was that of murder, and that it was not a scientific inquiry. However, at the end of the following page it is suddenly taken for granted that cannibalism did occur: 'notwithstanding the time spent over the different trials, and despite the fact that whenever the subject of cannibalism came up the Court was keenly on the alert to fathom its objects, *it is not possible to state definitely why the members of the Human Leopard Society ate their victims*' (pp. vi/vii; my emphasis). The judge then expressed his view that, since the men were of mature age, the purpose was to increase their virility. He admitted that 'There is no sentence in the notes of evidence which I can quote in support of this theory', but argued that it was based on his 'extended experience of the point of view of the West African mind' (p. vii). The body of the work itself contains no shred of evidence regarding cannibalism. If one stopped at this point, one might be inclined to suppose that it was all in the judge's mind.

However, going on to consult the standard work on the Mende of Sierra Leone by Kenneth Little (1951), I found an account of how (African) people in the town reported being chased by 'cannibals'. Little commented: 'The fear is the greater because it rests, very occasionally, on objective facts in that associated outbreaks of "cannibalism" still occur, the object being to obtain human fat for the purpose of re-invigorating certain medicines' (pp. 232/3). Little went on to comment that in modern times such 'cannibal medicines' were being used for the purpose of gaining political or economic power, by striking fear into the community.[7] As Little made clear, such practices did not form part of the institutions of Mende society, and were in fact strongly condemned. Moreover, whether or not the bodily substances were obtained by killing a victim (and that is not necessarily the case), the resulting medicines could then be sold to third parties. I have heard rumours about this in other parts of West Africa, and while there is no proof it is quite plausible. Would this be different in principle from drinking a mixture of powdered bones, which even Frank would not categorize as 'cannibalism'?

What I am trying to demonstrate is that 'ritual' cannibalism is a vague notion which covers a wide range of behaviour, from mild to ferocious. There are indications that even the latter kind has not altogether disappeared. Quite recently a case was reported of a French mercenary accused on the basis of photo-graphic evidence of having taken part in a cannibal meal (*The Times*, 22 January 1996). He admitted having eaten the livers of two Burmese soldiers, stating in his defence that 'he did not want to appear cowardly in front of his comrades by refusing to take part in what he called a "local tradition" during which the Karen warriors symbolically "devour" the bravery of their enemies'. The Karens' cannibalism would by this account clearly fall into the 'ritual' rubric, but the cannibalism of the French mercenary is less easily categorized.

Enough has been said to show why, in my view, cannibalism of various kinds cannot be dismissed as mere fantasy but has some foundation in fact. Saying this is of course not to defend the numerous groundless allegations epitomized in Frank's title, taken from a letter by Columbus: 'They are man-eaters, as is evident from their horrid appearance.' There is no doubt that belief in the cannibalism of others has always greatly exceeded its actual practice.

## The universality of notions about cannibalism

Even as far as the *image* of cannibalism is concerned, it differs significantly from those of the other two mentioned above, in so far as it was frequently *reciprocal*. There is no evidence that any savages attributed animality to Europeans – if anything, they were perceived as supernatural beings. Similarly, it was only in exceptional cases, when Europeans tried to learn the skills of other peoples, that they were regarded as child-like. But it has often been shown that not merely hostile neighbours but also Europeans were feared as cannibals. This is mentioned by Frank, who cites the example of a group of Indios of eastern Peru known as 'Cashibo', once regarded as typical cannibals; they themselves apparently in turn attributed cannibalism to Europeans.[8] Frank saw this kind of reciprocity as an indication that ferocious cannibalism never really existed; but there is no logical reason why it should be so regarded.

Beginning with attributions of cannibalism to Europeans, there are numerous accounts of this. In Africa they date back at least to the period of the 'Atlantic trade', when slaves were kept in depots on the coast awaiting shipment. There was a widespread belief that they were being fattened up as food for Europeans (Baker 1974). Several recent examples are given by Lewis (1986), such as that of the Belgian firm, whose picture of an African baby on the tins of meat they tried to market in Africa was misunderstood. Lewis also provides a valuable discussion of the various factors, including political ones, that influenced the cannibal image of Europeans.

As mentioned above, it has been common for peoples in many parts of the world to suspect their neighbours of cannibalism. For instance, Turnbull (1976), who worked with pygmies, related the following incident. He had taken one of them, Kenge, on a trip beyond his forest to a people called BaLese who had an evil reputation:

Kenge was getting more and more nervous . . . and refused to move from the safety of the car, and stood there with his hand on the door, ready to lock himself inside at a moment's notice. For him this was a foreign world indeed, for these were not only villagers, but villagers who had a reputation for devouring corpses.

(p. 217)

It is usually outsiders who are suspected, but they are not necessarily so in geographical terms, nor is the cannibalism always conceived in a physical sense. Thus among the Akan in Ghana it was thought that witches eat the vital essence of a person who will then die (Field 1960); similar notions are to be found in many other cultures (cf. Lewis 1986, pp. 66–7). Generally speaking, cannibalism is a pervasive theme of myths and beliefs throughout the world, and hence is presumably deeply rooted in the human psyche.

## Some interpretations

At least since the time of Herodotus, the idea of cannibalism has been deeply repugnant within the western tradition; yet at the same time a morbid interest has been displayed, suggesting that the *frisson* caused by it is not altogether disagreeable. Once again this can be illustrated with reference to Defoe ([1719] 1972, p. 159), who seems to dwell almost lovingly on the horrors:

When I was come down the hill to the shore . . . I was perfectly confounded and amazed; nor is it possible for me to express the horror of my mind, at seeing the shore spread with skulls, hands, feet, and other bones of humane bodies; and particularly I observed a place where there had been a fire made, and a circle dug in the earth . . . where it is supposed the savage wretches had sat down to their inhumane feastings upon the bodies of their fellow-creatures.

. . . all my apprehensions were bury'd in the thoughts of such a pitch of inhuman, hellish brutality, and the horror of the degeneracy of human nature . . . I turned away my face from the horrid spectacle; my stomach grew sick and I was just on the point of fainting, when nature discharged the disorder from my stomach, and having vomited with an uncommon violence, I was a little relieved.

The graphic description, it must be remembered, was designed to appeal to the reader as well as providing an object lesson on the depravity of savages. As will be shown in more detail below, *Robinson Crusoe* had a long-lasting effect on the European image of the savage.

The combined repulsion and – usually unacknowledged – attraction of cannibalism points to deep-rooted sources within the psyche. It is therefore not surprising that discussions of the topic have commonly resorted to speculations based at least partly on depth psychology. Although such discussions are usually aimed at throwing light on the psychic processes of those who engage in cannibalism, rather than on European images which are the focus here, some aspects are pertinent.

One of the most ambitious projects to explain not only why some peoples engage in cannibalism, but also why it enters into the mythology of others who abhor it, is by Sanday (1986). Her highly abstract theoretical concepts are drawn from a range of sources, philosophical, psychoanalytic as well as anthropological. What is central for her, as for Sahlins (1983), is 'the system of symbols that predicates a people's understanding of their being-in-the-world and formulates their strategies vis-à-vis social regeneration, reproduction, and dominance' (Sanday, 1986, p. 26). It would of course not be possible to summarize here her complex arguments, which follow a dual track of cannibalism as both a cultural system and the manifestations of certain psychological tendencies. Sanday attempted to specify the conditions under which cannibalism would or would not be likely to become a social practice, and also what would be likely to make it a symbol of evil. As regards the latter, one of her statements of interest in the present context is that 'an ethos that emphasizes accommodation and integration with cosmic or social forces, as opposed to domination and control of these forces, finds in cannibalism a ready symbol of evil' (p. 55). If one tries to apply this to the European case, it does not seem to fit. Domination and control are prominent in European ideology, yet cannibalism is a powerful symbol of evil.

Another commentator, Sagan (1974), takes an unadulterated Freudian line, proposing that emotional ambivalence regarding aggression is crucial in cannibalism; and that may well be true. However, when it comes to spelling this out in concrete detail concerning mortuary cannibalism, some remarkable claims are made:

> The undeveloped imagination of the cannibal does not deal very adequately with metaphorical usage. *He is compelled* to take the urge for oral incorporation literally. He eats the person who, by dying, has abandoned him. This act of literal oral incorporation has an affectionate and an aggressive dimension.
>
> (Sagan 1974, p. 28; my emphasis)

The first thing to note is the assumption of a 'primitive mentality' à la Lévy-Bruhl, the savage being unable to distinguish between literal and metaphorical usage. Hence he is 'compelled' to eat the dear departed, against whom he feels (unconscious) aggression for having abandoned him. In this respect Sagan displays an outdated European image of the savage.

Apart from that, the suggestion that the aggression is not conscious, so that only affection is manifest, is more interesting. One might speculate that the opposite would apply to the European response to cannibalism – the aggression is overt, and the positive feelings suppressed or at any rate not readily displayed. But why should there be any positive feelings at all? The answer may lie in the link between eating and sexuality, examined in some detail by Lewis (1986, pp. 75–6). This becomes more plausible when one recalls the ancient association between savagery and unrestrained sexuality in the European mind.

All this may seem far-fetched, and perhaps it is, but there are indications that it may not be entirely so. Charles Dickens is a case in point. Most of his biographers mention his life-long preoccupation with cannibalism, and Stone (1994) devoted a whole book to this. Apparently he was addicted to 'twopenny dreadfuls', such as the *Terrific Register*, which regaled its readers with a constant diet of cannibal stories, illustrated with grisly pictures. These dealt with themes like '"Anthrophagi or Men-Eaters" who "subsisted on human flesh" or the famished multitudes of India who often "devoured their own children" ' (Stone 1994, p. 73). One piece is worth quoting in full, since it not merely bears most directly on the present theme but, as will be shown below, had more recent echoes. It was offered in the *Terrific Register* in the guise of 'useful knowledge':

> [There are] in South America, and in the interior of Africa . . . people who feed upon human flesh merely on account of its delicacy, and as the height of gourmandize. These nations not only eat the prisoners they take in war, but their own wives and children; they even buy and sell human flesh publicly. To them we are indebted for the information that white men are finer flavoured than negroes, and that Englishmen are preferable to Frenchmen. Farther, the flesh of young girls and women, particularly of new-born children, far exceeds in delicacy that of the finest youths, or grown men. Finally, they tell us that the inside of the hand and the sole of the foot are the nicest parts of the human body.
>
> (Cited in Stone 1994, p. 76)

Apparently these lurid stories fired Dickens' imagination, and prompted hints of thinly disguised near-cannibalistic scenes in several of his works. For instance, the Fat Boy in *Pickwick Papers* is about to eat a meat pie when he notices Mary, the pretty housemaid, sitting opposite. He leans forward, knife in hand, and slowly remarks: ' "I say! How nice you look." There was enough of the cannibal in the young gentleman's eyes to render the compliment a double one.' This and other such cannibal images with a sexual tinge are described by Carey (1973).

It could be argued that Dickens' proclivity towards cannibalism, and his frequent portrayal of women as delicious in both senses, was an idiosyncratic one. Yet it should be stressed that during the 19th century, when Dickens was writing, cannibalism was very much in the air. As will be shown in the next chapter, travellers and explorers seemed to find it in numerous places; and their tales, however improbable, were often accepted quite uncritically by scientific authorities.

# 9

# THE FASCINATING HORROR

In analysing the European images of savages, the notion of 'inversion' is a useful one. It refers to a process whereby an imaginary ethnography is generated by inverting something close and familiar, so that the outcome may be likened to a photographic negative; and these inverted features are then attributed to the savages. This was the kind of interpretation used by Mason when discussing the European image of the Other in antiquity, the Middle Ages and the 16th to 17th centuries (e.g. Mason 1990, pp. 124–7). The same interpretation fits the European images of savages in the 19th century, and Hegel provides a prototypical example. He saw Africa very much as a kind of inversion of Europe,

*Figure 9.1* An obviously posed photograph dating from about 1890, purporting to show 'Fijian cannibals'. A good deal of the alleged evidence for cannibalism is of this kind.
*Source:* Royal Anthropological Institute Photographic Collection (RAI 35418).

113

painting it in the most lurid colours. For Hegel the values of humans lay in their connection with 'the Absolute', and, since Africans do not recognize that entity, he inferred, in a convoluted argument, that they attach no value to human life. Hence they slaughter their fellows, drink their blood and eat them, practise polygamy and are apt to suddenly explode in blind destructive fury (Hegel [1832] 1992, Vol. 12, pp. 120–9). These fearsome images were not dreamed up by the philosopher in his armchair, but originated from a stream of colourful reports by travellers and explorers, a stream which barely abated in the course of the 19th century. It shaped the image of Africa in particular, and rendered not only public but also scientific opinion credulously receptive to the most fantastic claims. Even if some of the reports of cannibalism were accurate, these were almost certainly greatly outnumbered by cases where the travellers and explorers were either led astray by their preconceptions or, one suspects, wanted to increase the impact of their reports by sensationalizing them in the expected direction (see Figure 9.1).

At the outset I propose to concentrate on two significant episodes that are worth examining in some detail. The first is the relatively little known case of the Niam-Niam, which combines the topics of ape-likeness and cannibalism. The other concerns the German explorer Schweinfurth, still regarded by some as having provided conclusive proof of cannibalism. I shall try to demonstrate the slender basis of his claims, and the manner in which his strong prejudices coloured his perceptions.

## Strange tales about the Niam-Niams

In the mid-19th century, reports began to circulate in France about cannibals with tails who had been found in Central Africa. They were variously called Gnamgnam, YamYam or Ghilanes, but have entered history as the Niam-Niams. The reports originated from Louis Ducouret, who after his conversion to Islam called himself Hadj Abd-El-Hamid-Bey. He was an adventurer who from 1832 travelled widely for fifteen years in Egypt, Abyssinia, the Sudan, Arabia and Persia. He had heard stories about the Niam-Niams – people with tails – from Arab slave traders and various African ethnic groups such as the Nubians and the Nuer. In 1848 he passed on this information to the *Société Orientale* who published it. In 1849 he submitted a note to the *Académie des Sciences* (Comptes Rendus 1849, pp. 231–4) about a people well known among neighbouring tribes for 'une particularité d'organisation très étrange'. It was stated that Ducouret had not himself been able to penetrate into their land, but that he had personally seen one in Mecca in 1842. A few months later he added to this the testimony of two explorers and merchants who had obtained information about such people with tails (p. 451). Another willing recipient of his claims was the *Société de Géographie* in 1851, and subsequently an article of his appeared in *La France Médicale*. In 1854 he published a pamphlet on the Niam-Niams (Abd-El-Hamid-Bey 1854). This contained a biographical sketch of the author by Alexandre Dumas, the famous novelist, in which he stated that Ducouret was in the process of convincing the

*Académie des Sciences* of the existence near the Equator of monsters intermediate between monkeys and humans who had language like humans and tails like monkeys.

The fact that so many learned societies, and notably the august *Académie*, were prepared to receive such communications indicates that they were taken seriously. Not only that, but he received an official commission to travel to the Sudan in order to collect further evidence.

Ducouret's description of the Niam-Niams was very detailed, considering that by his own admission he had only seen one single specimen:

> [They] constitute a special race of men, who have many similarities with the ape . . . their arms are long and spindly; their feet and their hands are longer and flatter than those of other races of men. They have a strong and and very extended lower jaw, prominent cheeks, a short forehead strongly angled backwards, long and deformed ears. . . . What particularly distinguishes this tribe is the exterior extension of the spinal column, which, with each individual whether male or female, forms a tail of two or three inches in length. . . . They often seek out quarrels with neighbouring negro tribes, with the sole aim of taking away their women, to whom they are very partial [i.e. as food], children, and other victims, whom they devour without pity.
>
> (Abd-El-Hamid-Bey 1854, pp. 84–7)

As documented in full detail by Pénel (1982), Ducouret's claims were followed by a multitude of other testimonies, nearly all of which consisted of nth-hand hearsay. For instance, one report to the *Société de Géographie* mentioned a reliable Abyssinian who saw fifteen tailed men at a market near Aden. Moreover, a European in Cairo assured the witness that a young female slave had eaten an infant. Another contributor reported having seen in Paris two Negroes from Central Africa, one of whom spoke French quite well. This man did not claim to have personally seen cannibals with tails, but he sang a song about them! There was general agreement that belief in the existence of such a people was widespread among Africans. Slave-traders were also said to be anxious to avoid buying slaves with tails, since they were wild, hard to domesticate and ate children.

Especially revealing is the case of Francis de Castelnau who had been French consul in South America, where he had interrogated slaves who had come from Central Africa and were said to have fought against tailed men. On this basis he felt able to write a small book (Castelnau 1851), so phrased that one might imagine he had been an eyewitness:

> and a few days later one came across a group of the savage Niam-Niams . . . they all had a tail approximately 40cms in length and which might have a diameter of some two or three; this organ is smooth . . . these

people are similar to other negroes; they were absolutely naked. The following day the expedition encountered several other groups . . . one was occupied in eating human flesh and the heads of three men were still cooking over the fire, suspended on poles pushed into the ground.

(p. 15)

It will be noted that while Ducouret gave the length of the tails as merely two to three inches (about 5–7cms), Castelnau was far more generous. Not that Ducouret was particularly scrupulous: when he produced what was supposed to be an authentic drawing of the tail, the distinguished naturalist Geoffroy St Hilaire observed that it would be anatomically impossible to have an extension of the coccyx from the location shown; unabashed, Couret shifted it to the correct place. Pénel (1982, pp. 151–5) presents a systematic overview of the physical descriptions of the Niam-Niams, showing them to be completely lacking in consistency. The only aspect on which there was complete agreement was that the Niam-Niams practised the sharpening of their teeth, widely taken as evidence of cannibalism and of their wish to identify with carnivorous animals.[1]

One might well wonder how it was possible for members of the French educated elite to be so readily taken in. Perhaps one reason was the feeling, dating back to Pliny (Ex Africa semper aliquid novi), that mysterious Africa still harboured unexplored phenomena. This would help to account for the credulity of someone like Dumas.[2]

Most intriguing is the change of position by Geoffroy St Hilaire: initially highly sceptical as indicated above, he became, oddly, a believer, as a result of the threadbare and highly tendentious testimony of Ducouret. Once having accepted the reality of the tailed Niam-Niams, he went on to propose that the biological classification of monkeys and apes would have to be modified, since the higher apes had previously been regarded as lacking tails.

The lively discussions of the issue went on throughout the 1850s, and mention was frequently made of earlier writings, from antiquity onwards, about all kinds of near-human beings. The name of de Maillet (cf. Chapter 4) cropped up repeatedly, his speculations being linked to the puzzle of the Niam-Niams. As late as 1862 the Marquis d'Antinori contributed a report to the *Bulletin de la Société d'Anthropologie*. On the basis of information from a neighbouring tribe he stated that only one sub-group, namely the 'Banda-Gniam-Gniam' had tails. He himself had seen an individual with a rudimentary tail at a slave merchant's in Constantinople. He added that Turkish and Arab slave merchants did not want tailed Niam-Niams, especially not women who eat their children. Simonot, a commentator on this piece, maintained that owing to the multiplicity of observations the existence of tailed people must be accepted as an authentic scientific fact. They constitute a link between human and animal, filling a gap in the Great Chain of Being and confirming its harmonious progression. This of course harks back to the theories of the 18th-century naturalists.

The debate about the existence of people with tails took place mainly in France, though its echoes could be found in other European countries (cf. Gleisberg 1868). It only gradually came to be generally accepted that tailed humans were just a myth; as late as 1896 the case of a tribe of tailed people in Indo-China was reported in *Nature* (Vol. 55, p. 82), albeit in a somewhat sceptical manner.[3]

Stories of cannibalism, which had routinely accompanied those of tails, met with little if any scepticism. During the whole of the 19th century, travellers and explorers returned with such reports. Mission maps listed certain people as 'Menschenfresser-anthropopagi', a claim confirmed by Richard Burton (1860, Vol. II, p. 114) as regards the Wabembe, 'who devour, besides man, all kinds of carrion and vermin, grubs and insects ... they prefer man raw, whereas the Wadoe of the coast eat him roasted'. Similarly, on the basis of a stay of a single week with the Fans, Burton felt able to write extensively about their cannibalism.[4] There were many others, notably Henry Stanley, whose popularity as a result of his finding of Livingstone made him a celebrated writer.

## Schweinfurth in pursuit of cannibals

Among the explorers claiming to have obtained conclusive evidence of cannibalism, one of the most famous and influential was the botanist Georg Schweinfurth (1836–1925). He travelled widely in Central Africa between 1868 and 1871, spending much time with the Niam-Niams (later known as Azande) and their neighbours. While heaping ridicule on the stories of the Niam-Niams' tails, he had taken those about cannibalism very seriously. One of his aims was to investigate the matter, and as a result he came to the conclusion that not only the Niam-Niams but numerous other African peoples practised it. Owing to the weight of his scientific authority, Schweinfurth's testimony powerfully reinforced the European belief that cannibalism was widespread in Africa, a belief which persists to the present. A recent writer on African exploration commented as follows:

> When Schweinfurth turned for home, he had every reason to be pleased with his achievements ... he had acquired a veritable thesaurus of information on the Mangbetu, Mittoo and Niam-Niam peoples, including incontrovertible evidence of cannibalism, for Schweinfurth was far too erudite and subtle to be unable to distinguish between fact and fantasy in this controversial area.
>
> (McLynn 1992, pp. 115–16)

It will be instructive to look at this case in a more critical fashion. The very title of his book, *In the heart of Africa* (Schweinfurth 1874), was apt to evoke in the minds of 19th-century readers all the exotic mystery and horror associated with the 'dark continent'. It is relevant to mention that he was hoping that the book would help him to gain financial security, which provided a motive to sensationalize his account. It indeed became a bestseller that was translated into several languages and established his fame. His descriptions of flora and fauna, unlike those of humans, tend to be cloyingly sentimental.

The account of his first entry into 'the true jungle' is coupled with reminiscences about his youthful readings about jungles in adventure literature. As a botanist, he was fascinated by the rich flora and contrasted the 'holy temple of nature' with the malice and dirt of the 'human devils' around him. The Niam-Niams, whose very name was synonymous with cannibalism, seemed to him to have a facial expression that was 'an indescribable mixture of bestial savagery, war-like determination and an openness inviting trust'; among these the former prevailed, for he kept referring to their 'uninhibited savagery' (Vol. II, pp. 5 and 13). It should be added that he was not much more complimentary about other peoples, except the occasional ones who had caught his fancy. Thus he remarked on the simian physiognomy of the Dinka.

As was the usual practice in his time, and in contrast to modern fieldworkers, Schweinfurth kept himself rigidly apart from the peoples he was studying, coming somewhat closer only to the Nubians who formed his armed escort; and he relied heavily on whatever the Nubians told him. Schweinfurth at all times explicitly claimed the right to be regarded as a being of a superior kind, justifying this by what he felt was the ever-present danger of falling into savagery oneself. Interestingly, and significantly, this seems to have been a common fear at the time; and not only a fear, since there were Europeans, including lapsed missionaries, who 'went native'. In 1897 Johnstone (cited in Brantlinger 1985, p. 194) wrote: 'I have been increasingly struck with the rapidity with which such members of the white race as are not of the best class, can throw over the restraints of civilisation and develop into savages of unbridled lust and abominable cruelty.'

Anxious to preserve his European identity, Schweinfurth clung to material symbols such as European dress, knife and fork, handkerchief and so on. He also revealed his fear of attacks, being killed, and perhaps worse. Under the circumstances his feeling of desperate loneliness is understandable. He may also have experienced sexual frustration, though in a work of this kind, and at that time, one could hardly expect that this would have been mentioned. One may speculate, however, that his vile characterization of African women may have been a reaction formation. This is how he described an old woman, who had been helpful to him: 'Words fail to portray her ugliness: a naked, wrinkled, bent bundle of bones, covered by tough Negro skin, toothless, with thin strands of hair drenched in fat . . . (Vol. I, p. 141). The accompanying sketch (see Figure 9.2) is probably more truthful than his words, showing a woman with a finely chiselled, open face. In referring to women he always used the then common pejorative term *Weib*, and his drawings of Bongo and Dinka women are rather nasty caricatures (see Figure 9.3). He complained of the unpleasant sight of Bongo women: 'The long raffia tail makes its own contribution [to the ugly sight], and the silhouette of a gravely prancing Bongo woman is highly reminiscent of a dancing baboon' (Vol. I, p. 324).

*Figure 9.2* 'Words are inadequate to convey the ugliness' was Schweinfurth's comment. His drawing tells another story.
*Source:* Schweinfurth (1874).

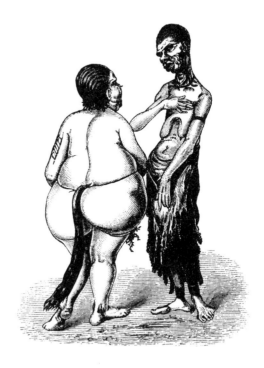

*Figure 9.3* Schweinfurth's nasty caricatures of African women: a case of sour grapes?
*Source:* Schweinfurth (1874).

Schweinfurth also waxed highly indignant about some women who 'before the whole world made the most shameless propositions to the stranger by means of an obscene finger language and gestures of more than plastic nature' (Vol. II, p. 96). He was clearly intent upon showing that African women are not desirable, but at times one feels that he protests too much.

Schweinfurth's isolation, which stemmed from an unwillingness to enter into closer relations with his African hosts, was relieved by his dog. When the dog died, he wrote that he had lost his only true friend while living among 'devilish humans'. Comparing dogs favourably with Africans, he was particularly disgusted with groups that were fond of eating dog meat, suggesting that this might be associated with a tendency to consume human flesh.

Let me turn now to some of the main evidence Schweinfurth offered of cannibalism, beginning with a quote about the Niam-Niams (Vol. I, p. 556):

> Numerous witnesses, testifying unambiguously to the tendency of the inhabitants to engage in cannibalism, appeared before my astonished eyes. In the vicinity of the huts that served as living quarters, on the heap of kitchen scraps of all kinds, there were human bones or pieces thereof; all had marks of having been hacked with knives or axes. Here and there, on the branches of neighbouring trees, arms and feet were hanging, half reduced to skeletal state; and having been badly dried in the shadow of the dense greenery, they were evil-smelling and polluted the air of much of the surroundings.

A most graphic and horrific account, requiring careful reading: after the initial brief reference to testimonies, it is written as though Schweinfurth had seen it all himself; in fact it was only hearsay. Schweinfurth's keenness to be told something about cannibals must have been obvious to all and sundry, and they were no doubt happy to oblige.

Other passages seem to be based on his own experience (Vol II, p. 19):

> One can confidently describe the Niam-Niams as a people of anthropophagi . . . they themselves proclaim their wild greed before all the world . . . carry ostentatiously the teeth of the people they have eaten . . . [in their cooking] human fat is most commonly used.

This is intended to sound like a confession by Niam-Niams, but of course it is nothing of the kind. The fact that they wore teeth in no way proves that they had eaten their former owners. One is also inclined to wonder how Schweinfurth could have known about the human fat, since he stated that in principle he never ate any meals with his village hosts.

One passage clearly refers to a personal observation, whose context has to be explained. Schweinfurth was an avid collector of human skulls, but this was not peculiar to him – explorers of the period were expected to do so in order to provide material for the craniology then so much in vogue.[5] In one rhetorical display he said that, given the well-founded reputation of the Niam-Niams, no one was likely to have any illusions about the source of much of his collection. This in itself is of course mere assertion, but elsewhere he stated that some of the skulls given to him 'seem to have come directly from the meals of the natives, for they were still damp and carried the smell of something freshly cooked' (Vol. II, p. 60).

This may sound suspicious unless one knows more about the circumstances, information which Schweinfurth himself provided.

The Niam-Niams, returning from war expeditions, brought him freshly cooked skulls for which he paid with copper rings. So also did his Nubian followers after they had been involved in a fight, though he never accused them of cannibalism. There is another piquant fact, somewhat sheepishly acknowledged by Schweinfurth. If the heads had not been cleaned, he retired to his tent with them (so as not to offend the susceptibilities of his Muslim retainers), and discreetly boiled them! Hence there was no good reason to believe that the flesh of the heads had been eaten. Ironically, the avid search for skulls led Africans to occasionally suspect that it was the explorer who had a predilection for cannibalistic practices.

Although the Niam-Niams were Schweinfurth's primary target, they were by no means the only one. In the course of his travels he liberally scattered accusations or insinuations of cannibalism, casually stating that 'it is supposed to be common among them'; or again, seeing the dying child of a slave woman he remarked, 'it was destined to find use as a delicious roast' (Vol. II, p. 240). Underlying the expressions of horror and digust, one senses a great deal of quiet satisfaction that the objective of winkling out the evil deeds had been amply achieved.

Schweinfurth was the epitome of smug European superiority over the 'dark races'. Condescendingly tolerant of Islamic peoples ('of an eternal childhood'), he seems to have disliked and despised most Africans, trotting out common stereotypes in the then usual way. Some peoples, he maintained, suffer from a lack of articulate linguistic expression, and when he reached a group of pygmies he described them as follows: 'the ever-changing play of facial expression, which . . . makes the Bushmen more similar to apes than to humans, applies to the Akka in a high degree' (Vol. I, p. 152). As this passage indicates, he mistakenly believed that pygmies and Bushmen were one and the same ethnic group.

The extent to which Schweinfurth was pandering to the preconceptions and prejudices of his prospective readers is uncertain; but there can be no doubt of his genuine conviction regarding the wide prevalence of cannibalism. What is also certain is that the success of his book strongly reinforced the popular myths in Europe about 'the heart of Africa', and especially the belief that most of the inhabitants were cruel savages. Evans-Pritchard, whose work on the Azande is a classic, made the following comment: 'It would be a mistake to suppose that because Schweinfurth had a well-deserved reputation as a botanist his ethnographical observations are equally to be relied upon. They are not' (1965, p. 139).[6]

## Seek, and ye shall find

In addition to the numerous supposedly first-hand reports about cannibalism, there grew up a considerable secondary literature drawing on these reports and often embellishing them. What Pagden said about 16th-century Europeans applied also to late 19th-century ones – cannibalism had become something of an obsession. This was equally true of German writers, who published extensively on the topic. Some examples will illustrate this, as well as the manner in which travellers sometimes obtained their 'evidence'.

Rich material is provided in an article on the anthropophagy of South American Indians by Koch (1899). Koch was a serious scholar who began with a discussion of the psychological aspects of anthropophagy, such as beliefs in the transmission of personal qualities by ingesting the meat of animals or the flesh of humans. When it came to describing various forms of cannibalism, any kind of source, however remote and indirect, was quite uncritically cited. Hence the reports bear an uncanny similarity to what had been written about American Indians three centuries earlier. This is perhaps not so surprising, since some of the reports were very old ones. Thus under the heading 'anthropophagy of relatives', one of the items goes back to the previously mentioned 18th-century traveller Castelnau. A missionary had told Castelnau, 'qu'il avait vu une femme Camacan manger son enfant qui venait de mourir en disant qu'il était sorti de son sein et qu'il devait y retourner' (Koch 1899, p. 85). Similarly, 'The famous Brazilian explorer Conto de Magalhaes heard from a reliable man that the Chavantes consume their deceased children' (ibid.). Koch quoted a certain Herrera to the effect that for the natives of Cauca in Columbia the living are the graves of the dead: 'The man eats his wife, brother the brother or the sister, the son the father' (p. 86). There are stories of missionaries being killed and eaten, and one could go on at length in the same fashion. Let me cite one further revealing report derived from Wied, an early 19th-century traveller in Brazil:

> The Botokudes mostly deny that they themselves are cannibals, shifting it on to tribes hostile to them. – Wied's servant, the Botokude Quäck, had long shied away from acknowledging the truth about this matter, until he was eventually made to confess. – He described the following scene, about whose veracity there can be hardly any doubt, *in view of the fact that it was so hard to get him to confess.*
>
> (Koch 1899, p. 102; my emphasis)

Having finally been persuaded, Quäck then obliged with highly imaginative stories which were all evidently lapped up eagerly, however improbable. For example, he said that after a body had been cut up for cooking, the head was fixed on a post and string passed through the ear into the mouth, so that by pulling on the string the mouth moved up and down. Quäck clearly had a lot of fun at the expense of his gullible master; that a scholar of ethnography should also be prepared to swallow such a story is more surprising.

Lest it be thought that Koch was exceptionally credulous, I will give another example from a relatively recent academic work by Volhard (1939). It is packed with descriptions of cannibalism from all over the world, reproducing old material quite uncritically. Among the profusion of cannibal stories there is one concerning the Makkarika on the west bank of the White Nile, where a horrible scene is said to have taken place: 'Samuel White Baker was given a detailed account of [it] by a widely travelled Negro who had himself been a witness of the events' (Volhard 1939, p. 69). There follows a verbatim quotation from Baker about a slave girl who tried to escape and was shot in the side.

> The girl was remarkably fat, and from the wound, a large lump of yellow fat exuded. No sooner had she fallen, than the Makkarikas rushed upon her in a crowd, and seizing the fat, they tore it from the wound in handfuls, the girl still being alive, while the crowd were quarrelling for the disgusting prize. Others killed her with a lance, and at once divided her by cutting off the head, and splitting the body with their lances, used as knives, cutting longitudinally from between the legs along the spine to the neck.
>
> (Baker 1866, Vol. I, p. 298)

What Volhard omitted to mention was that Baker had described the 'widely travelled Negro' as being 'excessively fond of recounting his adventures, all of which had so strong a colouring of the "Arabian Nights" that he might have been the original "Sinbad the Sailor"'. Then, no doubt in order to increase the plausibility of the tale of Makkarika atrocity, Baker referred to an additional witness who had been in his service.

None of this of course excludes the possibility that among the spate of reports some might have had some basis in fact. But it does confirm the contention of Arens and Frank that a great deal of the evidence is open to doubt, and some of it is ludicrous. The climate of opinion was one of belief, and stories of man-eating found an eager readership – Charles Dickens was not exceptional, as the popularity of a magazine devoted to such tales indicates. Moreover, this applied not merely to popular opinion, but also affected prominent scientists such as Thomas Henry Huxley, the distinguished follower of Darwin. In his book on *Man's place in nature* (1863) he discussed the proximity between Africans and the anthropoid apes, mentioning also the belief by an African tribe that they were once closely related to apes. He added to this a totally irrelevant note about 'African cannibalism in the 16th century', based on an old Portuguese account; it was illustrated with a gruesome woodcut showing a human butcher's shop, with severed arms and legs, a severed head, and the 'butcher' in the act of hacking at what appears to be a mutilated torso. It is evident that sinister fantasies must have lurked beneath the surface of even so rational a mind.

At the turn of the century Joseph Conrad published his *Heart of darkness*, whose central figure, Kurtz, had abandoned civilization and taken part in 'unspeakable rites'. Before the mysterious Kurtz died, 'He cried in a whisper at some image, at some vision – he cried out twice, a cry that was no more than a breath – "The horror! The horror!" (Conrad [1902] 1994, p. 100). The use of these epithets was no doubt deliberate; and although he did not spell it out, the words by their association almost certainly evoked in contemporary readers the image of cannibalism.

## The cannibal image in the 20th century

The brief outline offered here mentions only some salient trends to show the continuity of the image, beginning with authoritative sources. During the first half of the 20th century cannibalism was still regarded as a social practice commonly found among 'savage' peoples, and crude ideas persisted. In the eleventh edition of the *Encyclopaedia britannica* (1910–11) part of the entry under the heading 'Negro' reads as follows:

> Cannibalism is found in its simplest form in Africa. In that continent the majority of cannibal tribes eat human flesh because they like it, and not from any magical motive or from lack of any other animal food.

1er NÈGRE. — Moi, je préfère la carcasse.
2e NÈGRE. — Moi, les ailes.
3e NÈGRE. — Moi, les cuisses.
4e NÈGRE. — Moi, les pieds.
LE CROCODILE. — Moi, la tête.
L'EXPLORATEUR. — Eh bien, alors, qu'est-ce que vous allez me laisser, à moi?                    Dessin de DÉPAQUIT.

*Figure 9.4* A variation on the more usual 'cannibal' joke showing a missionary in a pot
*Source: Le Rire*, 28 April 1900.

In 1930 a table was published listing the geographical distribution of seventy peoples to whom 'real' (as distinct from 'ceremonial') cannibalism was attributed, i.e. the eating of human flesh as a regular part of the diet. Africa led, with twenty-five cases, followed by South America with fifteen, and Australia with twelve. The authors suggested that the incidence of 'real' cannibalism was about one in four among 'lower cultures' (Hobhouse *et al.* 1930, p. 241). The impression given is that the peoples listed were still actively engaged in the practice, since those said to have abandoned it (noted as 'formerly') were excluded.[7]

The article on 'Cannibalism' in the 1930 edition of the *Encyclopaedia of the social sciences* (unchanged in the 1962 edition) suggested the possibility that all peoples at one time practised the custom. The general tenor may be gauged from its statement that people like the Fan of West Africa sold human flesh in their butcher shops.[8] The credulity of some scholars writing in the 1930s has already been illustrated above.

At the popular level there appears to have been some decline in the reports and stories about cannibalism, paralleled by a surge of cannibal jokes (see Figure 9.4) – the missionary in the pot, surrounded by grotesque savages, became a stock figure. It was just another way of ridiculing the savage and asserting white superiority.[9]

Later, when the former colonial territories gained their independence, this kind of humour ceased to be acceptable. However, this did not mean that the light-hearted treatment of the 'cannibalism' topic, with its underlying barb, ceased altogether. For instance, the *Observer Magazine* (19 March 1995) contained the following feature for the titillation of its readers under the the jocular title 'And the foe was soundly eaten'. A lead paragraph in bold type ran as follows:

> The tribesmen of the Markham Valley apparently prized the feet and hands as delicacies, cooked with sago and cabbage, although I am more inclined to believe the tour guide I once met in Fiji, who told me that the tastiest portion of a human being was the underside of the upper arm of a young girl.

There appears to be an insatiable appetite for this kind of material, and popular books on the topic are published periodically, among the more recent ones *The flesh eaters* (Haining 1994). As these examples show, and as will others, images of cannibal savages are still circulated and perpetuated at the popular level.

One also encounters the image in more serious writing, in the tradition of the image as indicative of savagery and evil, though this does not necessarily mean that all of the accusations are groundless. It tends to be evoked in relation to disliked and despised African rulers, as the following two passages will illustrate:

> Marvellous Emperor Jean-Bedel Bokassa, eating up little black babies, lavishing diamonds upon the Western Dignitary! . . . . The West will be hard pressed to rid itself of this generation of simian and prosaic despots.
> (Baudrillard 1983, p. 46)

[Idi Amin Dada] lives now with one of the wives he didn't eat . . . Jean-Bédel Bokassa . . . who once ate people.

(*Independent*, 17 April 1995)

It is not my intention to defend the reputation of what were certainly unsavoury characters; but whether the rumours of their cannibalism are true is an open question.[10]

Enough has been said to show that the image is still alive and well, and there is no point in multiplying examples. But the question arises why this should be so, in spite of socio-political and cultural transformations.

## Deeper roots of the image?

As already discussed in Chapter 8, the revulsion against cannibalism, often coupled with a usually unacknowledged fascination, is deeply embedded in western cultural tradition. Already at the dawn of recorded history, anthropophagi were thought to be among the 'monstrous races'. Two major surges amounting almost to cannibal mania coincided with highly active phases of colonization, by the Spaniards in America and by several European powers in Africa. This clearly points to an ideological cause: the need to rescue the benighted savages, sunk in sexual depravity and the evil of cannibalism, provided one of the ostensible motives for colonization in both cases.

However, while this is certainly part of the answer, it can hardly be the whole of it. For in order to be able to mobilize these sentiments, the potential for them must already have been present at the level of individuals. This issue has been discussed mainly on the basis of psychoanalytic theory, sometimes in a rather naive way, as by Money-Kyrle (1932, pp. 90–1). He proposed that the origin of cannibalism and of the feelings attached to it derive from the supposed fact that the 'primal father' was not merely killed, but also eaten. This, and even subsequent more sophisticated speculations, is unconvincing. But it is likely that our double-edged responses combining horror and fascination do have unconscious roots.

This is not altogether mere speculation, since there is a line of evidence arising from the recent spate of allegations concerning so-called 'satanic cults'. Whether these are real or only imaginary is irrelevant for my purpose. What matters is that a considerable number of people believe that as children they had been forced to take part in satanic rites, and there now exists a number of clinical studies of such individuals. Young *et al.* (1991) reported on thirty-seven such patients, all of whom claimed to have suffered sexual abuse in the course of the rituals; a further thirty-one mentioned witnessing or even having been forced to participate in human adult or child sacrifice, and nearly all of these (thirty) also alleged forced cannibalism. A subsequent study of twenty such patients by Shaffer and Cozolino (1992, p. 189) confirmed these findings:

All subjects reported witnessing the sacrificial murder of animals, infants, children, and/or adults. Corpses were often subjected to sexual violations and cannibalistic feasting. The vast majority of subjects in this study reported severe and sadistic forms of sexual abuse by multiple perpetrators.

On the basis of these and other studies, Ross (1995, p. 117) summarized the gruesome events purported to have taken place, noting that these correspond to popular stereotypes of satanism:

> Survivors report ceremonies and rituals involving intercourse on altars; chanting; wearing of robes; use of black, white or red candles; ceremonial cutting with daggers; ritual murder with cannibalism of the heart and other organs; pentagrams; collection of blood, urine and semen in goblets for group drinking; elaborate preparations of the survivor before the rituals; and murder of victims at the point of orgasm.

Most, if not all of these, are probably sick fantasies. Yet the fact that such fantasies can be buried in the unconscious of ordinary people is itself highly significant. An anthropologist was commissioned to prepare a report on a recent epidemic in Britain of allegations of sexual abuse of children, accompanied by rituals involving perverted sex, bestiality, human sacrifice and cannibalism. Although finding no substance for the allegations, she was struck by their similarity to old accounts of the witches' sabbath: 'the more I read of the historical record, the more similar the two epidemics seemed'; she further commented:

> Perhaps it is another skin of our ethnocentricity that must be peeled off: we are not rational beings, using science in contrast to those others, our subjects, whose thinking is based on non-scientific premises. Not so: we are all afraid of witches now.
>
> (La Fontaine 1996, p. 263)

It seems highly likely that similar kinds of fantasies, even if less extreme, lurked in the minds of both the explorers who ventured into savage lands, and those at home who received their reports. As Mannoni suggested, they 'project upon the colonial peoples the obscurities of their own unconscious' (1956, p. 19). Such a process would go a long way in explaining why the image of cannibalism was and remains a key symbol of unbridled savagery.

# Part III

# THE IMAGE OF THE SAVAGE AS CHILD-LIKE

# 10

# FROM ANCESTOR TO CHILD

The image of the savage as child-like began to be widespread by the middle of the 19th century, and its effects lasted a long time. As recently as the 1950s, when I lived in West Africa, some of the 'old coasters' among the Europeans would still call an elderly African servant 'boy'. The image has a pre-history concerning mainly the American savages that has been described in previous chapters.

Subsequently, during the 18th century, the comparison of savages with children acquired a different meaning for a time. During the Enlightenment there was widespread concern with human origins and development, and more generally with the character of human nature and its relation to what is now known as 'culture'. This led to an interest in childhood as well as in primitive mentality, and may have been responsible for the equation of primitiveness and childhood, viewed positively.

From the early 19th century onwards the trope reverted, and the attribution of child-likeness once again became derogatory. After the middle of the 19th century two major theories became associated with the notion of savages as 'grown-up children'. But contrary to what is sometimes supposed, neither originated it; rather, they provided a rationale for the trope. One was social evolutionism,[1] the other the 'biogenetic law'. The second of these, which had wide-ranging implications, will be discussed in Chapter 12. However, most of the people employing the trope later were innocent of its theoretical justifications. Even among sophisticated people, be it travellers, missionaries, adminstrators or scholars, it is generally far from clear whether their usage was connected with either or both theories, or whether its appeal was merely intuitive and absorbed from the social world surrounding them.

Prior to the 18th century there were relatively few references to the child-likeness of savages, with the exception of early Spanish writers concerning American Indians. Ovideo's comment that Amerindians are like 6- or 7-year-old children has already been cited (p. 19). Later the images of American savages as immature became part and parcel of a broader conception of the New World in general. In the 17th century Raynal expounded the then common theme of the physical (especially sexual) and mental weakness of the Indians:

The indifference of the males toward that other sex to which nature has entrusted the place of reproduction suggests an organic imperfection, *a sort of infancy of the people of America similar to that of the individuals of our continent who have not reached the age of puberty.* It is a deep-rooted failing of that other hemisphere, a sort of impotence that reveals clearly how new the continent is.

(Raynal [1770] 1820–1, Vol. IX, p. 23; my emphasis)

It has already been shown how this line of argument was more powerfully developed by Cornelius de Pauw, who described the Americans variously as little more than animals or idiot children. Although his views were strongly disputed by others de Pauw was highly influential, and Meiners in particular echoed his ideas. Yet the case of the American savages, though important, was an exceptional one.

## Savagery as the infancy of humanity

The increasingly negative portrayal of savages during the latter part of the 18th century, described in Chapter 6, was in conflict with the dominant ethos of the Enlightenment before its decline. This ethos entailed a belief in the continuous progress of humanity from primitive conditions to civilization. At the time this did not imply that savages were stupid, only ignorant: all humans, even early ones, were regarded as being endowed with 'reason'; what changed was the ability to *apply* reason effectively (cf. Jahoda 1992). It was not so much that savages as individuals were looked upon as children, but that their society was regarded as embodying an earlier stage – the childhood – of *humanity*. Lord Kames (1779 Vol. 2, pp. 468–9), for instance, suggested that

> as, with respect to individuals, there is a progress from infancy to maturity; so there is a similar progress in every nation from its savage state to its maturity in arts and sciences.

In the same spirit, Joseph-Marie Degérando (1772–1842) declared that travelling to see primitive peoples in distant lands is to travel back in time, to discover the state of our own ancestors (Degérando [1800] 1978). It is in this sense that several other 18th-century characterizations of savage child-likeness have to be understood. The German dramatist Friedrich Schiller (1759–1805) presented an image of different peoples grouped around Europeans just as children of different ages may surround a male adult. But then he added, significantly, 'So waren wir' – we used to be like that.

Francois LeVaillant (1753–1824) was a follower of Rousseau who travelled in southern Africa during the 1780s. Unlike most of his contemporaries, he took a rather romantic view of the Hottentots; and when he called them 'ces grands enfants' it was because he saw them as the innocents of humanity's state of infancy. This romantic outlook did not prevent him from staging various demonstrations of the power of his firearms, which 'gave them a high opinion of my superiority' (LeVaillant 1792, Vol. III, p. 243). Another characterization of the romantic kind is due to Sylvain de Golbéry, a captain of engineers who travelled in Senegal around 1785. He saw in Africa a lost paradise:

> Similar to children, blacks of the most mature age devote the whole day to futile occupations, to conversations which, to our mind, would seem mere blether, but which by this very fact are inexhaustible and are carried on with an abundance, a confidence, a gaiety, of which our societies in Europe can hardly any more offer an example.
>
> (cited in Bitterli 1970, p. 85)

The mode of conceptualizing savages as child-ancestors lacked the heavily pejorative connotation, the implication of inferiority, which the label of 'child' as applied to non-European peoples acquired later. It is significant that it was not uncommon for 18th-century writers to stress the similarity of savages to the Ancient Greeks rather than employing the metaphor of childhood. Lafitau (1724) so compared American Indians, and it was frequently done in relation to the inhabitants of the South Sea Islands. For instance, the explorer Georg Forster waxed lyrical over the parallels between powerful Tahitian district chiefs and classical Greek heroes (cf. Goldmann 1985a).

Generally, the child metaphor as applied to the development of humanity was common, and its most systematic elaboration was undertaken by a prominent figure of the Swiss Enlightenment, Isaak Iselin (1728–82). Iselin wrote a history of humankind intended as a polemical answer to Rousseau's *Discourse on the origin of inequality*. Iselin (1779), elaborating on Kames' formulation, put forward a theory of parallels between individual and collective life stages, with corresponding psychological and cultural characteristics:

| Childhood | sensuousness [Sinnlichkeit] | savagery |
| Adolescence | imagination | barbarism |
| Adulthood | reason | civilization |

The Australians, Fuegians and Greenlanders were, according to Iselin, approximately at the level of a group of children aged between 6 and 8, deprived of education and given mere physical care, who had been abandoned on an island and left to fend for themselves.[2]

Iselin's general thesis was not altogether consistent. On the one hand he maintained that the human advance is rather fragile. Everyone is potentially a savage and would revert to this state, were it not for what we would call 'socialization':

> by means of the wise and careful supervision by a gentle father or a severe master who keeps him in check; or if he had not, by fortunate

illumination, acquired the notions of decency, of order, of justice, or the lofty truths of religion which provide a noble and softening nourishment for his spirit.

(Iselin 1779, Vol. 1, pp. 237–8)

On the other hand, he postulated a general law that results in humanity transcending the limits imposed on animals and moving forward towards ever higher steps of perfection: 'In his soul every thought generates another thought, and every desire another desire' (Vol. 1, p. 168). However, the rate of progress was also said to be affected by climatic and geographical factors, whose influence Iselin discussed at some length.

In the course of the subsequent decades, a gradual and subtle shift occurred away from the notion of savages as kinds of 'contemporary ancestors' towards one of savages as eternal children, whose child-likeness constituted a permanent trait, usually regarded as unmodifiable.

The work of Iselin was published at a time when, as previously described, biological theorizing about human differences began to be in the ascendant. After a period of transition, some of the fundamental ideas of the Enlightenment were reasserted later in the 19th century by the social evolutionists, though often tainted by the then pervasive influence of biological racism.

## The influence of social evolutionism

Initially in direct line of succession to 18th-century progressivists, social evolutionists sought to trace the natural history of the development of humanity. In contrast to the race theorists, they placed the emphasis on environmental conditions rather than biology. This was very clearly stated by Lewis Morgan (1877, p. 8):

> the experience of mankind has run in nearly uniform channels . . .
> human necessities in similar conditions have been substantially the same
> . . . the operations of the mental principle have been uniform in virtue of
> the specific identity of the brain of all the races of mankind.

In order to arrive at that lawful sequence of development, social evolutionists had recourse to the 'comparative method'. This involved the identification of similarities in institutions and artefacts separated in space and time. For instance, ancient Swiss lake habitations were similar to those of 19th-century Maoris, and were taken to show that the same evolutionary track had been followed by both peoples, though the Maoris were well behind. The broad aims of such an approach have been summarized by McLennan (1865):

> If within the scope of my inquiry I can connect the ancient civilizations
> with the forms of civilizations existing among barbaric races of which we

have trustworthy accounts; and the latter with the lower forms prevailing among neighbouring races more barbaric than themselves; and these again with still lower forms in use among peoples counted by common consent to be savages; and if I succeed in showing the connections throughout the series of connected stages to be connections of growth and development – the higher to have in every case passed through the lower in becoming itself, then I shall be entitled to conclude . . . that the doctrine of development is established as applicable to human society.

(McLennan, cited in Voget 1967, p. 139)

Among the most prominent social evolutionists were Herbert Spencer (1820–1903) and Edward Burnett Tylor (1832–1917), who both later came to dilute their social evolutionism by adopting some of the ideas of the race theorists about the immaturity of savages. Spencer (1877) in particular devoted a great deal of attention to the problem, and cited reports concerning the Australians, the Negroes in the United States, those on the Nile and in East, West and Equatorial Africa, the Andamanese, the New Zealanders, the Sandwich Islanders, the Hindus and the Aleuts of Alaska – implying that the evidence was overwhelming. Spencer went on to analyse in detail 'the intellectual traits of the uncivilized', seeking to show how they parallel the mentality of European children. This implies that for Spencer, as for many others, the image was double-edged, i.e. the modern child was a savage, just as the savage was a child:

> Infancy and nursery life, show us an absorption in sensations and perceptions, akin to that which characterizes the savage. . . . Children are ever dramatizing the lives of adults; and savages, along with their other mimicries, similarly dramatize the actions of their civilized visitors. Want of power to discriminate between useless and useful facts, charac- terizes the youthful mind, as it does the mind of the primitive man. . . . The mind of the child, like that of the savage, soon wanders from sheer exhaustion when generalities and involved propositions have to be dealt with. . . . The child, like the savage, has few words of even a low grade of abstractness, and none of a higher grade . . . its extreme credulity, like that of the savage, shows us the result of undeveloped ideas of causation and law.
>
> (Spencer 1877, Vol. 1, pp. 102–3)

Spencer's explanations for these alleged phenomena are neither very clear nor altogether consistent. When he referred at one point to 'the higher intellectual powers [the European child] inherits from civilized ancestors' (p. 103), one cannot be sure whether he meant a biological or social inheritance. Later he commented that the higher intellectual faculties could not develop in the absence of 'a fit environment', which suggests non-biological causes; but elsewhere he also invoked 'biological laws' in the same context.

135

Tylor in his early work of the 1860s did not believe in radical race differences in mental functioning, although he was inclined to accept what he called the 'trite comparison' between savages and children. It is noteworthy that by then it had already become 'trite'. He held at that time that there is a continuity of modes of thought from childhood to maturity even among highly educated people: 'the mental process . . . though it never disappears, must be sought for in the midst of more complex phenomena' (Tylor 1865, p. 109). But later in life he came to accept some of the claims of the race theorists, citing the then common reports by European teachers about the intellectual weaknesses of their charges. Generally, pupils from 'lower races' were said to absorb very rapidly elementary instruction that relies on memory and imitation, considered to be inferior capacities shared with animals. Yet, it was claimed, as soon as one gets to a certain level demanding abstraction and the understanding of logic, development stops.

The theme of resemblances between children and savages was also taken up by other scholars. Mid-19th-century social evolutionists relied heavily on philology for their theories, arguing on the basis of linguistic changes. For this purpose they commonly sought to show parallels between the language of European children and that of savages:

> A word formed on the principle of imitation is said to be formed by onomatopoeia. . . . How universal and instinctive this procedure is may be observed among infants and savages.
>
> (Farrar 1860, p. 73)

Much the same point was made by Sir John Lubbock (1834–1913) (later Lord Avebury), who stated that 'Savages . . . have a great tendency to form words by reduplication, which is also characteristic of childhood among civilized races' (Lubbock [1863] 1913, p. 564). Lubbock was extremely influential, having been one of the most widely quoted authorities until the early 20th century, as indicated by the fact that his work was repeatedly reprinted. In several books he sought to present a portrait of 'the primitive condition of man' and, as was the practice at the time, drew rather indiscriminately on the writings of numerous travellers and missionaries. Although sceptical of some of the most extravagant stories, he was generally rather uncritical. Unlike his 18th-century predecessors, he believed that the mind of the savage is bound to be utterly alien to Europeans: 'The whole mental condition of a savage is so different from us, that it is often very difficult to follow what is passing in his mind, or to understand the motives by which he is influenced' (Lubbock 1870, p. 3). One of the grounds he offers for this state of affairs is that the mind of the savage is like that of a child: easily tired, the savage then just gives random answers to save himself the bother of thought. The equation of savages with children runs as a constant thread throughout Lubbock's writings, as exemplified in the following passage:

Savages may be likened to children, and the comparison is not only correct, but also highly instructive. Many naturalists consider that the early condition of the individual indicates that of the race, that the best test of the affinities of a species are the stages through which it passes. So also it is in the case of man; the life of each individual is an epitome of the history of the race, and the gradual development of the child illustrates that of the species. Savages, like children, have no steadiness of purpose.

In fact, we may fairly sum up this part of the question in a few words by saying, as the most general conclusion which can be arrived at, that savages have the character of children with the passions and strength of men.

(Lubbock [1863] 1913, pp. 562–5)

These passages illustrate different strands of ideas all converging on the child-like nature of savages. Some are in the socio-evolutionist tradition, while others seem to anticipate the biogenetic theory that had yet to be formulated when Lubbock first wrote.

In documenting the 'childishness' of savages, Lubbock drew his information largely from 18th- and early 19th-century accounts such as that of James Cook, who had written, for example, that the king and queen of Tahiti amused themselves with large dolls. This and other titbits were then taken up by later writers and used in support of their arguments. James Sully (1842–1923), in his classical work on childhood, relied very heavily on Lubbock for the numerous parallels he drew between children and savages. For instance, after discussing the intense sentimental attachment girls often feel for their dolls, he went on: 'And here we have the curious fact that the doll exists not only for the child, but for the "nature man". Savages, Sir John Lubbock tells us, like toys, such as dolls, Noah's Arks, etc.' (Sully [1895] 1903 p. 45). In a book republished as recently as the inter-war years, Lubbock was still being cited as an authority on the nature of savages (Moore [1918] 1933). Although Lubbock was far from complimentary about savages and, like other social evolutionists, had not altogether escaped the influence of biological race theorists, he was in the last analysis not convinced that they were forever condemned to backwardness.

The examples given so far may give the impression that the child image was based almost exclusively on the supposed lack of intelligence of savages, but this would be mistaken. There was one particular strand of ideas, discussed below, which did have such an emphasis. However, the child image in general comprised a whole range of other elements, character traits viewed as signs of immaturity. These included impulsiveness, emotionalism, lack of forethought, inability to concentrate and so on. A fairly comprehensive picture of such images was provided by Letourneau (1881) in his section on the 'Comparative psychology of human races'; I shall quote from it at some length, partly to indicate that such attributions were by no means confined to black Africans:

The very inferior savage, like our own infant children, does not know what tomorrow means.

The Tasmanians . . . express a wish for every kind of trifle, but drop them immediately afterwards; everything seems to distract them, nothing can occupy their minds.

All travellers are agreed in saying that the majority of the black races in Africa may be compared to our young European children. They have all the light-headedness, the capriciousness, the want of prudence, the volubility, and the same quick and confined intelligence, as a child.

The Fuegians. . . . Their soddened mind is not capable of astonishment or of curiosity. . . . A missionary, who complained of the heat, was answered by a young Fuegian that he was wrong to reproach the sun, for if the star hid himself they would soon have an icy cold south wind. [A reasonable enough comment one would have thought.]

Like the Caribs, who will sell their hammocks in the morning for less money than they could have done the evening previous, the Red Skins will destroy a whole herd of bisons and take only their tongues, without thinking that in two days' time they may again be hungry.

But of all savage races none are more childish than the Polynesians. Their thoughtlessness and their light-headedness are extraordinary. It is impossible to fix their attention upon anything for two minutes.

(Letourneau 1881, pp. 553–7)

The underlying assumption should be noted that savages are pretty much the same everywhere, an assumption sometimes openly declared. For instance, another French writer stated that 'The more primitive people are, they more they are alike' (Fouillée 1903, p. xvii), the reason being that they are almost entirely governed by instinct. The general pattern of key features attributed to savages remained remarkably constant over a long period. This can be illustrated by the following quotation from Freud's account of group psychology, which contains essentially the same basic ideas:

the weakness of intellectual ability, the lack of emotional restraint, the incapacity for moderation and delay, the inclination to exceed every limit in the expression of emotion and to work it off completely in the form of action – these and similar features . . . show an unmistakeable picture of a regression of mental activity to an earlier stage such as we are not surprised to find among savages or children.

(Freud [1921] 1955, p. 117)

As will be demonstrated in more detail below, Freud's portrayal of the savage–child equation was based on a biological theory. What is striking is that the picture he draws closely resembles characterizations inspired by social evolutionary theories. In other words, it would seem that the theories merely sought to account for what at the time were believed to be 'facts' about the savages. If the theories were secondary, one has to ask what could have given rise to such beliefs, and why they became so popular.

## What lies behind the child image?

Although the image has often been described, there have been few attempts to analyse it further. One such attempt was by Boas (1966), who suggested a number of ideas 'which could have led to an identification of the child with primitive men' (p. 62). He went back as far as Vico (1668–1744), who had proclaimed that the first, 'divine' age, following the emergence from mere animality, had been one when people were incapable of abstract thought and governed by 'poetic logic'. This was followed by the 'heroic' and finally the 'humane' ages. Boas referred to the 'obvious' similarity between the development of nations and individuals, and children's liking for fables and nursery rhymes, the implication being that children are poetic like early humans. Since no poetry or anything like it ever came into the comparisons between children and savages, this is rather unconvincing.

Boas also referred to Auguste Comte's (1798–1857) 'Law of the Three Stages', from theological via metaphysical to positivistic. Comte actually wrote that the mentality of the theological stage corresponded to that of the modern child. It is indeed likely that Comte's views contributed to the notion of the similarity of savage and child.[3] Comte's work came out at the right time and had a considerable impact. Although Spencer vigorously denied having taken over Comte's ideas, he was certainly familiar with them; and his later theorizing about the mental processes of children and savages may well have been influenced by Comte's writings on the topic. Nonetheless, this can hardly have been the whole story, since it does not explain the ready acceptance of the idea well beyond intellectual circles, and its persistence long after Comte's star had faded.

An approach by Cairns (1965) is a good deal more pertinent and realistic, based as it was on a clear grasp of the broader context. Cairns provided a series of interesting examples of what he terms the 'child analogy', some of which I shall borrow in due course. As regards the basis of the analogy, he noted that it embodied the assumptions of social evolutionism, without mentioning biological theories. Cairns made the useful point that Africans were sometimes also compared to the poorer classes in Britain, for example, by Livingstone, 'But the much more frequent comparison of Africans to children had a general basis in the hierarchical framework of concepts through which Britons viewed the racial divisions of the world' (p. 93). He might have said 'Europeans' rather than 'Britons', although his discussion of the role of the 'gentleman' in relation to both inferior classes and races is particularly relevant to Britain. Cairns further suggested that 'The comparison of the African to the child . . . rested on a common ethnocentric inability to judge alien cultures in terms of their own values. All individuals will appear as children if observed and judged from a cultural background irrelevant to their way of life' (p. 94). While the cultural perspective is undoubtedly an important factor it is questionable whether it could be the only one, since there are a variety of different ways of branding the culturally alien Other, as has already been amply demonstrated. This leaves open the issue of the special significance of the child image, though Cairns correctly identified one of its major functions, namely that of justifying white control. Yet there remain other issues concerning the trope which require more detailed scrutiny.

Taken literally, the proposition put forward by Lubbock that whole peoples have the minds of children in the bodies of adults is of course absurd. Therefore the practice of describing savages as children is to be understood symbolically, reflecting the preconceptions of the users concerning certain characteristics of both children and savages; and the particular features singled out are likely to relate to particular contexts.

At the outset it will be useful to glance at least briefly at European images of childhood, on which a good deal has been written (e.g. Ariès 1973; De Mause 1976; Stone 1977). While these writers differ – sometimes quite radically – in their interpretations, there is a consensus that the images have fluctuated between those of purity and innocence and those of original sin. Other characteristics have remained constant since antiquity, notably the absence of mature 'reason', also generally ascribed to savages. Other negative stereotypes about savages widely prevalent through the ages, such as excessive sexuality and cannibalism, are more problematic. It is hard to see how these could be regarded as 'childish', yet in so far as these might be construed as 'depravity', a link with original sin afflicting children, is at least conceivable. It will therefore be necessary to look in more detail at the images of childhood prevalent in Europe and America.

# 11

# RESCUING THE 'BENIGHTED SAVAGE'

## Missionaries and colonial administrators

### The child, original sin and original innocence

Stone (1977) documented the harshness of the treatment of children in England during the 17th century, followed by permissiveness during the 18th century, with a reversion to authoritarianism – especially among the middle classes – from the turn of the century onwards. These changes paralleled shifting conceptions of the nature of the child, from being innately bad to good and back again.

The last of these changes began with the Puritans in America and was followed by other Protestant sects, notably Methodists. In 1737 a Puritan preacher in America wrote that young children are subject to 'unbridled appetites and passions' (cited in Walzer 1976), precisely the moral failures long attributed to savages. John Wesley (1703–91), in his sermon *On the education of children*, advised parents as follows:

> Show them that, in pride, passion, and revenge they are now like the Devil. And that in foolish desires and grovelling appetites, they are like the beasts of the field.
>
> (Wesley 1825, Vol. 2, pp. 498–9)

In the same vein Hannah More (1811) wrote a treatise on female education in which she stated that the young lack a standard of moral good and evil, an absence whose deeper roots are a 'consequence of their already partaking of the . . . corruption . . . and which in perverting the will, darkens understanding also' (Vol. 2, pp. 278–9). Hannah More had numerous followers in her view that the main aim of juvenile literature should be to teach children that they are naturally depraved creatures. This was also the message of *The history of the Fairchild family*, a book published by a Mrs Sherwood in 1818; it was said in the *Dictionary of national biography* to have been the bible of child rearing for the English middle classes in the first quarter of the 19th century (Quinlan 1951). Thomas Arnold, who became headmaster of Rugby in 1828, had no doubts about the depraved nature of young boys, 'the natural punishment of their age'. The sight of a group of boys clustered around the schoolhouse fire elicited from him the comment: 'It makes me think that I see the Devil in the midst of them!' (Stanley 1846, p. 137).

Given such views of children's depraved nature, the comparison with licentious savages would make some sense. However, in a fairly extensive survey of child-likeness passages by a wide variety of authors I have not come across any that would unambiguously lend themselves to such an interpretation. The only possible exception may be that of the previously mentioned eccentric view of Joseph de Maistre (1753–1821), who was exiled from France and appointed Sardinian ambassador to St Petersburg. He wrote that even a cursory glance at the savage would reveal the anathema written in his body and soul, describing the savage as a robust, ferocious and misshapen child (de Maistre [1821] 1888).

Although the 'anathema' implies divinely ordained monstrosity, this had nothing to do with the Anglo-American type of Protestant sects which were virtually non-existent in France. Moreover, crassly negative images of childhood were rare there (Robertson 1976), yet the child trope was at least as commonly employed in France as in Britain. It is therefore highly unlikely that the concept of innate child depravity was a significant source of the trope.

The romantic idealization of childhood innocence, by contrast, does seem to have been an important factor. This image is usually attributed to the heritage of Rousseau, especially his *Emile ou de l'éducation* ([1762] 1992). Rousseau, as is well known, regarded savages positively, and sometimes held them up as models to be emulated. After citing an account of the way savages give up childish things in adolescence he went on: 'Emile, having been brought up in the full freedom of young peasants and young savages [note the juxtaposition] should change and stop being like them when growing up' (Rousseau [1762] 1992, p. 391). From this tradition stems the benevolent, even though patronizing, label of savages as 'nature's children'.

The comment by Harriet Beecher Stowe, the author of *Uncle Tom's cabin*, is of this kind. She maintained that 'The negro race is confessedly more simple, docile, childlike and affectionate, than other races' (Stowe [1853] 1968, p. 41). While to the modern reader this sounds intolerably patronizing, it was well meant at the time. Henry Drummond (1851–97) in his *Ascent of man* sought to christianize evolutionary theory by stressing altruistic elements in natural selection, and his picture of savages is unusually rosy:

> here in his virgin simplicity dwells primeval man, without clothes, without civilization, without learning, without religion – the genuine child of nature, thoughtless, careless and contented. This man is apparently quite happy; he has practically no wants.
>
> (Cited in Cairns 1965, p. 94)

Or again, a couple rhapsodizing about life with Kikuyu of Kenya described their sense of space and freedom 'which springs from daily and nightly intercourse with nature and nature's children' (Routledge & Routledge 1910, p. xxi). The general tone of such passages is rather different from that of the large majority of 'child' attributions, which tend to be distinctly pejorative.

## Savage and child as dependent

On scanning a wide range of references to savages which employ the child image from the early 19th century onwards, it becomes clear that the predominant conceptions expressed or implied were those of immaturity, lack of responsibility and inability to properly order one's own affairs. The underlying message is that savages, like children, cannot be trusted to behave sensibly. Therefore, just as children require the guidance of their parents, so savages need that of civilized Europeans.

The notion that the relationship between savages and Europeans is analogous to that between parents and children probably stems from, and is certainly closely associated with, two ideologies which became increasingly salient in the course of the 19th century. They embodied the dual aims of *christianizing* and *civilizing* the savages, commonly taken to be more or less synonymous. If Europeans stood, as it were, *in loco parentis*, this also implied certain obligations on their part in helping the 'children' to grow up by seeking to stamp out undesirable (from the European cultural perspective) beliefs and practices and to introduce more wholesome ones.

The initial impetus, already mentioned in another context, was provided by the missionary movement from the end of the 18th century onwards. With the onset of modern colonialism during the second half of the 19th century, European governments became involved in dealings with indigenous populations. By that time the label 'savages' was slowly beginning to be supplemented by somewhat less offensive terms like 'primitives' in English or *Naturmenschen* in German.

Missionaries and colonial administrators shared certain aims, such as the elimination of cruel customs and the encouragement of habits of steady work, beyond that necessary for meeting modest needs. The term 'encouragement' is appropriate mainly as regards missionaries; colonial governments often employed such means as forced labour, or the imposition of head taxes. In other respects there were some considerable divergences owing to conflicting interests.[1] Colonial administrations had an economic agenda, which led to different priorities from those of the churches. Enforcing radical changes in cultural practices ran the risk of being costly, and, when these were central to the traditional order, could even lead to resistance. This happened, for instance, in relation to the Ashanti 'Golden Stool'.[2]

Customs that were neither grossly offensive to European sentiment, nor affected European rule directly, were usually left alone. An example would be polygamy, strongly opposed by missionaries.

While there were thus areas of conflict of interests between church and state, they were united in their perceptions of the 'natives' as child-like and in need

*Figure 11.1* Missionaries and colonial officers tended to convey images of African traditional religions that were horrific and repulsive. These pictures show 'fetish worship' in Ashanti (left) and the Belgian Congo.
Source: *Illustrated London News* (1873) and *Le Congo Belge en images* (1909).

of firm guidance. Missionaries as well as colonial officers were apt to refer to 'child-races' or 'child-peoples' (e.g. Ogilvie 1924, *passim*). It was an image that was presented to church members and the public at large in the home countries. It served as a justification for actions which, had they been concerned with people held to be responsible adults, might have been regarded as intolerable. The forms taken by these images will now be surveyed in more detail.

## Savages in the eyes of missionaries

Mary Kingsley (1862–1900), an independent-minded woman and intrepid traveller, wrote in her *West African studies* [1899] (1901): 'The portrait painted of the African by the majority . . . of West African missionary reports has been that of a child' (p. 273), a view with which she strongly disagreed. She did not mean that the 'child' label was always actually applied, but that the characterizations were of a kind to suggest child-likeness. The same is true of my discussion, which will borrow extensively, though by no means exclusively, from a work by Raoul Allier (1925) dealing with 'the psychology of conversion' among what he called 'the non-civilized'. Since the nature of this material might produce a somewhat biased impression, some preliminary remarks are indicated.

The missionaries who went into the field usually did so with a set of pre-conceived ideas about the 'degraded' savages whom they wanted to deflect from their 'path of error'. Hence they commonly shared, at least initially, a disparaging attitude towards indigenous beliefs and traditions. This was probably a psychological necessity, especially for the early missionaries, since it provided the motivation for their efforts. They struggled to give the savages the best they had to offer, in surroundings that were both physically and socially hostile. It is all the more creditable that there were those among them who developed respect and profound sympathy for the people with whom they lived. It would therefore be inappropriate to tar them all with the same brush.

Returning to Allier, he wanted to show how fundamentally different the 'non-civilized' are from Europeans, in order to highlight the achievements of missionary work.[3] This can be seen from a paragraph in his conclusions:

> We have come to assist at a spectacle which some, *a priori*, would have judged impossible: the spectacle of individuals and races who, from a mental and social state which constitutes a radical antithesis to our own, pass to a mental and social state which constrains us to recognise in them fellow creatures and, to say the word, brothers in humanity.
>
> (Allier 1925, Vol. II, p. 423)

Some hesitation may be noted before he took the plunge and mentioned brotherhood. Similarly, at the outset, Allier explained that he did not wish to offend by using the term 'uncivilized', because he hoped that his book would help to bring them back into the 'human family'.

For the purpose of his argument Allier drew upon an extensive survey of the European missionary literature over a century, which provides ample grist for my very different mill. Many of the quotations are from secondary or even tertiary sources, for example, Lubbock citing someone else; but here I shall confine myself to reporting either Allier's own opinions or direct citations from the writings of missionaries.[4] With regard to the latter, a rough chronological order will be followed within particular themes.

### Weak personality and lack of emotional control

They are allegedly unable to conceal their feelings which 'shake their souls and their bodies; their pains like their joys manifest themselves by laughter or crying; in this way they are rather like children' [1842] (Vol. I, p. 496). The guiding role envisaged for the missionary is very clearly expressed in the following passage:

> Our Blacks [*sic*] have not yet arrived at a degree of personality to be able to follow a coherent line of conduct . . . one has to supervise them a great deal, making them advance step by step, holding them all the time by the hand. They have to be very dependent on their missionary.
>
> [1906] (Vol. II, pp. 156–7)

145

There are plenty more characterizations of this kind, one report of 1916 listing stereotypical attributions such as happy-go-lucky, little self-esteem, no ambition or concern for the future, no real will, and acting purely on impulse (Vol. II, pp. 15, 58–9).

### Lack of intelligence

An example is given of stupidity on the part of a Surinam woman, with the comment that 'The starting point of this kind of reasoning is furnished by child psychology' [1886] (Vol. II, p. 142). Another quotation shows that the old legend of the origin of blacks still survived: 'Let us not forget that these poor descendants of Ham do not know how to think' [1888] (Vol. II, p. 157). One is struck by the uncharitable, even sarcastic tone of some of the judgements: 'A Black is capable of believing anything, provided it is incredible' [1916] (Vol. I, p. 84).

It was widely held by missionaries that their charges were quite incapable of knowing where their real interests lay, and one missionary put this very plainly at a conference in 1888:

> What now does Africa need? If Africa were standing on this platform she could not tell you; she does not know her needs. She might stand here and say, 'Give us the things we want; give us calico, give us gunpowder, give us all the articles that as traders you produce in your country.' But these are not your Africa's needs. It is only the Missionary who knows Africa's needs.
>
> (Johnston 1889, Vol. I , p. 290)

In a number of passages Allier sought to show that the non-civilized themselves accept their intellectual inferiority.

### Lack of morality

Not surprisingly, this theme is very heavily stressed, often to absurd lengths: 'Theft, lying, murder, atrocities, the most revolting forms of corruption do not seem to astonish anyone' (Vol. I, p. 478). They are said to be inveterate liars; some parents, it is stated, sell their daughters even for a shameful life; and some 'engage in orgies every day' ([1888] Vol. I, p. 490). Their 'purely negative morality' is rooted 'in the depth of the mentality' (Vol. II, p. 64). Moreover, parents do not provide any moral instruction for their children, and examples are given of total permissiveness. This is not to say that their observations were necessarily wrong, but presented in an ethnocentrically moralistic fashion. For instance, one missionary decribed the Bambara as 'hideously degraded', having been particularly upset by the fact that sexual matters were openly discussed in the presence of children:

And without any shame, they talk about all these villanies, in front of their little brothers, in front of children of ten or twelve years, in front of little girls, and it is not rare to see an older girl pressed against the door of the hut, with ears well open, so as not to lose a word, and to have occasion to burst into laughter.

(Henry 1910)[5]

It was an almost universal belief during the 19th century that savage parents provide no kind of education or training for their children:

In Africa family life is not very far above the plane of mere animalism, modified, of course, by human instincts; yet there is really no family training. Children run wild and grow up with untamed and grossly tainted natures.

(Dennis 1899, Vol. 1, p. 128)[6]

The belief that savages do not train their children in turn served to reinforce the child image. Thus one missionary wrote that adults themselves are 'from the standpoint of morality, veritable children incapable of self-control, of mastering their passions and their greed' ([1888], Vol. II, p. 157). The passions in question were sexual, regarded as being at the root of polygamy. As might have been expected, polygamy featured prominently and itself presented moral problems for missionaries, especially Protestant ones: should one require converts to get rid of all surplus wives? If so, would it be acceptable for the convert to keep just the youngest and most beautiful (Vol. II, p. 34)?

### Other aspects

The image of the savage as a childish, happy-go-lucky creature that was sometimes put forward carried the risk that supporters of the missions at home would wonder why it was necessary to disturb such an idyllic state. Hence the frequent claim that their lives were pervaded by perpetual uncertainty and irrational anxieties: 'into whatever situation life puts them, fear tyrranizes them' (Vol. II, p. 264); or again: 'Every act, thought and influence of life is connected in some way with the power of evil spirits. He is not a free agent. Malign influences are ever seeking his destruction' (Roome 1927, pp. 18–19). Hence it was often suggested that Africans themselves eagerly welcomed the Europeans as liberators from these burdens: 'We can realise what a deliverance there comes with the message of Christianity to those poor slaves of ignorant terror' (Roome 1927, p. 29). It was sometimes claimed that savages believed themselves to be lost and helpless children. According to the wife of one missionary, Africans were like 'a lot of passionate children . . . [who would] with scarce an exception, instinctively hail with joy the advent of the adult power, which would secure them mutual peace and happiness' (Hore 1889, pp. 167–8). The child trope was not confined to those who, like Allier, regarded them as intellectual and emotional cripples. In 1926 a missionary to the Congo chided some of his fellow-missionaries for failing to understand Africans and underestimating their abilities. Yet in spite of all this his conclusion was that 'The blacks are children, and are to be treated like children, i.e. in a just and friendly manner' (Fraessle 1926, p. 49).

Enough has been said to show that the kind of characterization of the savage espoused by many missionaries may have helped to create, and unquestionably propagated, the child image. While some missionaries sought to protect 'their people' from the harshness of colonial authorities, thereby coming into conflict with them, others shared similar prejudices. Allier reported a conversation he had with a person who, from the context, must have been either a colonial officer or a 'colon'. When recounting this man's stories about the puerility of the 'natives', Allier added the comment that such incidents 'lead the colonial administrators to ask themselves if they do not have to deal with unintelligent and purely emotional beings' (1925, Vol. I, p. 85).

Before moving on to consider more generally the opinions of those who held power in the colonies, it is worth remembering that Allier's book was published as recently as the first quarter of the 20th century. By that time there had already emerged from the ranks of the 'non-civilized' considerable numbers of highly educated and articulate men who resented the slurs on their people and culture.[7]

## The stance of colonial administrators

The increasing expansion overseas of the European powers from the mid-19th century onwards was mostly justified in the lofty terms of the 'civilizing mission', as famously expressed by Rudyard Kipling (1865–1936):

> Take up the White Man's burden –
> Send forth the best ye breed –
> Go, bind your sons to exile
> To serve your captives' needs;
> To wait in heavy harness
> On fluttered folk and wild –
> Your new-caught, sullen peoples,
> Half-devil and half-child.

It is worth pausing over these lines which neatly capture the mixture of sentimental idealism and crude prejudice that lay at the heart of the colonial enterprise. The 'best' are to accept exile and dedicate themselves to the needs of those who, with brutal frankness, are described as 'captives'. The generous spirit the verses are supposed to convey is also spoilt by the phrase 'new-caught, sullen peoples', which rather gives the game away: how ungrateful of these peoples to be sullen! The last line reflects the profound ambivalence with which the 'captives' were regarded. Kipling was writing at a time when imperialism was at its height, but the child trope began to be used long before that, and was by no means confined to Africans. For instance, during the first Afghan war (1838–42) a political officer in occupied territory dismissed threats of unrest with the words, 'these people are perfect children, and should be treated as such. If we put one naughty boy in the corner, the rest will be terrified' (cited in Pottinger 1983, p. 109). In the event this turned out to be a miscalculation that was to have tragic consequences. Half a century later, in William Fitchett's (1901) *Tale of the Great Mutiny*, the author attributed the Indian Mutiny almost entirely to the character of the instigators who, according to him, 'had the petulance and the ignorance of children' (cited in Brantlinger 1988, p. 204).

This kind of attitude was typical also of most colonial officials in Britain, France and, judging by Schultze (p. 88ff.), in Germany as well. A French colonial officer wrote in 1888 that the Negro 'is like a little child, expecting everything from his father and not thinking of giving anything back in return' (Barret 1888, p. 130).[8] Some years later another French administrator who subsequently became a governor referred to the 'infantilism of [Africans'] character' (Cureau 1904, p. 652). One of the outstanding British colonial administrators was Lord Lugard (1858–1945), founder of 'indirect rule', whose declared aim was to educate the 'natives' and help them to acquire the capacity for self-rule. In a book written at the end of his career, he described Africans in a manner that deserves to be quoted in some detail:

> The character and temperament of the typical African is a happy, thriftless, excitable person, lacking in self-control, discipline and foresight . . . naturally courteous and polite, full of personal vanity, with little sense of veracity, fond of music. . . . His thoughts are concentrated on the events and feelings of the moment, and he suffers little from apprehension for the future, or grief for the past. . . .
>
> He is by no means lacking in industry. . . . He has the courage of the fighting animal – an instinct rather than a moral virtue. He is very prone to imitate anything new in dress or custom. . . .
>
> In brief, the virtues and the defects of this race-type are those of attractive children, whose confidence when once it is won is given ungrudgingly as to an older and wiser superior.
>
> (Lugard [1922] 1965, pp. 69–70)

Later (p. 72) he again referred to Africans as one of the 'child races of the world'; and while he clearly had a liking for them, it was a paternalistic and patronizing one, lacking in any respect. A rather less sympathetic view was expressed as late as 1943 by Général Paul Azan, a French colonial administrator:

> If one tries to characterize all Blacks, he can say that they have remained very primitive – that they are 'large children'. They love gaiety, laughter

and noise, the drums that accompany dances and songs, and long palavers that develop into endless discussions.

(Cited in Milbury-Steen 1980, p. 30)

Europeans in the lower echelons of their respective colonial services, in direct contact with the 'natives' and with near-absolute power of them, must have been well aware of these views of their political masters. True, they were supposed to be responsible for the welfare of their charges, but temptations were ever-present. The image of the benevolent whites doing their utmost to help the benighted blacks, while widespread in their home countries, was far from accurate. Without wishing to deny the existence of idealistic motives among Europeans, or their positive contributions, there was a great deal of not only collective economic but also personal sexual exploitation. Most of this was of course kept under wraps, but occasionally some of the more flagrant cases found their way into the archives. I shall provide some illuminating details of one of the best documented ones.

The events concern a man called Raikes, Assistant Native Commissioner for a district in Mashonaland in what was then Southern Rhodesia. Raikes came from a good family of fervent church people, his father having been Member of Parliament for Cambridge University and Postmaster-General. Raikes himself, having graduated in classics from Trinity, and failed the entrance examination for the Indian Civil Service, joined the Colonial Service.

In 1903 the sexual conduct of Raikes led to an official inquiry. He had employed an African to seek out attractive African girls and, when they refused his advances, threatened to arrest their father or even to shoot them; one girl was in fact accidentally shot and her death not reported. The story that came out in the course of the inquiry was lubricious:

> Several witnesses told how he went to kraals and took liberties with messengers' wives, patting their breasts, opening their legs, 'examining their private parts', and generally 'playing disgusting tricks with them'. Sometimes the women were laid across his knees for mutual fondling. He rewarded them with bars of soap, except for one whose breasts he complained were too small. One of these married women told the inquiry, 'I thought he had the right to do what he liked, as he is the Native Commissioner here'. Raikes denied there was any indecency: '*I have always treated these people as children.* I have chafed them and played with them but I have never had any evil design . . . towards them'.
>
> (Hyam 1991, p. 172; my emphasis)

Remarkably, Raikes' immediate superior pleaded for him to be merely reprimanded and transferred, on the grounds that he was a good chap troubled only by an 'unruly member'. The Colonial Office decided to dismiss him. But this whole affair reveals the extent to which not merely multiple concubinage but abuse of power for the purpose of obtaining sexual favours must have been widely tolerated. It is also worth noting that Raikes evidently perceived treating Africans as children as the proper and officially accepted way of doing things.

The image lingered on well into the 20th century, as may be seen from the remarkable case of Julian Huxley, grandson of Thomas Henry Huxley. In the early 1920s he visited the southern states of the USA and seems to have become thoroughly infected by local prejudices. He related numerous examples of behaviour indicating the child-likeness of blacks, and with surprising naivety accepted 'evidence' of the following kind:

> They are often childlike in their intellect. I used occasionally to stay with a Southern friend who used his cook as an exhibition and object-lesson to doctrinaires from New England. 'Bring me my saucer, Julia,' he would say, after a discussion on racial equality; and Julia always appeared with a saucer, a small plate, and an apology for disremembering which was which.
>
> (Huxley 1924, p. 821)

His general conclusion was that 'The negro mind is as different from the white mind as the negro from the white body. The old characterization "the minds of children" is perfectly true.' Some fifteen years later he had changed his own mind, and was one of the signatories of an anti-racist manifesto by eminent biologists (in the *Journal of Heredity* 1939, Vol. 30, No. 9).

There is little doubt that the colonial situation was a major factor in the emergence and persistence of the most common type of child image, which clearly symbolized the then prevailing power relationships. This is further indicated by the fact that, although its traces lingered on after the Second World War, the image became practically extinct after the breakup of European colonial empires. However, the child trope was not confined to those missionaries and colonial officials in direct contact with indigenous peoples. Just as the 'ape' image came to acquire the backing of scientific theories, so did that of the savage as close to the child; and that will the theme of the following chapters.

# 12

# WHY SAVAGES ARE
# CHILD-LIKE

## 'Arrested development' and the
## 'biogenetic law'

Just as the popular comparison of savages and apes had come to be buttressed by scientific theories from the end of the 18th century onwards, so biological explanations of child-likeness began to emerge a few decades later. They will be surveyed in this and the following chapter.

The first theory to be put forward was the notion of 'arrested development', which had become firmly established by the mid-19th century. Unlike the 'child image' discussed in Chapter 11, it was as a rule strictly confined to what was then regarded as the intellectual deficiency of savages. Its mere title adequately conveys the very simple basic notion, which persisted in some circles until the middle of the 20th century.

The second theory to be discussed is a version of the so-called 'biogenetic law', which is at an altogether more sophisticated level. The initial idea stemmed from Karl von Baer (1792–1876) who formulated what became known as von Baer's rule of embryonic resemblance. It states that characteristics held in common by large animal groups usually develop earlier in an embryo than unique features. Darwin took up and elaborated on this notion, observing that 'Embryology rises greatly in interest, when we look at the embryo as a picture, more or less obscured, of the progenitor' (Darwin [1859] 1928, p. 429).

Ernst Haeckel (1834–1919) was the one who developed the idea most extensively and with whose name the 'biogenetic law' has become associated. He enunciated it first in his *Generelle morphologie der organismen* published in 1866, and later in his more popular *The evolution of man* ([1870] 1905), where he referred to it as 'the fundamental law of organic evolution':

> This general law . . . may be briefly expressed in the phrase 'The history of the foetus is a recapitulation of the history of the race'; or, in other words, 'Ontogeny is a recapitulation of phylogeny'. It may be more fully stated as follows: The series of forms through which the individual organism passes during its development from the ovum to the complete bodily structure is a brief, condensed repetition of the long series of forms which the animal ancestors of the said organism, or the ancestral forms

of the species, have passed through from the earliest period of organic life down to the present day.

(Haeckel 1905, Vol. I, p. 5)[1]

While Haeckel's concept had been confined to embryology, the general idea came to be extended to include *post-natal* human development in order to account for race differences; and this is the particular aspect to be considered here. The 'biogenetic law' has been extremely influential, having been adopted by a wide range of prominent thinkers, and still stands in its original restricted version.

The last theory to be briefly examined, 'neoteny', refers to a relative slowing down of development coupled with the retention of some juvenile characters. As such, it conflicts in the present context with the postulates of the 'biogenetic law'.

## The doctrine of 'arrested development'

It seems likely that this notion was originally derived from the observation that ethnic differences tend to be much less marked in childhood than in maturity. Hence the idea that some kind of change takes place between these stages, a change that was believed to be innately determined. Nowadays, of course, we would attribute this mainly to the effect of cultural influences.

The earliest appearance of this idea which I have come across was by the 16th-century Dominican Tomas Ortiz, whose derogatory views of the South American Indians have already been quoted. He also commented on them as follows:

> The higher the age reached by these people, the nastier they become. While they are still ten or twelve years old, one can still believe that they possess some civility and virtue, but later they truly degenerate into brute animals.
>
> (Cited in Todorov 1985, pp. 182–3)

Some two hundred years later de Pauw, writing about North American Indians, expressed similar notions:

> One has to admit that the children . . . display some glimmer of intelligence up to the age of 16 or 17 years . . . but towards the 20th year, stupidity suddenly develops.
>
> (de Pauw 1770, Vol. 2, p. 156)

De Pauw anticipated later interpretations by seeking to relate the change to the onset of puberty, suggesting that its 'juices' in some way 'thicken the vital spirits'.[2]

The beginnings of a wider discussion on this issue coincided with the burgeoning of publications by European travellers and explorers during the early part of the 19th century. It had come to be accepted that such exploration should concern itself also with the 'characters' of savage peoples – what we would call their psychological features. Most of the reports observed that savage children were as lively and bright as European ones; frequently it was even suggested that they were precocious by European standards. But there was a consensus of opinion that they progressively declined in intelligence with increasing age.

It is a claim that was discussed by Theodor Waitz (1831–64), an early opponent of racial explanations, who reviewed several such reports. He agreed with the commonly expressed view that Negroes are relatively better in memory as compared with reasoning. But Waitz was more doubtful as to whether the notion of rapid progress followed by arrest was accurate; and even if it were, he contended, it would not prove innate inferiority, but could be attributed to such external factors as climate and social conditions (Waitz 1860, p. 235). In this he was probably influenced by the statements of some competent observers like Peter Leonard, a Royal Navy surgeon on a ship operating in West African waters with the duty of suppressing the slave trade. Leonard (1833) not only stated that African children 'appeared to me equal in intelligence and acquirements to European children of the same age' (p. 91), but also denied 'any defect of natural ability' among adults. Later there were further occasional challenges to the notion of 'arrested development'. Thus when the subject came up in the course of a discussion during a meeting of the London Ethnological Society, one of the contributors strongly disagreed. Robert Mann, then Superintendent of Education in Natal, described not only the children of the Kaffir tribes as quick on the uptake, but said that 'the men grow with advancing years in intelligence and sagacity in a remarkable degree' (Mann 1867, p. 195). Such voices were, however, in a small minority and 'arrested development' came to be generally accepted as an established fact. Curiously enough, the precocity of African children was affirmed even by those convinced of racial inferiority:

> With the Negro, as with some other races of man, it has been found that children are precocious; but that no advance in education can be made after they arrive at the age of maturity; they still continue, mentally, children.
>
> (Hunt 1865, p. 27)

The notion of black precocity followed by 'arrest' persisted until quite recently. The distinguished scientist Charles Richet, who was a firm believer in the inferiority of blacks, considered the possibility of verification by systematic comparisons of black and white children. He went on to dismiss it on the following grounds: 'The precocity . . . not being similar, one will not be able to compare a negro of twelve years with a little white of the same age, who will still be altogether a child' (Richet 1919, p. 65).

Many of those who believed in 'precocity' followed by 'arrested development' accepted it simply as a biological fact, without seeking any further explanation. Others referred in vague terms to brain development, as did the social evolutionist Tylor after he had become 'contaminated' by biological race theories. Before citing him, it should be mentioned that anecdotal reports by teachers about the academic weaknesses of their indigenous charges were widely circulated at the time:

> The account generally given by European teachers who have had the children of lower races in their schools is that, though these often learn as well as the white child up to about twelve years old, they then fall off, and are left behind by the *children of the ruling race*. This fits with what anatomy teaches about the less [*sic*] development of the brain in the Australian and African than in the European.
>
> (Tylor [1881] 1930, Vol. I, p. 58; my emphasis)

Carl Vogt, whose ideas have already been presented at some length (Chapter 7), discussed the matter in considerable detail, for he viewed 'arrested development' as fitting neatly into his thesis of the simian character of blacks: 'It is undeniable that the sudden metamorphosis which at the time of puberty takes place in the Negro . . . is a repetition of the phenomena occurring in the anthropoid apes' (1864, p. 191). Young apes, according to Vogt, are intelligent and 'very apt to learn and become civilised', but afterwards they become

> obstinate savage beasts, incapable of any improvement. And so it is with the Negro. The Negro child is not, as regards the intellectual capacities, behind the white child. All observers agree that they are as droll in their games, as docile and as intelligent as white children. Where their education is attended to, and where they are not, as in the American Slave States, intentionally brought up like cattle, it is found that the Negro children in the schools, not only equal but even surpass the white children in docility and apprehension. But no sooner do they reach the fatal period of puberty than, with the closure of the sutures and the projection of the jaws, the same process takes place as in the apes. The intellectual faculties remain stationary, and the individual – as well as the race – is incapable of further progress.
>
> (Vogt 1864, pp. 191/2)

It will have been noted that Vogt referred to 'the closure of the sutures', meaning the gaps between the bones of the skull which grow together as the child matures. By that time the theory had gained ground that early closure prevents further growth of the brain, and thereby of mental development. It is not clear who originated the theory. According to some, it was first mooted by the French anatomist Gratiolet. Vogt credited Pruner-Bey, who did mention early closure and the 'infantile form of the brain of the Negro' (Pruner-Bey 1861, pp. 328, 335), but without referring to 'arrested development'. Chamberlain (1900) attributed the idea to an Italian anatomist, Filippo Manetta (1864), but Vogt had clearly anticipated him.

Whatever the origin of the theory, it continued to hold sway until at least the end of the century. Ellis (1890, pp. 9–10), whose work on the Ewe of West Africa is a classic, had this to say:

> The Ewe-speaking people of the Slave Coast present the ordinary characteristics of the uncivilized negro. In early life they evince a degree of intelligence which, compared with that of the European child, appears precocious; and they acquire knowledge with facility till they arrive at the age of puberty when nature masters the intellect, and frequently completely deadens it. This peculiarity has been observed amongst others of what are termed the lower races, and has been attributed by some physiologists to the early closing of the sutures of the cranium, and it is worthy of note that throughout West Africa it is by no means rare to find skulls without any apparent transverse or longitudinal sutures.

Probably the most detailed elaboration of 'early closing hypothesis' is that of Augustus Henry Keane (1833–1912). A prominent ethnologist, he was Professor of Hindustani at University College London and does not seem to have had qualifications in anatomy or physiology. This did not prevent him from embarking upon grandiose speculations, based entirely on sometimes rather old secondary sources.

> The development of the cellular tissue, with a corresponding increase in mental power, apparently goes on until arrested by the closure of the cranial sutures. All the serratures are stated to be more complex in the higher than in the lower races, and their definite closing appears to be delayed till a later period in life amongst the former than amongst the latter.
>
> (Keane 1896, p. 44)

Keane further cited a finding by Broca to the effect that such early closing also happens with idiots, in line with Vogt's notion concerning the status of the idiot as intermediate between that of the Negro and the ape. Keane regarded the duration of the delay as being a function of mental activity; in other words, the more mental exercise, the later the closure. He stated that a direct relation between 'mental and cerebral expansion' seems 'beyond doubt', a view then widely shared; and this would account for racial differences in intelligence. He then ventured even further towards proposing a physical cause (p. 45):

> It would therefore seem probable, or at all events possible, that intense cerebration acts almost mechanically on the brain-cap, tending by its throbbing to keep the frontal sutures free till late in life, and even causing an expansion of the cranium itself in energetic and highly intellectual races.

156

This naive physiologizing is not very far removed from de Pauw's notion of 'the thickening of the vital spirits'. Perhaps that was the reason why the 'early closing' notion faded away thereafter. The issue was still considered worthy of detailed discussion by Franke (1915), who did however come to a negative conclusion as regards this particular cause.

Another type of causal explanation of 'arrested development' began to become popular towards the end of the century, though it was rooted in very old ideas. These ideas, about the excessive sexuality of savages, have already been amply documented. Travellers commonly reported both on the lasciviousness of the savages and their stupidity, and these came to be combined into cause and effect. It boiled down to the proposition that after the onset of puberty, savages become so obsessed with sex as to be incapable of any intellectual activity. No attempt was made to provide any kind of evidence, and it was just a case of 'putting two and two together'.

The first systematic study of the development of non-European children was the classic work on *Savage Childhood* by Dudley Kidd ([1906] 1969), dealing with 'Kafir' children in South Africa. It consists of a vivid and sympathetic account of the lives of the children, of whom he was evidently very fond. Moreover, in several places Kidd did his best to expose European stereotypes and myths, and he displayed his liking and respect for adult Africans in several passages, as when he thanked his 'many Kafir friends' who with great skill collected information he would not otherwise have been able to obtain. And yet his preface contains the following passage:

> As a matter of fact the savage is at his best, intellectually, emotionally, and morally, at the dawn of puberty. When puberty is drawing to a close, a degenerative process seems to set in, and the previous efflorescence of the faculties leads to no adequate fruitage in later life. If we consent . . . to treat the savage child as the zero of our scale . . . we must remember that the adult Kafir, on this scale, is often a *minus* quantity. . . . Not a few observers have pointed out that the imagination in the Kafirs runs to seed after puberty: it would be truer to say that it runs to sex.
>
> (Kidd 1969, pp viii–ix; emphasis in original)

It is remarkable that in spite of his personal experience over many years, and his generally favourable attitude, Kidd still declared his adherence to what by then had become the conventional wisdom, and continued as such for almost half a century. The French medical man who later became governor of the Congo expressed the classical formulation:

> after the Native reaches the age of twelve or fifteen his faculties, which are at first fairly quick, grow blunted and dull, his understanding becomes sluggish, he withdraws into himself, the childishness of his

157

primitive nature crystallizes, and henceforth he will never exceed the height to which the swift progress of his early days has carried him.

(Cureau [1912] 1915, p. 73)

In subsequent pages, when discussing 'Negro education', Cureau withdrew even the limited credit he gave them for their early years; in Cartesian terms, he equated them to animals:

Children taught in African schools learn reading, writing and the rudiments of arithmetic. . . . But the education they receive is never of further use to them for their own improvement. They copy, but they do not revise, *for they are simply machines*.

(Cureau [1912] 1915, p. 76; my emphasis)

Some two decades later Miller described the precocity of 'the primitive child' and said that there is 'a unanimity of opinion' that it comes to a halt with the onset of puberty. He then quoted a number of authors, summarizing the supposed cause by saying that the primitive then 'falls into a slough of sensuality' (Miller 1928, p. 125).

When planning his first field trip, the distinguished anthropologist Meyer Fortes put forward research proposals to the International African Institute in 1932 which included the following item:

It has been maintained that the African child's mental development ceases at puberty. . . . The question arises whether the African child's apparent cessation of intellectual development is not due to a puberty crisis, and what the relation of childhood experience is to this crisis.

(Cited in Goody 1995, p. 164)

The word 'apparent' indicates a degree of scepticism, and Fortes (1938) in due course carried out a study of child development that was to become a classic.

After the war, Davidson, a psychiatrist in what was then Northern Rhodesia, had no such reservations. He cited with approval the thesis of a psychoanalyst (Ritchie 1943) who had apparently analysed several Africans. The title of a subsequent article by Ritchie (1944) epitomizes his views: 'The African as grown-up nursling.' According to Davidson, Ritchie's work provided proof that as a result of an excessively indulgent infancy followed by traumatically sudden weaning,

the typical African is somewhat arrested in mental development. An observation which I myself have made also arises from the weaning situation, from which the ambivalent attitude of the African develops. This is that up to puberty there is in my opinion very little difference in the intelligence and learning ability between Bemba and European children. After that a marked difference occurs, the European far outstripping the African child. This, I think, is due to the early release and gratification of the genital sexual impulse in the average African child.

(Davidson 1949, p. 77)

Apparently Davidson was under the illusion that he had made a new discovery, which is remarkable in view of the extensive dissemination of that notion over a century. Finally, and most astonishingly, similar ideas were expressed in a monograph commissioned by the World Health Organization dealing with 'the African mind'. Its author, Carothers (1953), was a psychiatrist whose work was widely read, well received and extensively cited.[3]

His colleagues do not seem to have objected to parallels he drew between brain-damaged Europeans and normal Africans (shades of Vogt!). Furthermore, he put forward a theory alleging that the African experience of infancy and childhood is such that it prevents the formation of an integrated personality. After reviewing some of the literature claiming that early indulgence in sexual activity stifles further intellectual progress, he suggested that this misses the point:

The trouble is much more deeply seated; and the whole-hearted concentration on sex which characterizes the African adolescent is, in the present writer's view, merely one symptom of a general condition – one more example of the all-or-none attention which is part and parcel of the lack of personal integration which has now become the clearest feature of African mentality.

(Carothers 1953, pp. 106–7)

Some two decades later he published a book that showed he had not changed his mind, since it consisted essentially of a restatement of his original thesis.

Once again, the continuity of this line of thought over a century is striking. Although the actual term 'arrested development' gradually faded away during the latter part of the 19th century, belief in the supposed phenomenon to which it referred remained constant, with relatively few dissenters. What changed were the explanations proffered in order to account for the supposed facts. Initially, in a climate of opinion where craniology was dominant, the answer proposed was purely anatomical. Then sexual behaviour was said to be responsible, often with the implication that it was biologically determined. By the mid-20th century a predominantly psychological interpretation was put forward, with precious little evidence to support it. Thereafter the whole notion seems to have quietly faded away, probably as a result of fundamental changes such as the crumbling of colonial empires, the scientific critiques of racism after the Second World War, and an official rejection of ethnic discrimination in western countries.

One might be tempted to dismiss the whole business as a fanciful aberration; but that would be a mistake, as it almost certainly had significant practical

159

implications. While the tracing of detailed causal chains is not feasible, even a limited perusal of sources suggested that the idea of arrested development was initially put forward by explorers and travellers and taken over and in turn reinforced by European teachers in colonial territories. It was certainly not confined to writers in ivory towers. This was shown by the Belgian psychologist Ombredane (1952), who undertook research in the Belgian Congo during the years after the Second World War. He interviewed people who held responsible positions in the then colony about the idea of 'arrested development' of blacks. While it was of course rejected by black Africans themselves, he found that many of the whites firmly believed it to be true:

> A senior magistrate: The black, when he is young, can be more alert than the white, but when he reaches puberty he becomes mindless.
>
> A senior administrator: The arrest of intelligence at puberty is *a reality*. This can be seen in the infantile behaviour of the adult, in his exhibitionism. Up to 8 or 9 years, the black kid is at least as smart as the white kid. Towards puberty a sclerosis sets in due to sexual excesses.
>
> (Ombredane 1952, pp. 522–3; emphasis in original)

There is little doubt that such beliefs are likely to have influenced the behaviour of colonial officials towards the people over whom they exercised authority. Perhaps even more serious would have been the educational effects, since low expectations on the part of the teachers are likely to have resulted in correspondingly low performance.

From the latter half of the 19th century onwards the notion of 'arrested development' became associated with the 'biogenetic law', purporting to provide an evolutionary account of the backwardness of the 'lower races'.

## The 'biogenetic law'

The theory to be discussed has become known in psychology as 'the phylogenetic principle' or 'recapitulation theory'. If the 'biogenetic law' had remained confined to the anatomical structures of the embryo, it would be of no concern for psychology. However, during the latter part of the 19th century the biological concept came to be applied increasingly to the interpretation of cultural phenomena. Social evolutionists believed in unilinear development through a series of stages to its culmination in western civilization. Existing savage peoples were believed to have become 'arrested' at an earlier stage. Such a scheme was readily compatible with a concept of parallelism between organic and mental evolution. The latter was viewed as the genetically determined ascent of mind from animals to humans and, thereafter, human races advancing at differing rates, indicated by their levels of culture, towards the true rationality of the West.

Such a broad scheme left the processes involved rather vague, and that is where an extended version of the biogenetic law filled the gap: it was postulated that the cultural stages of the progress of humanity were functionally related to the biologically fixed phases of the psychological maturation of individuals. These phases recapitulate, in miniature as it were, the mental capacities and dispositions corresponding to the hierarchy of cultural stages; and the progress of individuals in the lower races is arrested when they reach their biological limit. This provided a theoretical rationale for equating the mentalities of savages and children, as shown very clearly by the arguments of Sir James Frazer. One of the great anthropological theorists of the period, he had come to adopt recapitulation in later life:

> by comparison with civilized man the savage represents an arrested or rather retarded stage of social development, and an examination of his customs and beliefs accordingly supplies the same sort of evidence of the evolution of the human mind that an examination of the embryo supplies of the evolution of the human body. To put it otherwise, a savage is to a civilized man as a child is to an adult; and just as the gradual growth of intelligence in a child corresponds to, and in a sense recapitulates, the gradual growth of intelligence in the species, so a study of savage society at various stages of evolution enables one to follow approximately the road by which the ancestors of the higher races must have travelled in their progress upward through barbarism to civilization.
>
> (Frazer 1913, pp. 162–3)

The extrapolation of the 'biogenetic law' from embryology to *post-natal* development to maturity led to a context in which the phrase 'recapitulation of the history of the race' took on the meaning given to it by Frazer.

One of the most prominent exponents of the biogenetic law in its extended version applied to mind was George Romanes (1848–94). As a young biology student Romanes had come into contact with Darwin, who befriended him and passed on to him an unpublished chapter of his own on instinct, as well as notes on psychological topics. Thus encouraged, Romanes duly embarked upon work on comparative psychology that was to occupy him for the rest of his life.

By the 1870s there was widespread acceptance of evolutionary theory among scientists, at least in so far as animals and the bodily structures of humans were concerned; but there was still considerable reluctance to accept that the same processes could have been responsible for the emergence of the human mind. Most prominent among the sceptics was what Romanes called 'the school of Mivart and Wallace'. St George Mivart (1827–1900) was then a prominent naturalist, but it was the opposition of Alfred Russell Wallace (1823–1913) that most upset Darwin, who went so far as to refer to Wallace's murder of 'your own and my child' (cited in Gould 1983, p. 47). The aim of Romanes was to persuade the doubters that 'one cannot draw a hard and fast line at the mind of man' (Romanes 1880, p. 4); the differences between animal species and human races were to be explained in terms of the biogenetic law.

In 1878 Romanes gave an address on mental evolution to the British Association that received a standing ovation, though *The Times* reporter present evinced a certain amount of scepticism:

> In the absence of actual ancestors, *The Times* reported, he lined up an ugly ersatz collection of 'savages, young children, idiots and uneducated deaf-mutes'. These dubious stand-ins seemed to show that 'man and brute have much more in common intellectually, and perhaps, even morally, than is dreamt of'. Each was 'arrested' at some lowly stage.
> (Cited in Desmond and Moore 1991, p. 633)

Romanes continued his missionary activities by giving lectures, and in 1888 he published his major work on *Mental evolution in man*, in which he presented a grand theme of the continuous transition from mere sensation to self-conscious thought, which is the essential distinction between man and brute. Comparative philology shows the emergence of human intelligence over historical time, while what he called 'linguistic psychology' reveals a parallel unfolding of mind in the individual child. This provides direct evidence of the evolutionary process within the life-history of every human.

A lecture delivered in Glasgow and subsequently printed (Romanes 1880) contains the gist of his arguments in succinct and rather drastic form; in particular it has a remarkable table, some of whose major contents are reproduced in Table 12.1.[4] I have left out two columns on 'the products of emotional and intellectual development', and another column showing the ordinal positions of deaf-mutes; for example, 'half-educated deaf-mutes' were shown as equivalent to imbeciles.

At first sight it is hard to credit that Romanes really meant what he appeared to say in the table. Comparing savages to children aged between about 3 and 5 years went well beyond what even extreme racists had claimed. Yet it is clear from his explanation of the table that everything was intended to be taken literally:

> You see that at birth I have placed the infant, in respect of its intellectual development, on a par with the jelly-fish. I have had some quarrels with young mothers on this subject. When an infant is three weeks old I consider it to be on a level with the worms . . . when they understand words they are on a level with pigs, horses and cats.
> (Romanes 1880, p. 13)

It is amusing to note that young mothers evidently had more sense than the learned scientist. Again, by multiplying arbitrary minor categories (not shown in detail in Table 12.1) the impression of continuity between ape and man is fostered: between 'very brutal man' and 'very human ape' the developmental gap was indicated as just six months! The whole scheme clearly lent strong support to the idea of the child-likeness of savages and the early arrest of their intellectual development.[5]

*Table 12.1* Developmental phases according to Romanes

| The psychological scale | Human age equivalent | Idiots |
|---|---|---|
| Existing man | adult | – |
| Highly civilized | 15 yrs | – |
| Civilized | 10 yrs | – |
| Savages & partly civilized | 5 yrs | Feebleminded |
| Low savages | 3 yrs | Imbeciles |
| Lowest savages | 30 mths | High idiots |
| Primitive man | 28 mths | Counting idiots |
| Almost human ape | 20 mths | Talking idiots |
| Anthropoid apes | 9 mths | Babbling idiots |
| Horses, pigs, cats, etc. | 5 mths | |
| Birds | 18 wks | Low idiots |
| Reptiles | 16 wks | Cretins |
| Spiders & crabs | 14 wks | Low cretins |
| Higher molluscs(?) | 12 wks | Microcephalic |
| Worms(?) | 3 wks | |
| Medusae | Birth | Acephalic |

It is paradoxical that Wallace, whom Romanes tried to convert, had a much more realistic appreciation of the intellectual potential of savages. Unlike most of his contemporaries, Wallace believed that their brains are not significantly different from those of Europeans; at the same time the demands of their simple way of life on their intellect are modest, leaving a great deal of unused capacity. This was Wallace's reason for denying that natural selection could have created the human mind: such selection, in his view, could only operate in response to specific needs and would be incapable of developing into a brain with so much surplus capacity. Wallace's concept of natural selection was unduly narrow, ignoring possible wider indirect consequences of particular changes. With hindsight, Romanes was right about the general principle of the evolution of mind, but his arguments about savages were absurd; Wallace was wrong about natural selection, but right about savages.

# 13

# HEADS I WIN, TAILS YOU LOSE

## From 'recapitulation' to 'neoteny'

The biogenetic formula that ontogeny repeats phylogeny was alluring, owing to the apparent facility with which it could be applied to all manner of spheres.[1] It became well known far beyond the range of specialists, and it is most likely that some of the writers on the child-likeness of savages quoted in Chapter 12 had been directly or indirectly influenced by it. The 'law' held out the promise of revealing humanity's past and the linkage of that past with mental disturbances in the present; it explained the causes of social problems, justified imperialist policies and so on. Here I shall merely illustrate some of these issues, beginning with the last point.

At the turn of the century The Reverend Josiah Strong (cited by Gould 1977, p. 131) put forward biogenetic arguments for the annexation of the Philippines by the USA; he declared that 'Filipinos' as a race were no more capable of self-government than undeveloped children. The famous criminologist Cesare Lombroso (1836–1909) taught that, owing to recapitulation, each child passes through a savage (more or less equated with criminal) phase; most grow out of this, but some remain biologically anchored at that stage and this is one major (though not the only) source of criminality.

The psychoanalytic movement was highly receptive to the biogenetic law. Freud read Romanes' *Mental evolution in man*, said to have been the most annotated book in his library (Sulloway 1980, p. 247). Recapitulation, coupled as it almost invariably was with the Lamarckian assumption of the inheritance of acquired characters, certainly constituted a central plank in his theoretical edifice. It recurred in many of his writings (Cf. Hallowell 1948; Gould 1977), and there follows an example in relation to dreams from his *General introduction to psychoanalysis*:

> The era to which the dream-work takes us back is 'primitive' in a two-fold sense: in the first place, it means the early days of the *individual* – his childhood – and, secondly, in so far as each individual repeats in some abbreviated fashion during childhood the whole course of the development of the human race, the reference is phylogenetic.
>
> (Freud 1938, p. 177; emphasis in original)

In *Totem and taboo* Freud linked 'our' European ancestors, children and primitives. His followers, who originally included Jung, steadfastly maintained the same ideas.[2] Marie Bonaparte (1934, p. 22), a psychoanalytical anthropologist, was particularly sanguine:

> The 'infantile return of totemism' can furthermore be observed in the animal phobias of so many of our children. The wolf, the horse, the dog and other animals are, for the child they terrify, so many substitutes for the father, at the same time loved and feared. Moreover, the child generally reproduces, in the course of its development, the attitudes of the primitive. The biogenetic law is verified in the psychic as well as in the physical sphere; in it ontogeny reproduces phylogeny.

Later (p. 24), reiterating Freud's thesis, Bonaparte noted that obsessional neurosis is singularly apt to manifest the archaic mode of thought of child and primitive. There is no indication that Bonaparte herself had worked with children, but her views had long been shared by child psychologists such as James Sully (1842–1923). His comparisons between children and savages, a context in which he frequently referred to Romanes, have already been mentioned. A particularly interesting early case is that of the famous art historian and literary scholar Hyppolite Taine (1828–1893). In 1877 there appeared an English translation of a piece in which he recorded in great detail the language development of a young child, truly a pioneering work. Such interpretations as he offered were clearly inspired by recapitulation theory:

> One evening (at three years) on inquiring for the moon and being told that it had set [qu'elle est allée se coucher] she replies 'But where is the moon's *bonne* [maid]?' All this closely resembles the emotions and conjectures of primitive peoples. . . .
>
> Speaking generally, the child presents in a passing state the mental characteristics that are found in a fixed state in primitive civilisations, very much as the human embryo presents in a passing state the physical characteristics that are found in a fixed state in the classes of inferior animals.
>
> (Taine 1877, pp. 258, 259; emphasis in original)

In America James Mark Baldwin (1861–1934) subscribed in his *Mental development in the child and the race* (1895) to a modified version of recapitulation theory. But his was an entirely theoretical exposition, overshadowed by that of a famous expositor whose name is prominently associated with the theory.

## Stanley Hall and recapitulationism

Granville Stanley Hall (1844–1924) was the guru of child and educational psychology in America and founded the so-called 'child study movement'. It was a label for a very broad and rather vague set of ideas, as he himself was aware when attempting to define it:

> It is a nondescript and, in some sense, an unparalleled movement – partly psychology, partly anthropology, partly medico-hygiene. It is closely related at every step to the study of instincts in animals, and to the rites and beliefs of primitive people.
>
> (Stanley Hall 1900, p. 689)

Like many of his generation of American psychologists, Stanley Hall studied in Germany at the time when Haeckel propounded his ideas. He was also familiar with the writings of Romanes and Baldwin, and another influence was Henry Drummond's *Ascent of man* (1894), whose version of evolutionism was then much in vogue. Drummond, largely inspired by Romanes, portrayed the development of both body and mind in terms of the recapitulation theory. Following Romanes, he suggested that emotions emerge in the child's mind in the same order as that found in the animal scale, and he proposed that the same applies to all aspects of mental functioning.

In fact Stanley Hall's evolutionism had little to do with Darwinism, being more akin to the social evolutionism that essentially concerned historical stages. The further step taken by Stanley Hall was to suggest that in the course of the development of the child these stages are 'recapitulated'. His 'genetic psychology' proposed that parallel stages of infancy, childhood and particularly adolescence are characterized by typical modes of thought, feeling and behaviour. Moreover, though later overlaid, these aspect of the psyche continue to exist in adulthood:

> we are influenced in our deeper more temperamental dispositions by the life-habits and codes of conduct of we know not what unnumbered hosts of ancestors, which like a cloud of witnesses are present throughout our lives and our souls are echo-chambers in which their whispers reverberate . . . we have to deal with the archaeology of mind, with zones and strata which precede consciousness as we know it.
>
> (Stanley Hall 1904, Vol. II, p. 61)

This is of course reminiscent of psychoanalysis, also based as we have seen on recapitulation, and as such congenial to Stanley Hall; it is thus not surprising that it was Stanley Hall who invited Freud and Jung to America in 1909.

Stanley Hall postulated that the modes of psychological functioning at each stage of child development correspond to some primitive ancestral ones, and it is only during adolescence that the latest advances of the race become dominant. Such a theory postulating sequences of development based on evolutionary history would of course have important educational implications, which Stanley Hall sought to demonstrate by means of questionnaire studies. But as Ross (1972) observed, the results were quite inconclusive. Even Stanley Hall himself seldom felt confident of having isolated age-specific patterns of the kind his theory predicted, and which could have been used for curriculum planning:

> Often he suggested that the child's impulse was a hereditary survival from a much earlier age and that it had features in common with certain characteristics of primitive cultures, but he was never able to show that the timetable of evolution indicated to what age of childhood the impulse belonged.
>
> (Ross 1972, p. 306)

Edward L. Thorndike challenged both the theory and Stanley Hall's question-naire methods, which prompted Stanley Hall to try again to prove the theory; but, not surprisingly, he failed. Nonetheless, a whole series of studies came to be published, two of which will be considered here. The first, comparing the activities of children and primitives, illustrates the incredible naivety of some of this work. Following the usual practice, Acher (1910) gave a questionnaire to teachers who observed children's activities. Here are the comments relating to activities with 'string':

> Most primitive people use the string in connection with religious rites, ceremonies and magic. . . . It undoubtedly became of survival value to many primitive tribes . . . [account of findings follows].
>
> The analogy between children's use of strings and those of primitive man is thus seen to be very close. Undoubtedly many of the uses children make of them today are given us by social inheritance as is generally maintained. But the aptitude which children show in their use and the intense interest with which they play with them, and even save them, point to something more than mere imitation. It has been said that the younger the child is the racially older it is. If this be true it can be readily conceived how the early struggles of the race with the string as a means of evolution, could give to the modern child's mind a psychic stringward tendency.
>
> (Acher 1910, p. 137)

Someone who believes in a 'psychic stringward tendency' will believe anything! The second study is of quite a different kind; and although open to criticism, constitutes a more serious effort to examine the validity of Stanley Hall's theory. This was a Ph.D. dissertation by Appleton [1910] (1976) supported, and probably inspired, by Stanley Hall. She also acknowledged the help of L.T. Hobhouse whose *Morals in evolution* (1929) constituted an attempt to apply evolutionary principles to ethics by a comparative diachronic study of customs and institutions; and that of Alfred Haddon, the distinguished anthropologist who had led the famous Cambridge Expedition to the Torres Straits. This indicates that the project was taken seriously by some outstanding contemporary figures.

The theoretical basis of the work was the so-called 'culture–epoch theory', characterized by the author as:

> the theory that the child recapitulates the psychical as well as the physical evolution of his race, and hence that his mental growth is best promoted by assimilation of the cultural products belonging to that stage of *race* development, which corresponds to his own.
>
> (Appleton [1910] 1976, p. 1)

Although this was not spelled out, it implies a parallel series of stages of development in the individual 'civilized' child that corresponds to mental dispositions present at successively higher cultural levels. Appleton's aim was to test this theory, at least in a preliminary way. Doing it comprehensively would have entailed covering the whole range of the then existing cultures, taking these as reflecting a linear evolutionary progression. In practice that was not feasible, and the project was confined to:

> an attempt to make a beginning of an unprejudiced study of the actual mental characteristics of some of the lowest of savage tribes with a view to finding whether their mental life does or does not reveal any definite types similar to those found in ontogenetic development.
>
> (Ibid., p. 1)

In much of the later discussions this limitation was lost sight of, and conclusions were drawn as though the whole of the supposed 'phylogenetic series' had been examined. The method of investigation consisted of using existing studies of children's play, of the kind favoured by Stanley Hall, and ethnographic data about tribes 'low in savagery', one from each continent. For the classification of play some broad and rather vague categories were used.

While ample information was provided on the five tribes, that about 'civilized children' remained rather sparse. The analysis consisted of a comparison of the two sets of samples according to types of play. Given the looseness of the categories, such comparisons must have involved a great deal of arbitrary judgement. The general conclusion reached was one of at least partial support for recapitulation theory:

> So far as somatic characteristics of play activities are concerned, very close though not perfect correspondence is found between the savage and the child. In the matter of organization of play activities, wide differences appear, while in the psychological characteristics of their play those qualities, such as, for example, rhythm, dramatization, and competition, which, with civilized children, are very strong in very early life, are also very strong with the savages. . . . On the other hand, the more purely abstract and intellectual phases of children's play are almost absolutely lacking.
>
> (Ibid., p. 4)

The actual text indicates that the last of these claims was, even within the given framework, far too extreme. In the conclusions at the end of the monograph it is conceded that the tribes do have some 'purely intellectual play', but this resembles that of 'civilized children' between the ages of 6 and 11. The lesson to be learnt from all this for educational practice was said to be that

> it is necessary to bring the specific products of the culture epochs coresponding most closely to [the child's] own, into the realm of formal instruction. But to do this intelligently, it is necessary that the teacher add to his knowledge of genetic pedagogy a genetic anthropology.
>
> (Ibid., p. 83)

Thus in spite of the acknowledged weakness of the support lent to the 'culture–epoch theory' by the study, it ended with a recommendation that presumes its validity. As in the case of her mentor, Stanley Hall, faith in the theory prevailed over hard evidence.

Recapitulation theory as formulated by Stanley Hall implied the inferiority of primitives, whose intellectual development was said to cease sooner. Stanley Hall believed that non-whites were lower on the evolutionary scale, on a level with either white children or adolescents (Muschinske 1977). Lowest on his scale were American Indians, then African blacks, and highest American blacks, since he thought that the best and most evolved had been selected for slavery. This did not mean that he harshly denigrated non-whites as did so many other racists. His attitude was tolerant but of course patronizing – childish traits are often attractive. Non-whites develop so far, and then they stop. But why and how do they stop? It is important to note that the supporters of recapitulation theory had no better answer to this question than did their predecessors, who had lacked the benefit of an evolutionary theory. So Stanley Hall had to fall back on the old chestnut of sexuality: up to the age of 12 the black child develops in the same way as the white child; then there comes for the black a burst of sexual impulse, inhibiting for the average black (and he had to grant the existence of exceptions) any further progress (Stanley Hall 1905).

By the time Stanley Hall wrote, the biogenetic law had already passed its zenith and come under increasingly critical scrutiny. Nonetheless, its influence remained a powerful one. Pierre Bovet, Director of the Jean-Jaques Rousseau Institute in Geneva (a post occupied later by Piaget), though aware of the attacks on the theory, continued to regard it as important for the educator:

> However we may regard Haeckel's theory as a definitive formulation of a law, it is not in doubt that it constitutes a very fruitful working hypothesis. It is eminently fitted to bring to the inquirer's notice many facts that would otherwise pass unperceived. And it is a valuable theory for the educationist too; for many of the child's instincts and likings, which were formerly a dead weight on the teacher's hands, take on a

positive interest, as soon as the latter ceases to regard them as individual and passing whims, and accustoms himself to look on them as the living prolongation of the great forces which have fashioned mankind during thousands of years.

(Bovet 1923, p. 150)

Elsewhere in the same context Bovet referred to the relationships between various aspects of child behaviour and that of our primitive ancestors. One in particular concerns the then often discussed issue of the drawings of children and those of primitive peoples. This harks back to an intriguing story that deserves to be told since it was inspired by, and in turn reinforced, the image of savages as children.

## Drawings of savages and children

The recapitulation theory was employed in an ambitious, albeit misguided attempt to rank savages into an evolutionary order.

The story began early in the 19th century when there was a growing interest among travellers and explorers in the artistic endeavours of the peoples whom they visited. They would sometimes actively invite them to demonstrate what they could do by handing them pencil and paper, and asking them to draw. Until the latter years of the century, their comments were often favourable. For instance, the members of an early British expedition to the Torres Straits during the 1840s, and those of a Dutch expedition to New Guinea some twenty years later, were impressed by the drawing abilities of the savages.[3] Similarly Wallace, the co-discoverer with Darwin of the theory of evolution through natural selection, had this to say about the Papuans of New Guinea:

> It is curious that a rudimental love of art should co-exist with such a low state of civilization ... we could hardly believe that the same people are, in other matters, utterly wanting in all sense of order, comfort, or decency. Yet such is the case. They live in the most miserable, crazy and filthy hovels. ... If these pople are not savages, where shall we find any?
>
> Yet they have all a decided love for the fine arts, and spend their leisure time in executing works whose good taste and elegance would often be admired in our schools of design!

(Wallace 1869, pp. 324–5)

Wallace, who had travelled widely in the Malay Archipelago, was certainly exceptional in the extent of his praise, of a kind which would not recur again until 'primitive art' became fashionable in the 20th century. Yet more restrained appreciation of indigenous art in various parts of the world including Africa (especially Bushmen), Australia and South America was by no means lacking. It may be mentioned in passing that the apparent inability of some of these peoples to *understand* pictures presented to them gave rise to some astonishment.[4] At any rate, by about the 1880s a great deal of information about 'savage art' had been accumulated.

At that time a German ethnographer, Steinen, worked among the Bororo, a Brazilian Indian group. He had come across a book on children's art published in 1887 by Corrado Ricci, which enjoyed great success and led to the collection of large masses of children's drawings. When Steinen returned to the field he carried out systematic studies of the drawing abilities of the Bororo Indians, which he compared to those of European children. He found many striking similarities, but also some significant differences (Steinen 1894). It is unlikely that this was the first time such similarities had been noted, though I have not been able to find any earlier examples. What is certain is that, from then onwards, comparisons between drawings of European children and savages multiplied. Moreover, owing to the prevalent vogue of social evolutionary theory, such comparisons tended to be couched in evolutionary terms. There was considerable interest in the evolution of art, and various 'stages' were proposed (cf. Balfour 1893), 'savage art' of course being an early one. Haddon (1895), in his *Evolution in art*, commented on the resemblance between the drawings of European children and those of the 'less advanced peoples'. At the same time, unlike the majority of the writers of the period, Haddon acknowledged the close observation of nature apparent from the drawings, which made it possible to identify the particular species of animals represented.

The evolutionary approach was cast in a much more rigorous mould by Lamprecht, who sought to employ it as a tool for reconstructing historical epochs. Karl Lamprecht (1856–1915) was a German historian who shocked his academic colleagues by proposing that history, generally regarded as a humane discipline (Geisteswissenschaft) should strive to become a rigorous science. Rather than confine itself to description, concentrating on the actions of particular heroic figures, it should attempt to discover the determining causes of historical change. According to Lamprecht, this effort should be based on psychology, which he regarded as the key discipline for all social sciences; and he drew an analogy in this respect with mechanics which he (mistakenly) believed served the same purpose for the natural sciences. He suggested that history corresponds to biology, and can only become truly scientific if it is reduced to general concepts.

Lamprecht justified this by claiming that all historical events are psychical in nature, and that any given phase of social evolution can be regarded as a collective mental state that characterizes a period, a diapason which penetrates all mental phenomena and thereby all historical events of the time. He first tried to apply these principles to the periods of German history (Lamprecht 1900), maintaining that they were bound to follow each other in a definite order determined by the mental diapason and its modifications, according to certain principles that need not concern us here. The whole approach is somewhat reminiscent of Auguste Comte's 'social dynamics'.

While ample documentary material was available for the higher civilizations, this was not true of the various primitive societies around the globe, whose evolutionary status was unclear. Lamprecht then hit upon the idea of utilizing the 'biogenetic law' for the purpose of obtaining objective evidence that would make it possible to order 'primitive' societies into an evolutionary sequence. The means whereby this was to be achieved consisted in the analysis of drawings. He therefore appealed for children's drawings from various cultures to be collected (Lamprecht 1905a and b).

In order to understand the rationale of such a procedure, it is necessary to look briefly at events following the publication of Ricci's book. There was a great surge of interest leading to numerous attempts at analyses of European children's drawings.

A regular age progression was identified, roughly from mere scribbles via schemata to phenomenal representations.[5] Comparing the drawings of European children with those of savages, the resemblances were interpreted as the latter apparently having been 'arrested' at one of the earlier stages. Just as savage languages were believed to be simple and to correspond to the language of European children, so the drawings of savages remained crude.

For Lamprecht these child/savage comparisons suggested the answer to his problem. Remember that he viewed the mental states in a population at a given time as basically homogeneous, so that any particular manifestation of the collective psyche would be as good as any other and constitute, in our terminology, a valid sample. Moreover, in accordance with the extended version of the 'biogenetic law' , he assumed a parallelism between ontogenesis and phylogenesis. Finally, the ontogenetic stages were known from the studies of European children; this seemed to provide a kind of normative scale against which the productions of savages could be set, with a view to establishing their evolutionary status.

Lamprecht's ideas were taken up by Levinstein (1905) and Buschan (1906), who closely followed the teaching of the master and thought that their findings confirmed his theory. Others disagreed, pointing out that matters were more complicated, and it is not possible to pursue the lengthy debate (for details cf. Jahoda 1991). At any rate, no one succeeded in determining the evolutionary status of any population, which is hardly surprising.

In spite of this failure, faith in the promise held out by the biogenetic law remained undiminished for quite some time. A German ethnographer who had worked in East Africa and elicited numerous drawings which he published in 1926 made the following comment:

> [the African drawings] correspond perfectly to the drawings of our small pre-school children and can thereby be counted as solid support for the biogenetic law.
>
> (Weule 1926, p. 95)

While expressing reservations about the then still prevalent view that 'the Negro is a large child', Weule did regard blacks as people representing humanity in its earlier, youthful stage. The same enduring faith in the biogenetic law was voiced a few years later by the distinguished child psychologist Karl Bühler:

> We know very little about primitive times and yet a resigned '*ignorabimus*' would be premature; for the science of prehistory has not yet exhausted its best source of information, nor yet indeed in many respects succeeded in recognizing it. This source, I feel convinced, is the mental development of *our* children. We are beginning to see, e.g. in the language and drawing of children, certain fundamental laws of mental progress manifesting themselves quite independently of external influences, laws which, as they govern the evolution of childhood, in like manner presumably governed that of prehistory.
>
> (Bühler 1930, p. 2; emphases in original)

Hilda Eng's [1931] (1954) well-known work on children's drawings mentioned alleged common features in the 'psyche of the child and the primitive man', basing herself on the biogenetic law. Referring to Lévy-Bruhl (about whom more in Chapter 14), she listed 'want of firm voluntary attention, of penetrating analysis and higher synthesis, [and] the power of abstraction and of logical and realistic thinking' (p. 213).

If I have devoted a good deal of attention to the topic of drawing, it is not only because it was widely discussed for several decades. The main reason is that underlying these discussions was the firm assumption, based on recapitulation theory, that the minds of savages, children, and sometimes also pre-historic humans, were fundamentally alike. Given these assumptions, the conclusions drawn were not as such unreasonable. However, the wide recourse to recapitulation theory in order to explain the characteristics of savages also prompted some extraordinary flights of fancy that are worth illustrating briefly.

## Some curious aberrations

A German scholar came across a book on the Congo, in which one particular passage inspired him to write a piece on 'The psychology of the Negro race'. The passage in question ran as follows:

> It seems that . . . the porters on their own initiative band together in . . . groups and elect a leader. What is very astonishing is that these leaders, who enjoy great prestige with the members and sometimes thrash them, are often children aged eight to ten. It seems generally to be the case . . . that boys of that age are held in high regard by the tribes. This is readily explained, since as all those who have lived among the Negroes know,

> Negro children are about as intelligent as our children until puberty, and only start at that age to become stupid and brutish. It is only surprising that adults take account of this fact and defer to the relatively better intellect of the young ones.
>
> (von den Velden 1906/7, p. 111)

It does not seem to have occurred to the learned doctor that this report might have been unreliable. Rather, he embarked upon a discussion of recapitulation in which he dwelt, for no apparent reason, on the development of apes. He claimed that children go rapidly through the stages which their ancestors went through, and cavalierly added an improbable hypothesis necessary for his argument: namely that the Congolese had degenerated from a much higher level of culture. This led him to the following conclusion:

> When the Negro boys . . . are mentally as developed as the children of the white races, they recapitulate the nature of their human ancestors. At 10 years they are as far as their ancestors were 10000 years ago (the figure is of course arbitrary), then they recapitulate their degeneration, centuries in a year or two, and finally they become like their close forbears brutal, stupid but crafty, bestial beings.
>
> (von den Velden 1906/7, p. 112)

Another *Gelehrter*, Woltmann (1906/7), took issue with this analysis. Not that he disputed what in his title he called 'the mental inferiority of the Negro race', but he suggested another cause, namely 'the law of the physiological interaction between brain and sexual system'. This was just another, rather more pretentious restatement of the view that sexual maturity inhibits further growth of the brain. However, Woltman added an ominous twist: the same applied, to a lesser extent, to mental differences between dark-haired and blond 'races', and between males and females. Later sexual maturity and consequent greater development of the brain explain, according to him, the high intellectual endowment of the blond race. If the consequences of that kind of thinking had not been so tragic, its absurdity would be amusing.

Unlike the above, which was based on mere speculation, the second case to be described involved an empirical study. Hrdlicka (1931), working from the prestigious Smithsonian Institution in Washington, advertised to solicit information about children who run on all fours. This was prompted by his notion that 'the child after birth recapitulates and uses for a time various phases of its prehuman ancestral behavior' (p. 93). He obtained 369 responses concerning white children, eighteen relating to 'colored' children and mostly reported by whites from other parts of the world (who often compared these children to monkeys); and only from one single black American family. Notwithstanding, he felt able to conclude that 'The indications are that the manifestation is more common among the colored, the negroes in particular, than it is among the whites' (p. 13). The implication is obvious.

As this last example shows, crude forms of recapitulation theory were still acceptable at respectable scientific institutions as late as the third decade of the 20th century. By that time, however, a rival theory had gained ground.

Before going on to an alternative theory, it is worth mentioning that the issue still lingers on. This is indicated by a recent article which finds it necessary to argue that the biogenetic principle, while relevant for anatomy (though in a narrower sense than postulated by Haeckel), is not applicable to behavioural ontogeny (Medicus 1992).

## Neoteny: different theory, same outcome

From the turn of the century onwards doubts began to be voiced about the biogenetic law in general, and recapitulation in particular. The theoretical debates took place primarily among biologists, and it is neither necessary, nor would I be competent, to rehearse them here (cf. Gould 1977). Let me just repeat at the outset that 'neoteny' refers to the retention after sexual maturity of some juvenile characters, produced by a relative slowing down of bodily development. From an evolutionary point of view this means that descendants display some of the childish attributes of their ancestors. It is generally accepted that this process has played an important part in evolution, and also that in comparison with animals humans are far more paedomorphic, i.e. they retain juvenile ('paedo-morphic') characteristics. It will be apparent that this formulation is almost exactly the opposite of recapitulation, where descendants pass beyond their ancestors, leaving childish characteristics behind. This comes out very clearly in the statement by Brinton, a supporter of the biogenetic law:

> The adult who retains the more numerous fetal, infantile or simian traits, is unquestionably inferior to him whose development has progressed beyond them. . . . Measured by these criteria, the European or white race stands at the head of the list, the African or negro at its foot.
>
> (Brinton 1890, cited in Gould 1977, p. 128)

Given this opposition, one might have thought that supporters of the rival theory would have had a more positive image of blacks; but that did not happen. There was no disagreement about the supposed 'facts' of the inferiority of other peoples. For instance, Havelock Ellis, an early proponent of paedomorphosis, repeated the hoary myth that Africans become dumb with increasing age, while Europeans retain their childish vivacity. Thus the retardation theory merely became an alternative explanation for their inferiority.

The best-known formulation of neoteny was by the Dutch anatomist Louis Bolk, which began to supplant recapitulation during the 1920s and 1930s. Bolk maintained not merely that humans experience increasingly retarded devel-opment in comparison with their animal ancestors, but also that the rates of change differ as between human races – some are more evolved than others. The greater the retardation, and thereby the retention of juvenile characteristics, the more advanced the race. It is in this sense that one has to understand his statement that 'In his fetal development the negro passes through a stage that has already become the final stage for the white man' (Bolk 1926, cited in Gould 1977, p. 135). Bolk was convinced that his theory provided firm biological grounds for dividing races into higher and lower levels. Ashley Montagu (1962) demonstrated that this was a fallacious conclusion. In a table (p. 331) he listed the relative distributions of infantile traits among major human groups, and it becomes immediately apparent that no one group has a monopoly of 'fetalization' when a wider range of characters is taken into account. Yet in the same year[6] a book by the prominent German 'philosophical anthropologist' Arnold Gehlen was republished, entitled *The human being* [Der Mensch]. In it Gehlen provided a detailed exposition of Bolk's theory, which he regarded as having been unduly neglected; nor did he exclude from this Bolk's ideas about the inequality of races. In some of these, notably Australian Aborigines, retardation was said to be be considerably less, and this was interpreted as a race-specific form of development resulting in greater similarity to animals. The same theme was spelled out in more detail as regards Africans:

> The conspicuous race differences in pigmentation, hair, prognathism, as well as in the physiological life course [Lebenstempo] (i.e. more rapid development, shorter period of flowering, rapid decline in the Negro race) may be viewed from the same standpoint. Thereby one could draw an important parallel between, for instance, the much greater similarity to Europeans of the Negro child compared with the adult Negro, and the much greater similarity to humans of the young anthropoid ape.
>
> (Gehlen 1962, p. 112)

Moreover, all the old stereotypes, already peddled by Vogt a century earlier, were rolled out again in support of a totally different theory. The inversion of similarity judgements may be noted: instead of the adult Negro resembling the European child, it is now the Negro child who is supposed to resemble the adult European, albeit in physique rather than mentality. Once again it is the continuity of the unfavourable images that is striking, which appears unrelated to the theories. Recapitulation postulated that blacks remain fixed at an ancestral level, while whites go on developing and thereby overtake them. Neoteny as applied to humans postulated that the development of whites is relatively retarded, so that they retain more paedomorphic characters, while blacks go on developing further. Yet both these opposite theories were put forward as explanations for the inferiority of blacks, a bedrock belief that remained unquestioned. The game of theory was rigged: heads, whites win; tails, blacks lose.

The argument for neoteny was resurrected not long ago by Eysenck (1971). He referred to a number of articles published during the 1950s suggesting an African infant precocity in sensori–motor development (e.g. Géber and Dean 1957; Géber

1958). This led him to propose that such precocity explained the alleged intellectual inferiority of blacks. The key passage runs as follows:

> the observed precocity lasts for about three years, after which time white children overtake the black ones. These findings are important because of a very general law in biology according to which the more prolonged the infancy, the greater in general are the cognitive or intellectual abilities of the species.

(Eysenck 1971, p. 84)

The 'general law' to which Eysenck referred is of course that of neoteny. Now, first of all, the drawing of such inferences from neoteny as regards human behaviour is highly questionable (cf. Gould 1977). Moreover, even if it were defensible, Eysenck's argument could not be sustained, as its assumed empirical basis has collapsed: more recent and better controlled studies have shown that African infant precocity applies only to those skills that have been specifically taught by the caretakers (cf. Super 1981; Bril 1986).

There appears to be no direct link between the early 19th-century claims of African precocity followed by arrested development, and the views expressed by Eysenck. It is intriguing, therefore, that there is a certain similarity between the basic notions put forward by 19th-century writers and a late 20th-century psychologist.

This is an opportune point to go back to a previous generation of psychologists and psychiatrists who, unlike Eysenck, were partly the inheritors of 19th-century thought, and partly influenced by the persuasive writings of the sociologist Lévy-Bruhl.

# 14

# HOW CHILD-LIKENESS LINGERED IN 20TH-CENTURY PSYCHOLOGY

The bearing of biological theories on images of the savage has been described in previous chapters. Vogt, it will be recalled, proposed the following descending scale: Europeans, blacks, idiots and apes. Darwin in one passage linked monkeys, microcephalous idiots and the 'barbarous races of mankind'. Comparisons of this kind were adopted by the emerging science of psychology as it became progressively more oriented towards an evolutionary stance. This was reflected in the ways the sub-divisions of the discipline came to be seen. An early example is that of Wundt (1862: XIV) who then envisaged two main branches of the subject, namely 'the evolutionary history of mind [Seele]' and comparative psychology; the second of these whould deal with differences in the animal kingdom and the races of man. A generation later Charles Peirce (1839–1914), the founder of pragmatism, proposed a classification of the sciences. As far as psychology was concerned, he also suggested two main divisions, the second of which included animal, pathological and race psychology (Vidal 1994). This of course was not an arbitrary categorization, and the supposed 'animality' of the 'lower races' has already been extensively discussed. What may seem stranger today is the coupling of savagery with pathology, to which infancy also came to be added. It was a linkage that had been foreshadowed by the social evolutionists, and was still widely taken for granted during the 1920s. The underlying idea was that savages have less impulse control than civilized people, a characteristic they share with infants. Savages were thought to display openly some of the seamier side of human nature that is suppressed among the civilized, and mental disorder was conceptualized as a *regression* to the features of infancy and savagery. This was expressed very clearly by Rivers (1919, p. 891):

> Of even more interest to the physician should be the study of mental process in rude and backward forms of human society. Much as we may disagree in detail, there is general agreement that in neurosis and psychosis there is in action a process of regression to primitive and infantile states. Anything which helps the physician to a knowledge of the primitive and infantile in man should therefore come within his circle of interests. In so far as the thought and behaviour of savage man

178

are primitive, they furnish material which helps us to understand and deal with the regressive states exhibited by sufferers from disorders of mental function.

Rivers had at the time still been under the influence of social evolutionist ideas, which he later came to abandon.

Within the sphere of child psychology, early writers such as Preyer (1894), Sully (1903) or Stern (1914) often made comparisons between children and savages. The prevailing intellectual climate in psychology was saturated with a cluster of ideas loosely based on evolutionary theories. The same applied to Freud, Jung and their followers, whose theories implied recapitulationism, as has already been noted above. For instance, Fenichel (1945) equated schizophrenic thinking with that of primitives and small children. Such views were by no means confined to psychoanalytically oriented writers. In France, which had been slow to accept Darwinism, several psychologists and psychiatrists discussed such notions extensively and sought to mould them into a more coherent shape.

One of the first to champion evolutionism in French psychology was Henri Piéron (1909, p. 125), who suggested that it would be important to carry out research on the development of primitive children, and

> generally, the study of the mentality of primitive peoples [peuples incultes] compared on the one hand with that of the anthropomorphic apes and on the other with that of civilized peoples [would be desirable], resorting to 'educability' as the method of choice for animals which would not be less precious with humans; such a study would make possible the integration of man into zoological evolution, and enable us to finalise the general sketch of the curve of psychic development.

Piéron also made some bizarre comments in which he mentioned that criminals who dig up corpses are often found to be anosmic. This is not true of primitives, he averred, who have a highly developed sense of smell; yet that of stinking corpses does not affect them, because they are lacking in disgust, 'especially if their life remains very animal-like' (p. 121). Thus he linked, albeit unsystematically in his case, child development, animals and primitives.[1]

A year after Piéron's article was published there appeared Lévy-Bruhl's first book entitled *Les fonctions mentales dans les sociétés inférieures*, not very accurately translated as 'Mental functioning in the lower societies'. This and his subsequent works on this topic made an enormous impact, and the views he expressed have been discussed ever since. His ideas exerted great influence on several prominent psychologists, though not in a way he had intended. The work of Lévy-Bruhl appeared to many psychologists to be admirably suited for the purpose of documenting and confirming the child-likeness of what were by then called 'primitives'.

## Lévy-Bruhl's thesis

In his early formulations Lévy-Bruhl ([1910] 1951, 1922) sought to demonstrate that there is a profound and qualitative difference between the 'pre-logical' mode of thinking of 'primitives' and the logical thinking of 'moderns'. His views triggered debates and disputes about what are now called 'cultural differences in cognition'; these have continued in modified form ever since. As a result of powerful critiques by field anthropologists such as Thurnwald (1928) and especially Evans-Pritchard (1934), Lévy-Bruhl later came to abandon the sharp dichotomy he had originally postulated, and to accept that both modes of thought coexist in varying degrees in all cultures (Lévy-Bruhl [1949] 1975). General accounts of Lévy-Bruhl's work are available elsewhere,[2] and since my aim is to examine certain reactions to his initial position, this alone will be considered more closely.

Lucien Lévy-Bruhl (1857–1939) was trained as a philosopher; in 1900 he was appointed Professor of the History of Philosophy at the Sorbonne. At that time the generally accepted view propounded by the so-called 'English School' of the social evolutionists Tylor and Frazer was that psychological differences between human groups are to be explained in terms of levels of evolutionary stages through which everyone has to pass. According to Tylor and Frazer, the human mind is always and everywhere logical and essentially rational, though working 'in a mental condition of intense and inveterate ignorance' (Tylor [1871] 1958, p. 23).

Lévy-Bruhl was about 50 years old when he had an experience that led him to challenge this view and which determined the direction of his interests for the rest of his life. A friend who was a sinologue sent him a translation of an ancient Chinese text, which in spite of his efforts he felt unable to understand. Consequently he came to ask himself whether there might not be radical variations in modes of thinking, depending not on linear evolutionary stages but on *types of society*. He was influenced by Durkheim's notion of 'collective representations' of social origin, that are seen as imposed on the members of a given society from without.

Ideally this would have involved the construction of a general typology of a multiplicity of 'mentalities', but this was not feasible practically. Such a task would have been beyond the capacities of an individual, and in any case the then available ethnographic resources would have been inadequate. Accordingly, Lévy-Bruhl decided to concentrate on a dichotomy of contrasting types of thought across a wide range of world cultures. This entailed the immense labour of perusing the reports of travellers, missionaries and ethnographers in search of common elements characterizing what he called 'primitive mentality'.[3]

Lévy-Bruhl, as is well known, contrasted the pre-logical mentality of primitives with its antithesis, an occidental mentality. The former he regarded as characterized by indifference to logical contradictions in particular; the latter by rationalistic philosophy and positive science. Since his thesis is frequently misunderstood as attempting to portray two quite different types of *homo* – one *sapiens* and the other not – it is necessary to stress that this was never his intention. He well understood that in their everyday life, primitives are every bit as rational and competent in coping with their environment as occidentals are in relation to theirs. It is not what they are doing, but their *representations* of the world.

It is important to stress that Lévy-Bruhl himself never directly compared savages with children. In the rare instances when he referred to children, he explicitly objected to such comparisons. One passage concerns a report about the Bororo Indians of South America, who beseeched the explorer not to show women his drawings of bull-roarers, since such a sight would kill them:

> Are these [cases] to be explained from a purely psychological point of view, as is so frequently the case, by the association of ideas? Must we say, with de Groot, that it is impossible for them to distinguish a mere resemblance from identity, and admit that primitives suffer from the same illusion as the child who believes her doll to be alive? First of all, however, it is difficult to decide whether the child herself is quite sure of it. Perhaps her belief is part of the game and at the same time sincere, like the emotions of grown-up people at the theatre, shedding real tears about misfortunes which they nevertheless know to be feigned. On the contrary, it is impossible to doubt that the primitives' beliefs which I have just mentioned are serious; their actions prove it. How then can a portrait be 'materially and physically' identified with its original ? To my mind, it is not on account of childish trust in analogy, nor from mental weakness or confusion; it is not due to a naive generalization of animist theory, either. It is because, in perceiving the similitude, as in looking at the original, the traditional collective representations imbue it with the same mystical elements.
>
> (Lévy-Bruhl [1910] 1951, pp. 48–9)

Again, with regard to certain peculiarities of indigenous languages, he made the following comment:

> We may be inclined to say perhaps: 'It is merely a childish way of speaking, not worth the trouble of listening to.' The truth is quite the contrary, however. The naturally versatile and ready-witted mind of the race is reflected in this picturesque language.
>
> (Ibid., p. 167)

Yet in spite of such clear statements, a number of prominent psychologists used Lévy-Bruhl's material as a springboard not only for making comparisons between primitives and children, but often also for emphasizing alleged similarities in their mental processes; and this was extended by some to the mentally ill as well. It may be noted that in seeking to show the parallels between primitive and childish modes of thought, several writers implicitly or explicitly based themselves on a version of recapitulation theory. A clear example is Murphy, who claimed that 'the child . . . recapitulates the character of truly primitive man' (Murphy 1927, p. 103) and tried to support his case by alleged 'facts' of brain development. The views of some of the most prominent figures who were influenced by Lévy-Bruhl in their comparisons of children and primitives will now be sketched.

## Janet and Vygotsky: savages, children and the insane

During the 1920s a number of mainly but not exclusively francophone psychologists were occupied with this theme. They included Henri Wallon (1928) and Jean Piaget (1928). Piaget had a high regard for Lévy-Bruhl, and also at that time broadly accepted the prevailing primitive–child equation. But his analysis of the reasons for the similarity was quite different from that of his contemporaries, being directed at what we would now call socio-cultural factors. His approach was too complex and subtle to lend itself to a brief summary.

Janet was aware of Piaget's ideas, but developed his own very diferent approach. In his early writings Pierre Janet (1859–1947) regarded some mental illnesses as due to 'arrested development', a view criticized by Binet and Simon (1919) as vague and unsatisfactory. Subsequently he put forward a theory of hierarchical evolutionary stages of human behaviour, expounded in a work (Janet 1926, 1928) sub-titled 'studies concerning beliefs and sentiments'. In it he distinguished three broad dispositions labelled respectively as 'superior, average and inferior'. The 'superior' applies to normal civilized humans characterized by 'scientific, logical and moral' conduct. The 'inferior' refers to animal tendencies based on the functioning of the nervous system; their malfunctioning gives rise to organic mental illness. Those of the 'average' are the most puzzling and interesting ones, relating to savages. While to some extent governed by logic and morals, savages are also influenced by inferior needs and passions. These are related to neuroses and other forms of non-organic mental illness, and they manifest themselves most strikingly in the domain of beliefs.

While psychopathology is concerned with abnormalities, there are, Janet states, two other major fields of psychology: namely child psychology and what he called 'sociology'. It is his discussion of 'sociology' that is of primary interest here, since it deals with the ideas of Lévy-Bruhl. Its object is human social conduct which, according to Durkheim, differentiates it from psychology. Janet would have none of that: since humans live in society, all behaviour with the exception of simple reflexes and suchlike is in some way social.

Sociologists such as Durkheim or Lévy-Bruhl, Janet contended, have concerned themselves neither with the 'superior' nor the 'inferior' in the above sense, but with the 'average'. Just as psychopathology had been seduced by suggestive hysterics, so sociology has been conquered by the Arunta of Australia and the North American Indians. Janet then went on to outline Lévy-Bruhl's seemingly startling conclusions before challenging his interpretations.

Lévy-Bruhl, he wrote, attributes the strange beliefs of savages to the institutions of their societies, and that may have a certain influence. But we must remember that small children have egocentric and irrational beliefs; moreover,

> There remains the brutal fact that adult individuals living in our time and in our milieu present under certain circumstances a form of thought and of belief identical to that of small children and of savages. . . . Inversely, one can say that the primitives give us the impression of children or half-crazy people.
>
> (Janet 1926, pp. 240–1)

There follow case-histories to illustrate the parallels. For instance, as regards contradiction, a woman believed that her mother was in Grenoble, and at the same time in Paris under the carpet of a room; and she declared this to have been a sacred revelation. In relation to Lévy-Bruhl's recognition that savages behave sensibly in their ordinary life, he contends that this is equally true of his cases. As an example, he cites a woman who believed herself to be a lioness and accordingly ate photographs of children; yet at mealtimes she refused paper and ate her soup with a spoon.

Janet dismissed the more cautious stance taken by Piaget regarding comparisons between the logic of children and of savages. He maintained that the pre-logicality of primitives corresponds to his own stage of 'assertive belief', i.e. one that is adopted prior to rational reflection. Janet pounced on Lévy-Bruhl's comment to the effect that Africans cannot be troubled to reflect on anything unless forced to do so. From this alleged fact Janet concluded that, contrary to Lévy-Bruhl's interpretation, it is not the collective representations and corresponding institutions that govern the savages' mental processes; rather, the institutions are the *consequences* of the feeble mentality of these Negroes. Janet also drew a distinction between two stages at the 'average' level, a distinction which I must confess is not very clear to me; but he claimed that it is highly relevant to an understanding of the mentally ill, children and primitives:

> The stage of immediate belief, the assertive stage, extends from 3 to 7 years . . . Lévy-Bruhl's Australian savages, whom he calls pre-logical, seem to remain all their life at the assertive stage.
>
> (Janet 1926, p. 331)

In other words, it is a case of 'arrested development'. In his conclusions, Janet summarized the relationships between the three types. The mentally handicapped (débile) person in our society is surrounded by people who think for him and provide him with a set of ready-made beliefs which might give the illusion that he has thought them out for himself. The savage is not surrounded by such individuals, and hence his beliefs are more primitive and absurd. The child is in between the two, getting a great deal from adults; but the main difference is that children change and develop rapidly. According to Janet, it should be a future task of genetic psychology to carry out studies examining these relationships.

Janet's writings, as well as those of Lévy-Bruhl, were among Vygotsky's sources of inspiration. In 1930 he published, jointly with Luria, a monograph with the title *Essays on the development of behaviour: ape, primitive, child.*[4] Although this title is apt to evoke the central theme of the present work, its aims were in fact totally different: namely to discuss the historical conditions of what they called the 'psychological evolution' from the apes up to the higher mental processes found in humans. The first two chapters, authored by Vygotsky, deal with apes and primitives respectively.

Vygotsky characterized the use of tools as the critical evolutionary change among apes, while a different kind of (socio-historical) development occurred among primitives as a function of labour and the use of psychological signs. It is only his notions about primitives that are directly relevant in the present context.

Already in an early paper on what he called the 'cultural development of the child', one can find a comparison between children and primitives:

> Contrary to the magical thinking of primitive man when the connection between ideas is mistaken for the connection between things, in this case the child takes the connection between things for the connection between ideas. In the former case the magical reasoning is due to insufficient knowledge of the laws of nature, in the latter, to insufficient knowledge of its own psychology.
>
> (Vygotsky 1929, p. 425)

According to Vygotsky, both primitives and children at a certain stage engage in magical thinking, but the causes differ. Such comparisons are not infrequent in Vygotsky's writings, and the question has been raised whether they imply an equation of children and primitives. In her insightful discussion of Vygotsky's use of ethnographic material, Scribner (1985) admitted to a certain ambiguity in Vygotsky's writings on the topic; but she nevertheless sought to show that his comparisons between children and primitives do not really mean what they appear to mean on the surface. In support of this contention she advanced a number of arguments: he was not a recapitulationist, nor did he subscribe to a theory of 'culture stages' as did the social evolutionists; moreover, Vygotsky confined his child–primitive comparisons to specific 'functional systems', i.e. to patterns of psychological processes within particular domains. Moreover, she claims that Vygotsky held that 'modern children [are] unlike primitive adults in real life' (Scribner 1985, p. 131).

This defence does not seem to me to be altogether convincing, since one can find passages like the one below in which Vygotsky clearly echoes the old equation of primitives, children and the insane:

There is another very interesting trait of primitive thought that shows us complex thinking in action and points up the difference between pseudo-concepts and concepts. This trait – which Lévy-Bruhl was the first to note in primitive peoples, Storch in the insane, and Piaget in children – is usually called *participation*. The term is applied to the relationship of partial identity or close interdependence established by primitive thought between two objects or phenomena which actually have neither contiguity nor any other recognizable connection. . . .

Primitive peoples also think in complexes, and consequently the word in their languages does not function as the carrier of a concept but as a 'family' name for groups of concrete objects belonging together, not logically, but factually. Storch has shown that the same kind of thinking is characteristic of schizophrenics, who regress from conceptual thought to more primitive levels of mentation, rich in images and symbols. He considers the use of images instead of abstract concepts one of the most distinctive traits of primitive thought. Thus the child, primitive man, and the insane . . . all manifest participation.

(Vygotsky [1934] 1962, pp. 71–2)

It is perhaps more likely that Vygotsky, a radical innovator, was not always consistent in his views. He certainly held that the emergence of what he called 'the higher mental processes' was a result of socio-historical changes and had nothing to do with biology as such. Yet at times he slipped back into a familiar traditional framework of a kind which his work as a whole had been intended to undermine. It is interesting that he adduced the testimony of Piaget, with whom he shared an acceptance of the main Lévy-Bruhlian thesis, though their analyses of the causes of 'primitive mentality' differed considerably.

## Werner: a 20th-century theoretical edifice built from 19th-century materials

Werner bridges the pre- and post-Second World War periods, since his work was begun during the 1920s and was still regarded as a major contribution half a century later. I should explain at the outset that only part, albeit a substantial part of his theory will be considered here. Werner's (1957) 'comparative organismic theory' is a Gestalt-oriented 'genetic' (i.e. developmental) psychology, which holds that development proceeds in a dialectical manner through progressive differentiation. It is of course neither possible nor necessary in the present context to provide much detail about this complex theory. What I am concerned to demonstrate is that Werner displayed a strong tendency to equate 'primitive' forms of mental organizations not merely with those of the child, but also with those of what he called 'primitive' peoples. I shall do so at some length since the theory has been, justifiably, highly regarded and widely cited; but Werner's treatment of 'primitives' has been, unjustifiably in my opinion, widely ignored.

On the very first page of the first introductory chapter Werner's assumptions become manifest, when he refers to 'the comparison of the child, the primitive man, and also the animal with one another and with *mature man*' (Werner 1957, p. 3; my emphasis). As was common in the 19th century, Werner drew inferences about 'primitive thought' from the nature of indigenous languages:

> It is often said that primitive people do not think as logically as civilized people. How could it be otherwise when, for instance, Australian aborigines designate wood and fire by the same name? . . .
> Does this plurivalence in concept or name reveal a logical weakness? It is obvious that the primitive man exhibits a different mode of thinking in his naming of things. But it is pointless merely to define it negatively, from our own standpoint, as representative of an inadequate, un-advanced logic . . . more primitive forms are not so much lacking in logic as based on a logic of a different kind.
>
> (Ibid., p. 15)

Werner listed examples, partly drawn from Lévy-Bruhl, which he claimed violated the premises of Aristotelian logic, whereby supposedly an object cannot be A and B at the same time. Thereby he followed Lévy-Bruhl in committing a fallacy: an object obviously can be both A and B (for example, short and red) logically, but it cannot be both A and non-A (for example, short and long). The examples cited usually involve *physical* as distinct from *logical* impossibilities. Yet in other respects Werner wanted to distance himself from Lévy-Bruhl, stating that such thinking is neither illogical nor 'pre-logical'. Nevertheless, he stressed primitive indifference to contradiction just as much as had Lévy-Bruhl.

Werner also strongly affirmed the existence of a 'primitive mentality'. He claimed that anthropologists who maintain the opposite, namely that all mental differences are due to culture, are guilty of serious misrepresentation:

> Any argument which tends to reduce differences in mentality to differ-ences in culture appears to move in a circle. It fails to recognize that culture is not something that conditions the mentality of the group, but it is the objective aspect of this mentality.
>
> (Ibid., p. 17)

Werner then tried to deal with an objection to the notion of a 'primitive mentality' originally raised against Lévy-Bruhl, namely that primitive thought can be found in advanced cultures. While admitting this, he argued that there is a critical difference, since the primitives are permanently tied to their modes of thinking as a result of a specialized adaptation to their environment, while the 'higher group' creatively expands its thought in the course of development:

> 'The aborigines of Australia and Tasmania' says Duckworth, 'furnish the examples of the greatest concentration of ape-like characters. But we

must not conclude that the aborigines present us with facsimilae of a human ancestor, for these very aborigines are themselves remarkably specialized in adaptation to their surroundings.' From this it may be inferred that the 'primitiveness' found among the more advanced groups is still different from the primitiveness existing in lower civilizations.

(Ibid., p. 19)

Werner then raised the issue of the legitimacy of comparisons between child psychology and ethnopsychology. He argued that they are fully justified, since there are certain 'genetic' (in the sense of 'developmental') parallels between the mentalities of the child and of primitive man. However, he rejected the recapitulation theory as propounded by Stanley Hall. The similarities, he stated at this point, are merely 'formal', and he listed certain obvious differences. Yet in the subsequent discussions such reservations were usually forgotten. Thus he claimed that the western child has greater 'plasticity' than the primitive child, since 'Development among primitive people is characterized on the one hand by precocity and, on the other, by a relatively early arrest of the process of intellectual growth' (ibid., p. 27). Thereby he reverted to 19th-century beliefs,[5] though in a footnote he paid lip-service to more modern ideas by saying that 'these differences should not be interpreted as differences in innate potentialities' (p. 28). Yet in general he stoutly defended comparisons between children, primitives and pathological individuals, much as some of his predecessors described above had done.

Some of the topics covered by Werner will be reviewed to show how in each case he sought to establish the child–primitive link. One of his contributions concerned what he called 'physiognomic perception' characteristic of an early stage of development. He proposed that for children objects are predominantly understood 'through the motor and affective attitude of the subject. . . . Things perceived in this way may appear "animate" and, even though actually lifeless, seem to express some inner form of life' (p. 69). Werner claimed that physiognomic perception is more salient in the 'primitive world' as compared with our more usual 'geometric-technical' kind of perception. This helps to account for animism and anthropomorphic conceptions of nature: 'Everything is understood to behave dynamically, quite apart from and prior to the differentiation between object and subject' (p. 80). Perceptual processes of primitives are highly syncretic and 'percepts are deeply conditioned by emotional and motor behavior' (p. 83). This account is strikingly similar to that put forward by Lévy-Bruhl, who wrote 'les primitifs ne perçoivent pas comme nous' ([1910] 1951, p. 40), their perception being suffused with affect and mystical elements, as contrasted with the conceptual and objective perception of Europeans.

Again like Lévy-Bruhl, Werner constantly sought to buttress his arguments with illustrative anecdotes drawn from ethnographic reports: primitive Veddas 'when angry throw themselves on the ground and thrash about with their legs just like children' (Werner 1957, p. 83); similarly Andaman Islanders and Negritoes in the

Philippines. In addition, Werner claimed that verbal expressions support this interpretation; for example, an Aranda woman pining after a stolen object will say that her bowels long for it; or in the Congo the phrase 'his heart is hung fast to his ribs' indicates courage. However, Werner was content to ignore parallel expressions in European languages such as 'her heart was broken' or 'he has guts'.

Other characteristics allegedly shared by children and primitives are 'diffuse forms of sensori-motor organization'. This refers to an inability to conceive of things outside the concrete situation in which they are embedded. It would be redundant to cite his numerous examples, with one exception: children as well as primitives are apt to produce what are known as 'chain-type drawings', in which the spatial relationships between the parts are ignored or distorted. Specific parts that appear salient are reproduced without relating them spatially to others; often a serial sequence or a combination of incompatible angles of view results. Thus he mentioned that South Sea Islanders and children represent a cube by five squares.[6]

Werner claimed that this 'peculiarity of the primitive mode of experience' (p. 135) is reflected in the languages of primitives. They will have different words for the successive phases of an action, where in Indo-Germanic languages there are grammatical changes. They have names for specific objects, but not for the general class of which these objects constitute a part; for example, specific colours, but no name for 'colour'; names for particular peaks, but not for the mountain range as a whole. 'What appears as a self-subsistent, rigid unity to the mind of the primitive man submits to the domination of a larger inclusive whole only with extreme reluctance' (p. 139). Here again, Werner was rehearsing hoary notions of the past: the paucity of abstract terms in primitive languages had long been regarded as evidence for the poverty of primitive thought.

According to Werner, the primitive world is dynamic and ever-changing, so that 'the things of the world exhibit this or that property, depending on the changing frame of activity in which they are bound fast' (p. 140). He called this the 'fluidity of meaning in things' (p. 141) which is supposed to result, in ways that are not explained, in a relatively high sensitivity to change. From this, he concluded, stems their rigid adherence to customs and practices: any changes create anxiety and are viewed as unlucky, fraught with dangerous consequences. This was said to account for the conservatism of primitive societies; but if, as he claimed, their phenomenal world is ever-changing, how is it that they can perceive their customs as constant?

Finally, I shall examine Werner's concept of syncretic versus diffuse organization. In advanced persons, as distinct from children and primitive individuals, percepts as contrasted with imagination are felt to be external and independent of ego. Primitives are said to be in an intermediate state of 'syncretism', of which the eidetic image is a prime example. Primitives are subject to the 'compulsion of visions' which are highly valued. There is also the 'amazing sensuous memory' of the primitive who thus is very like an eidetic child. Werner cited Galton's report of an Eskimo who was able to draw a remarkably accurate map of a coastline extending over 960 nautical miles (Galton [1883] 1928, p. 72). So-called 'naturalistic art' of primitives like Eskimos or Bushmen are based on eidetic images. Generally, Werner stated, percepts and images tend to be closely related if not confounded in the primitive, and invested with emotional loading. Things are exaggerated in memory by this affective element, also strongly present in children, who draw those things large that are important to them. A primitive syncretism of image is also found as a feature in such pathologically regressive types as the hysteric or the schizophrenic: 'Primitive images, like primitive perceptions, are much more undifferentiated than their intellectualized counterparts' (Werner 1957, p. 159) and thus not merely syncretic but diffuse: 'In many primitive stories there is little distinction between what is essential in the situation and what is not' (p. 160).

With regard to the last observation, one is led to wonder whether Werner had read many 'primitive stories' with a sufficient knowledge of the culture to decide what is or is not 'essential'.

The wonderful memory of primitives which he mentioned is also an old chestnut going back centuries. But the most telling instance of confusion relates to what he said about drawings and eidetic imagery, where he referred to Jaensch. If primitives are *Eidetikers*, why is it that they produce chain-type drawings? In addition, to try and explain the Eskimo skill in drawing maps as due to a 'sensuous memory' linked to an eidetic capacity is absurd: how could one form an eidetic image of a vast coastline?

It would be possible to continue at length to deal with other topics such as 'primitive notions of space and time', 'classification and naming', the 'structure of thought in primitive man' and so on, but it would serve no useful purpose. Enough has been outlined to show that the tendency to bracket primitives with children runs as a pervasive theme through Werner's exposition of his theory. It is all the more remarkable, therefore, that the many relatively recent discussions of Werner's theoretical edifice almost invariably omit any critical discussion of his juxtaposition of children and primitives. For instance, Langer (1970) contributed a whole chapter in the prestigious *Manual of child psychology* to Werner's ideas. Yet there is no mention whatsoever of Werner's key postulate of the existence of a 'primitive mentality'. The only reference to what, significantly, Langer called 'nonliterates' occurs in the following passage:

> The general idea to be drawn from all these considerations is that childhood, nonliterate and schizophrenic activities are not assumed to be synonymous with primitive stages of development.
>
> (Langer 1970, p. 748)

This sanitized version is disingenuous, and certainly very misleading.

Finally, it is an intriguing question how Werner came to acquire the old-fashioned ethnocentric views so prominently present in an otherwise highly respectable theory, and politely ignored by his followers. The answer is that his original formulation dates back to the 1920s when he first published his *Introduction to developmental psychology* (Werner 1926).[7] At that time, as is clearly evident from the earlier part of this chapter, the conviction still largely prevailed that children, primitives and the mentally ill share many important psychological characteristics. These notions were supported by old-style ethnographies, whose authors themselves usually subscribed to the notion of 'primitive childishness'. They were therefore apt to select and present their material accordingly. In order to test this interpretation I arranged Werner's ethnographic references, numbering over 300, in terms of their dates of publication. It turned out that about 70 per cent of them had appeared prior to 1920 (25 per cent before 1900), and only 30 per cent between 1920 and 1940; not a single one was later than that. This seems to confirm that Werner was misled by his sources, and unable or unwilling to correct this either in his first English edition (1940), or in the revised edition (1948) that was reprinted twice.

Following Werner, what one hopes will be the last gasp of claims that the primitive is like a child was advanced by an anthropologist who based himself on Piagetian theory.

## Hallpike: on the pre-operative primitive

From the inter-war years onwards the new generation of field anthropologists, who lived among the peoples they studied, were sceptical of the views of Lévy-Bruhl. Moreover, they also questioned the claims of psychologists who applied their intelligence tests to non-literate peoples and on that basis declared them to be intellectually inferior. As one of them put it, 'Most tests seem to contradict completely the knowledge which the anthropologist has gained of their cultural achievements and their intellectual capacity' (Nadel 1939, p. 185). After the Second World War very few if any reputable anthropologists would have countenanced any comparison of the intelligence of non-literate peoples with that of European children. The most notable exception is Hallpike (1979).

Hallpike is critical of Lévy-Bruhl, but his critique is chiefly focused on Lévy-Bruhl's interpretations of phenomena: 'if we substitute the term "pre-operatory" for "pre-logical" in his work, many of his observations on primitive thought have some justification' (Hallpike 1979, p. 50). Several passages in the book refer to Werner, whom he cites in support of his own thesis. Like Werner, Hallpike himself seeks to explain 'primitive thought' by means of developmental psychology, basing himself not on Werner's theory but on that of Piaget. Here it is only necessary to mention that Piaget envisaged four main developmental stages in approximate chronological order: sensory-motor (birth to 2 years); pre-operatory (about 2–7 years); concrete operational (about 7–11 years), and finally formal operational (about 11 years onwards).

Hallpike contends that the cognitive capacities of most primitive individuals do not develop beyond the pre-operatory stage. This was precisely what Janet, in different terminology, had also claimed half a century earlier. Moreover, Hallpike's fundamental argument is also identical with that of both Janet and Werner:

> the collective representations of a society must themselves reflect or manifest, in their basic cognitive aspects, the level of cognitive development of the great majority of the adult members of that society.
>
> (Hallpike 1979, p. 32)

While there are faint echoes of the 19th-century doctrine of 'arrested development' here, the differences are more marked. 'Arrested development' was supposed to be biologically determined, while Hallpike ascribes it to environmental influences and assumes no innately determined barrier to further development under alternative circumstances. In the course of his detailed and lengthy exposition he deploys a massive apparatus of scholarship, and unlike most of his predecessors he has many nice things to say about primitive peoples. However, the bottom line is still a comparison between primitive adults and European children:

> One of the great mistakes of anthropologists, both in the 19th century and today, is to suppose that there is a contradiction between saying that the cognitive processes of primitive man are more childlike than those of educated men, and that they can also attain more complex and profound representation of reality than those of which children are capable.
>
> (Ibid., p. 39)

One could document Hallpike's views in more detail, but I shall give only one more example. He presents a dichotomous list of eleven rational attributes and their non-rational counterparts, stressing that several of these can apply equally to primitives and to educated and civilized members of our society. The remaining pairs, where the non-rational is confined to primitives, are as follows: sanity versus insanity/absurdity; wisdom versus folly; objectivity versus subjectivity; articulate versus inarticulate; discussion versus violence. In spite of the protestations, this is a very dismal as well as highly questionable picture.

An extensive critique of Hallpike's thesis would not be appropriate here, and in any case others as well as myself have discussed it elsewhere (e.g. Jahoda 1982; Lave 1981; Shweder 1982). Let me just say that, in spite of Hallpike's pleading to the contrary, the statement that the mental capacity of most primitive adults is no greater than that of European children aged about 7 is as absurd as it sounds. What is interesting in the present context is the fact that even in the second half of the 20th century the old notion of the child-likeness of savages could still be seriously argued by a scholar.

## The relativity of 'child-likeness'

The whole issue of savage–child comparisons has been extensively discussed by Lévi-Strauss (1949, pp. 122–3), who described it as a 'subjective illusion' and went on to explain:

> It is not surprising that . . . differences strike us more than similarities, so much so that, for any given society, it is always their own children who offer the most convenient point of comparison with strange customs and attitudes. Modes of life very remote from our own always appear to us, and very naturally so, as puerile.

Before concluding, I should perhaps clarify my own position, since the discussion may have conveyed the impression that I regard the whole issue as a mere pseudo-problem. This is not the case – the problem is real, but it is one that has in the past often been bedevilled by the image of the 'inferior' and dominated 'Other' as childish. This image was created, and then reinforced, by the perplexity of early travellers and ethnographers when they encountered peoples whose mental world was totally strange to them; and the 'child' trope came readily to hand in the attempt to make sense of it. Lévy-Bruhl, in spite of having been an armchair scholar, had the great merit of seeking to interpret the mental processes of 'the Others' without reducing them to just childishness. Those like Janet or Wallon, who also lacked any first-hand knowledge, not only took their cue from Lévy-Bruhl but equated 'pre-logicality' with childishness which he had explicitly denied. By accepting the traditional 'child' image, they were misled into con-structing theoretical schemes that were misconceived. On the other hand, Piaget followed Lévy-Bruhl more consistently by proposing that people in traditional cultures are *constrained* in their thinking within the bounds created by their cultural environment. Evans-Pritchard (1937, p. 338) expressed this lucidly in his discussion of Azande ideas about their poison oracle and the reason why they cannot see its futility:

> Their blindness is not due to stupidity, for they display great ingenuity in explaining away the failures and inequalities of the poison oracle and experimental keenness in testing it. It is due rather to the fact that their intellectual ingenuity and experimental keenness are conditioned by patterns of ritual behaviour and mystical belief. Within the limits set by these patterns they show great intelligence, but it cannot operate beyond these limits. Or, to put it another way: they reason excellently in the idiom of their beliefs, but they cannot reason outside, or against their beliefs because they have no other idiom in which to express their thoughts.

However, later critics (e.g. Gellner 1973) have shown that even Evans-Pritchard exaggerated the rigidity of the boundaries constraining the thinking of people in pre-literate cultures.

Nonetheless, it would be idle to deny that modes of thought (though almost certainly not basic cognitive processes) differ across cultures, and these differences have been and continue to be extensively discussed, but no longer in terms of 'childishness'.

Theories have also ceased to operate with simplistic dichotomies such as 'civilized' versus 'primitive', which tacitly assume – as did the early Piaget – a normative rational European adult as the hidden *tertium quid*; as has often been shown, such a European is a mere man of straw. Anthropologists have concentrated mainly on the content of adult thought, while cultural and cross-cultural psychologists have been mainly concerned with cognitive development. Moreover, there has been considerable convergence in their respective approaches.[8]

Today, traditional societies, such as the Azande used to be, have become extremely rare. Such intellectual bounds within which they were once to some extent confined have burst, and it has become evident that all peoples have much the same latent potential.

# Part IV

# PERSPECTIVES AND INTERPRETATIONS

# 15

# IMAGES MIRRORED AT THE POPULAR LEVEL

While there are many scattered accounts of particular aspects of popular images, detailed systematic surveys of the whole area seem to be lacking. Moreover, the existing accounts do not correspond to the particular conceptual framework adopted here. The topic is an important one for understanding how certain images, such as that of blacks as monkeys, have persisted. Hence without presuming to fill this gap comprehensively, I shall seek to indicate at least in a general way how the images came to be diffused among people at large. The discussion will focus in the main on the period after the middle of the 19th century, when the spread of literacy facilitated communication and propaganda. This is of course not to say that the images had previously been confined to a small specialized elite. Stories told by travellers and sailors, who had been in direct contact with savages, are likely to have percolated in the first instance to the populations of maritime towns, and subsequently beyond. Miner (1972, p. 89) noted that 'Certain images constantly recur in the naturalistic description of savages . . . dirt and darkness, bestial appearance, sexuality, and especially cannibalism'. He went on to document the ways in which these themes were reflected in 16th- and 17th-century literature and drama.

During the latter part of the 18th century the heated debates about slavery must have resonated through much of the population. Travel literature about savages flourished, though Samuel Johnson did not favour it:

> Johnson: There can be little entertainment in such books; one set of savages is like another.
> Boswell: I do not think the people of Otaheité can be reckoned savages.
> Johnson: Don't cant in defence of savages.
> Boswell: They have the art of navigation.
> Johnson: A dog or a cat can swim.
> Boswell: They carve very ingeniously.
> Johnson: A cat can scratch, and a child with a nail can scratch.
>                         (Boswell [1777] 1909, Vol. II, pp. 532–3)

Johnson's comments epitomized the image of savages as uniform in character, comparable to animals and children, and therefore of little interest to him; but his attitude was unusual, judging by the popularity of the numerous accounts of voyages then circulating among the reading public. The contents of such works, usually including descriptions of savages, are likely to have filtered down to the common people in simplified and probably more colourful versions. More directly, various entertainments featuring 'tame' savages of a kind that, as will be shown, became even more widespread during the 19th century no doubt had their effects. Among the most important factors was probably imaginative literature, above all *Robinson Crusoe*, already cited in connection with cannibalism. Published in 1719, Daniel Defoe's book had enormous success and was translated into several European languages. The relationship depicted between Crusoe and his man Friday typified that prevailing at the time, and long thereafter, between Europeans and savages. Defoe had numerous imitators who created 'Robinsonades'. A German version first came out in 1779 and went through numerous editions, one in 1848, from which the following key passage is taken:

*Father* When the joy about his fortunate rescue was over, he began to reflect on his unhappy state. He looked around; but there was nothing except wild bushes and trees that bore no fruit! Nowhere he saw anything that could have led him to suppose that this country was inhabited by humans.

That was really a frightful thought for him, that he should live all alone in a strange country! But even more hair-raising was the further thought: what if there were wild animals or savage people here, from whom one could not feel safe for a moment?

*Fritzchen* Are there also savage peoples, father?

*Johannes* Yes, Fritz! Have you not heard that yet! There are – who knows how far from here – such people who are as wild as beasts.

*Gottlieb* Who go almost entirely naked; imagine that, Fritzchen!

*Dietrich* Yes, and who don't understand anything, who don't build houses, don't plant gardens and cannot plow any field.

*Lotte* And who eat uncooked meat and raw fish; I have certainly heard it! Isn't that so father, did you not tell us about it?

*Johannes* Yes, and what do you think: the poor people don't even know who has created them, because they have never had a teacher who told them.

*Dietrich* That's also why they are so barbaric. Imagine, some of them eat human flesh!

*Fritzchen* Ugh! The horrible people!

*Father* The unfortunate people! you wanted to say. It is enough misfortune for the poor rogues, that they are stupid and have grown up like beasts.

(Campe [1779] 1848, cited in Kappeler 1992, pp 58–9)

These brief passages, it will be noted, contain practically the whole gamut of images previously reviewed: nakedness, beastliness, unsuitable food including cannibalism, and there is even an echo of child-likeness in as much as they are incapable and have never been taught anything. The one aspect that distinguishes it from the more common vilifications is the missionary tone of pity rather than revulsion; but even that is ambivalent, since they are described as 'poor rogues'. No less a figure than Goethe commented that the book had been of inestimable value for children, and was their delight and bible. This evidently was one of the ways in which the images came to be diffused among the young.

There is clearly a great deal more to learn about earlier periods, but they are unlikely to offer such a wealth of material as the decades following the middle of the 19th century. I shall in due course return to a consideration of the factors that seem to have been responsible for that surge. For the present it is necessary to briefly mention some classificatory problems. One of these stems from the fact that the distinction between 'scholarly' or 'scientific' and 'popular' is far from clear-cut. For instance, Virey was certainly taken seriously as a scientist by his contemporaries, and his ideas were therefore discussed under that rubric. However, he later came to be described by the French anthropologist Paul Topinard as a 'vulgarisateur' (1885a, p. 85). Similarly Schweinfurth, who figured in a previous chapter, was not only regarded as an authoritative scientist, but his book reached a wide public. Another marginal case is that of the notorious racist James Hunt, founder of the London Anthropological Society. While its declared object was 'to establish a *de facto* science of man', in practice Hunt used it to propagate his ideas. Since these ideas were essentially derivative, he will be dealt with here.

It must be stressed that the material presented below in no way constitutes a representative sample – obtaining that would be an enormous task well beyond the capacity of a single researcher. It is no more than a selection of relevant passages which I came across in the course of my reading. Nevertheless, it should help to convey at least a rough picture of the various ways in which the images seem to have percolated to the population at large.

## Writings of explorers and missionaries

Books by explorers were exceedingly popular with the Victorian reading public, and Brantlinger (1985, p. 176) suggests that they 'exerted an incalculable influence on British culture and the course of modern history'. While this may be going rather far, there is little doubt that the manner in which most of the explorers described the savages must have left its mark. This applied even to the explorers who described their adventures in letters to *Nature*; before becoming the august scientific journal it is now, letters such as the one from which an extract is cited below were a regular feature:

> I could fill volumes were I to relate all my experiences at the court of this
> wild brown Caesar [the Mombuttu King Munsa] covered all over with

red copper spangles, and looking like a well-furnished kitchen; of his numerous wives, painted in all colours of the rainbow; of his immense palace, resembling a railway station. . . . It would be impossible for me, however, to pass over in silence the horrible cannibalism which is here, as well as among the real Niam-Niams, everywhere in vogue. Munsa dines off human flesh every day of his life.

(Nature 1871, 3, p. 215)

One of the most popular of the authors catering to the taste for the exotic was Henry Stanley, probably partly owing to his 'folksy' style – his *In darkest Africa* sold 150,000 copies in English alone. Below is a passage from *Through the dark continent* where he describes in typically flamboyant manner his repeated encounters with alleged cannibals, while travelling down the Congo river. Seeing some men on the bank waving their spears, he reports them as shouting:

> Meat! meat! Ah! ha! We shall have plenty of meat! Bo-bo-bo-bo, Bo-bo-bo-bo-o-o!
>
> Undoubtedly these must have been relatives of the terrible 'Bo-bo-bo's' . . . we thought, as with one mind we rose to respond to this rabid man-eating tribe. Anger we had none for them. It seemed to me so absurd to be angry with people who looked upon one only as an epicure would regard a fat capon. Sometimes also a faint suspicion came to my mind that this was all but part of a hideous dream. Why was it that I should be haunted with the idea that there were human beings who regarded me and my friends only in the light of meat? Meat! *We?* Heavens! what an atrocious idea!

(Stanley 1878, Vol. II, p. 201)

It sounds like a caricature of a boys' adventure story, but in reality it was less amusing: on mere suspicion of being cannibals, Stanley shot them. On another similar occasion he mused that he would have to sacrifice either a few of the men, women or children who were with him, or a few cartridges; nobly, he decided on the cartridges. It is astonishing that a recent writer expressed the view that 'Stanley was prudent to take no chances, to shoot first and ask questions later' (McLynn 1992, p. 270).

While other explorers wrote in a more dignified way, the contents were usually of a similar character. Among the most prolific was Richard Burton, already mentioned in connection with cannibalism.[1] According to him, 'The African preserves the instincts of infancy in the higher races' (1860, Vol. I, p. 147), and this was later elaborated: '[The East African] seems to belong to one of those childish races which, never rising to man's estate, fall like worn-out links from the great chain of animated nature' (Burton 1860, Vol. II, p. 324). The imagery of the Great Chain is used in poetic phrasing to suggest, as was not infrequent at the time, that savages are doomed to die out.

Another widely read explorer, who followed some twenty years later in Burton's footsteps, was Joseph Thomson. The way he perceived many Africans is shown by the following passage:

> [The Wakhutu] are now as Burton found them, one of the most degraded tribes to be found in Africa. With their black sooty skins and miserable withered bodies, they present . . . a picture of apathy. . . . Nothing disgusted me more than to see them gather round me in crowds, watching me with an idiotic lack-lustre gaze. . . . Nothing I could show them elicited the least mark of surprise . . . and without doubt they were beneath the monkey in the extent of their curiosity.
>
> (Thomson 1881, Vol. I, pp. 159–60)

Seemingly, Thomson had been disappointed by their failure to be impressed by the marvels he showed them. It is perhaps worth juxtaposing the above with a piece from a book entitled *Missionary heroes in Africa* intended for children, with the evocative sub-title 'True stories of the intrepid bravery and stirring adventures of missionaries with uncivilized man, wild beasts and the forces of nature'. One of the stories quotes a letter from a missionary uncle to his nephews and nieces:

> Fancy a set of hideous savages regarding your uncle as a strange, outlandish creature, frightful to behold! 'Are those your feet, white man?' 'No, gentlemen, they are not. They are my sandals.' 'But, do they grow on your feet?' 'No, gentlemen, they do not. I will show you.' So I would unlace a boot. A roar of astonishment followed when they saw my blue sock, as they thought my feet must be blue and toeless.
>
> (Lambert 1909, pp. 50–1)

Here the 'hideous' savages, ironically addressed as 'gentlemen', are ridiculed *because* of their curiosity. There are of course numerous cases of such inconsistencies, not merely between different writings but often by the same author. For instance, Lord Lugard's belief that Africans are children was mentioned in Chapter 11. Yet he appears to have attributed to these children an acute grasp of the British class system: 'To maintain [European prestige] a missionary must, above all things, be a gentleman; for no one is more quick to recognize a real gentleman than the African savage' (Lugard 1893, Vol. I, p.74).

It seems to me that in placing so much emphasis on explorers, Brantlinger tends to underestimate the role of the missionaries in shaping opinions and images. There was an extensive literature, examined by Moorhouse (1973), aimed in no small part at the young. It consisted of periodicals, books (e.g. *Among the cannibals of New Guinea*), and even games for children. This material had a very wide circulation. For instance, a book sub-titled *Thirty years among South Sea cannibals* was a story especially 'told for young folks'. In 1902 it was in its eleventh edition, totalling 68,000 copies. This missionary had left for Australia in 1858, and his first letter to the church at home contained the following passages:

> We found the Tannese to be painted savages, enveloped in all the superstitions and wickedness of Heathenism. All the men and children go in a state of nudity. The older women wear grass skirts, and the young women and girls, grass or leaf aprons like Eve in Eden.

Subsequently he described their frequent warfare and went on:

> In one case, of which we obtained certain information, seven men were killed in an engagement; and, according to Tannese custom, the warriors and their friends feasted on them at the close of the fray, the widows of the slain being also strangled to death, and similarly disposed of. . . . It is said that the habitual Cannibal's desire for human flesh becomes so horrible that he has been known to disinter and feast upon those recently buried.[2]
>
> (Paton 1902, pp. 59, 61–2)

The depiction of blacks in comic books was almost invariably unflattering. A particularly crass example in a 1929 Dutch book bears the caption 'A man-eater'. It shows a humanoid creature on all fours, with two large fangs and holding a bone in its left hand. It also has a rudimentary tail, reminiscent of the Niam-Niam.[3]

All this must have had a very substantial impact in transmitting the dominant images. Even in less sensational writings the prejudices of some missionaries were conveyed to the young. In one book especially written for boys who might consider contributing to the 'moral and spiritual regeneration of Africa', the author suggested that 'the darker the skin, the deeper the degradation' (cited in Moorhouse 1973, p. 164).

As Cairns (1965) pointed out, missionaries were faced with a dilemma when addressing their audiences at home. If those who were sympathetic to the savages presented them in the light of 'children of nature', people might ask themselves why one should disturb such an idyllic existence and withdraw their support. Hence most felt obliged to stress the negative, the savages' ignorance, their lack of morals and pervasive superstitious fears, all evils from which they had to be freed. Others, who seemingly disliked and despised those they had come to teach, had no such problems in presenting them as evil wretches. An example of this can be found in a relatively recent collection of stories about missionaries, one of whom went to Madagascar in 1907, and described the Anativolo people as follows:

> Sly, lazy, filthy in person and morals, brutal, cunning, superstitious, they were creatures of fear and elemental passions, haunted by their dread of

vindictive and malignant spirits, everyone loaded with charms either to protect themselves or to strike with evil.

(Hemmens 1945, p. 61)

This man complained that the people were not keen to hear him preach, which is understandable. Eventually he succeeded in attracting them by obtaining a gramophone, and playing them Harry Lauder records!

Henry Drummond was an altogether different person, an evangelical Christian who had travelled widely. He sought to reconcile Christianity with evolution and is well known in this connection for his *Ascent of man* (1894). An earlier work of his began as follows:

> It is a wonderful thing to start from the civilization of Europe . . . and work your way into that unknown land . . . meeting tribes which have no name, speaking tongues which no man can interpret. . . . It is a wonderful thing to look at this weird world of human beings – half animal half children, wholly savage and wholly heathen.
>
> (Drummond 1888, p. 4)

Though clearly kindly and relatively liberal, Drummond's vision was totally ethnocentric: he perceived the tribes as lacking names and intelligible languages, even the animal and child tropes were applied, and the whole thing was 'weird'. Hence not merely writers who denigrated the savages, but also those who were on the whole well disposed, served to create or reinforce the central images of the savage. The missionaries, however noble their intentions, did have a lot to answer for.

## Savages in popular science, fiction and the press

The 19th century, with its zest for 'improvement' and for the creation of an educated public that would appreciate the contribution of science to 'progress', witnessed a mushrooming of journals, societies and lectures dedicated to diffusion of scientific ideas among the general public. In Britain this was epitomized by the foundation, in 1831, of the British Association for the Advancement of Science. There were of course numerous others, among them the Ethnological Society of London which was founded in 1843 and whose aim was the study 'of the varieties of Mankind'. It was predominantly under the influence of the monogenist James Pritchard, and its perspective was primarily philological and historical. While its 'Proceedings' naturally reflected the prevailing stereotypes to some extent, its tone was relatively restrained. One of its members from 1854 was James Hunt, who was to become one of the most vociferous propagandists for extreme racist views. In 1863 he, together with some other members, broke away to found the Anthropological Society of London and became its first president. His ostensible reason for the secession was the move by the Ethnological Society to admit ladies to its meetings, but the real reason was ideological (cf. Burrow 1966, p. 121).

Hunt's inspiration came from Robert Knox, the Edinburgh professor of anatomy whose career had been shattered by the Burke and Hare affair. Knox, regarded by Philip Curtin (1965, p. 377) as the 'real founder of British racism', was a complicated person who in his book on *The races of men* (1850) proclaimed the inferiority of blacks, and yet was an opponent of colonialism. He gave numerous popular lectures on the theme of race which, according to his Preface, is all-important in human affairs (cf. Collinson 1990). Hunt himself was essentially a publicist who trawled assiduously through the publications of others, seeking out ammunition for his racist stance. The main theme of his writings concerned the *animality* of blacks, most extensively treated in his essay 'On the Negro's place in nature' (1865). Some of the salient passages from this tirade will be summarized or cited, omitting numerous repetitions, so as to convey the unpleasant flavour of his smears. An underlying assumption derived from Vogt should initially be noted: men, women and children display an increasing resemblance to apes, in that order.

The pelvis of the male Negro is said to resemble closely that of their lower mammalia, while the shortened humerus of the Negress appears as 'a return to the animal form' (p. 15). African women generally are very inferior beings, as shown by 'their very virtues, with their affections and their industry, [which] are those of well trained domestic animals' (p. 46). The Negro brain is like that of European females or children, 'while the Negress approaches the ape still nearer' (p. 17). All this means that efforts to civilize the Negro are bound to be futile – there is no point in trying to civilize creatures that are so ape-like.

Hunt's attitude to slavery is of particular interest. Generally, even racist writers felt themselves obliged to make appropriate noises about their abhorrence of the slave-trade, and Hunt at first was no exception. In his Introductory address (1863a, p. 4) at the first meeting of the Anthropological Society of London, he had this to say:

> I would therefore express the hope that the objects of this Society will never be prostituted to such an object as the support of the slave-trade, with all its abuses.

Much the same pious litany can be found in the 1865 essay (p. 54):

> No one can be more conscious of the horrors of the 'slave trade' as conducted at this time. Nothing can be worse for Africa generally than the continual capture of innocent men and women by brutal Europeans. Few things can be more horrible than the manner in which it is attempted to carry these people across the Atlantic.

All very noble and moving sentiments, which might lead one to imagine that at least in this respect Hunt's heart was perhaps in the right place. But it is hard to reconcile this with what he had penned on the immediately preceding page:

> Our Bristol and Liverpool merchants, perhaps, helped to benefit the race when they transplanted some of them to America; and our mistaken legislature has done the Negro race much injury by their absurd and unwarrantable attempts to prevent Africa from exporting her worthless or surplus population.

Although Hunt was probably the outstanding popularizer of scientific racism, he was by no means the only one. The theme of the animality of blacks percolated increasingly into the semi-scientific and popularizing literature of the period, serving to strengthen existing preconceptions. The traveller and writer Winwood Reade provided a condensed version of prevailing ideas in his *Savage Africa* (1863 pp. 508–9; my emphasis):

> It has been discovered that . . . the growth of the brain in the negro, as in the ape, is sooner arrested than in those of our race; that its convolutions are less numerous and more massive; that . . . the brain itself has a smoky tint.
>
> Therefore, in the muzzle-like extension of the jaws, in the manual application of the foot, and in the early cessation of brain growth, the negro, speaking physically, approaches the ape.
>
> In his flattened nose, elongated cranium, simplicity of cerebral convolution, rounded larynx, and less strongly marked curves of the vertebral column, the negro approaches the child; for all these features are found in the foetus or child of the Aryan race in its different periods of development.
>
> And in the curvature of his arteries, in the flatness of his cornea, in the feebleness of his muscles, in his general lack of enthusiasm, and love of repose, the negro presents the characteristics of old age.
>
> *Thus it has been proved by measurements, by microscopes, by analyses, that the typical negro is something between a child, a dotard and a beast. I cannot struggle against these sacred facts of science.*

The final paragraph implies regret at having to say such unpleasant things, but he passes the responsibility on to unassailable scientific authority.

At about the time when Hunt joined the Ethnological Society, Joseph Arthur de Gobineau wrote his book on *The inequality of human races* (1853). When it first appeared his work received little attention, but it subsequently became immensely popular, going through many editions. Here is an extract from his characterization of what he called 'the Melanesian variety':

> The Melanesian variety is the humblest and lies at the bottom of the scale. The character of animality imprinted on the form of its

pelvis imposes their destiny on them, from the moment of conception.
. . .

> All nourishments are good for him, none disgusts him . . . what he
> wants is eating, eating to excess, with fury; there is no decaying carcass
> unworthy of being crammed into his stomach. It is the same with smells,
> and his sensuality accommodates itself not only to the crudest, but the
> most odious ones.
>
> (Gobineau [1853] 1967, p. 205)

Although Gobineau did not mention him, this sketch seems to owe much to
Virey; and as regards smell and taste he referred to Pruner-Bey. Through numerous writings of this kind the notion of the 'animality' of savages, and particularly
blacks, came to percolate wide sections of the educated public. These ideas
gained further dissemination in encyclopaedias, such as the *Britannica* already
mentioned (p. 124). Similarly, the first edition of *Larousse* included the following
passages:

> The colouring of the skin is not the most characteristic difference which
> exists between the black species and the white species. The anatomical
> structure offers an interest of quite another order of importance, since it
> approaches the Negro almost as closely to the orang-outan as to the
> white or caucasian species. . . .
>
> The Hottentot speaks only with difficulty, especially because of the
> oblique forward angle of his teeth; he clucks almost like a Guinea-fowl,
> which provides again a manifest relationship to the orang which emits
> muffled clucks.
>
> (*Larousse* 1866–76, article on Nègre)

*Larousse* explicitly invoked the authority of Virey, and the remarks about Hottentot
speech echo those of travellers in earlier centuries.[4]

Turning now to fiction, this can be dealt with in summary fashion, since there
exists a substantial literature dealing with the topic.[5] It should come as no surprise
that, by and large, the representation of savages mirrors the images already
discussed at some length. The major emphases are on simian features, unbridled
sexuality and, to a somewhat lesser extent, cannibalism. Interestingly, Cohen
(1980, p. 284) comments that French 'Colonial novels in the interwar years were
particularly powerful in conveying an image of African savagery and bestiality;
their accusations of black cannibalism were even stronger than those made prior
to the colonial era'. French novels, more so than British ones, deal with black
concubines of colonial officers. They are portrayed as animalized: 'the black
woman is at best a "gentil animal" bursting with physical vitality but devoid of
mind; at worst she is "la bête humaine à son plus bas degré"' (Steins 1972, p. 91).
Viewed as incapable of any proper feelings, she is painted as though she were not
really a person at all. Since at least some of the writers had themselves experienced

life in the colonies, this was probably a veridical account of the way the women were regarded and treated.[6]

The negative images of savages were not confined to adult literature, and in the age of imperialism they also frequently appeared in children's books, glorifying the heroic deeds of European supermen in defeating the dastardly savages.

By the latter part of the 19th century mass newspapers and the illustrated press had reached a circulation of millions, so that they were unquestionably most important in shaping ideas and images. In view of this it is unfortunate that the section on the press will have to be as short as that concerning fiction, but for the opposite reason: there appear to be no similar comprehensive analyses in this sphere. Hence I shall confine myself here to examples relating to animality and sexuality, and some further ones will form part of subsequent discussions. The Bushmen had a particularly bad press, and the passage below is a report from a traveller published early in the 19th century:

> they bear a marked resemblance to the baboon, orang-outan, or chimpanzee. . . . The facial line resembles that of the monkey. . . . There is a rolling restlessness in the eye which marks the extent of cunning but want of reason in some inferior animals.
>
> (Lichtenstein 1811, cited in Guenther 1980, p. 126)

Charles Dickens, like Dr Johnson before him, strongly objected to cant about noble savages in a piece that originally appeared anonymously in the magazine *Household Words*; his concluding emotional outburst is worth noting:

> Think of the two men and the two women who have been exhibited about England for some years. Are the majority of persons – who remember the horrid little leader of that party in his festering bundle of hides, with his filth and his antipathy to water, and his straddled legs, and his odious eyes shaded by his brutal hand, and his cry of 'Qu-u-u-u-aaa!' . . . – conscious of an affectionate yearning toward that noble savage, or is it idiosyncratic in me to abhor, detest, abominate, and abjure him?
>
> (Dickens [1868] 1958, pp. 468–9)

Then, remarkably, in 1929 a newspaper claimed that the Bushmen had been newly discovered as the lowest, most animal-like form of humanity:

> Scientists find the lowest living race of mankind. African bushmen who have no homes, own nothing but bows and arrows, have a mating season like the birds but no family life – animals in human form.
>
> (Cited in Langness 1974, p. 37)

Let me turn now to a second example, drawn from a study by Reinders (1968) concerning an episode that took place in 1920, following the First World War.

There was an incident when French Moroccan occupying troops fired on a German mob in Frankfurt, and it triggered an outburst of racist sentiment in an unexpected quarter. A few days later the *Daily Herald*, then the main organ of the British Labour Party, printed a front-page article by Edmund Morel headed

# BLACK SCOURGE IN EUROPE
## SEXUAL HORROR LET LOOSE BY FRANCE ON RHINE
### DISAPPEARANCE OF YOUNG GERMAN GIRLS

Morel's article referred to 'black savages', 'primitive African barbarians', their 'barely restrainable bestiality'. There were also claims (unsubstantiated and later shown to be untrue[7]) of an epidemic of rapes by 'over-sexed blacks'. Of particular interest is the statement that 'for well-known physiolgial reasons, the raping of a white woman by a negro is nearly always accompanied by serious injury and not infrequently has fatal results'. This harks back to the writings about race mixture by Broca and Serres previously mentioned, only greatly sensationalized.

The editor approved of the article, denying that it had anything to do with race prejudice – 'we champion the rights of the African native in his own home'; but, he added, nature has equipped us to live where we were born, the clear impli-cation being that they should stay in Africa. Morel continued his campaign, joined by others who went even further, referring to the 'black faces of African cannibals'. Morel's socialist credentials were impeccable: he was associated with the left wing of the Labour Party and, paradoxically, had long been dedicated to a fight against the exploitation of African labour in the Congo. Morel's agitation about the supposedly aggressive sexuality of blacks for a while created a stir abroad as well as in Britain, before it eventually subsided.

This episode brought to light a whole cluster of images of blacks, indicating that they had lost little of their strength.

It is also noteworthy that it began from the left of the political spectrum, just as Vogt, who likened blacks to apes, had been a rather extreme political radical. It shows that the present-day association between left-wing political views and opposition to racism, far from being a law of nature, is a function of a particular historical and socio-cultural setting.

## Savages as show-pieces

A little-known but very relevant feature of 19th- and early 20th-century life in the West was the display of 'savages' in museums, zoos and places of entertainment. The 'Hottentot Venus', discussed in Chapter 7, was far from being an isolated case. Over the centuries it had been common for 'savages' to be exhibited at fairgrounds and markets, but a radical increase in scale began at that period.

At the outset it is worth mentioning a relatively minor but nonetheless highly significant aspect. The popular museum, open to scholars and general public

*Figure 15.1* A stuffed Bechuana tribesman, displayed as recently as 1997 in the museum of
the Catalan town of Banyoles
*Source: The Times*, 5 March 1997. Associated Press.

alike, was the product of the educational ideas of the 19th century. In these newly
established museums, it was not uncommon for the bodies of representatives of
'savage races' to be stuffed and exhibited. For instance, the Austrian Imperial
Museum of Natural History contained at one time the preparations of three
African males and a girl, displayed side by side with exotic animals (Debrunner
1979). A remnant of this practice could still be found in 1991 in the Catalan town
of Banyoles, where the presence of a stuffed Bechuana tribesman in the Municipal
Museum of Natural History (see Figure 15.1) threatened a boycott of the Olympic
rowing events that were to take place there (*The Times*, 16 November 1991).

More usual were displays of live specimens, like the 'Hottentott Venus'. She
was followed in 1822 by the 'Venus of South America', who was received with a
mixture of sexual titillation and disgust, the latter apparently aroused by her
manner of eating.

209

At the Egyptian Hall in London, Laplanders were shown in the same year and proved very popular, while a subsequent troupe of Eskimos aroused little enthusiasm. Then in 1840 George Catlin, famous for studying and painting American Indians, brought some of them to London for a display that was used for educational purposes during the day and popular entertainment on some weekday evenings. In the course of the former, questions could be asked about the Indians, and some of the answers to the questions most often asked have been recorded. They are indicative of then prevailing preconceptions, and there follow some examples of answers:

No, there are no tribes that go entirely naked;
Mr Catlin was amongst the Indians eight years, and was never killed during that time;
The Indians *do* lend their wives sometimes to white men. . . .
They *never eat* the scalps.
Reason! Yes; why, do you think they are wild beasts?
The Indians speak *their own* language.

(Cited in Altick 1978, p. 276; emphasis in original)

A Bushman family was also shown at the Egyptian Hall in 1847, leading *The Times* to comment as follows:

In appearance they are little above the monkey tribe. They are continually crouching, warming themselves by the fire, chatting or growling, smoking etc. They are sullen, silent and savage – mere animals in propensity, and worse than animals in appearance.

(Quoted in Guenther 1980, p. 125)

During the second half of the 19th century the number and scale of such displays of exotic peoples increased substantially. So-called 'ethnographic exhibitions' (a label designed to indicate a seriousness of purpose that became increasingly spurious) were held in zoos, exhibition centres and fairgrounds, becoming popular in Europe and America. The development of such exhibitions in France has been studied in detail by Schneider (1977). Initially their purpose was informative, portraying the daily life of 'these most strange and rare examples of far-distant peoples', as one observer commented. Members of the Paris Anthropological Society paid frequent visits – probably in some cases their first opportunity of seeing live specimens of the peoples about whom they had been busy theorizing. Subsequently the exhibitions became increasingly commercialized and sensationalized, intended to make money for the promoters and to dramatize French colonial conquests. The display areas were fenced off, and it became the practice for spectators to throw coins into the areas for the pleasure of seeing the performers (who were very poorly rewarded) scrabbling for them; it was much like visitors to a zoo throwing food to the animals. Hence it is not surprising that the accounts of such exhibitions in the press often tended to 'reflect the traditional European predilection to find animal-like qualities in Africans' (p. 107). Since these exhibitions attracted several million visitors over a ten-year period, their impact is likely to have been considerable.

In Germany the movement began in the 1870s, initially with the intention of arousing interest in the newly acquired colonial territories among the population at large. The famous Africanist Leo Frobenius first encountered Nubians, Eskimos and other distant peoples as a child in the Berlin Zoo, where his grandfather had been director (Luig 1982). It was also a place to which physical anthropologists paid frequent sponsored visits, accompanied by a photographer, in order to carry out extensive anthropometric measurements.[8] As a recent commentator noted wryly, covert sexual voyeurism seems to have been masked by ostensible scientific concerns:

> Breast forms and genitalia were subjected to detailed investigation. The search for knowledge thereby remained unconstrained by any shame responses [of the victims]; when the search encountered these among female Falklanders, [the investigators] were puzzled; for according to a general consensus these people, together with the Australian Aborigines, were to be placed at the lowest level of the development of humanity.
>
> (Goldmann 1985, p. 263)

While it seemed perfectly acceptable for men to try and inspect the genitalia of female savages under the banner of 'anthropological science', any interest displayed by European women in black males incurred severe censure. When a group of Matabele, described as 'hordes of savages', were displayed in the setting of their huts, the *Daily Mail and Evening News* (12 August 1899) waxed indignant:

> Women, apparently of gentle birth, crowd round the near-naked blacks, give them money, shake hands with them, and even go down to their hands and knees in order that they may investigate further the interior of the overcrowded huts. . . . At night it is even worse, for under the cover of partial darkness, the manners of the Matabele grow very offensive and they are encouraged by the behaviour of female visitors whose impropriety is plain.

Some pygmies who were brought to Britain were taken to Parliament, and a photograph (see Figure 15.2) shows a pathetic group dressed up in children's sailor suits, robbed of all dignity. The accompanying text states:

> Surely extremes meet when the little folk from the heart of the Ituri Forest, in Central Africa, mixed with the Members on the terrace of the House of Commons. They are supposed be of the lowest type, mentally, as well as the smallest, physically, of the human race.
>
> (Stone 1906, Vol. 2, p. 18)

*Figure 15.2* Members of Parliament on the terrace of the House of Commons with a
pathetic group of Pygmies. The men had been dressed in children's sailor suits,
an evident symbolism of how they were regarded

*Source:* By courtesy of the National Portrait Gallery (Benjamin Stone, 1905).

Even worse than such exhibitions was the exploitation of 'exotics' by showmen, of
the kind suffered by the 'Hottentot Venus'. This was sometimes done under a
scientific guise, as when in 1884 'The Great Farini' displayed the hairy girl Krao
at the Royal Aquarium, Westminster, as 'The Missing Link'. A particularly sad
story was that of a group of nine Australian Aborigines, brought first to America
by the showman R.A. Cunningham, and then to Europe, by which time two had
died. In Britain in 1884 the seven remaining Aborigines were publicized as
'ranting man eaters' and 'veritable blood-thirsty beasts'. Examined the same year
in Brussels by the Société d'Anthropologie, they showed signs of tuberculosis. By
May 1885 only five remained, and later that year when being examined by
the famous anthropologist Topinard in Paris, only three survived to undergo the
examination. One of these was Jenny, whose father had just died in a Paris
hospital, and who was so distraught that she took little notice of what was
happening to her. It is revealing of the then prevailing attitude that Topinard
attributed this to her 'stupidity' (Poignant 1992; Topinard 1885b).

In the United States, where show business prevailed from the start, 'Fiji cannibals' were the main attraction from the 1830s onwards, with P.T. Barnum in the forefront. When the show came to York in Pennsylvania, the crowd were disappointed, since the 'cannibal dwarf' had died. The local paper running the story added the following (purely invented) details:

> Shortly after the corpse was placed in the coffin last evening, S.S. Smith, the keeper, locked the door upon the three companions in an adjoining room and left the building for the purpose of consulting the manager at the National Hotel. He states that he was not absent 30 minutes, but that upon returning, a scene presented itself too horrible to detail. The two male associates had gained access to the corpse and were biting and gnawing at the fleshy part of the body with all the eagerness of their native cannibalism.
>
> (Bogdan 1988, pp. 181–2)

In 1893, Barnum and Bailey's Circus featured their 'Great Ethnological Congress', where some seventy non-western people were shown in their menagerie tent. During the 1920s another showman displayed a Bushman, described in the publicity pamphlet as being 'as near like the ape as he is like the human' (Bogdan 1988, p. 192). In the early 1930s another circus advertised 'genuine monster-mouthed Ubangi savages'.

Whether the purpose of these shows was the glorification of the colonial enterprise, or whether they were staged for financial gain, there was one thing which most of these various spectacles had in common: they reduced the Other to an object of pity, ridicule and scorn.

Finally, mention should be made of advertisements, in many of which not only savagery but animality was suggested. A particularly clear-cut case is that for 'Monkey Soap' which appeared during the 1880s. It portrays a figure dressed in jacket, trousers, collar and tie, but with hands and bare feet that are distinctly human. However, the dark face is ambiguously drawn, half-way between ape and man.[9]

Even this brief outline of a vast topic will have been sufficient to indicate the powerful convergence of a whole range of different influences. These served to maintain and even enhance the traditional images of lascivious ape-likeness and cannibalism among the European populations at large.

# 16

# THE RELATIVITY OF IMAGES

So far the main images have been treated separately, and in each case specific background factors have been discussed. In the two final chapters a more global perspective will be adopted. The issues to be addressed in this chapter concern the sources of variations in the nature and targets of images in the long term, and in particular some of the historical and situational factors that seem to have affected them.

## The images compared

In terms of their temporal ordering, the images of animality and cannibalism date back to antiquity and still survive, while that of child-likeness appeared late and proved transitory. This in itself suggests that it was less deeply rooted than the other two. All three images are associated with the idea of lack of impulse control, and in the cases of cannibalism and animality mainly within the spheres of sexuality and aggression.

As regards the targets on to which the images were (and in some cases still are) projected, they are more diverse than the prototypical 'savages' on which my discussion has mainly concentrated. Cannibalism has not only been attributed to distant savages, but also to close peoples with a pigmentation not unlike one's own: as late as the 17th century 'cannibalism' was attributed even to such alleged European savages as the Irish (Carlin 1984); when Bonnie Prince Charlie's army had taken Derby in 1745 and was threatening London, the journals in the capital encouraged the rumour that the Highlanders ate babies. In the 18th and 19th centuries rumours of cannibalism were rife in France (Corbain 1992), and contemporary instances have already been described. Historically, cannibalism has also been alleged concerning Others whose sole or main difference was their beliefs, regarded as so abhorrent that by a 'halo effect' they were thought capable of almost anything; early Christians were thus accused, and they in turn later accused Jews.

When it comes to animality, there is a semantic problem if one tries to compare it with cannibalism, since the term 'bestial' employed in relation to all kinds of distant savages sometimes, but not necessarily, implied the practice of cannibalism; furthermore, from the Enlightenment onwards 'bestiality' tended to give way to the more neutral 'animality'. Ape-likeness, an increasingly prominent sub-division of animality, began dimly during the Middle Ages and reached its apogee during the 19th century. The terms 'ape' or 'monkey' were applied almost exclusively to darkly pigmented savages from distant parts. Inevitably, educated Africans became aware of the label and resented it. An anonymous writer at Fourah Bay College in Sierra Leone published a poem containing the following verses:

> Dispersion brought Ham to the African land;
> The Bible tells this, but it never doth say
> That Ham was become a baboon any way:
> Some ignorant men of the proud-colour tribe
> The notion that Negroes are monkeys imbibe.
> (*Sierra Leone Weekly News*, 17 November 1888;
>     cited in Spitzer 1972, p. 125).

Knowledge of the offensive appellation gradually filtered down to all sections of the population, including illiterates. When I worked in West Africa during the 1950s, African labourers in a public works department went on strike because, they alleged, an expatriate foreman had told them they were like children, and called them 'black monkeys'. The foreman denied this, but having personally observed the manner in which some expatriates talked about Africans among themselves, I was inclined to believe the labourers' version. In Europe and America the ape image ceased to be acceptable in educated circles (at least in public discourse) after the Second World War, but persisted at the popular level.

Moving now to the 'child' image, this is only rarely encountered prior to the 19th century. Its targets were in the main all kinds of 'subject races', including 'Orientals' (cf. Said 1978). It was even suggested that the people of so ancient a civilization as China's were in some respects child-like. For instance, Sir William Lawrence, noted anatomist and follower of Cuvier, wrote that the languages of China 'betray . . . all the imperfections of the first attempts at speech. . . . They form plurals as children do' (Lawrence 1819, pp. 471–2). But the circle, in more attenuated fashion, was even wider: women were seen as closer to children than to men, and thereby also closer to savages (see p. 85); the lower classes in Europe were close to savages, and thereby also child-like. Thus the child image appeared in a whole cluster of contexts.

Another topic of interest is the relationship of the images to states of scientific knowledge. As far as cannibalism is concerned, it would seem that the supposed practice was for a long time merely taken for granted as one of the key manifestations of savagery. It was not until the latter part of the 19th century, with the rise of anthropological theory, that discussions about its origin and nature began. As far as the former is concerned, it was speculated that the practice dates back to prehistoric times; a number of psychological motives, mainly in terms of supernatural beliefs, were put forward as explanations. As already indicated, the whole issue remains highly controversial even today.

The case of the ape image is particularly noteworthy in this connection. Street (1985), who commented on its persistence, assumed that it was derived from 19th-century science. Although this is probably correct, it tells only part of the story, and the less interesting part at that. A top-down movement from science to the popular level is not unexpected, while a bottom-up movement is more surprising. As has already been shown in more detail (Chapter 4), the ape image had long been present among travellers or sailors, and from them spread to ordinary people, being reinforced during the 18th century by entertainments featuring 'ape-men'. In a socio-political context where the issue of 'race' had become salient, the image was taken up first by Edward Long in his quasi-scientific but largely propagandist work. Thereafter it became an important topic for 'normal science', notably anatomists and the proponents of the emerging 'new biology'. By the mid-19th century the 'apishness' of savages had become extensively adopted as a 'scientific fact'. The process could therefore be seen as resembling an inverted U-shape: from bottom to top and back again.

The situation was not so clear with regard to the child image, which is rarely encountered prior to the 19th century, except in a metaphorical sense during the Enlightenment. Specialized research would be needed to establish the detailed sequence of events, and the following comments are somewhat speculative. The duration of the 'child' image overlapped extensively with the rise, full bloom and eventual demise of modern colonialism, and it therefore seems tempting to interpret it simply as a consequence of colonialism. But this takes no account of the fact that the child image emerged and spread prior to extensive European colonization. Another objection is that colonies existed before the 19th century, which failed to give rise to a stereotypical child image.

It would seem likely that the impetus for the postulation of child-likeness stemmed from the pre-existing belief in the stupidity of savages. The observation that savage children do not appear backward in comparison with European ones presented a puzzle. In an attempt to find a scientific explanation for this phenomenon, it was suggested that their mental growth stopped while they were still children, *ergo* they remained child-like. In due course the explanation became modified and elaborated by recourse to the 'biogenetic law'.

Now it so happened that the new label also meshed admirably with the ideology of later 19th-century colonial paternalism: we have an obligation to care for the poor benighted savages, and they are dependent upon us, as children are on their parents. Paternalism of this kind did not, even theoretically, define the relationship between the ruling power and the savages before the middle of the 19th century. During the period of colonial expansion, administrators and missionaries eagerly seized upon the image, giving it another twist by adding *dependence* to stupidity. Thus it is likely that the image began as a scientific concept, albeit one of 'race science', and was taken over by the colonial elite.

The discussion so far has been confined in the main to descriptions of the images, and it might be supposed that in the course of actual encounters Europeans would have treated savages not merely as inferiors, but as barely human. While this did occur under certain circumstances, notably the slave-trade, it was not the rule. Quite apart from the fact that the images, while widespread, were not universally shared, attitudes are not necessarily reflected directly in personal interactions. Moreover, Europeans were only able to treat savages with contempt when it was safe for them to do so, and this was by no means always the case.

## Situations where the Europeans were powerless

When savages were enslaved, or subjected to colonial conquest, Europeans were in positions of overwhelming power, and the ape or child image could serve as justification for such dominance. There were, however, frequent circumstances where Europeans found themselves dependent upon the good will of the savages. The two main categories of people to whom this applied were missionaries and traders. Prior to the European colonial expansion during the latter part of the 19th century, missionaries and traders were often not able to count on the actual or potential military power of their homelands. Hence they were not in a position to antagonize the peoples with whom they had to deal by an overt display of arrogant superiority. Coming from a background where such superiority was normally taken for granted, they found themselves in a situation which one would have thought conducive to 'cognitive dissonance', and it is of interest to consider how they reacted.

Missionaries in particular found themselves in an ambiguous situation: on the one hand they had to present to their home audience and supporters a picture of savages as depraved, irrational, irresponsible and lawless; on the other hand they were in practice obliged to defer to those same savages in order to be able to pursue their task. This can be illustrated in relation to the missionary's letter from the New Hebrides (cited in Chapter 15, p. 202), in which he presented the Tannese as 'painted savages' who indulge in the most repulsive cannibalistic practices. Yet from his subsequent account of the progress of the mission, it is clear how much it depended upon the willingness of the chiefs to allow them to carry out their work. For instance, it was described how it was necessary to conciliate the chiefs; and when things went wrong, as, for instance, when a serious theft occurred, the chiefs had to be approached for help.

Another example is from the Journal of the Reverend Wilson of the Victoria Nyanza Mission (1878, p. 33):

> The men here . . . smear their bodies with red clay, and dress up their hair with a paste of red clay and rancid butter, and the odour of a crowd of Wagogo is most overpowering . . . they are all great thieves, and at the same time great cowards, not daring to go out after dark . . . they are,

like all these negroes, thinking only of the moment's gratification, without any regard for the future.

Later he tells of an audience with the local 'king', who kept him waiting, and to whom he was most respectful.

There is little indication in most of the records of any awareness on the part of the missionaries, and consequent unease, about the divorce between their words and their actions. Generally they appear to have regarded the intrusion of Europeans into indigenous cultures as being in the best interests of the indigenous populations, and wholly beneficent. There were some exceptions, notably the Reverend Robert Cust (1891, p. 7) who had a less rose-tinted view of events:

> The European lands on the coast of Africa, as a Man of Science, or a Man of Commerce, or a great Hunter, or a mighty Explorer, totally regardless of the rights of others; he treats the tribes, who have had the prescriptive possession of the country for centuries, as if they were in the category of the wild beasts, mere 'ferae naturae': he cares neither for their souls, nor their bodies . . . he sets at nought their customary game laws: he steals their fetishes from their joss-houses, the skulls and bones of their forefathers from their places of sepulture, and often defiles their women.

Needless to say, Reverend Cust was not popular with his fellow missionaries: by exposing in plain terms the other side of the coin, he was undermining their comforting rationalizations. Without these, they would have found it difficult to endure the many hardships to which they were exposed. But the main point I wish to bring out is the contrast between the dismal portrait of the savage they had to paint for home consumption, and their unavoidable reliance on these same people in their roles as local authority figures.

While missionary activity in Africa did not effectively start until the latter part of the 18th century, trading had a much longer history, especially the notorious slave-trade. While Europeans had initially attempted to capture the slaves themselves, this was soon abandoned for the more efficient means of buying them from the local rulers. After the abolition of the 'evil trade', there was a substantial increase in trade in other commodities; and until the imposition of colonial rule, traders had to establish good relations with local chiefs in order to be able to pursue their activities. Such situations will be illustrated with examples drawn from the late 17th to the mid-19th centuries.

The first is an extract from the journal of a voyage to the Guinea Coast by the slave-trader Thomas Phillips in 1693/4 (in Churchill 1746, Vol. vi, p. 213; emphasis in original).

> I was astonished when first they came near the ship, to hear no other speech come from them but *Qua, Qua, Qua, Qua*, like a parcel of ducks. . . .

> The negroes of this part are called the *Man-eaters*, and that they eat their enemies they take prisoners, and their own friends when dead, as I was told by my old mate Captain *Robson*, who had long used this Guiney voyage. How true that is I know not; but in truth their looks are very savage and voracious; and all their teeth, I observed, are pointed at the end as sharp as bodkins, which looks very terrible . . . they are all well limb'd, and strong men, but the most hideous in their aspect of any negroes I have met with. Each canoe brought a broker with him, who, as he enters the ship, demands a dashy [gratuity] of a knife or two, for he pretends to bring the trade to you.

It will be clear from the above that the captain shared the then accepted image of Africans, including the likelihood that they were cannibals. Their pointed teeth were taken as an indication of this, as was still the case in the 20th century (see Chap. 9, note 1, p. 252). But it should also be noted that a 'dashy' was *demanded*, and that Phillips was obliged to accede to the demand (pp. 227–8).

> I bought a five-handed canoe here of the *Black* general, who had surprized and seized the *Danes* fort here, forced the *Danes* general to fly to the *Dutch* to save his life, murdered his second and several of the [Danish] soldiers, and now trades with the *Dutch* interlopers. . . .
>
> This *Black* general sent two of his servants to invite Mr. Bloome, Mr. Buckridge and myself to dine with him, which we accepted . . . we were treated at dinner with plenty of punch and victuals, and indeed pretty well dressed, considering the swinish manner it is the custom of the Negroes to eat . . . he drank the king of England, the African Companies', and our own health frequently, with vollies of cannon . . . the flag he had flying was white, with a black man painted in the middle brandishing a scymitar.

Africans at the time took full advantage of the rivalries between the several Europeans powers who had forts there, which served as trading stations. All Europeans were ultimately dependent on good relations with the Africans, who had permitted them to build the forts. Note how Phillips referred to 'the General' with considerable respect, excepting him from the usual 'swinish' customs.

Phillips and his companions then travelled to another town where they teamed up with an East India Merchant vessel and came to live on shore until they had achieved their main task of acquiring 1,300 slaves. As soon as the local king heard of their arrival he sent two of his nobles asking them to 'pay [their] devoirs to his majesty'. They were invited to stay the night, an invitation they did not dare refuse, though Phillips commented rather sarcastically on the poverty of the 'palace'. They were again wined and dined, with the usual drinking of toasts. When it came to the sales, they had to take those offered by the king first, though these were generally the worst as well as the most expensive; but they could not avoid this, 'it being one of his majesty's prerogatives' (p. 234). The indications are that the homage paid to the king was more than superficial – he may have had to conform on the spot, but there was no need for him to refer invariably to 'his majesty' in the book.

When the slaves were brought to the ship, several drowned themselves and others starved themselves to death, as commonly happened. Phillips explained that according to their belief, they would return to their country and friends again after they died – actually a misinterpretation of ancestor worship. They were also said to believe that such a return would only occur if their bodies remained whole. Some of the ship's officers therefore suggested cutting off the arms or legs of some, thereby terrifying the rest – as was apparently done by some commanders. After reporting this, Phillips wrote (p. 235):

> but I could not be persuaded to entertain the least thoughts of it, much less to put into practice such barbarity and cruelty to poor creatures, who, excepting their want of Christianity and true religion (their misfortune rather than a fault) are as much the works of God's hands and no doubt as dear to him as ourselves; nor can I imagine why they should be despised for their colour, being what they cannot help, and the effect of the climate it has pleased God to appoint them. I can't think there is any intrinsic value in one colour more than another, nor that white is better than black, only we think it so because we are so, and are prone to judge favourably in our own case.

This remarkable effusion by a slave-trader was written well before the onset of the anti-slavery movement. The negative stereotypes, oddly coupled with more or less subservient behaviour towards the Africans on whom his business depended, were to be expected; but these sentiments, which could have come from a 20th-century liberal, are a surprise; they indicate a constellation of motives and attitudes that is well-nigh incomprehensible today.

William Smith (1744) traded in the same region, and his report puts the sexual laxity of which Africans were constantly accused in a different light. He was a man who, in the context of his time, appeared relatively enlightened, though he had no doubts about the inferiority of blacks. When offered a girl by a local king (p. 251) he

> asked the Reasons for such a Practice; I was soon answered, that it was to keep me chaste and regular. [He then inquired at length how that could be, since he was being tempted to fornication] Why, said the King, is it a Sin to lie with a woman? Yes, I said, unless I was married to her. And did you never, said the King, in your Country, lie with a Woman unmarried? Here I hesitated, and found I could not answer this question, and there begged to be excused.

The outcome was that he accepted the girl, praising her beauty and manners: 'At midnight we went to bed, and in that Situation I soon forgot the complexion of my Bedfellow . . . greater pleasure I never found' (p. 354). What is unusual here is not the event itself, for such intercourse was no doubt commonplace, but the frankness with which Smith recorded the affair, including the shrewdness of the king. Such frankness in print would have been almost inconceivable a century later, and it is of interest to compare Francis Galton's reaction in the same situation:

> I did much to make myself agreeable, investing Nangoro with a big theatrical crown that I had bought in Drury Lane for some such purpose. But I have reason to believe that I deeply wounded [the king's] pride by the non-acceptance of his niece as, I presume, a temporary wife. I found her installed in my tent in negress finery, raddled with red ochre and butter, and as capable of leaving a mark on anything she touched as a well-inked printer's roller. I was dressed in my one well-preserved suit of white linen, so I had her ejected with scant ceremony.
>
> (Galton 1908, p. 143)

The same air of condescension and moral superiority is displayed in the introductory part of my previous example. It concerns another Smith (1851, p. vi) who described himself as a 'surgeon and trading captain', again on the Guinea Coast.

> The author regrets the occasions of some coarse expressions to be found in this work; but, as the people he gives an account of are in so debased a state as to render the conveying anything like a correct notion of them otherwise, impossible, he deems any further apology unnecessary.

As may be gathered from the above, Smith had plenty of unpleasant things to say about African manners, customs and so on, including the usual tirade about their general inferiority. Yet suddenly one comes across the following passage (pp. 182–3):

> Many of the kings and chiefs possess great powers of discriminating character. During the first interview with a European, not a word, nor the movement of a muscle of the face, nor an expression of the eye, can escape their notice; and if a man have a character at all, they are sure to find it out, and treat him accordingly. Some they bully, some they flatter and coax, while others they reason with; their prominent characteristic, however, in their intercourse with Europeans, is a mild, bland, gentle, confident mannerism you hardly expect to meet with but in refined society, well calculated to mislead those ignorant of their true character.
>
> They are keen, cunning men of business, very grasping, and leave no means untried to overreach you in bargain-making. Europeans generally

suppose that the white traders take advantage of their innocence, ignorance and simplicity. It is true they sometimes have done so, but as a general rule, never was there a greater mistake. If you prevent them cheating and robbing you, you do very well, and ought to be perfectly satisfied.

The author had initially rehearsed a series of negative stereotypes. Yet when it came to a description of actual trading situations, where equality reigned, the tone changed radically. Almost miraculous psychological insight was attributed to the black trading partners. They were said to be able to bully the whites, or reason with them; and if they were not very careful the blacks would get the better of them.

In sum, these examples show the effects of situations where Europeans lacked power advantages over the savages. On a superficial level they did not shed the negative images which constituted the conventional wisdom of the period – they were even apt to parade them emphatically for the benefit of their readers. However, when they described their interactions with the savages, it transpired that they had gained a healthy respect for them.

It will also have been noted from the records of Phillips (above) that as late as the 18th century Europeans were sometimes driven from their forts by Africans. The power balance shifted only gradually, as a function of European technical advances. The following section examines this process in a wider historical perspective.

## The effects of changes in European societies

In the eyes of post-Renaissance Europeans, the great divide between themselves and the savages was the fact that they were civilized and the savages, like animals, were not. From this point of view the image of the ape was that of a near-human animal epitomizing this lack, and the child was a human not yet civilized. But the terminology I am using is anachronistic as far as the earlier periods are concerned, and its history is not without interest and relevance in this context.

At the time of the first contacts between Europeans and savages, the term 'civilization' did not yet exist, and 'civility' – discussed further below – was beginning to gain currency. Other terms were 'police', not in the modern sense of course but in the archaic sense of the adequate regulation and control of the community, or 'polite' in the broad sense of 'orderly'. The distinction between 'us' and 'them' who are neither 'policed' nor 'polite' was based on a variety of elements. The main ones concerned 'loi, foi et roi', i.e. the existence of laws, the right kind of religion and some form of government – none of which savages were generally believed to possess. Other aspects included knowledge and technical skills, and not least 'polite' manners and customs. The verb 'to civilize' and the adjective 'civilized' made their appearance during the 16th century, and it is probably no coincidence that this occurred just when the debates about the possibility of bringing savages out of their deplorable state were taking place. The noun 'civilization' did not come into being until the Enlightenment with its vision of a unitary humanity on an upward path of progress, and its plural was first used during the 19th century when that vision had faded.

By the above-mentioned criteria Europeans themselves had not always been civilized, or even 'polite'. In the light of this fact it becomes understandable why, during much of the Middle Ages the distinction between 'us' and 'them' was primarily expressed in terms of religion. Until the late Middle Ages the differences between the ways of life of the bulk of European populations, and those later attributed to savages, were not very great. This was true especially of the two critical spheres of food and sex – the sins of gluttony and lechery were closely coupled. As far as table manners were concerned, these were exceedingly crude by later standards. All ranks of society ate with their hands, dipping them into a common dish; and in spite of the preachings of the Church against 'carnal lust', sexual mores were lax, extra-marital relationships common, and not even shrouded in secrecy. It is interesting that some modern historians view the 'common people' of the Middle Ages in a manner rather similar in certain important respects to the way in which savages were seen during the 19th century. Thus an inability to think in abstractions has been attributed to medieval Europeans:

> Another feature of the consciousness which interests us here is its disinclination for abstract concepts. General and abstract notions are comprehended exclusively in their concrete and tangible forms. The most spiritual beings are transformed into demonstrably material things, are personified and embodied. An educated man, priest or monk, may have perceived, for example, personifications of sins and virtues as metaphors or allegories, but his listeners almost certainly added flesh and blood to the metaphor and believed in its real existence.
>
> (Gurevich 1988, p. 11)[1]

As Europe emerged from the Middle Ages, the life-styles of the upper layers of society underwent a gradual transformation away from the crude simplicity that had characterized it before. The nature of this process has been lucidly analysed by Elias (1978) in his famous account of the development in Europe of the notion of 'civility'. A crucial turning point in this transition was the publication in 1530 by Erasmus of Rotterdam of a book on the teaching of manners that became extraordinarily popular, was translated into many European languages and went through numerous editions. It gave instructions about desirable manners and what to avoid in a range of contexts from meals to the bedchamber. For instance, one should not spit on the table, lick one's fingers or wipe them on one's coat; also one should not needlessly expose 'the parts to which nature has attached modesty' (cited in Elias 1978, p. 58).

The period of transition in manners coincided with an increase in travel and exploration. It is striking to note how often such travellers seemed shocked by exotic eating habits – the manners of eating as well as what was eaten. The Venetian nobleman Ca' da Mosto ([1507] 1895), who entered the service of Henry the Navigator, visited the Wolofs of the Senegambia region on the West African coast at the end of the 15th century. He gave a relatively cool and factual description of many aspects of life on the coast: ordinary people go naked except for a piece of goat leather, while 'nobles' wear cotton shirts, but all go barefoot. In contrast to the later stereotype of 'dirty savages', he noted that they were very neat and washed several times a day – much more than the 'civilized' Europeans of the period. He gave an account of standards of female beauty (the longer the breasts the better), and referred to the multiple wives of the king, and to his right to sleep also with their 'chambermaids'. Although commenting that 'custom permits it', he took it as evidence of lasciviousness. Ca' da Mosto appeared more upset by their eating habits, which he mentioned more than once in derogatory terms (pp. 82, 101):

> But one eats there in a very dirty way, without observing a single point of civility . . . they eat brutally, lounging on the ground, without observing the least point of civility. . . . The populace eats in groups of ten or twelve, having in their midst a pot full of meat into which they all put their hand.

Even relatively minor breaches of good form greatly upset some travellers such as Champlain (1604). He wrote about Canadian Indian savages, calling them 'bestial', apparently mainly on the grounds that: 'they eat in a very dirty manner; for when their hands are greasy, they wipe them on their hair or on the fur of their dogs' (p. 4).

Another explorer, Stefansson [1577] (1938), who visited the Eskimo, went further and inferred from their observed eating habits that they must be cannibals:

> What knowledge they have of God, or what Idol they adore, we have no perfect intelligence. I think them rather Anthropophagi, or devourers of human flesh, than otherwise: for there is no flesh nor fish, which they find dead (smell it never so filthily), but they will eat it, as they find it, without any other dressing. A loathsome spectacle, either to the beholders or the hearers.
>
> (Stefansson [1577] 1938, Vol. II, p. 23)

The passages cited so far, while registering disgust at the lack of 'civility' in eating, did not deny the essential humanity of the savages, even if they were cannibals. Later this very humanity often came to be regarded as questionable. In addition to the deplorable 'table manners' of the savages, other negative features came increasingly to be invoked as reasons for such a judgement. Thus Bergeron (1649, Vol. 2, p. 2) had this to say about North American Indians:

Here there are peoples who are so savage that they hardly know how to speak, so dirty that they eat the intestines of beasts full of excrement without washing them, and so brutal that they more resemble famished dogs than humans who have the use of reason.

The idea of the excessive sexuality of savages was old and has already been discussed. During the Renaissance the Catholic clergy conducted a campaign intended to improve sexual conduct, to the extent of removing from churches religious pictures they supposed might evoke impure thoughts. This was connected with the emphasis on sexual restraint by the Protestant Reformation, which led in Elizabethan England to denunciations of neighbours for alleged sexual transgressions (Hale 1993). These movements resulted in progressively more rigid restraints on the overt expression of sexuality. At home this probably rendered reports of the sexual abandon of savages more piquant; among the travellers there were certainly those who indulged in the free living-out of their fantasies, often at the same time denouncing the excesses of the savages. These aspects have already been extensively illustrated in previous chapters.

Within European societies, 'civility' spread from the nobility to lower strata, though the peasantry retained many of their traditional habits. Knowledge and technical skills, especially military ones, advanced steadily. By contrast, savage societies with limited contacts to the outside world long remained relatively stationary. Thereby the psychological distance between European and savage cultures progressively widened in the course of time, reaching a maximum during the 19th century. Thereafter, increasing 'westernization' progressively narrowed the gap again. The great psychological distance during the 19th century perhaps helps to account for a seeming paradox: in spite of the fact that Europeans' scientific sophistication and knowledge of savages improved steadily, their image of the savage as ape-like persisted, and that of child-likeness became firmly established. The main change during the 19th century was that these images took on a more (pseudo-)scientific guise. It should also be remembered that most of the late 18th- and 19th-century men of science, who pontificated about the simian or child-like nature of savages, usually lacked any first-hand knowledge of them. One important factor that subsequently contributed to the fading of the images among the educated public was an increasing understanding of non-European cultures during the 20th century. Thereby the savage, in Goody's phrase, became 'domesticated'.

In addition to the influence of increasing cultural differences over time, which affected the character of the images, there were also considerable shifts in terms of the populations regarded as savages or near-savages, and this issue will now be briefly considered.

## Who is a savage?

'Who are the savages?' is a question that would have received very different answers at different periods. In antiquity and the early Middle Ages the criteria were mental rather than physical: savages were regarded as having no proper languages or true religion, even though their pigmentation was the same. Slavery was the fate of numerous white as well as non-white savages. During the later Middle Ages the position became more ambiguous: while (partly mythical) black Christians were held in high esteem, the blackness of the 'burnt faces' came to be associated with the devil and savagery.

Once the whole of Europe had become christianized, and thereby the slavery of whites abolished, the savages became generally confined to more distant places; but as will be shown below there were exceptions. The linkage between blackness and savagery probably began with the Portuguese importation of slaves from West Africa. The case of the American Indians was somewhat different, since there was little emphasis on skin colour. Rather, they came to be thought of in terms of the 'Wild Men of the Woods', who had been conceived as hairy but not coloured. It was the fact that they were heathen, and had repellent customs, that made them savages. Once blackness had become established as a sign of savagery, it was extended to other newly discovered populations such as the Andaman Islanders, and until well into the 19th century all 'black savages', wherever they were located, were usually treated as an undifferentiated category in the 'racial' literature.

The 'colour' issue was not always clear-cut however, as is evident from the wide variations in classifications of races; and not only by different authors, but as with the most famous of them, Linnaeus, by the same author in successive editions. In his *Systema Naturae* from 1740 onwards there was a sharpening as regards American Indians from 'reddish' to 'red', and similarly for Europeans from 'whitish' to 'white'; the greatest change was for Asiatics, from 'dark brown' to 'yellow'.

The settlers in New England knew the indigenous peoples as 'Indians' until after the 17th century, and expressions such as 'dark-skinned heathen' and 'red-skins' only gradually gained currency thereafter in the context of bloody conflicts. There were other instances where the state of inter-ethnic relations influenced the perception (in a loose sense) of skin colour. A particularly revealing case is that of the Chinese, as documented by Demel (1992). A Florentine traveller to China reported in 1515 that the Chinese were 'of our kind', and another a few years later explicitly called them 'a white-skinned people' and like others of the period referred to them in very positive terms. With few exceptions, this characterizations continued until the 18th century. Then, with the opening up of trade, ensuing friction, and increasingly vocal assertions of European superiority ('China is the most stupid empire in the world' wrote a German scholar), the Chinese turned yellow! They were of course never actually called 'savages'.

The effects of conflict situations on perceptions is seldom more apparent than in the case of the Irish, which also exemplifies the fact that savages need not always be non-Europeans. During some seven hundred years of English occupation of Ireland, punctuated by uprisings, the Irish were long characterized by their conquerors as savages, and here again (as mentioned above in connection

with the ape image) Victorian ethnologists offered scientific confirmation of
the old images. One of them was D. Mackintosh, whose description of Irish
physiognomy was entirely based on – obviously biased – observation. It was
allegedly 'marked by his bulging jaw and lower part of the face, retreating chin
and forehead, large mouth and thick lips ... projecting eyebrows ... and
protruding ears' (cited in Curtis 1968, p. 71). This is somewhat reminiscent of the
'low facial angle' attributed to blacks, and the 'thick lips' also fit the stereotype.
Another more well-known ethnologist, John Beddoe, sought to establish such a
linkage more directly:

> Beddoe contended that in Ireland one could still find the residual
> survivals of a primitive people who had certain affinities with Cro-
> Magnon or 'Africanoid' man. His index of negrescence served to prove
> that the Irish were darker than the people of eastern and central
> England, and that they were closer in physical type to the aborigines of
> the British Isles, who in turn had traces of Negro ancestry in their
> appearance.
>
> (Curtis 1968, p. 72)

In this slightly roundabout way the African origin of Irish savagery was
convincingly explained! These notions, originally derived from the popular level
and given 'scientific' blessing, in turn served to support them and make them
respectable. Victorian caricatures of Irishmen closely parallel those of 'African
savages', both having pronounced 'simian' features (Curtis 1971).

Apart from such special circumstances, the attribution of savagery to certain
Europeans was often merely a function of distance from metropolitan centres and
the perception of a primitive way of life. For instance, during the 18th century
Edinburgh was one of the foremost intellectual capitals of Europe. Yet the
inhabitants of remote Scottish islands were commonly viewed as near-savages.
Lord Bougham, who visited St Kilda in 1799, had this to say about the islanders:

> A total want of curiosity, a stupid gaze of wonder, an excessive eagerness
> for spirits and tobacco, a laziness only to be conquered by the hope of the
> above mentioned cordials, and a beastly degree of filth, the natural
> consequence of this renders the St Kildan character truly savage.
>
> (Cited in Steel 1975, p. 51)

The similarity of this effusion to the then prevailing images of African savages is
striking.

Before concluding this chapter, some views that have been put forward
about significant changes that are supposed to have taken place, or did actually
occur, will be briefly considered. With regard to the ape image, it has been
suggested that the association between blacks and apes resulted from the fact that
'European explorers had stumbled across Negroes and the most man-like of apes

simultaneously' (Jordan 1968, p. 229). While the exact date of the European discovery of anthropoid apes is disputed, scattered reports during the Renaissance aroused hardly any interest. Precise knowledge of them was not recorded until the 17th century, and blacks had of course been known in Europe for millennia before that. In any case, as Janson (1952) rightly observed, the discovery of the great apes had initially little impact on European thought. The increasing salience of the ape image towards the end of the 18th century, and its elevation into a scientific doctrine, therefore seems to have had little to do with the initial European discovery of the great apes. It is more likely to be directly connected with Edward Long's reaction to the anti-slavery movement and the ensuing debate, which rendered the 'ape' issue salient and resulted in its being taken seriously, whereas before the label had been applied only casually.

The temporal coincidence of anti-slavery sentiment and the emergence of racialist theories has been noted several times in previous chapters, and its presumptive causes discussed. One attempted explanation was in terms of 'the unfolding of bourgeois social relations' (Fields 1982, p. 152), i.e. viewing it as part of a wider ideological change. But without further elucidation, the invoking of 'ideology' is an alternative description rather than an explanation. Another suggestion was that, slavery having been abolished, another form of anti-black thinking came to the fore: '*Race* emerged as the buffer between abolition and equality' (Pieterse 1992, p. 59). Apart from in a very loose sense, this interpretation is not borne out by the facts, since the first race theories preceded the advent of abolition. Moreover, such a claim appears to exaggerate the differences between the views of abolitionists and their opponents. The equality of all men before God preached by the evangelical movement in Britain, and the revolutionary ideal of human brotherhood in France, remained largely theoretical. In neither case did this imply a belief in full racial equality, and the disagreement between abolitionists and those who favoured continuation of the slave trade concerned not present inferiority but future potential. The limitations on benevolence were humorously epitomized in a cartoon by Honoré Daumier. It was drawn as late as 1848, when both slavery and the trade had finally been abolished in France. The cartoon shows 'an abolitionist giving a black slave a violent kick in the behind while yelling at him "I have already forbidden you to call me 'master' . . . know that all men are brothers, animal!"' (Cohen 1980, p. 209).

It should be apparent from these examples that there were no abrupt discontinuities of the kind sometimes suggested. There were of course various changes, on the whole fairly gradual ones. Yet the overriding impression from my reading of the evidence is that of continuity.

# 17

# THE CONTINUITY OF IMAGES

Although the persistence of similar images of the Other over the centuries has been mentioned several times in these pages, the remarkable nature of this phenomenon may have been obscured by the focus on detail. Hence at the outset, as a reminder, an extensive illustration is provided.

In the 5th century St Jerome commented on the long list of savages known to him, not having a good word to say for any of them. Here is an extract from his lengthy disquisition:

> The Nomads and Troglodytes and Scythians and the new savages, the Huns, eat half-raw meat . . . the Sarmatians, Quadi, Vandals, and innumerable other people, delight in the flesh of horses and foxes. What shall I say of the other heathen, since as a boy in Gaul I saw Attocoti, a British people, eat human flesh; when they come upon herds of swine and cattle and sheep, they slice off the buttocks of the herdsmen and the breasts of the women and esteem them the most delicious of foods. The Scottish nation do not practice monogamy; but, as if they had read the *Republic* of Plato and were following the example of Cato, there is no individual wife among them, but as each pleases, they satisfy lust in the manner of brutes. The Persians, Medes, Indians, and Ethiopians . . . mate with their mothers and grandmothers, with their daughters and nieces.
>
> (Boas 1948, p. 131)

Here one finds already most of the salient components of the image of the savage: they eat unsuitable foods, including human flesh; they are beastly and unrestrained in their sexuality. The ape image first made its appearance during the later Middle Ages, after the beginning of the great voyages. Then came the conquest of the New World, and the pronouncement of Tomas Ortiz concerning American Indians, cited on pp. 16–17, closely echoes these censures.

In 1866, some three hundred years after the Dominican Ortiz, a Church of England clergyman gave an address to the Ethnological Society on the classification of races (Farrar 1867). Some of his descriptions of what he called 'the irreclaimable savage' are cited below:

the tallow-coloured Bosjesmen . . . when not living on worms and pismires [ants], are glad to squabble for the putrid carcass of the hyaena and the antelope . . . the degraded, gibbering Yamparico, whose food consists of vermin; the aborigines of Victoria, among whom new-born babes are, when convenient, killed and eaten by their parents and brothers; the Alforese of Ceram, who live in families in the trees . . . the pygmy Dokos, south of Abyssynia, whose nails are grown long, like vultures' talons, that they may dig up ants, and tear the skins of serpents, which they devour raw; the Veddahs of Ceylon, who have gutturals and grimaces instead of languages.

Farrar mentions that many tribes attribute their origin 'with contented unanimity to the ape', going on to comment on the account of primitive races in the Book of Job, before remarking that his

> picture is not half so revolting as that photograph of modern savages, with which several modern travellers have presented us . . . take Dr. Mowatt's picture of dead [*sic*] Andamaners. 'Their expression as it had been settled by the hand of death was truly repulsive and frightful. Their features distorted by the most violent passions were too horrible for anything of human mould, and I could regard them only as the types of the most ferocious and relentless fiends. Their aspect was really that of demons. . . . '
> Gross ignorance, total nudity, and promiscuous intercourse, will give a notion of their moral condition; and to complete the picture of other savages would demand the introduction of features darker and deadlier still. To read one such description of savage life is to read all.
>
> (Farrar 1867, pp. 118–19)

Like Dr Johnson, Farrar believed that all savages are the same; the 'darker and deadlier' aspects probably refer to cannibalism. Allowing for the fact that Farrar's tirade is considerably more intemperate than the passage from Ortiz, the contents of the images presented are strikingly similar;[1] nor do the characterizations of either of them differ greatly from those of St Jerome. When one considers that this spans a range of about one-and-a-half millennia, in the course of which Europe underwent immense transformations, this is astonishing and also puzzling. What changed over this extensive period was mainly the *object* of the images. With the exception of the relatively short-lived child image, key aspects of the others remained remarkably constant: how is this to be explained? This is an intriguing question that has seldom been posed, since with a few exceptions there seems to be little awareness of that constancy. At the outset some disciplinary approaches that might seem to hold the promise of contributing to an answer will be briefly surveyed, only to show that they are unlikely to help.

## Some blind alleys

Images may be regarded as psychological phenomena; as such, one would expect that psychology, and especially social psychology, would help to throw light on their nature, origin and persistence. This is true to some extent, as indicated in the preface (p. xiv): Tajfel's work has uncovered one of the fundamental processes underlying ethnocentrism. However, it does not tell us what form it will take, or how particular forms come to endure.

The extensive literature dealing with such topics as stereotypes, prejudice and social representations may, at first sight, appear to be directly relevant. But the bulk of the stereotype literature refers to adjectival qualifiers like the 'stingy Scot', 'cruel Indian' or 'dumb Negro'. Not until quite recently have there been studies of noun-stereotypes of the kind relevant in the present context. It has been shown that

> compared to trait-based categories, these noun categories (1) are richer, having more features that afford a wider variety of inferences about category members; (2) are more imaginable, due to the fact that their features include not only traits but also physical characteristics, typical behaviors, and demographic characteristics; (3) are more distinctive in that they have idiosyncratic features not shared with other categories; and (4) function more efficiently in information processing tasks.
>
> (Hamilton *et al.* 1992, p. 122)

These conclusions certainly apply to the images as embodied in noun labels. However, the above theoretical formulation focuses on 'categories', i. e. mainly cognitive aspects, and fails to deal with the often extremely powerful emotional loading. In the literature on stereotypes this is dealt with in terms of the favourable or unfavourable *content* of stereotypes, said to be determined in part by the extent of group similarity or difference, and also by the nature of intergroup relations (Triandis 1994). As implied in the formulation by Triandis, most of the conventional 'stereotypes' literature, from the classic text of Allport (1954) onwards, postulates that the content of stereotypes varies in different periods and under different circumstances; hence the problem of continuity is not even on the social-psychological agenda, and it is difficult to see how it could be tackled from within its current theoretical framework, which largely excludes history.

The universalist stance of mainstream psychology was radically challenged by the French school of historiography founded during the inter-war years by Marc Bloch and Lucien Febvre, known as the 'Annales' historians. Their position was succinctly stated in Febvre's essay on 'History and psychology' (1953, p. 213):

> When psychologists . . . talk to us about the emotions, decisions, and modes of reasoning of 'man', they deal in reality with our emotions,

decisions, and modes of reasoning, with our particular situation as West European whites forming part of groups with a very ancient culture. But how could we historians rely on the help of a psychology based on the observation of 20th-century people for the purpose of interpreting the actions of men of the past?

It is the contention of these historians that each historical period is characterized by its own *mentality*, and that it is the task of historians, jointly with psychologists and especially social psychologists (Le Goff 1974), to study these mentalities. Or again Gurevich, discussing the problem of mentality as an explanation in history, states that 'The historian of mental structures is concerned with the intersection between social psychology and the history of culture' (1983, p. 187). The clarity and simplicity of the original thesis of the 'mentalities' historians has given way to more subtle and complex formulations (cf. Burke 1986), but the fundamental claim has not been abandoned. Hence if each period is characterized by its own 'mentality', this could be expected to result in *differences* between images in successive periods.

Then there is psychoanalysis, which deals primarily with the emotional side of human nature. Since the images under discussion are often heavily charged with emotion, and since the emotional responses of humans have certainly remained more stable over time than modes of thought, one would expect that depth psychology should be able to throw some light on the problem of continuity. There is a sense in which this is certainly true. The themes of sexuality and aggression in relation to Others recur throughout history. But this in itself does not explain the continuity of specific images.[2]

More interesting in the present context, since it deals with historical material, is Cohn's well-known work *Europe's inner demons* (1975) that has already been mentioned (p. 99). He provides an Appendix described quite frankly as 'psycho-historical speculations', explicitly based on psychoanalytic ideas. He lists various fantasies about witches consorting with the devil, cannibalistic infanticide, promiscuous orgies and so on, attributed to various out-groups. These are inter-preted as the results of projection on to these out-groups of 'obsessive fears' and 'terrifying desires' that formed part of the accusers' innermost selves, or are produced by 'wishes and anxieties experienced in infancy or early childhood, but deeply repressed and, in their original form, wholly unconscious' (Cohn 1975, pp. 259, 261). It is not possible to decide how far such speculations may be correct; but when one reads the literature there can be little doubt of the frequently deep emotional anchoring of images.

Apart from Cohn, psychoanalytically oriented writers have not addressed the particular issues considered here. But from another direction (not without occasional resort to psychoanalytic concepts) bold efforts have been made to throw light on western responses to 'the Other' in a broad culture-historical perspective.

## Over-arching analyses of 'alterity'

Both approaches to be discussed deal with 'myths' rather than 'images', and it is therefore necessary to indicate why I believe that they are, nevertheless, relevant. Myths are traditional stories embodying in symbolic form deeply entrenched cultural beliefs. As such, they contribute to shaping a particular outlook on the world, and this includes the mediation of the modes of feeling and perceiving which I have called 'images'. This seems to be implicit in a passage from Lévi-Strauss (1964, p. 346) on whom the authors rely to a considerable extent. The passage defies ready translation, and I shall therefore cite it in the original:

> Les nythes signifient l'esprit, qui les élabore au moyen du monde dont il faith lui-même partie. Ainsi peuvent être simultanément engendrés, les mythes eux-mêmes par l'esprit qui les cause, et par les mythes, une image du monde déjà inscrite dans l'architecture de l'esprit.

Lévi-Strauss seems not merely to be saying that myth links intellect to the emotions, but also hinting at the complex ways in which myths are perpetuated. Since certain myths, notably those of the 'monstrous races' and of the 'Wild Men of the Woods' have been shown to be implicated in the genesis of images, the study of myths is obviously pertinent. Moreover, if the nature of particular long-enduring myths is elucidated, this will also illuminate the sources of dominant images.

With this we return first to the post-structuralist and semiotic work of Mason (1990). While Mason's primary concern was with the impact of the discovery of the New World on European thought, he used this as a springboard for a wider consideration of European as well as Amerindian images of the Other. As already indicated (p. 103), his complex argumentation, inspired mainly by Emmanuel Levinas and Jacques Derrida, defies any concise rendering. The bold sweep of his intellectual flights frequently left this reader with a mixture of admiration and perplexity. Singling out some strands from so delicate and intricate a web is bound to be somewhat misleading, but I have neither the competence nor the space to do more.

The key to Mason's exposition of the images of the Other are the 'monstrous' or, as he prefers to call them, 'Plinian' races. The style of his approach may be typified by extracts from a chapter entitled 'The monstrous idiom', where it is proposed that the various forms taken by the body and its orifices in mythical representations have a semiotic function. 'The body communicates':

> The bodily orifices under discussion here are the ears, the nose, the mouth, the vagina and the anus. In fact, the system could be widened: the eyes, the navel and the penis may also be considered as bodily orifices . . . [and they] may be said to constitute a system.

> As Lévi-Strauss remarked, the terms for 'eat' and 'copulate' are identical in a very large number of languages. . . . This already indicates a linking of the sexual and alimentary codes, and enables us to pass from the orifices of the digestive system . . . to those of the genital system.
>
> (Mason 1990, p. 139)

There follow examples of numerous Amerindian myths, as well as an analysis in these terms of 'Plinian races'. In all such myths various modifications of body orifices are said to occur, and also associated variations in body articulation. Orifices and articulated movements are regarded as constituting homologous systems, expressing in parallel the same messages. This imaginary quasi-body language is then said to be analogous to writing, though the content of the messages appears to be left somewhat vague. The virtue of this kind of interpretation is that it seeks to find some meaning in creations like the Plinian races, which usually seem mere senseless fictions. The imaginary Plinian races with their bodily oddities, originally dreamed up to give form to the radically Others, are in turn used later to construct the images of newly encountered Others.

When relating this kind of scheme to a particular historical setting, Mason takes a vast leap which is apt to strain credulity (p. 149):

> the opening of the body is an opening to externality in general, and thereby to the Other. The Plinian races, as we have repeatedly pointed out, are of crucial importance for any theory of alterity. Is it more than a coincidence that the foundations of European anatomy, the dissection of the human body and the revelation of its inner world, coincide with the discovery of the New World and the European interest in cannibals there . . . ? At this point, the innermost parts of the body and the outermost parts of the world coincide.

If Mason's argument were confined to that particular period, it would not be relevant here. But he is clearly aiming at a *general* discourse[3] about alterity. He calls it 'Ethno-anthropology', which 'studies the possible accounts of possible worlds and their inhabitants' (p. 7) and is designed as a critique of empirical social anthropology. As I understand it, the images of the Other he analyses, and which overlap extensively with the ones discussed here, are trans-historical in character. The savage (my term) 'is constructed from European images of Europe's own repressed and outward projected Others' (p. 8). Or again 'The images are all products of a process of exclusion: witches, Wild Men, madmen and animals are aspects of the European self that self cannot tolerate' (p. 41).

In spite of Mason's disclaimer that he is only concerned with texts, his whole edifice rests on a foundation of psychological assumptions. These only emerge occasionally, as in the following passage (p. 175) concerning images of 'humanoids', said to result from sexual fantasies:

if we look at the information on spirit beings collected among the Guajiro of Venezuela by M. Perrin, we find two kinds of supernatural beings, *keeralia* and *akalakui*, which form a mutually reinforcing system in which the specific qualities attributed to one of these categories are simply the product of a mental operation seeking to define the complement of the other.

The word 'simply' here suggests that the whole thing is obvious, which is far from being the case. Moreover, the example is supposed to illustrate 'the existence of mental operations which precede zoological data', a claim whose meaning is obscure.

Generally, what Mason seems to be saying in his fascinating yet often exasperating volume is not only that the imaginary Others of Europeans and non-Europeans consist of similar patterns, but also that they are independent of time and place. In this sense it could be said that he takes continuity for granted, rather than explaining it. For explanation would entail an empirical approach of the kind he regards as mistaken and is anxious to eschew.

While Mason sometimes mentions Wild Men, these are clearly secondary in his scheme to the Plinian races. By contrast, the other general work on 'Otherness' to be considered virtually ignores them altogether. The bulk of Bartra's (1994) study is devoted to a detailed documentation of what he terms 'the myth of the wild man' over the centuries, from the Middle Ages to its traces in the present. It represented an underground movement, in opposition to the prevailing theological doctrines: 'The wild man was the pagan symbol of the Middle Ages most openly linked to sexual pleasure, erotic passion, and carnal love' (p. 100). Until the Renaissance the myth was transmitted by a persistent oral tradition, which then entered literature and thereby moved 'from popular culture to a sophisticated bourgeois culture' (p. 183). Bartra contends that the myth of the Wild Man contributed in a significant manner to the formation of a western identity, and among other things to its 'separation between nature and culture, which gives rise to the notion of *civility*' (p. 146). This is said to account for 'the Western distaste for peoples submerged in nature and [the] fear of a political vacuum' (p. 111) of a kind that has been illustrated in the present work from at least the 16th century onwards. Bartra goes so far as to claim that the myth created a new western individualist mentality. He stresses the 'astonishing continuity of a myth pregnant with modern reverberations'. Since the myth is a product of the imagination, it also shows that 'otherness is independent from the knowledge of others' (p. 204), which is an important point, clearly manifest in the image of the savage. The Wild Man takes on a distinctive character in each epoch, yet remains part of a continuous chain. The fundamental thesis advanced is summarized in the following passage:

> I believe that when confronted by a *logos* unable to fully explain the *mythos*, one must drastically change course and attempt to explain the *logos* through the *mythos* . . . .

> I want to reinterpret wild thought (producer of myths) not as a rational idea, but as a myth, thereby acknowledging the presence of a profound mythical impulse in the heart of Western culture, i.e., in the ancient horror and fascination for wildness. Thus escaping and fleeing from the natural bestiality of the wild man becomes a necessity.
>
> (Bartra 1994, p. 206)

The 'enigma' of the enduring presence of the myth is interpreted in terms of a kind of quasi-evolutionary adapation to the needs of different periods. This entails changes in 'the idea of otherness without which any notion of modern civilization is inconceivable' (p. 207).

Bartra's approach was considerably influenced by Lévi-Strauss, and he seems to agree with the latter that 'the Europeans were incapable of opening themselves to Otherness, since they only conceived it as a slight difference or as a radical and unsolvable contrast to their own identity' (Bartra 1995, p. 242).

Compared with Mason's rather esoteric discourse, Bartra's argument seems to be relatively more straightforward, though in my sparse exposition it also loses much of its subtlety and force. His demonstration of the pervasiveness of the myth during the Middle Ages and beyond, as well as its subsequent reverberations, is impressive. Bartra seeks to show that what he seems to regard as a foundation myth, shaped western mentality, including its modes of thought (*logos*) about Otherness, and perhaps more. He further makes an attempt to explain its continuity, an attempt which appears to imply something like a Jungian collective unconscious specific to the West. In this connection his position contrasts sharply with that of Mason, who states that broadly similar processes occur in all cultures.

Both authors agree in attributing far-reaching consequences to their respective myths, and the fact that they differ in their selections (Plinian races versus Wild Men) is perhaps not of critical importance. On the other hand, if one asks which of them contributes more towards an understanding of the images of the savage discussed in the present volume, my answer would be Bartra. Whether or not he is correct in detail – which would be hard to decide – one tends to feel that his is a plausible analysis of the type of mental soil from which the images grew. He also offers a rationale for the long-term effectiveness of the myth, said to manifest itself in varying forms at different periods. At first sight it would seem that this still does not account for the close similarity of images of the savage across epochs. However, it is arguable that changes in the forms of the myth (for example, from popular to scientific) may not affect the images it generates.

Both Mason and Bartra suggest that the function of the myths was that of shaping western identity. The same would have been true of the associated images, but this does not explain their persistence once a western identity had become firmly established. At a time when the cultural distance between the West and others was relatively small, it makes sense that there was a need for the West to differentiate itself from others. By the 19th century western scientific and technological superiority was so glaring that it is hard to see why it required bolstering. Yet it was precisely during that period that the ape and child images of the savage reached their apogee.

## An alternative view

Bartra argued that the forms of the myth (and presumably the associated images) underwent successive adaptations, while the function remained constant. However, in order to avoid the above-mentioned difficulty, it seems equally plausible to assume that the functions of the images changed in accordance with historical circumstances. On this basis I would venture an alternative interpretation: while accepting that at the outset the images are likely to have been primarily connected with the establishment of a western identity, their subsequent elaborations may have served the additional function of bolstering the status of dominant sub-groups in western societies.

This becomes particularly clear during the second half of the 19th century, when the 'otherness' of the savage came to be extended to a whole series of European 'Others', as viewed from the pedestal of the educated male middle class. Instances have been mentioned in passing in several of the preceding chapters, and the matter will be examined more closely here. Savages, in this context, form part of a cluster that includes not only children but also the rural and urban poor, criminals, the mentally ill, and even women.

The theoretical bases for these links are of two kinds. One is 'degenerationism', which originally held that savages had at one time been more advanced, but had degenerated to their current state. It subsequently became more directly biologized into 'atavism', a reversion to an earlier state. The other view was derived from Darwinism, and its interpretation from this point of view is analogous to a 'temporalized Great Chain'. Just as some 18th-century thinkers had believed that apes and savages were created before proper humans, so many 19th-century writers regarded several categories of their contemporaries as being 'less evolved'. Such theoretical assumptions were of course not necessarily stated explicitly, being commonly taken for granted. Especially in a literary context, the use of images was probably unreflective, drawn from the community pool of such images; but the pool itself was fed from prevailing scientific speculations or theories. In this manner a kind of self-perpetuating system operated, one that was slow to change.

While this topic would certainly deserve special study, only a few examples can be cited here. Thus Walter Bagehot ([1872] 1905, pp. 100–1) likened savages to 'gregarious beasts', attributing to them a tendency to imitate which they share with children, and to some extent also with 'uneducated people in civilised nations'. The frequent parallels in Victorian Britain between attitudes to savages and to the urban poor are extensively documented in Lorimer (1978) and McClintock (1995). The latter even has a quotation from Engels stating that the working class had been reduced to 'bestiality' (p. 43), the very epithet commonly attributed to savages. The tendency to equate the 'lower classes' with savages was by no means confined to Britain; here is a French example:

> Among the primitive and inferior races – *and there is no need to go to the pur savages to find them, since the lowest layers of European societies are homologous with primitive beings* – one always discerns a more or less greater incapacity to reason.
>
> (LeBon 1894, pp. 28–9; my emphasis)

Perhaps the most sweeping claims were made by Lombroso (1887), who cited numerous sources to show that savages lacked a conscience: 'In the savage state man does not know remorse; he derives vanity from his criminal exploits' (p. 413). Moreover, he claimed that women, being less evolved than men, also resemble savages in being less sensitive to pain. Lombroso's equation of the mentality of the born criminal with that of savages, wild beasts, the mentally ill and children was widely known, and continued to be accepted even after the methodological foundations of his work had been discredited. Lombroso's extravagant notions are mentioned in Russett (1989), who cites many other examples of this kind concerning women, for example, their child-likeness. Savages were sometimes linked to a whole cluster of undesirable European types:

> In the lower races the hollow of the foot does not exist, and the condition known as flat foot occurs. . . . It occurs among the stigmata of degeneracy, and is not rarely associated with grave moral defects and intellectual distortions. It and other feet degeneracies have been found frequently among paranoiacs, moral imbeciles, and prostitutes. This is particularly true of the prehensile power of the foot.
>
> (Talbot 1898, pp. 280–1)

That 'prehensile power' of course evokes a feature of apes. Havelock Ellis (1904, p. 422) argued in similar fashion about a tribe

> remarkable for the position of the big toe, set at a considerable angle to the foot, and almost opposable to the other toes . . . this atavistic peculiarity . . . is met with more especially among women. There can be little doubt that the smaller size of women as compared to men is connected with the preservation of a primitive character.

All these perceived resemblances clearly serve to affirm the identity, and superiority, of Victorian upper-middle-class males. It may be objected to such an interpretation that, over most of history, women were regarded as inferior to men, and the rich to the poor. In earlier ages, however, such status differentials were believed to have been instituted by God, and thus were not open to question. By the 19th century theological sanctions had lost much of their strength, and it was therefore convenient that a biological substitute had become available.

## On the processes underlying the continuity

This is an intriguing problem that has so far received relatively little attention. Bartlett touches upon it when critically discussing Jung's notion of the 'collective unconscious'. In this connection Bartlett (1932, p. 282) refers to 'that terrific persistence of apparently dead culture', and suggests that two factors may help to explain it. One consists of 'social tendencies' of a group embodied in institutions and customs; the other is the age overlap that renders such tendencies independent of the life of particular individuals. Unfortunately he fails to provide any concrete illustrations, so it is not altogether clear what he had in mind.[4]

Some years later Maurice Halbwachs began his studies of what he called 'collective memory', and a book with that title was posthumously published in 1950. It is a seminal work, neglected for some time, that has more recently inspired empirical studies. These are, however, largely confined to short time-spans for which not only ample documentation is available, but where people themselves can be interviewed (e.g. Galliker 1990; Middleton and Edwards 1990). Still, Halbwachs' central thesis is clearly relevant here:

> Collective memory . . . is a continuous current of thought, a continuity that has nothing artificial about it, since it retains from the past only that which is still living or capable of living in the mind of the group that maintains it. By definition, it does not go beyond the limit of that group. When a period ceases to interest the period that follows, it is not a case of the same group forgetting part of its past: there are, in reality, two groups which succeed each other.
>
> (Halbwachs 1950, p. 71)

The 'groups' Halbwachs was thinking of concerned relatively small-scale social units rather than nations, let alone 'the West' as a whole. Nonetheless, the important point made by him is that collective memories persist only as long as their content is of active concern to the members of a social unit; and that probably remains valid, whatever its size. It seems to make sense to regard the images of savages as part of the 'collective memory', and it follows from Halbwachs' analysis that such images must have performed some functions for them to be transmitted over numerous generations. Provided they do perform important functions, it is presumably not essential that such functions remain unchanged. Thus in the present case the initial function, as proposed by Mason and Bartra, will have been that of establishing and subsequently enhancing a 'western identity'; later it widened to underpin western superiority, the status of dominant groups in western societies, and to justify colonialism; latterly this changed to the function of providing a feeling of superiority over underpriviledged sections of western societies. While 'animality' remained as a constant, 'child-likeness' was most functional from about the mid-19th to almost the mid-20th century.

Halbwachs did not say a great deal about the actual processes of transmission, presumably since in small groups these are hardly problematic. In the case of the images, the modes of transmission were clearly multiple. Prior to the Renaissance, oral communication was probably predominant. Thereafter, as shown in detail by Bartra and Mason, literature and art played important roles, followed from the late 18th century onwards by scientific publications as well as popular journals and the press. However, at the popular level it is likely that oral transmission of the lore about savages continued to be salient. It may be questioned whether such transmission could take place over long time-spans, but there is evidence indicating that it is possible. For instance, Bastide (1960) showed that slaves imported from Yorubaland into Brazil were able to maintain a considerable part of their cultural heritage over centuries. Or again, there is the well-known study of children's lore and games:

> Like the savage, [schoolchildren] are respecters . . . of custom; and in their self-contained community their basic lore and language seem scarcely to alter from generation to generation. Boys continue to crack jokes that Swift collected from his friends in Queen Anne's time . . . they ask riddles which were posed when Henry VIII was a boy. Young girls continue to perform a magic feat . . . of which Pepys heard tell . . . they hoard bus tickets and milk bottle tops in distant memory of a love-lorn girl held to ransom by a tyrannical father; they learn to cure warts . . . after the manner which Francis Bacon learnt when he was young. etc.
>
> (Opie and Opie 1959, p. 2)

The authors emphasize that the learning of these games was not mediated by adults, but passed on solely through the cohorts of children. Hence the importance and long-term effectiveness of transmission through person-to-person interaction can hardly be doubted.

## A new version of the ape image in recent science

While ape images at the popular level persist with little notable change, scientific positions have undergone some substantial modifications since the Second World War. Prior to it, as has been documented, 19th century ideas were slow to disappear. The process was greatly accelerated by the rise of Nazi race doctrines. The revulsion occasioned by these led to *ex cathedra* statements by groups of anthropologists, biologists, geneticists and psychologists condemning them. This stance has never been abandoned, though some theories, like that of Rushton already discussed, or of Herrnstein and Murray (1994), come fairly close to doing so.

Then during the 1960s, on the margins of mainstream science, a group of 'pop ethologists' postulated that modern man and savages alike have innate behavioural tendencies, inherited from our animal ancestry. This is already implicit in Desmond Morris' (1967) title *The naked ape*; and Robert Ardrey (1967) had no qualms proposing that fighting for ones's country, or fencing in one's property, are basically the same in-built responses as an animal chasing off intruders from its territory. While such effusions were not taken too seriously by 'normal science', it was a different matter when sociobiologists came on the scene; yet their theories, while more subtle, were not fundamentally different. Wilson's (1978) *On human nature*, Diamond's (1991) *The rise and fall of the third chimpanzee* and Ridley's (1993) *The red queen* all reassert in varying degrees the proneness of 'savages' to aggression, lawlessness, adultery, murder and warfare – omitting only cannibalism. Such claims have been heavily criticized (e.g. Rose *et al.* 1984), but this literature nevertheless remains influential.

It is particularly to be noted in the present context that the unpleasant behaviours attributed by sociobiologists to hunter-gatherers (the prototypical 'savages') is closely connected to ape behaviour as described in recent primatological studies. The point of these comparisons is to show that modern humans share many of the traits of savages and apes, which have evolved through natural selection and are constitutive of human nature itself. This represents a striking reversal from past centuries, when the alleged resemblance between savages and apes was used to contrast them with the fully human Europeans. What was regarded as one of the main dividing lines was the possession of language, savages being seen as having either none, or at best a very imperfect one; another criterion was the absence of any technical skills. It has now been established that apes are capable of not inconsiderable symbolic communication (De Luce and Wilder 1983; Savage-Rumbaugh *et al.* 1993), and use a rich variety of tools even in the wild (Boesch 1993; McGrew 1992). Moreover, other quasi-human traits, such as cooperation and warfare, have also been discerned in chimpanzee societies.

These parallels are less surprising in the light of our present knowledge that we (i.e. all humans) share more than 98 per cent of our DNA with chimpanzees. Hence modern humans, the hunter-gatherers, and the apes, are linked by shared, genetically determined, attributes. While in the 19th century both social evolutionists and Darwinists saw animality and savagery as the starting point of a development culminating in the superiority of westerners, the new perspective is one that telescopes time, showing the continuity – and by implication, inevitability – of many features of modern culture with our savage and pre-human ancestry.

All this harks back to some of the main concerns of Enlightenment thinkers: they saw savages as ancestors, with whom they had much in common; and they struggled with the problem of the relationship between humans and apes, and with that of the boundary of humanity. In this way they were closer to the modern position than much of 19th-century thought. In recent decades there has been a re-evaluation of the ape to the extent that it has even been suggested in 'A declaration on great apes' that these close relatives of ours should be bracketed together with *homo sapiens* and accorded the same basic rights of life and liberty (Cavalieri and Singer 1993). This re-evaluation of the ape greatly diminishes, without precisely specifying it, the distance between the ape/savage and the civilized. Thereby the images evoked by the ape/savage trope have gained a new lease of life in recent scientific discourse. Hence it could be said that continuity of images has been maintained, but is accompanied by a radical shift in discursive function.

# POSTSCRIPT

## The images as symptoms and supports of racism

What does all this signify? Was it merely a stirring around in what Augustine Birrell described as 'The great dust-heap called "history" ', to come up with some intriguing facts that no longer concern us today? Has the continuity now been broken, so that in our modern age we can dismiss these absurdities from the past as no longer relevant? Or perhaps the continuity itself might be questioned as an unlikely phenomenon. Beginning with this last issue, I would point out that such continuity is by no means confined to images of savages. It applies, for instance, to a different kind of Other, namely the mentally ill; and the parallel is rather close: Jodelet (1991, p. 176) specifically referred to the notion of the 'animality' of mental patients. Non-rational, 'superstitious' beliefs and practices have persisted, sometimes for millennia. In some European communities even the use of sorcery is, or was until quite recently, still alive (Favret-Saada 1977). An outstanding example is that of astrology, which has not merely survived but regained a certain amount of respectability as well as enjoying considerable commercial success. The reason is that such beliefs continue to serve psychological functions which I have discussed elsewhere (Jahoda 1969).[1]

These examples of enduring 'superstitions' are on a par with emotionally based beliefs in racial inferiority. Underlying them is an uncomfortable fact that tends to be ignored, often even by psychological theories. Most texts on child development describe a linear trend from early animism and quasi-magical ideas to adult rationality. However, it has been shown that scientific-logical and early magical modes of thinking, fused with emotion, coexist in varying degrees in adult minds, coming to the surface and overshadowing rationality in certain contexts (for a review, cf. Cole and Subbotsky 1993). What Piaget called the 'ego-centrism' of the small child is not, as he postulated, necessarily outgrown, but becomes the ethnocentrism of numerous adults.

All this helps to account for the continuity of the images, whose relevance for current concerns has already been documented in several chapters in this volume. While it is true that the images no longer have the support of the majority of political and scientific establishments, and have to some extent been driven underground, they are far from having become extinct. The images, it should be remembered, are of course tokens which stand for clusters of – predominantly negative – beliefs and feelings regarding out-groups. The key image in this connection, and the one that has survived most stubbornly, is that of 'animality'.

When one considers how long this has been a major theme in the western past, this survival is hardly surprising. Ideas and feelings about the imaginary Other, which had their remote roots in the Middle Ages, gradually became focused on the 'savages'. First the American Indians, and then the blacks, acquired in popular belief the attributes of sub-humans. In the crucible of the anti-slavery debate the issues were highlighted, and from the end of the 18th century onwards the 'new biology' began to buttress the old belief with its authority. This illustrates the now generally accepted fact that science is not an activity completely detached from mundane concerns, which deals only with objective truths. The precise manner in which the men of science at the turn of the 19th century came to be influenced by the prevailing climate of opinion remains an intriguing puzzle; but there is little doubt that it did influence them. There were of course dissenters, but the dominant ethos of the 19th century proclaimed the 'animality' of blacks and other ethnic groups. This in turn greatly strengthened the popular attitudes from which the scientists had drawn their original inspiration.

The retreat from this scientific position was more recent than is sometimes realized. In the United States the medical profession was in the forefront of racial denigration, and plenty of the 19th-century doctrines concerning blacks could still be found in the medical journals of the early years of the present century. They included allegedly simian features, 'bestiality', 'sexual madness', and even 'insanity' (cf. Haller 1970).

As late as the 1920s and beyond, prominent psychologists who lacked any first-hand knowledge of other cultures did not hesitate to compare 'primitives' with European children and the mentally ill. Furthermore, as has been shown, the decline of such notions even among professionals and academics has been gradual, and is not altogether complete. It would therefore be unrealistic to suppose that the ancient images are no longer present at the popular level. Indeed, anyone paying attention to informal conversations can verify this. As Street (1985, p. 102) noted:

> When I was doing research in the 1970s for a thesis on [racism], I was constantly amazed by the similarity between the popular symbols and myths of race that I would encounter in pubs, etc., and the representations of race in the obscure nineteenth-century anthropology journals that I was consulting in academic libraries.

Among the symbols, the 'monkey' image was and remains the most salient: Street mentioned its invocation by football crowds when a black player comes on to the field; symbolic bananas were sometimes thrown on to the pitch. There has been little change since he wrote. For example, when a football team from Zaire played against Scotland, there were reports that the Zairiens had brought monkeys with them to eat; this neatly combines the monkey image with a hint of cannibalism.[2]

The traditional images are by no means confined to football crowds, but are widely found among the police who are supposed to protect all citizens equally. There is evidence that they refer to blacks as being 'animals' and 'bestial' (e.g. Gilroy 1987).

While some of these may be specifically British aberrations, it has also been reported that one of the most common stereotypes of racist discourse in France is that of 'bestial sexuality' (cf. Lorreyete 1989), an image that goes back a very long way. Even a casual perusal of the daily press provides a constant flow of instances. As I am writing, a scandal is erupting at the oil giant Texaco, where executives are being accused of referring to blacks as 'orang-utans' or 'porch monkeys' (*The Times*, 18 November 1996). Or, again in Britain, a law report refers to repeated physical and verbal abuse of a fellow-worker of mixed descent: 'He was called "chimp", "monkey", and "baboon" ' (*The Times*, 16 December 1996). Even cannibalism has reappeared in popular writing, as, for example, in the best-selling book *Congo* (Crichton 1993), which was made into a film. In it the author, in a 'faction' style citing authorities, attributes deep-rooted cannibalistic tendencies to the inhabitants of Central Africa. Or again, in the United States a documentary film was released in 1994 dealing with the Korowai, an Oceanic pople. Significantly entitled 'Treehouse people: cannibal justice', it panders to the sensationalist appetite of viewers in the absence of any clear evidence:

> The film opens with rumors of cannibalism and then culminates in the elaborate description, analysis, and staged reenactment of anthro-pophagy. Using the cinematography of horror – close-ups, noir lighting, fastpans and point-of-view shots – the filmmakers make cannibalism a site of special aesthetic and emotional investment.
>
> (Morris 1996, p. 140)

It was even possible in the 1990s for a New York talk-radio host to say that in the United States there are millions of subhumanoids, savages who have not become civilized (Mukhopadhyay and Moses 1997). In sum, there can be no doubt that the images are alive and well, in spite of official condemnations.[3]

It hardly needs pointing out that owing to the radical tranformations that have taken place in the world during the present century, the 'savages' of old have largely disappeared.

The process actually began at the height of the colonial period, when missionaries and colonial administrators set up schools. The aim was partly the idealistic one of civilizing the savages, but also had the more practical purpose of providing a supply of catechists and clerks. The initial limits of such endeavours are shown by the fact that the schooling and training had been intended to remain rather basic, and to concentrate on practical skills. But once set in motion, the process became unstoppable. There were indications of the ambivalence with which this civilizing process was viewed by people in the home countries. Thus the sight of 'savages' in European dress evoked a negative reaction, as shown

THE "WINSTON WALK" IN CENTRAL AFRICA.
*(The effect on the natives of a visit from the Rt. Hon. W. Churchill.)*
" Oh, why do dey call me a Winston boy—Winston boy—Winston boy ?!! " etc., etc.

*Figure P.1* Africans were often ridiculed for 'aping' Europeans. The references to Winston
　　　　Churchill shows how close to our time this was.
*Source: Punch*, 1908.

by numerous caricatures of the period ridiculing the jumped-up savages, who
were seen as vainly seeking to 'ape' Europeans in a grotesque manner (see Figure
P.1). One comes across such derogatory labels as 'Hosennigger' (nigger in
trousers), sometimes coupled with a romantic idealization of the 'natural' savage.
The feeling of incongruity elicited by a person in European attire, yet whose face
was not pink, faded only gradually. Similarly, a wider acceptance that non-
Europeans need not be confined to menial occupations, since they have the same
potential as Europeans, was also slow to arrive. The other side of the coin is of
course that most traditional cultures have been extensively transformed as a result
of contact with the West.

　　Nowadays the process is well-nigh complete, and the remaining peoples who
have managed to more or less preserve their original cultures are portrayed in
television documentaries in a manner similar to that of endangered animal
species. Thus the savages to which the images once referred have largely ceased to
exist. This poses the question of why the images continue to persist in the absence
of their original objects. There is of course no simple answer, and current theories

246

are of little help, since they concern themselves with the images only marginally, if at all.

These theories may be broadly dichotomized into individual and societal ones. The former tend to attribute prejudice to certain character types, sometimes viewed as 'pathological', or to situational factors in persons' lives whereby they experience frustration which causes aggression that is then directed at convenient targets, notably the Other. Societal theories range from classical Marxist ones – where exploiters encourage prejudice and discrimination for their own purpose – to 'realistic conflict' ones. Straddling the two is the (mainly cognitive) learning approach, whereby children acquire prejudice from their social environment. In addition, there is Tajfel's 'social identity' theory, mentioned previously (p. xiv), which taps the root of 'Otherness'.

Since ethnocentrism is a complex phenomenon that has no single cause, it would be absurd to deny that each of the theories may be relevant in certain circumstances. However, in the discussions about racism there is seldom any reference to the historical factors examined here. At most, there is occasional mention of slavery and colonialism, without any detailed analysis of their effects.

There is even less awareness of the fact that the origins of ethnocentric images reach far back into the western past. Hence the continuity documented here must rest at least in part on permanent aspects of raw human nature, especially concerning the basic needs of sex and food, which are symbolically closely related. Conflicts and anxieties in these spheres have tended to manifest themselves in the attribution to savages of excessive sexuality, or shocking breaches of the civilized rules governing the consumption of food. These attributions were usually either grossly exaggerated or frequently just pure fantasy. From this it will become understandable that the fading away of the old 'naked savage', who was always in the main a *construction* of the European imagination, did not entail the dis-appearance of the images.

The civilized descendants of the savages, marked out merely by their pigmentation, will do just as well. For instance, a man once told an African doctoral student of mine, 'go back up the trees in the fucking jungle where you've come from'. Thus he was drawing on a store of traditional images still widely available in the culture. Moreover, in making this offensive remark he was, at the same time, asserting his superiority by virtue of being a member of a civilized society as contrasted with the 'jungle'. This brings in once again, but in a different form, the issue of identity. For in such cases the images serve to bolster the self-esteem of relatively disadvantaged white people in modern society.

Such conclusions are rather chastening regarding the aim of eliminating the images from what have become multicultural societies; for it would entail the abolition of social inequalities, which is utopian. Furthermore the usual cure-all, namely education, also has its limitations. Without wishing to deny the impor-tance of its potential contribution, it should be pointed out that there are at least two reasons why it cannot be expected to fully solve the problem.[4] One is that the images are largely non-rational in character, presumably serving emotional and ego-protective needs. Hence even scientific training does not necessarily eradicate them (cf. Jahoda 1968).

The second reason has to do with the stage at which the images are acquired, and this requires some elaboration. The key question here is how the images come to be transmitted. It is obvious that, nowadays at any rate, the transmission must be informal, since neither teachers, textbooks nor the media directly propagate them. An obvious possibility is that the images are transmitted from parents to children, or between peers. However, in my reading of the extensive literature on the development of children's awareness of ethnic differences, I have never come across any mention of such images. It therefore seems to me that, just as the Opies found lores and games being directly passed on through generations of children with minimal involvement on the part of adults, so the images are probably not usually transmitted before the end of formal schooling. This would mean that individuals only become exposed to them once they have entered the adult social world. They would then acquire them within informal social networks, in the course of casual conversations in such settings as the work place, during parties, in pubs and so on.

If this view is correct, it is difficult to see how such a process might be effectively blocked. There is only one suggestion that I might make, whereby people who deprecate the offensive images could, as individuals, make some modest contribution towards their eradication. Let me explain. Like everyone who does not lead too sheltered a life, I have from time to time witnessed talk in which the labels were bandied about, often in seemingly jocular fashion, in relation to blacks and Asians. On such occasions I have frequently noted that individuals, whom I knew to be opposed to any kind of racism, usually failed to intervene. On being questioned afterwards why they had not done so, a common response was that there was no point – 'you cannot change the views of bigots'. There was probably also an unavowed reluctance to set oneself apart from the group. However, as a consequence, there tends to result an illusory impression of unanimity among those present. One does not become more popular by shattering it, but if it were done on a substantial scale it might over time make some impact.

The analysis put forward in this volume leads to the conclusion that there is no easy answer to the problem. At the same time it would be wrong to end on a pessimistic note. When one compares the prevalence of images during the 19th century with that at the end of the 20th, it is clear that there has been substantial change for the better. At least in their cruder forms the images have been forced out of the public domain, ceasing to be respectable, and are now largely confined to the subterranean levels of popular culture.

# NOTES

1 For a modern, more sophisticated approach to stereotypes cf. Sherman (1996).
2 The year in square brackets always shows the date of first publication.

## 1 INTRODUCTION

1 The identity of Sir John Mandeville has been disputed, and his claims to have travelled to the Orient in the second part of his book (which contains the fantastic tales) have been shown to be false. For a recent assessment cf. Milton (1996).
2 On conceptions of humanity and animality cf. also Willis (1974) and Ingold (1988).
3 Curiously enough, Michiels was the translator of Harriet Beecher Stowe's *Uncle Tom's Cabin*, a task he must have undertaken only for financial reasons. For although he had never been to Africa, the preface to his own book consisted of a violent diatribe against Africans.
4 It should be mentioned that this interpretation, though long accepted, has been questioned by some modern scholars such as Lockhart (1994, p. 240 ff.).

## 2 THE SAVAGE AMERICANS

1 This was first demonstrated in a seminal essay by Leach (1958), and has since been shown to hold for women as well as for men (e.g. Delaney 1994; Mageo 1994).
2 Other examples of Indians being compared with animals, including dogs and pigs, can be found in Prien (1978).
3 An insightful study of images of South American Indians which bears upon the present theme is that of Taussig (1987).
4 Half a century later Wundt was to regret such statements and to express the view that 'the intellectual endowment of primitive man is in itself approximately equal to that of civilized man' (Wundt 1916, p. 113).
5 In Canada an Enfranchisement Act giving Indians civil (including voting) rights was passed as early as 1869, but it seems to have had little effect on images. This is indicated by Haycock (1971), who cites early 20th-century examples of animal and child comparisons. For a general survey covering all North American Indians cf. Washburn (1988); images in literature are described by Barnett (1975) and Monkman (1981).
6 'Today the consumers can eat, drink and dress "Indian" . . . one can wear Cherokee clothing, Seneca socks and Apache boots. During the day this consumer can drink native teas and snack on Hopi Blue Popcorn . . . to be "naturally" clean, one can shampoo with Native American Naturals and bathe with Zuni soaps' (Wesaw 1995, p. 10).

## 3  THE SAVAGE AFRICANS

1  The *locus classicus* is Lovejoy ([1936]1983); an excellent account of the last phase of the 'Great Chain' is by Bynum (1974).

2  Another source of confusion was the fact that in English 'ape' used to be the generic term before 'monkey' came into use; hence in early mentions of 'apes' one cannot be sure to what species reference was being made.

## 4  THE PUZZLE OF APES AND MEN

1  One naturalist, the Abbé Fontenu, claimed to have crossed a rabbit with a hen; and the brilliant experimenter Réaumur went so far as to make an attempt at replicating this feat. The rumour that he had succeeded created a sensation in Paris around 1740 (Poliakov 1975, p. 168).

2  A famous case was that of 'Wild Peter', a dumb boy unable to walk erect, who had been displayed at the English court. Linnaeus, evidently convinced by such cases, also listed such examples as the Lithuanian bear-man, the wolf-man from Hesse, and the Irish sheep-man; generally, he characterized wild men as shaggy-haired, mute and four-footed.

3  The Scottish associationist David Hartley took a similar view: 'Apes and monkeys, of the several Kinds, seem to approach nearest to Man, in the general Faculty of Reasoning, and drawing conclusions' (Hartley [1749] 1966, p. 410).

4  cf. Furth (1966) on the logical thinking of language-deprived children.

5  There circulated during that period a just-so story, attributed variously to Javanese natives and African Negroes, to the effect that orang-utans are perfectly capable of speech, but refrain from using this faculty in order to avoid being forced into unwelcome labour.

6  Elsewhere he assigned this position to the 'New Hollanders' (i.e. Australian Aborigines), who were then becoming known as the 'lowest' of black peoples (cf. Strong 1986).

7  In fact the penis of anthropoid apes is smaller than that of human males.

8  George Romanes (1848–94) in his *Mental evolution in man* (1888) characterized it as a proto-language, transitional between animal and human.

9  The Hottentots, belonging to a group now known as 'Khoisans', were in fact lighter than the Bantu populations further north.

10  This reputation continued well into the 19th century. The notorious American race theorists Nott and Gliddon (1854) stated that below 10° N. latitude 'the most degraded races of mankind' are to be found, with a 'cephalic conformation' that renders any hope of improvement futile (p. 185).

## 5  THE 'NEGRO' AND THE APE

1  For a detailed account of the behaviour of slave owners in Jamaica and elsewhere cf. Walvin 1992.

2  It is curious that even the most rabid detractors of blacks (in Europe, though not in the United States) felt obliged to voice their opposition to slavery.

## 6  TOWARDS SCIENTIFIC RACISM

1  He was able to establish that the famous 'Wild Peter' had been the mute mental defective child of a widower, turned out of his home by a new stepmother. Or again, he rebuked with gentle wit some of Linnaeus' categorizations:

> The custom of making women thin by a particular diet is very ancient, and
> has prevailed amongst the most refined nations, so politeness and respect
> forbid us to class it, with Linnaeus, amongst deformities.
>
> (Blumenbach [1795] 1865, p. 128)

2  During a visit to Switzerland,

> he saw from behind a female form which struck him by its harmonious
> and beautiful shape. He spoke to the girl, who turned her face on
> Blumenbach, and he saw to his stupefaction the features of an African lady
> ... Blumenbach was enchanted . . [and his] delight reached its height
> when he realised that the girl was not only beautiful, but also witty and
> sensible.
>
> (Debrunner 1979, pp. 142–3)

Blumenbach seems to have had quite a flirtation with her, and the experience clearly made a great impression on him.

3  Such topics include what Meiners described as their lack of visual judgement, which his examples indicate relate to what would now be called visual space perception (1815, Vol. 3, p. 222). On the other hand, he mentioned their good visual memory (pp. 224–5), and certain manual skills. Yet overall he asserted their complete unfitness for arts and sciences (p. 223).

4  For a detailed account of Virey's life and teachings cf. Benichou and Blanckaert (1988).

5  It is not clear whether Virey had actually read Long; although he referred to some publications in English, I have not come across any direct reference to Long. Nonetheless, in view of the prevalence of scholarly exchanges at that period it is virtually certain that Virey was familiar with Long's work.

6  At about the same time Daubenton (1764) proposed a measure of the angle of the head in both animals and men, relating to the position of the hole at the base of the skull ('Le grand trou occipital') through which the nerves pass into the brain. According to Barzun (1938), 'Daubenton was measuring in degrees the position of the head on top of the spinal column and correlating the measure of that angle with the amount of will-power in the several races' (p. 52). This was not in the *Mémoire* I consulted, nor was I able to trace any other one where it appeared.

7  The method which Camper devised may be briefly outlined as follows. He placed a skull in a position where the orifices of the ears and the lowest part of the nasal aperture were level, and this he somewhat arbitrarily designated as the horizontal. He then drew a line between the forehead and the foremost part of the front teeth, ignoring any intersection with the nasal bones. The angle between those two lines came to be known as the 'facial angle'. A high angle is one where the forehead is more or less on a vertical line with the chin, while a low value indicates a forward projection of the jaw in relation to the cranium, a characteristic that came to be known as 'prognathism' (cf. Baker 1974; Cowling 1989; Curtin 1965).

8  For more detail cf. Blanckaert (1987) or Gould (1991).

## 7  ON THE ANIMALITY OF SAVAGES

1  Those biographies of Cuvier I consulted were of no help. For instance, Viénot (1932) cited the early letter to show that Cuvier was without any prejudice, but failed to mention his subsequent stance.

2  Cuvier also said that the facial angle is relatively high in infants, which gives them a pleasant appearance. This was a shrewd observation, anticipating Tinbergen's (1951) view that the shape of an infant's head acts as an innate releaser of parenting behaviour. Tinbergen did not express the sign stimulus in terms of Camper's 'facial angle', characterizing it in part as 'a short face in relation to a large forehead' (p. 209); in the illustrations on that page the baby has a facial angle of approximately 110°.

3  Francis Galton [1883] (1928) claimed that 'Energy is an attribute of the higher races, being favoured beyond all other qualities by natural selection' (p. 18) and 'is eminently transmissible by descent' (p. 19). Accordingly, he suggested that maximizing it should

be the primary aim of any eugenics programme. Galton's views on eugenics are discussed by Richards (1997).

4 'Khoisanid' designates peoples consisting of two main ethnic sub-groups, one being the Sanid known as Bushmen, and the other the Khoid, a term used to cover a group of tribes collectively known in the past as 'Hottentots'.

5 In a footnote, LeBon complained that both he and Vogt had been 'persecuted' for reporting the facts that had emerged from research concerning women.

6 It is an inverted formulation of Spencer (1877, Vol. I, p. 102), who had written that the savage, like the child, 'exhibits a predominant perceptiveness with comparatively little reflectiveness'.

7 For a critical discussion of this and other similar theories cf. Kamin (1993); Kohn (1995); Richards (1997).

## 8 CANNIBALISM AT ISSUE

1 By Hulme (1986), whose book contains an extensive analysis of Defoe's work.

2 This is not to imply either that all science has become anti-racist, or that mainstream science has effectively transformed popular attitudes.

3 Sixel used 'public order' to denote this category instead of the now more usual one of 'government' because it was often stated that there was no such order. This is readily understandable, since the question as to how 'acephalous' tribes manage to maintain such order has only been satisfactorily resolved by anthropologists in the twentieth century.

4 The notion has been revived more recently by Harris (1977) and is known as 'the protein deficiency theory'; it has found few adherents.

5 This is of course merely a crude simplification. Mason explicitly rejects the metaphor of a *symmetrical* mirror image, suggesting that 'the worlds juxtaposed are incommensurable' (p. 166). This view appears to me logically flawed, for Mason cites examples of Amerindian cosmology obtained by anthropologists; if there were really incommensurability, this would have been impossible.

6 This is another debate not directly relevant in the present context; but it is worth mentioning that recent research provides some support for pre-historic cannibalism (Gibbons 1997).

7 Since this was written I saw a feature on the BBC evening news (30 January 1996) dealing with the civil war in Sierra Leone. Some of the young teenage boys, who had been recruited and who had subsequently either been captured or had deserted, were shown. The (African) psychiatrist active in their rehabilitation stated that many of them had taken part not only in mutilating people in the villages, but also in cannibalism.

8 Such attributions, at least in their mythology, also occurred among some 'native' (North- ) Americans such as the Western Soshoni (Clemmer 1996).

## 9 THE FASCINATING HORROR

1 Arens (1979, p. 175) refers to an introductory anthropological text which has a picture of an African with filed teeth and states that 'such filing is a frequent custom among cannibals'.

2 There was a more concrete reason why many competent scientists did not dismiss the matter out of hand, at least so far as the relatively short tail was concerned. At the embryological stage of normal humans there is a rudimentary caudal appendage that is later reabsorbed. There were also well-documented cases of anomalous individuals who retained such an appendage after birth. Hence it did not seem totally implausible that there might be a whole group genetically primed to retain such an appendage. The authorities were divided, the sceptics arguing that it was at best a case of very

infrequent monstrosities (the reports varied, some stating that only men had a tail, others that both sexes had it, while others again mentioned isolated individuals). The noted physical anthropologist Quatrefages, took a balanced view, suggesting that if the stories of the Niam-Niam were not fables, and if one assumed that the singularity is hereditary, then it would not be extraordinary to find it in some individuals.

3 It begins by noting that 'Tailed men have again turned up' and ends as follows: 'As this somewhat sensational account has been published by our esteemed contemporary *l'Anthropologie* . . . we must treat it with respect; and we hope it will not be long before these tailed men are carefully described by a trained scientific observer.'

4 Although Burton had a low opinion of most Africans, and the above reports are not credible, it should be said that he also made very significant contributions in other respects.

5 For instance, when an expedition was due to leave for Senegal, a distinguished panel of scientists prepared a set of research instructions (Geoffroy St Hilaire *et al.* 1860). They requested that skulls should be obtained; if that were not possible owing to scruples arising from people's respect for the dead, measurements of the 'facial angle' and suchlike should be carried out. They were also asked to check a previous finding that certain teeth of some Negroes were the same as those of apes. At the time Broca was actively searching for anatomical similarities between blacks and apes.

6 As regards the question of whether the Azande had ever been cannibals, Evans-Pritchard remained sitting on the fence. After stating that 'no one will deny that the evidence of the travellers each considered independently ranges from the dubious to the worthless' went on, 'but there is no smoke without fire, and . . . we may conclude, that there is a strong probability that cannibalism was practised at any rate by some Azande' (1965, p. 153). His procedure of adding together probable negatives to yield a highly probable positive has since often been held up to ridicule. Lewis (1985) discusses the reasons that were likely to have led Evans-Pritchard to such a conclusion.

7 In fact many of these alleged cases were based on unreliable 19th-century reports, with a good deal of attendant confusion; for example, Azande and Niam-Niam were recorded as separate units, yet the latter is merely an older name for the same people.

8 The entry on 'Cannibalism' was dropped from more recent editions.

9 On an occasion when I discussed race relations with African colleagues in Ghana, they cited the 'missionary-in-the-pot' cartoons as indicative of European attitudes. One of them mentioned that he had complained about them to an expatriate, only to be told that Africans lacked a sense of humour!

10 In Bokassa's case there are indications that the charge may have been justified. In his obituary in *The Times* (5 November 1996), reporting on his trial, it is stated that 'Despite the discovery of human corpses stuffed with rice in the presidential freezer, accusations of cannibalism were dismissed for lack of evidence'.

## 10  FROM ANCESTOR TO CHILD

1 For instance, Cole (1996, p.15) suggests that what he calls the 'child analogy' follows naturally from the assumptions of social evolutionism. Although correct logically, it does not correspond to the actual chronological sequence.

2 This is reminiscent of William Golding's well-known novel *Lord of the flies* (1971).

3 Comte recognized three main human races, namely white, yellow and black; these he characterized, respectively, as intelligence, industry and emotion. But unlike most of his contemporaries, he did not regard these differences as permanent: in his futuristic vision of an age of universal harmony, they would have disappeared (cf. Poliakov 1974, p. 224).

## 11 RESCUING THE 'BENIGHTED SAVAGE'

1 During the early stages of European expansion, no such clear distinction existed as yet. At the time of the Spanish conquest, the ostensible purpose of both state and church was the christianization of the benighted savages; but this noble aim had little practical effect on their treatment of them. It might also be objected to the present analysis that colonies had existed long before the 19th century, without the child image making more than a very rare appearance. The answer is that the aim of civilizing the savages which gave rise to the trope was almost entirely absent prior to the Enlightenment.

2 In 1900 the Governor of the Gold Coast demanded its surrender: he wanted to sit on it as a token of his authority. This demand was a fatal mistake: the 'Golden Stool' was a hallowed symbol of the nation, and for anyone to sit on it would have been sacrilege. The result was war.

3 As his title indicates, Allier also attempted some rather unconvincing psychological interpretations, referring to such figures as Freud and Lévy-Bruhl.

4 In citations from Allier, page references coupled with a year in square brackets denote a quotation from a missionary; page references alone are to Allier's own statements.

5 This may be compared with Meyer Fortes' famous monograph on child development in Taleland, where he reported in a neutral manner that even young children became sexually aware in the absence of any direct instruction (Fortes 1938).

6 This reverend gentleman painted a generally dismal picture of all non-European cultures, including the Orient, where one finds 'the most degrading customs and . . . the most puerile superstitions' (ibid., Vol. I, p. 183). But he was particularly scathing about Africa. On the East Coast 'the flesh of the old, the infirm, and the useless is dried and preserved' and then 'offered to guests'. On the West Coast 'Young boys are brought from the dark interior, kept in pens, fattened upon bananas, and finally killed and baked' (ibid., p. 156). It is interesting that this information was culled from an article by 'a correspondent' in the *Saturday Review* of 14 September 1895!

7 Since practically all of them owed their education to the missions, early criticisms tended to be rather muted, like that of Aggrey, who wrote, 'Africa is a child, but our paternalists fail to observe that this child is growing' (cited in Smith 1929, p. 2); it was only after the Second World War that sharp critiques came to be voiced (cf. Mobley 1970).

8 This is an interesting comment, echoed down the years and discussed by Mannoni (1956) in terms of the concept of 'dependence'. In certain African cultures a powerful person bequeathing a gift is thereby perceived as having established a 'client' relationship, whereby further favours can be expected in return for loyalty. For instance, a boy in West Africa whom I helped with his school fees expected me to send him to Britain for further education, which regrettably I was unable to do. This kind of behaviour is apt to be interpreted by Europeans as greed or ingratitude, whereas it is in fact a response rooted in traditional social relationships. Such misunderstandings continue, as shown by a recent complaint by two psychologists about what they called the 'pay me reaction' (Carr and MacLachlan 1993, p. 412).

## 12 WHY SAVAGES ARE CHILD-LIKE

1 Haeckel greatly exaggerated the uniformity of developmental stages. His work contained a picture purporting to illustrate the similarity of these stages in a variety of species, including fish, salamander, turtle, chicken, pig, cow, rabbit and human. It has since been shown that these drawings were largely imaginary and not based on actual specimens (Richardson *et al.* 1997).

2 The chapter on 'Natural selection and the human brain' in Gould (1983) provides a lucid overview of the arguments.

3  For details of Carothers' background and activities see McCulloch (1995).
4  The original heading of the middle column read 'Development of individual Man'; since this is liable to be misunderstood, I have replaced it.
5  By that time educated Negroes were well aware of such theories and sought to counter them. For instance, Edward Blyden (1888), a West Indian, wrote: 'The mistake which Europeans often make in considering questions of Negro improvement and the future of Africa, is in supposing that the Negro is the European in embryo – in the undeveloped stage' (p. 316).

## 13  HEADS I WIN, TAILS YOU LOSE

1  These are extensively illustrated by Gould (1977), to whom I am indebted for some of the examples.
2  Jung wrote:

> All this experience suggests to us that we draw a parallel between the phantastical, mythological thinking of antiquity and the similar thinking of children, between the lower human races and dreams. This train of thought is not a strange one for us, but quite familiar through our knowledge of comparative anatomy and the history of development, which shows us how the structure and function of the human body are the results of a series of embryronic changes which correspond to similar changes in the history of the race. Therefore, the supposition is justified that ontogenesis corresponds in psychology to phylogenesis. Consequently, it would be true, as well, that the state of infantile thinking in the child's psychic life, as well as in dreams, is nothing but a re-echo of the prehistoric and the ancient.
>
> (Jung 1944, p. 14)

3  Unless otherwise stated, these reports are cited from Andrée (1887).
4  The problems experienced in some cultures in 'understanding pictures' are discussed in Deregowski (1980).
5  For an annotated bibliography of studies of the period cf. Naville *et al.* (1951).
6  Actually the book was originally published in 1940, at a time when Nazi racism was rampant; it is significant, however, that the section discussed here was not eliminated.

## 14  HOW CHILD-LIKENESS LINGERED

1  For further details about Piéron cf. Jahoda (1995).
2  For a detailed examination of Lévy-Bruhl's ideas cf. Horton 1973; they are discussed in their broader context by Littleton 1985 and Tulviste 1987.
3  Critics rightly pointed out that in sifting through a vast mass of material he selected those items that tended to support his theory, a fatal flaw he himself was later to acknowledge.
4  For a translated reprint cf. Luria and Vygotsky ([1930] 1992); a concise introduction to Vygotsky's theory is provided by Wertsch (1991) and Van der Veer and Valsiner (1991).
5  Greenfield *et al.* (1966) who carried research on cognitive development among Wolof children in West Africa cited Werner's passage on precocity followed by early arrest with approval: 'This is an accurate formulation with respect to the difference between the performance of school children and those who have not been to a Western-style school in the present experiments' (pp. 317/18). It is evident, however, that the notion of 'arrested development' is used by them in quite a different sense from the old one, since they acknowledge that development continues when the setting is appropriate.

6 These so-called 'chain-type' drawings have been discussed by Deregowski (1969).

7 I have not been able to consult Werner (1926) and therefore do not know how closely his writings correspond to the more recent ones.

8 Here are some illustrative examples from the extensive literature: Boyer 1993; Cole 1990; Cole and Scribner 1974; Dasen 1984; Dasen and Ribaupierre 1987; Hollis and Lukes 1982.

## 15 IMAGES MIRRORED AT POPULAR LEVEL

1 Although I focus here on one of the least admirable sides of Burton, this is not intended to deny his remarkable achievements, including valuable ethnographic descriptions.

2 The account of the digging up of corpses is probably based on fact – Malinowski personally witnessed such a scene. But the alleged reason for doing so ('desire for human flesh') is totally inaccurate. In the Trobriands relatives of the dead were obliged to show their respect and piety by sucking on pieces of decaying flesh, a duty they performed with every sign of disgust (Malinowski 1929).

3 Reproduced in Pieterse (1992, p. 116).

4 For a detailed analysis of entries under 'Nègre' in French works of reference, cf. Brasseur (1976).

5 See e.g. Cario and Régismanset 1911; Dabydeen 1985; Hoffmann 1973; Killam 1968; Milbury-Steen 1980; Steins 1972; Street 1975.

6 British writers were less frank about this aspect of colonial life, and it only emerged into the open with the occasional scandal, as in the case described on p. 150.

7 More precisely, what was untrue was the story of an epidemic of rapes by *blacks*. There certainly were rapes, which usually remained unpunished, by both African and European troops (Tuohy 1931).

8 Invasive anthropometric investigations in the field were carried out during the 1920s. For instance, in the Ivory Coast, twenty-four measurements were taken of nude males and females, including the circumferences of the chest and of the uppermost part of the leg (Tauxier 1924).

9 Numerous examples of this kind of advertisement are reproduced in Pieterse (1990).

## 16 THE RELATIVITY OF IMAGES

1 A similar point was made by Rosenthal (1971) who discussed the nature of medieval intelligence, according to him very different from but not inferior to our own.

## 17 THE CONTINUITY OF IMAGES

1 It is worth mentioning that at the time he read his paper, Farrar had been Classics Master at Harrow, and was later to become Headmaster of Marlborough. These were of course among the major nurseries of future empire-builders, and it seems unlikely that Farrar would have kept his views from his pupils.

2 Psychoanalytical approaches to ethnocentrism and prejudice date back almost half a century, and are discussed by Allport (1954). They are generally interpreted in terms of individual (or sometimes group) psychopathology; a recent example is Young-Bruehl (1996). A different kind of elaborate theory has been put forward by Gilman (1985), who suggests that the 'deep structure' of stereotypes relates to the process whereby individuals split off their own 'bad self' and project it on to 'the Other'. Thus the image of 'the Other', while apparently located in the external world, in fact draws on internal representations that have been repressed. There are also such gems as 'the black, whether male or female, came to represent the genitalia through a series of

analogies' (Gilman 1985, pp. 109–10). While this kind of argument appears to me to be unconvincing, a more historically informed interpretation has been put forward by Kovel (1988); however, it is mainly concerned with the relatively recent American context.

3 Mason explicitly disclaims any ambition to put forward a theory, which would run counter to his deconstructionist stance: 'How to formalise rules when the very notion of a rule . . . is precisely that which is called into question by the method?' (p. 5).

4 In order to show that age overlap may not be necessary, he refers to the inheritance of intelligence, which from our present perspective entirely misses the point.

## POSTSCRIPT

1 In a different sphere there is the 'Robin Hood' theme, symbolizing opposition to the unfairness of established authority. It dates from the 14th century and was still evoked in the Lincoln green hoods of the poll tax protesters who broke into Nottingham Council Chambers in 1993 (cf. Seal 1996).

2 In Kuper (1994), which contains other examples of racism in football.

3 Although not concerned with images as such, Richards (1997) provides a comprehensive account of the persistences of race-thinking in modern psychology.

4 It may be noted that in the past education had directly the opposite effect. This is because it was precisely the educated elite (doctors, scientists, missionaries, social scientists and journalists) who were actively engaged in disseminating the images discussed here, thereby influencing the *content* of education at the time.

# REFERENCES AND FURTHER READING

Abd-El-Hamid-Bey (pseudonym of Louis du Couret) (1854) *Voyage au pays des NIAM-NIAMS.* Paris.

Académie des Sciences (1849a) Comptes Rendus, Lundi 20 Aout.

Académie des Sciences (1849b) Comptes Rendus, 22 Octobre.

Acher, R.A. (1910) Spontaneous constructions and primitive activities of children analogous to those of primitive man. *American Journal of Psychology* 21: 114–50.

Adam, Paul (1911) *La ville inconnue.* Paris: Ollendorf.

Ainsworth, M.D.S. (1967) *Infancy in Uganda.* Baltimore, MD: Johns Hopkins University Press.

Al-Azmeh, A. (1992) Barbarians in Arab eyes. *Past and Present* 134: 3–18.

Allier, Raoul (1925) *La psychologie de la conversion chez les peuples non-civilisés* (2 vols). Paris: Payot.

Allport, G.W. (1954) *The nature of prejudice.* Cambridge, MA: Addison-Wesley.

Altick, R.D. (1978) *The shows of London.* Cambridge, MA: Harvard University Press.

André, J. and Filliozat, J., (eds) (1980) *Pline l'ancien: histoire naturelle.* Paris: Société d'Edition 'Les Belles Lettres'.

Andree, R. (1887) Das Zeichnen bei den Naturvölkern. *Mitteilingen der Anthropologischen Gesellschaft in Wein* VII: 98–114.

Andrew, C. (1985) *Secret service.* London: Heinemann.

Anon (1854) Peuples ichtyophages et créophages. *Magasin Pittoresque* XXII: 224.

Appleton, L.E. [1910] (1976) *A comparative study of the play activities of adult savages and civilized children.* Chicago, IU: University of Chicago Press. Reprinted by Arno Press.

Ardrey, R. (1967) *The territorial imperative.* London: Collins.

Arens, W. (1979) *The man-eating myth.* Oxford: Oxford University Press.

Ariès, P. (1973) *Centuries of childhood.* Harmondsworth: Penguin.

Azurara, Gomes Eannes de (1896) *The chronicle of the discovery and conquest of Guinea* trans. and ed. by C. Beazley and E. Prestage. London: Hakluyt Society.

Bagehot, Walter [1872] (1905) *Physics and politics.* London: Kegan Paul, Trench, Trübner.

Baker, J.R. (1974) *Race.* London: Oxford University Press.

Baker, Samuel White (1866) *The Albert Nyanza, great basin of the Nile* (2 vols). London: Macmillan.

Baldry, H.C. (1965) *The unity of mankind in Greek thought.* Cambridge: Cambridge University Press.

Baldwin, James Mark (1895) *Mental development in the child and the race.* New York: Macmillan.

Balfour, Henry (1893) *The evolution of decorative art.* London: Rivington Percival.

Banton, M. (1987) *Racial theories*. Cambridge: Cambridge University Press.

Barker, A.J. (1978) *The African link*. London: Frank Cass.

Barley, Nigel (1986) *The innocent anthropologist*. Harmondsworth: Penguin.

Barnett, L.K. (1975) *The ignoble savage: American literary racism, 1790–1890*. Westport, Conn: Greenwood Press.

Barret, P. (1888) *L'Afrique occidentale* (2 vols). Paris: Baillière.

Bartels, F.L. (1949) *The provision and administration of education in the Gold Coast 1765–1865*. Unpublished MA thesis, University of London Library.

Barthelemy, A.G. (1987) *Black face maligned race*. Baton Rouge: Louisiana State University Press.

Bartlett, F.C. (1932) *Remembering*. Cambridge: Cambridge University Press.

Bartlett, R (1981) *Gerald of Wales*. Oxford: Clarendon Press.

Bartra, R. (1994) *Wild men in the looking glass: the mythic origins of European otherness*. Ann Arbor: The University of Michigan Press.

Bartra, R. (1995) The imperial dilemma. *Critique of anthropology* 15: 219–47.

Barzun, J. (1938) *Race: a study in modern superstition*. London: Methuen.

Bastide, R. (1960) *Les religions africaines en Brézil*. Paris: Presses Universitaires de France.

Baudrillard, J. (1983) What are you doing after the orgy? *Artforum* (October): 42–6.

Bauer, E., Fischer, E. and Lenz, F. (1931) *Human heredity*, trans. E. and C. Paul. London: Allen & Unwin.

Baumann, H. (1936) *Schöpfung und Urzeit des Menschen im Mythus der Afrikanischen* Völker. Berlin: Dietrich Riemer.

Beatty, K.J. (1915) *Human leopards*. London: Hugh Rees.

Becher, H. (1967) Die endokannibalistischen Riten als früheste Erscheinungsform der Anthropophagie. *Zeitschrift für Ethnologie* 42: 248–53.

Behn, W.F.G. (ed.) (1845) *George Cuvier's Briefe an C.H.Pfaff aus den Jahren 1788 bis 1792*. Kiel.

Bendyshe, Thomas (1865) *The anthropological treatises of Johann Friedrich Blumenbach*. London: Longman, Green.

Benichou, C. and Blanckaert, C. (1988) *Julien-Joseph Virey*. Paris: Vrin.

Bergeron, Pierre (1694) *Les voyages fameux du Sieur Vincent Le Blanc* (2 vols). Paris.

Berlin, I. (1990) *The crooked timber of humanity*. London: John Murray.

Bernheimer, R. (1952) *Wild men in the Middle Ages*. Cambridge, MA: Harvard University Press.

Binet, A. and Simon, T. (1919) L'arriération. *Année Psychologique* 16: 349–60.

Binger, L.G. (1892) *Du Niger au Golfe de Guinée*. Paris: Hachette.

Bitterli, U. (1970) *Die Entdeckung des schwarzen Afrikaners*. Zürich: Atlantis.

Bitterli, U. (1971) Der Eingeborene im Weltbild der Aufklärungszeit. *Archiv für Kulturgeschichte* 53: 249–63.

Blanckaert, C. (1987) Les 'vicissitudes de l'angle facial' et les débuts de la craniométrie. *Revue de Synthèse*, 4e série, No. 3–4, p. 417.

Blumenbach, Johann Friedrich (1787) Einige naturhistorische Bemerkungen bei der Gelegenheit einer Schweizerreise: von den Negern. *Magazin für des Neueste aus der Physik und Naturgeschichte Gotha* I: 1–12.

Blumenbach, Johann Friedrich [1795] (1865) *The anthropological treatises of Johann Friedrich Blumenbach*, trans. and ed. Thomas Bendyshe. London: The Anthropological Society.

Blyden, Edward W. (1888) *Christianity, Islam and the Negro race* (2nd edn). London: Whitingham.

Boas, Franz (1894) Human faculty as determined by race. *Proceedings of the American Association for the Advancement of Science* XLIII: 303–4.

Boas, Franz (1911) *The mind of primitive man*. New York: Macmillan.

Boas, G. (1948) *Essays on primitivism and related ideas in the Middle Ages*. Baltimore, MD: The Johns Hopkins University Press.

Boas, G. (1966) *The cult of childhood*. London: The Warburg Institute.

Boesch, C. (1993) Transmission aspects of tool use in wild chimpanzees. In T. Ingold and K. Gibson (eds) *Tools, language, and intelligence: an evolutionary perspective*. Cambridge: Cambridge University Press.

Bogdan, R. (1988) *Freak show*. Chicago, IU: University of Chicago Press.

Bolt, C. (1971) *Victorian attitudes to race*. London: Routledge & Kegan Paul.

Bonaparte, Marie (1934) Psychanalyse et ethnographie. In E.E. Evans-Pritchard, R. Firth, B. Malinowski and I. Schapera (eds) *Essays presented to C. G. Seligman*. London: Kegan Paul, Trench, Trubner.

Bonjan, J. (1981) Une image ethnologique: 'la mentalité primitive'. *Itineraires: Notes et Travaux*. Genève: Institut Universitaire d'Etudes du Développement.

Bonnet, Charles (1764/5) *Contemplation de la Nature*. Amsterdam.

Bonnetain, Paul (1895) *Dans la brousse: sensations du Soudan*. Paris: Lemerre.

Boswell, James [1777] (1909) *The life of Samuel Johnson* (2 vols). London: Dent.

Boswell, John (1991) *The kindness of strangers*. London: Penguin.

Bovet, Pierre (1923) *The fighting instinct*. London: Allen & Unwin.

Boyer, P. (ed.) (1993) *Cognitive aspects of religious symbolism*. Cambridge: Cambridge University Press.

Brantlinger, P. (1985) Victorians and Africa: the genealogy of the myth of the dark continent. *Critical Inquiry* 12: 166–203.

Brantlinger, P.B. (1988) *Rule of darkness*. Ithaca: Cornell University Press.

Brasseur, P. (1976) Le mot 'Nègre' dans les dictionnaires encyclopédiques Francais du XIXe siécle. *Cultures et Développement* 8: 579–94.

Bril, B. (1986) The cultural context of motor development. *International Journal of Behavioral Development* 9: 439–453.

Broca, Paul (1862) Sur les proportions relatives du bras, de l'avant bras et de la clavicule chez les nègres et chez les européens. *Bulletin de la Société d'Anthropologie de Paris*, Vol. 3, Part 2.

Broca, Paul (1864) *On the phenomena of hybridity in the genus homo* (ed. C.C. Blake). London: Longman Green.

Broca, Paul (1874) Sur la valeur des divers angles faciaux et sur un nouveau goniomètre facial median. *Bulletins, Scoiété d'Anthropologie de Paris* 9: 358–84.

Brown, R. (1995) *Prejudice: its social psychology*. Oxford: Blackwell.

Bryson, G. (1945) *Man and society: the Scottish inquiry of the eighteenth century*. Princeton, NJ: Princeton University Press.

Bucher, B. (1981) *Icon and conquest*. Chicago, Ill.: Chicago University Press.

Bucher, B. (1982) Die Phantasien der Eroberer. In K-H Kohl (ed.) *Mythen der Neuen Welt*. Berlin: Fröhlich & Kaufmann.

Bühler, Karl (1930) *The mental development of the child*. London: Kegan Paul, Trench, Trubner.

Burke, P. (ed.) (1973) *A new kind of history*. London: Routledge & Kegan Paul.

Burke, P. (1986) Strengths and weaknesses of the history of mentalities. *History of European Ideas* 7: 439–51.

Burnet, James (1773) *On the origins and progress of language*. Edinburgh.

Burrow, J.W. (1966) *Evolution and society*. Cambridge: Cambridge University Press.

Burton, Richard F. (1860) *The lake regions of Central Africa* (2 vols). London: Longman, Green, Longman & Roberts.

Burton, Richard F. (1864) *A mission to Gelele, King of Dahome* (2 vols). London: Tinsley.

Buschan, G. (1906) Primitive Zeichnungen von Kindern und von Wilden. *Die Umschau* X: 461–7.

Bynum, W.F. (1974) *The problem of man*. Unpublished Ph.D. thesis, University of Cambridge.

Byrne, R. (1995) *The thinking ape*. Oxford: Oxford University Press.

Ca'da Mosto, d'Alvise de [1507] (1895) *Relation des voyages à la Cote occidentale de l'Afrique 1455–1457*, (ed.) M.C. Schefer. Paris: Leroux.

Cairns, H.A.C. (1965) *Prelude to imperialism*. London: Routledge & Kegan Paul.

Camilleri, C. and Cohen, M. (eds) *Chocs de cultures* Paris: L'Harmattan.

Campbell, Joseph (1989) *Historical atlas of world mythology. Vol. II: The way of the seeded earth. Part 2: Mythologies of the primitive planters: the North Americas*. New York: Harper & Row.

Campe, J.H. [1779, 1848] (1977) *Robinson der Jüngere*. Munich: Weismann (cited in Kappeler (1992)).

Camper, Petrus (1794) *The works of the late Professor Camper*, trans. T. Cogan. London: Dilly.

Carey, J. (1973) *The violent effigy: a study of Dickens' imagination*. London: Faber & Faber.

Cario, L. and Régismanset, C. (1911) *L'Exotisme: la littérature coloniale*. Paris: Mercure de France.

Carlin, N. (1984) Ireland and natural man in 1649. In F. Barker *et al.* (eds) *Europe and its others*, Vol. 2. Essex: University of Essex.

Carlyle, Thomas (1853) *The nigger question*. London: Bosworth.

Carothers, J.C. (1953) *The African mind in health and disease*. Geneva: World Health Organization.

Carothers, J.C. (1972) *The mind of man in Africa*. London: Tom Stacey.

Carr, S. and MacLachlan, M. (1993) Asserting psychology in Malawi. *The Psychologist* 6: 408–12.

Castelnau, Francis de (1851) *Renseignements sur l'Afrique Centrale et sur une nation d'hommes a queue*. Paris: Bertrand.

Cavalieri, P. and Singer, P. (1993) *The great ape project*. London: Fourth Estate.

Chamberlain, A.E. (1900) Die Entwicklungshemmung des Kindes bei den Naturvölkern und bei den Völkern von Halbkultur. *Zeitschrift für Pädagogische Psychologie und Pathologie* 2: 303–309.

Chamberlain, A. F. (1896) *The child and childhood in folk-thought*. New York: Macmillan.

Champlain, Samuel (1604) *Des sauvages*. Paris.

Champsaur, Félicien (1926) *La caravane en folie – Afrique* (2nd edn). Paris: Fasquelle.

Churchill, A. and Churchill, J. (1746) *A collection of voyages and travels*. London: Lintot & Osborn.

Clemmer, R.O. (1996) Ideology and identity: Western Soshoni 'cannibal' myth as ethnonational narrative. *Journal of Anthropological Research* 52: 207–23.

Cleverley, J. and Phillips, D.C. (1976) *From Locke to Spock*. Melbourne: Melbourne University Press.

Cohen, W.B. (1980) *The French encounter with Africans* Bloomington: Indiana University Press.

Cohn, N. (1975) *Europe's inner demons*. London: Heinemann.

Cole, M. (1996) *Cultural psychology*. Cambridge, MA: Harvard University Press.

Cole, M. (1990) Cultural psychology: a once and future discipline? In J.J. Berman (ed.) *Cross-cultural perspectives*. Lincoln: University of Nebraska Press.

Cole, M. and Scribner, S. (1974) *Culture and thought*. New York: Wiley.

Cole, M. and Subbotsky, E. (1993) The fate of stages past: reflections on the heterogeneity of thinking from the perspective of culture-historical psychology. *Schweizerische Zeitschrift für Psychologie* 52: 103–13.

Collinson, S. (1990) Robert Knox' anatomy of race. *History Today* 40: 44–9.

Conrad, Joseph [1902] (1994) *Heart of darkness*. London: Penguin.

Copans, J. and Jamin, J. (1978) *Aux origines de l'anthropologie francaise*. Paris: Le Sycomore.

Cope, E.D. (1887) *The origins of the fittest*. London: Macmillan.

Corbain, A. (1992) *The village of cannibals*. Cambridge: Polity Press.

Cowling, M. (1989) *The artist as anthropologist*. Cambridge: Cambridge University Press.

Crichton, M. (1993) *Congo*. London: Arrow.

Cureau, A.L. (1904) Essai sur la psychologie des races nègres en Afrique tropicale. *Revue générale des Sciences pures et appliquées et Bulletin de l'Association francaise pur l'Avancement des Sciences* 15: 638–52.

Cureau, A. (1912) *Les sociétés primitives de l'Afrique Equatoriale*. Paris: Armand Colin.

Cureau, A. [1912] (1915) *Savage man in Central Africa*. London: Fisher Unwin.

Curtin, P.D. (1965) *The image of Africa*. London: Macmillan.

Curtis, L.P. Jr (1968) *Anglo-Saxons and Celts*. University of Bridgeport, Connecticut: Conference on British Studies.

Curtis, L.P. Jr. (1971) *Apes and angels. The Irishman in Victorian caricature*. Washington, DC: Smithsonian Institution Press.

Cust, Robert Needham (1891) *Africa rediviva. Or, the occupation of Africa by Christian missionaries of Europe and America*. London: Elliot Stock.

Cuvier, Georges (1800–5) *Lecons d'anatomie comparée* (5 vols). Paris: Baudouin.

Cuvier, Georges (1827–30) *The animal kingdom* (16 vols). London: Whittaker.

Cuvier, Georges [1817] (1994) *Etudes sur l'ibis et Mémoire sur la Vénus hottentotte*. Paris.

Dabydeen, D. (ed.) (1985) *The black presence in English literature*. Manchester: Manchester University Press.

Dalal, F. (1988) The racism of Jung. *Race and Class* XXIX: 1–22.

Dapper, Olfert (1670) *Beschreibung von Afrika*. Amsterdam.

Darwin, Charles [1859] (1928) *The origin of species*. London: Dent.

Darwin, Charles [1871] (1901) *The descent of man and selection in relation to sex*. London: John Murray.

Dasen, P.R. (1984) The cross-cultural study of intelligence. *International Journal of Psychology* 19: 407–34.

Dasen, P.R. and Ribaupierre, A. (1987) Neo-Piagetian theories: cross-cultural and differential perspectives. *International Journal of Psychology* 22: 793–832.

Daubenton, M. (1764) Mémoire sur les différences de la situation du grand trou occipital dans l'homme et dans les animaux. *Mémoires de l'Academie des Sciences* 1 September.

Davenport, C.B. and Steggerda, M. (1929) *Race crossing in Jamaica*. Washington, DC: Carnegie Institution of Washington.

Davidson, S. (1949) Psychiatric work among the Bemba. *Rhodes-Livingston Journal* 7: 75–86.

Debilius, H. (1991) Taxidermy threat to Olympics. *The Times*, 16 November.

Debrunner, H.W. (1979) *Presence and prestige: Africans in Europe*. Basel: Basler Afrika Bibliographien.

Defoe, Daniel [1719] (1972) *Robinson Crusoe*. London: The Folio Society.

Degérando, Joseph-Marie [1800] (1978) Considérations sur les diverses méthodes à suivre dans l'observation des peuples sauvages. In J. Copans and J. Jamin (eds) *Aux origines de l'anthropologie francaise*. Paris: le Sycomore.

Delaney, C. (1994) Untangling the meanings of hair in Turkish society. *Anthropological Quarterly* 67: 159–72.

De Luce, J. and Wilder, H.T. (1983) *Language in primates*. New York: Springer.

De Maillet (1755) *Telliamed*. La Haye.

De Mause, L. (ed.) (1976) *The history of childhood*. London: Souvenir Press.

Demel, W. (1992) Wie die Chinesen gelb wurden. *Historische Zeitschrift* 255: 625–66.

Dendy [?] (1869) Contributor to a debate on 'the character of the Negro' at the London Anthropological Society. *The Anthropological Review* VII: clxv.

Dennis, J.S. (1899) *Christian missions and social progress* (3 vols). Edinburgh: Oliphant Anderson & Ferrier.

Deregowski, J.B. (1969) Preference for chain type drawings in Zambian domestic servants and primary schoolchildren. *Psychologia Africana* 12: 172–80.

Deregowski, J.B. (1980) Perception. In H.C. Triandis and W. Lonner (eds) *Handbook of Cross-Cultural Psychology*, Vol. 3, Basic processes. Boston, Ill.: Allyn & Bacon.

Desmond, A. (1979) *The ape's reflexion*. London: Blond & Briggs.

Desmond, A. and Moore, J. (1991) *Darwin*. London: Michael Joseph.

Detienne, M. (1982) Between beasts and gods. In R.L. Gordon and R.G.A Buxton (eds) *Myth, religion and society*. Cambridge: Cambridge University Press.

Devisse, J. (1979) *L'image du noir dans l'art occidental* ,Vol. 2, Part 1. Des premiers siècles chrétiens aux 'Grandes Decouvertes'. Fribourg: Office du Livre.

Diamond, J. (1991) *The rise and fall of the third chimpanzee*. London: Radius.

Dickason, O.P. (1984) *The myth of the savage*. Edmonton: University of Alberta Press.

Dickens, Charles [1868] (1958) The noble savage. In *The uncommercial traveller and reprinted pieces*. London: Oxford University Press.

Dollard, John (1957) *Caste and class in a southern town* (3rd edn). New York: Doubleday.

Dragadze, T. (1988) Sex roles and state roles in Soviet Georgia. In G. Jahoda and I.M. Lewis (eds) *Acquiring culture: cross-cultural studies in child development*. London: Croom Helm.

Drummond, Henry (1888) *Tropical Africa*. London: Hodder & Stoughton.

Drummond, Henry (1894) *The Lowell lectures on the ascent of man*. New York: Pott.

Duchet, M. (1970) Monde civilisé et monde sauvage au siècle des Lumières. In *Au siècle des Lumières*. Paris: Ecole Pratique des Hautes Etudes.

Dudley, E. and Novak, M.E. (1972) *The wild man within*. Pittsburgh: University of Pittsburgh Press.

Dunstan, G.R. (1964/5) A note on an early ingredient of racial prejudice in western Europe. *Race* 6: 334–9.

Duval, Pierre (1685) *Geographia Universalis*. London.

Eickstedt, E. von (1940) *Geschichte und Methoden der Anthropologie*. Stuttgart: Enke.

Elfasi, M. (1988) *Africa from the seventh to the eleventh century*. London: Heinemann.

Elias, N. (1978) *The history of manners: the civilizing process*. New York: Pantheon.

Ellis, A.B. (1890) *The Ewe-speaking people of the Slave Coast of West Africa*. London: Chapman and Hall.

Ellis, Havelock (1904) *Man and woman*. London: Walter Scott.

Eng, Hilda [1931] (1954) *The psychology of children's drawings* (2nd edn). London: Routledge & Kegan Paul.

Evans-Pritchard, E.E. (1934) Lévy-Bruhl's theory of primitive mentality. *Bulletin of the Faculty of Arts* (Egyptian University, Cairo), 2.

Evans-Pritchard, E.E. (1937) *Witchcraft, oracles and magic among the Azande.* Oxford: Clarendon Press.

Evans-Pritchard, E.E. (1965) *The position of women in primitive societies and other essays in social anthropology.* London: Faber & Faber.

Evans-Pritchard, E.E. (1971) *The Azande: history and political institutions.* Oxford: Clarendon Press.

Eysenck, H.J. (1971) *Race, intelligence and education.* London: Temple Smith.

Farr, R.M. and Moscovici, S. (eds) (1984) *Social representations.* Cambridge: Cambridge University Press.

Farrar, Frederic William (1860) *An essay on the origin of language.* London: John Murray.

Farrar, Frederic William (1867) Aptitudes of races. *Transactions of the Ethnological Society* 5: 115–26.

Favret-Saada, J. (1977) *Les mots, la mort, les sorts.* Paris: Gallimard.

Febvre, Lucien (1953) *Combats pour l'histoire.* Paris: Armand Colin.

Fenichel, Otto (1945) *The psychoanalytic theory of neurosis.* New York: Norton.

Fernandez-Armesto, F. (1987) *Before Columbus.* London: Macmillan.

Field, M.J. (1960) *Search for security.* London: Faber & Faber.

Fields, B.J. (1982) Ideology and race in American history. In J. Morgan Kousser and J.M. McPherson (eds) *Region, race and reconstruction.* New York: Oxford University Press.

Figlio, K.M. (1976) The metaphor of organization. *History of Science* XIV: 17–53.

Fischer, Eugen (1955) Ueber die sogenannte Hottentotschurze. *Zeitschrift für Morphologie und Anthropologie* 47: 58–66.

Forde, Darryl C. (1963) *Habitat, economy and society.* London: Methuen.

Formigari, L. (1973) Chain of being. In P.P. Wiener (ed.) *Dictionary of the History of Ideas*, Vol. I, pp. 325–35. New York: Charles Scribner.

Formisano, L. (1992) *Letters from a New World.* New York: Marsilio.

Forster, Georg [1786] (1969) Noch etwas über die Menschenrassen. In *Werke* (4 vols). Frankfurt: Insel.

Forsyth, D. (1983) The beginnings of Brazilian anthropology: Jesuits and Tupinamba cannibalism. *Journal of Anthropological Research* 2: 147–78.

Fortes, Meyer (1938) *Social and psychological aspects of education in Taleland.* London: International Institute of African Languages and Cultures.

Fouillée, Alfred (1895) *Tempérament et caractère selon les individus, les sexes et les races.* Paris: Alcan.

Fouillée, Alfred (1903) *Esquisse psychologique des peuples Européens.* Paris: Alcan.

Fraessle, J. (1926) *Negerpsyche im Urwald am Lohali.* Freiburg im Breisgau: Herder.

Frank, E. (1987) Sie Fressen Menschen. In H.P. Duerr (ed.) *Authentizität und Betrug in der Ethnologie.* Frankfurt: Surkamp.

Franke, E. (1915) *Die geistige Entwicklung der Negerkinder.* Leipzig: Voigtländer.

Frazer, Sir James G. (1913) *The scope of social anthrolopogy.* London: Macmillan.

Fredrickson, G.M. (1981) *White supremacy.* New York: Oxfod University Press.

French, V. (1977) History of the child's influence: ancient mediterranean civilizations. In R.Q. Bell and L.V. Harper (eds) *Child effects on adults.* Hillsdale, NJ: Erlbaum.

Freud, Sigmund [1921] (1955) Group psychology. In J. Strachey and A. Freud (eds) *The standard edition of the complete psychological works of Sigmund Freud.* London: The Hogarth Press.

Freud, Sigmund (1938) *A general introduction to psychoanalysis.* London: Hogarth.

Friedman, J.B. (1981) *The monstrous races in medieval art and thought*. Cambridge, MA: Harvard University Press.

Froude, James Anthony (1895) *English seamen in the 16th century* (new edn). London: Longmans Green

Furth, H.G. (1966) *Thinking without language*. New York: The Free Press.

Galliker, M. (1990) *Sprechen und erinnern*. Göttingen: Hogrefe.

Galton, Francis [1883] (1928) *Inquiries into human faculty and its development*. London: Dent.

Galton, Francis (1908) *Memories of my life*. London: Methuen.

Géber, M. (1958) L'enfant africain occidentalisé et de niveau social supérieur en Ouganda. *Courrier* 8: 517–23.

Géber, M. and Dean, R.F.A. (1957) The state of development of newborn African children. *Lancet* 272 (1): 1216–19.

Gehlen, Arnold (1962) *Der Mensch*. Frankfurt-am-Main: Athenäum.

Gellner, E. (1973) The savage and the modern mind. In R. Horton and R. Finnegan (eds) *Modes of thought*. London: Faber & Faber.

Geoffroy St. Hilaire, Etienne and Cuvier, Georges (1795) *Histoire naturelle des orang-outangs*. Paris.

Geoffroy St. Hilaire, Isidore, Castelnau, Francis de and Broca, Paul (1860) *Instructions pour le Sénégal*. Paris: Bennuyer.

Gerbi, A. (1973) *The dispute of the New World*. Pittsburgh: University of Pittsburgh Press.

Gerbi, A. (1985) *Nature in the New World*. Pittsburgh, PA: University of Pittsburgh Press.

Gergen, K.J. (1973) Social psychology as history. *Journal of Personality and Social Psychology* 26: 309–20.

Gibbons, A. (1997) Archaeologists rediscover cannibalism. *Science* 277: 635–7.

Gillispie, C.C. (1959) *Genesis and geology*. New York: Harper.

Gillispie, C.C. (1951) *Genesis and geology*. Cambridge, MA: Harvard University Press.

Gilman, S.L. (1985) *Difference and pathology: stereotypes of sexuality, race and madness*. Ithaca, NY: Cornell University Press.

Gilroy, P. (1987) *There ain't no black in the Union Jack*. London: Hutchinson.

Gittings, J. (1996) *Real China*. London: Simon and Schuster.

Gleisberg, P. (1868) *Kritische Darlegung der Urgeschichte des Menschenlebens nach Carl Vogt*. Dresden: Weiske.

Gobineau, Arthur de [1853–5] (1967) *Essay sur l'inégalité des races humaines*. Paris: Pierre Belfond.

Golding, W. (1971) *Lord of the flies*. London: Faber.

Goldmann, S. (1982) Der Kasten des Alt-Vater Noah. In K. -H Kohl (ed.) *Mythen der Neuen Welt*. Berlin: Fröhlich and Kaufmann.

Goldmann, S. (1985a) Die Südsee als Spiegel Europas. In T. Theye (ed.) *Wir und die Wilden*. Reinbek: Rowohlt.

Goldmann, S. (1985b) Wilde in Europa. In T. Theye (ed.) *Wir und die Wilden*. Reinbek: Rowohlt.

Good, D. (1993) The problems of investigating social representations: linguistic parallels. In G.M. Breakwell and D.V. Canter (eds) *Empirical approaches to social representations*. Oxford: Clarendon Press.

Goody, J. (1995) *The expansive moment*. Cambridge: Cambridge University Press.

Gould, S.J. (1977) *Ontogeny and phylogeny*. Cambridge, MA: Harvard University Press.

Gould, S.J. (1981) *The mismeasure of man*. New York: Norton.

Gould, S.J. (1982) The Hottentot Venus. *Natural History* 91: 20–7.

Gould, S.J. (1983) *The panda's thumb*. Harmondsworth: Penguin.

Gould, S.J. (1991) Petrus Camper's angle. In *Bully for Brontosaurus*. London: Hutchinson Radius.

Grandpierre, Dralsé de (1718) *Relations de divers voyages*. Paris: Jombert.

Gratiolet, P. (1854) *Mémoire sur les plis cérébraux de l'homme et des primates*. Paris

Greenfield, P.M., Reich, L.C. and Olver, R.R. (1966) On culture and equivalence: II. In J.S. Bruner, R.R. Olver and P.M. Greenfield (eds) *Studies in cognitive growth*. New York: Wiley.

Grote, R.A. (1877) The early man of North America. *The Popular Science Monthly* X: 582–94.

Guenther, M.G. (1980) From 'brutal savages' to 'harmless people'. *Paideuma* 26: 123–40.

Gurevich, A. (1983) Medieval culture and mentality according to the new French Historiography. *European Journal of Sociology* 24: 167–95.

Gurevich, A. (1988) *Medieval popular culture*. Cambridge: Cambridge University Press.

Gwenebault, J.H. (1837) *The natural history of the Negro Race*. Dowling: South Carolina.

Haddon, Alfred C. (1895) *Evolution in art*. London: Walter Scott.

Haeckel, Ernest (1877) *Histoire de la création*. Paris: Reinwald.

Haeckel, Ernest [1876] (1905) *The evolution of man* (2 vols), trans. Joseph McCabe. London: Watts.

Haining, P. (1994) *The flesh eaters*. London: Boxtree.

Hakluyt, Richard (1904) *The principal navigations* (12 vols). Glasgow: MacLehose.

Halbwachs, Maurice (1950) *La mémoire collective*. Paris: Presses Universitaires de France.

Hale, J. (1993) *The civilization of Europe in the Renaissance*. London: HarperCollins.

Hall, G. Stanley (1900) Child study and its relation to education. *Forum* 29: 688–702.

Hall, G. Stanley (1904) *Adolescence* (2 vols). New York: Appleton.

Hall, G. Stanley (1905) A few results of recent scientific study of the Negro in America. *Proceedings of the Massachusetts Historical Society* 2nd series 19: 95–107.

Haller, J.S. (1970) The physician versus the Negro. *Bulletin of the History of Medicine* 44: 154–67.

Hallett, R. (1965) *The penetration of Africa*. London: Routledge & Kegan Paul.

Hallowell, A. Irving (1948) The child, the savage and human experience. In D.G. Haring (ed.) *Personal character and cultural milieu*. Syracuse, NY: Syracuse University Press.

Hallpike, C.R. (1979) *The foundations of primitive thought*. Oxford: Clarendon Press.

Hamilton, D.L. and Trolier, T.K. (1986) Stereotypes and stereotyping: an overview of the cognitive approach. In J.F. Dovidio and S.L. Gaertner (eds) *Prejudice, discrimination, and racism*. Orlando, FL: Academic Press.

Hamilton, D.L., Gibbons, P.A., Stroessner, S.J. and Sherman, J.W. (1992) Stereotypes and language use. In G.R. Semin and K. Fiedler (eds) *Language, interaction and social cognition*. London: Sage.

Hanke, L. (1965) *The Spanish struggle for justice*. Boston, MA: Little, Brown.

Harris, M. (1977) *Cannibals and kings: the origins of cultures*. New York: Random House.

Hartland, E.S. (1909) *Primitive paternity* (2 vols). London: David Nutt.

Hartley, David [1749] (1966) *Observations on Man*. Delmar, NY: Scholars' Facsimiles & Reprints.

Haycock, R.G. (1971) *The image of the Indian*. Waterloo: Waterloo Lutheran University.

Hegel, Georg Wilhelm Friedrich [1832] (1992) *Vorlesungen über die Philosophie der Geschichte*. In *Werke*, Vol. 12. Frankfurt-am-Main: Suhrkamp.

Helmuth, H. (1968) Kannibalismus in Paläanthropologie und Ethnologie. *Ethnographisch-Archäologische Zeitschrift* 9: 101–19.

Hemmens, H.C. (1945) *Adventures in Africa*. London: The Carey Press.

Henry, J. (1910) *Les Bambara*. Münster: Aschendorff.

Herbert, Thomas (1665) *Some years travels into divers parts of Africa and Asia*. London: Crook.

Herrnstein, R.J. and Murray, C. (1994) *The bell curve: intelligence and class structure in American life*. New York: Free Press.

Hernton, C.C. (1969) *Sex and racism*. London: André Deutsch.

Heyes, C.M. (1993) Imitation, culture and cognition. *Animal Behaviour* 46: 999–1010.

Hiraiwa-Hasegawa, M. (1992) Cannibalism among non-human primates. In M.E. Elgar and B.J. Crespi, (eds) *Cannibalism: ecology and evolution among diverse taxa*. Oxford: Oxford University Press.

Hobhouse, Leonard T. (1901) *Mind in evolution*. New York: Macmillan.

Hobhouse, Leonard T. (1929) *Morals in evolution*. London: Chapman and Hall.

Hobhouse, L.T, Wheeler, G.C. and Ginsberg, M. (1930) *The material culture and social institutions of the simpler peoples*. London: Chapman and Hall.

Hoffmann, L-F. (1973) *Le nègre romantique*. Paris: Payot.

Hollis, M. and Lukes, S (1982) *Rationality and relativism*. Oxford: Blackwell.

Hooton, E.A. (1938) *Apes, men and morons*. London: Allen & Unwin.

Hore, A.B. (1889) *To Lake Tanganyika in a bath chair*. London: Sampson Low.

Horsman, R. (1981) *Race and manifest destiny*. Cambridge, MA: Harvard University Press.

Horton, James Africanus (1868) *West African countries and peoples . . . and a vindication of the African race*. London: Johnson.

Horton, R. (1973) Lévy-Bruhl, Durkheim and the scientific revolution. In R. Horton and R. Finnegan (eds) *Modes of thought*. London: Faber.

Houston, James (1725) *Some new and accurate observations of the Coast of Guinea*. London.

Hoyme, L.E. (1953) Physical anthropology and its instruments: an historical study. *Southwestern Journal of Anthropology* 9: 408–30.

Hrbek, I. (1988) Africa in the context of world history. In M. Elfasi (ed.) *Africa from the seventh to the eleventh century*. Berkeley: University of California Press.

Hrdlicka, A. (1931) *Children who run on all fours*. New York: McGraw Hill.

Hulme, P. (1978) Columbus and the cannibals *Ibero-Amerikansches Archiv* 4: 115–39.

Hulme, P. (1986) *Colonial encounters*. London: Routledge & Kegan Paul.

Hulme, P. and Whitehead, N.L. (eds) (1992) *Wild majesty*. Oxford: Clarendon Press.

Humboldt, Alexander von (1856) *Cosmos* (4 vols). London: Murray.

Hunt, James (1863a) On the study of anthropology. *Anthropological Review* I: 386–91.

Hunt, James (1863b) On the physical and mental characters of the Negro. *Anthropological Review* I: 386–91.

Hunt, James (1865) On the Negro's place in nature. *Memoirs read before the Anthropological Society of London* 1863/4. London: Trübner.

Huxley, Julian S. (1924) America revisited III. The Negro problem. *The Spectator* 29 November, pp. 821–2.

Huxley, Thomas Henry (1863) *Man's place in nature*. London: Wiliams & Norgate.

Huxley, Thomas Henry (1906) *Man's place in nature*. London: Dent.

Hyam, R. (1991) *Empire and sexuality*. Manchester: Manchester University Press.

Ingold, T. (ed.) (1988) *What is an animal?*. London: Unwin Hyman.

Iselin, Isaak (1779) *Ueber die Geschichte der Menschheit* (2 vols). Basel: Schweighauser.

Jahn, J. (1964) *Wir nannten sie Wilde*. Munich: Ehrenwirt.

Jahoda, G. (1968) Scientific training and the persistence of traditional beliefs among West African university students. *Nature* 200, No. 5174, p. 1356.

Jahoda, G. (1969) *The psychology of superstition*. London: Allen Lane.

Jahoda, G. (1982) *Psychology and anthropology*. London: Academic Press.

Jahoda, G. (1991) Dessins primitifs, dessins d'enfants. *Gradhiva – Revue d'Histoire et d'Archives de l'Anthropologie* 10: 60–70.

Jahoda, G. (1993) *Crossroads between culture and mind*. Cambridge, MA/London: Harvard University Press.

Jahoda, G. (1995) Piéron et l'anthropologie psychologique. *Bulletin de Psychologie* XLVIII: 243–9.

Jameson, F. (1989) Foreword. In R.F. Retamar *Caliban and other essays*. Minneapolis: University of Minnesota Press.

Jancey, M. (1987) *Mappa Mundi*. Hereford: The Friends of Hereford Cathedral.

Jane, C. (trans. and ed.) (1930) *Journal of the first voyage of Columbus*. London: The Argonaut Press.

Janet, Pierre (1926) *De l'angoisse à l'extase* (2 vols). Paris: Alcan (Vol. 2 1928).

Janson, H.W. (1952) *Apes and ape lore*. London: The Warburg Institute.

Jaspers, R. (1972) *Die missionarische Erschliessung Ozeaniens*. Münster: Aschendorff.

Jensen, A.R. (1972) *Genetics and education*. London: Methuen.

Jodelet, D. (1991) *Madness and social representations*. Berkeley: University of California Press.

Johnston, Harry (1902) *The Ugandan protectorate* (2 vols). London: Hutchinson.

Johnston, J. (ed.) (1889) *Report of the Centenary Conference on the Protestant Missions of the World* (2 vols). London: James Nisbet.

Jordan, W.D. (1968) *White over black*. Chapel Hill: University of North Carolina Press.

Jost, J.T. and Banaji, M.R. (1994) The role of stereotyping in system-justification and the production of false consciousness. *British Journal of Social Psychology* 33: 1–27.

Jung, C.G. (1928) *Contributions to analytical psychology*. London: Kegan Paul, Trench, Trubner.

Jung, C.G. (1944) *The psychology of the unconscious*. London: Kegan Paul, Trench, Trubner.

Jüttemann, G. (ed.) (1986) *Die Geschichtlichkeit des Seelischen*. Weinheim: Beltz.

Kabbani, R. (1986) *Europe's myths of the Orient*. London: Macmillan.

Kames, Lord [Henry Home] (1779) *Sketches of the history of man* (3rd edn, 2 vols). Edinburgh.

Kamin, L. (1993) On the length of black penises and the depth of white racism. In L. J. Nicholas (ed.) *Psychology and oppression*. Johannesburg: Skotaville.

Kaplan, F. (1988) *Dickens: a biography*. New York: William Morrow.

Kappeler, M. (1992) Wie Robinson war, soll Emil werden. *Psychologie und Geschichte* 4: 53–87.

Keane, Augustus Henry (1896) *Ethnology*. Cambridge: Cambridge University Press.

Keay, J. (ed.) (1991) *History of world exploration*. New York: Mallard Press.

Kidd, Dudley [1906] (1969) *Savage childhood*. New York: Negro Universities Press.

Killam, G.D. (1968) *Africa in English fiction 1874–1939*. Ibadan: Ibadan University Press.

King, P. (ed.) (1983) *The history of ideas*. London: Croom Helm.

Kingsley, Mary [1899] (1901) *West African studies* (2nd edn). London: Macmillan.

Kirk, G.S. (1974) *The nature of Greek myths*. Harmondsworth: Penguin.

Knox, Robert (1850) *The races of men: a philosophical inquiry into the influence of race over the destinies of nations* London: Renshaw.

Koch, J. (1931) Sind die Pygmäen Menschen? *Archiv für die Geschichte der Philosophie* 40: 194–213.

Koch, T. (1899) Die Anthropophagie der Südamerikanischen Indianer. *Internationales Archiv für Ethnographie* 12: 78–110.

Kohn, Marek (1995) *The race gallery*. London: Jonathan Cape.

Kovel, J. (1988) *White racism: a psychohistory*. London: Free Association Books.

Kramer, F. (1981) *Verkehrte Welten*. Frankfurt-am-Main Syndikat.

Krauss, W. (1978) *Zur Anthropologie des 18. Jahrhunderts*. Berlin: Akademie-Verlag.

Kroll, J. (1977) The concept of childhood in the Middle Ages. *Journal of the History of the Behavioral Sciences* 13: 384–93.

Kuklick, H. (1991) *The savage within*. Cambridge: Cambridge University Press.

Kuper, A. (1988) *The invention of primitive society*. London: Routledge and Kegan Paul.

Kuper, S. (1994) *Football against the enemy*. London: Orion.

La Croix, A Pherotée de (1688) *Relation universelle de l'Afrique ancienne* (2 vols). Lyons.

Lafitau, J.F. (1724) *Moeurs des sauvages Amériquains comparés aux moeurs des premier temps* (2 vols). Paris.

La Fontaine, J. (1996) Key informants on the history of anthropology. *Ethnos* 61: 251–71.

Lambert, J.C. (1909) *Missionary heroes in Africa*. London: Seely.

La Mettrie, Julien Offroy de (1751) *Oeuvres philosophiques*. London.

Lamprecht, Karl (1900) *Die kulturhistorische Methode*. Berlin: Heyfelder.

Lamprecht, Karl (1905a) Aufforderung zum sammeln von Kinderzeichnungen. *Kind und Kunst* p. 359.

Lamprecht, Karl (1905b) De l'étude comparée des dessins d'enfant. *Revue de Synthèse Historique* 11: 54.

Langer, J. (1970) Werner's comparative organismic theory. In P.H. Mussen (ed.) *Manual of child psychology* (2 vols). New York: Wiley.

Langness, L.L (1974) *The study of culture*. San Francisco, CA: Chandler & Sharp.

Larousse, Pierre (1866/76) *Grand dictionnaire universel du XIXe siècle*. Paris.

Lave, J. (1981) How 'they' think. *Contemporary Psychology* 26: 788–90.

Lawrence, Sir William (1819) *Lectures on Physiology, Zoology and the Natural History of Man*. London: Callow.

Leach, E.R. (1958) Magical hair. *Journal of the Royal Anthropological Institute* 88: 147–64.

Leach, E.R. (1964) Anthropological aspects of language: animal categories and verbal abuse. In E.H. Lenneberg (ed.) *New directions in the study of language*. Cambridge, MA: The MIT Press.

LeBon, Gustave (1881) *L'Homme et les Sociétés* (2 vols). Paris: Rothchild.

LeBon, Gustave (1894) *Les lois psychologiques de l'évolution des peuples*. Paris: Alcan.

LeBon, Gustave (1895) *Psychologie des foules*. Paris: Bibliothèque de Philosophie Contemporaine.

Le Goff, J. (1974) Les mentalités – une histoire ambigue. In J. Le Goff and P. Nora (eds) *Faire de l'histoire*, Vol. 3. Paris: Gallimard.

Le Goff, J. (1985) *L'imaginaire médiéval*. Paris: Gallimard.

Le Roy Ladurie, E. (1975) *Montaillou, village occitan de 1294 à 1324*. Paris: Plon.

Leonard, Peter (1833) *Records of a voyage to the Western Coast of Africa*. Edinburgh: Tait.

Léry, Jean de [1578] (1990) *History of a voyage to the land of Brazil*, trans. Janet Whateley. Berkeley: University of California Press.

Letourneau, Charles (1881) *Sociology based upon ethnography*. London: Chapman and Hall.

Letourneau, Charles (1901) *La psychologie ethnique*. Paris: Schleicher.

Le Tour du Monde (1844) *1001 Merveilles des Voyages*. Bruxelles.

Letts, M. [1346?] (1953) *Mandeville's travels* (2 vols). London: The Hakluyt Society.

LeVaillant, Francois (1792) *Second voyage dans l'intérieur de l'Afrique* (3 vols). Paris: Jansen.

LeVine, R.A. and Campbell, D.T. (1972) *Ethnocentrism*. New York: Wiley.

Levinstein, S. (1905) *Kinderzeichnungen bis zum 14. Lebensjahr, mit Parallelen aus der Urgeschichte, Kulturgeschichte und Völkerkunde*. Leipzig: Voigtländer.

Lévi-Strauss, Claude (1949) *Les structures élémentaires de la parenté*. Paris: Presses Universitaires de France.

Lévi-Strauss, Claude (1964) *Mythologiques: Le Cru et le Cuit* Paris: Plon.

Lévi-Strauss, Claude (1966) *Tristes tropiques*. Paris: Union Générale.

Lévi-Strauss, Claude (1984) *Paroles données*. Paris: Plon.

Lévy-Bruhl, Lucien [1910] (1951) *Les fonctions mentales dans les sociétés inférieures*. Paris: Presses Universities de France.

Lévy-Bruhl, Lucien (1922) *La mentalité primitive*. Paris: Alcan. Translated (1985) under the title *How natives think*. Princeton, NJ: Princeton University Press.

Lévy-Bruhl, Lucien [1949] (1975) *The notebooks on primitive mentality*, trans. P. Rivière. Oxford: Blackwell.

Lewis, B. (1990) *Race and slavery in the Middle East*. New York: Oxford University Press.

Lewis, I.M. (1985) Social anthropology in perspective. Cambridge: Cambridge University Press.

Lewis, I.M. (1986) *Religion in context*. Cambridge: Cambridge University Press.

Lewis, R. (1994) *The Muslim discovery of Europe*. London: Phoenix.

Liauzu, C. (1992) *Race et civilisation*. Paris: Syros.

Lilienthal, G. (1990) Samuel Thomas Soemmering und seine Vorstellungen über Rassen-unterschiede. In G. Mann and F. Dumont (eds) *Die Natur des Menschen*. Stuttgart: Fischer.

Lilla, M. (1993) *G B Vico: the making of an anti-modern*. Cambridge, MA: Harvard University Press.

Little, K.L. (1951) *The Mende of Sierra Leone*. London: Routledge & Kegan Paul.

Littleton, C.S. (1985) Introduction to L. Levy-Bruhl: *How natives think*. Princeton: Princeton University Press.

Lloyd, G.E.R. (1990) *Demystifying mentalities*. Cambridge: Cambridge University Press.

Lockhart, J. (1994) Sightings: initial Nahua reactions to Spanish culture. In S.B. Schwartz (ed.) *Implicit understandings*. Cambridge: Cambridge University Press.

Lombroso, Cesare (1887) *L'Homme criminel*. Paris: Félix Alcan.

Long, Edward [under pseudonym 'A Planter'] (1772) *Candid Reflection upon a judgement . . . on what is commonly called the Negroe-Cause*. London.

Long, Edward (1774) *History of Jamaica* (3 vols). London.

Lorimer, D.A. (1978) *Colour, class and the Victorians*. Leicester: Leicester University Press.

Lorreyte, B. (1989) Francais et immigrés: des miroirs ambigus. In C. Camilleri (ed.) *Choc de culture*. Paris: L'Ahrmattan.

Loti, Pierre (1881) *Le roman d'un Spahi*. Paris: Calman-Lévy [cited from Oeuvres Complètes].

Lovejoy, A.O. (1936) *The great chain of being*. Cambridge, MA: Harvard University Press.

Lovejoy, A.O. (1960) *Essays in the history of ideas*. New York: Putnam.

Lovejoy, A.O. [1936] (1983) The study of the history of ideas. In P. King, (ed.): *The history of ideas*. London: Croom Helm.

Lubbock, Sir John (1870) *The origin of civilization and the primitive condition of man. Mental and social conditions of savages*. London: Longmans Green.

Lubbock, Sir John [1863] (1913) *Prehistoric times* (7th edn). London: Williams and Norgate.

Lugard, Frederick Dealtry (1893) *The rise of our East African empire* (2 vols). London: Blackwood.

Lugard, Lord F.D. [1922] (1965) *The dual mandate in British tropical Africa*. London: Frank Cass.

Luig, U. (1982) Introduction to Leo Frobenius *Vom Schreibtisch zum Aequator*. Frankfurt-am-Main: Societätsverlag.

Luria, A.R. and Vygotsky, L.S. [1930] (1992) *Ape, primitive man and child*. London: Harvester/Wheatsheaf.

Lyell, Sir Charles (1830/3) *Principles of geology* (3 vols). London: Murray.

Lynn, R. (1991) Race differences in intelligence: a global perspective. *Mankind Quarterly* XXXI: 255–96.

McClintock, A. (1995) *Imperial Leather*. London: Routledge.

McCulloch, J. (1995) *Colonial psychiatry and 'the African mind'*. Cambridge: Cambridge University Press.

McGrew, W.C. (1992) *Chimpanzee material culture*. Cambridge: Cambridge University Press.

MacGaffey, W. (1972) The West in Congolese experience. In P.D. Curtin (ed.) *Africa and the West*. Wisconsin: University of Wisconsin Press.

McLynn, F. (1992) *Hearts of darkness*. London: Hutchinson.

Mageo, J.M. (1994) Hairdos and don'ts: hair symbolism and sexual history in Samoa. *Man* 29: 407–32.

Maillet, Benoit de (1748) *Telliamed*. Amsterdam

Maistre, Joseph Marie de [1821] (1988) *Les soirées de Saint-Petersbourg* (2 vols). Paris.

Malfante, Antoine [1447] cited in George, C. (1968) The civilized West looks at primitive Africa 1400–1800. In Ashley Montagu, (ed.) *The concept of the primitive*. New York: The Free Press.

Malinowski, Bronislav (1929) *The sexual life of savages*. London: Routledge & Kegan Paul.

Malinowski, Bronislav (1989) *A diary in the strict sense of the term*. Stanford, CA: Stanford University Press.

Manetta, Fillipo (1864) *La Razza Negra nel suo stato solvaggio*. Turin.

Mann, Robert James (1867) Contributon to the debate. *Transactions of the Ethnological Society of London* V: 277–97.

Mannoni, O. (1956) *Prospero and Caliban. The psychology of colonization*. London: Methuen.

Marshall, P.J. and Williams, G. (1982) *The great map of mankind*. London: Dent.

Martin-Luther-Universität Halle-Wittenberg (1968) *Antonius Guilielmus Amo Afer aus Axim in Ghana*. Halle (Saale).

Marx, C. (1989) Der Afrikareisende Georg Schweinfurth und der Kannibalismus. *Wiener Ethnohistorische Blätter* 34: 69–97.

Mason, P. (1990) *Deconstructing America*. London: Routledge.

Mathey, Michel (1905) *La traite des blancs* (2nd edn). Paris: Juven.

Matthews, John [1788](1966) *A voyage to the river Sierra-Leone*. London: Frank Cass.

Medeiros, Francois de (1985) *L'Occident et l'Afrique*. Paris: Karthala.

Medicus, G. (1992) The inapplicability of the biogenetic rule to behavioral development. *Human Development* 35: 1–8.

Meiners, Christoph (1785) *Grundriss der Geschichte der Menschheit*. Lemgo: Meyer.

Meiners, Christoph (1787) Ueber die grosse Verschiedenheit der Biegsamkeit und Unbiegsamkeit, der Härte und Weichheit der verschiedenen Stämme, und Racen der Menschen. *Göttingisches Magazin* 1: 210–246.

Meiners, Christoph (1788) Einige Betrachtungen über die Schönheit der menschlichen Bildung und über den Hang aller hässlichen Völker, sich noch mehr zu verhässlichen. *Göttingisches Magazin* 2: 270–92.

Meiners, Christoph (1815) *Untersuchungen über die Verschiedenheiten der Menschennaturen* (3 vols). Tübingen: Cotta.

Métraux, Alfred (1967) *Religions et magies indiennes d'Amérique du Sud*. Paris: Gallimard.

Michiels, Alfred (1853) *Le Capitaine Firmin ou la vie des nègres en Afrique*. Paris: Garnier.

Middleton, J. (1970) *The study of the Lugbara: Expectation and paradox in anthropological research*. New York: Holt, Rinehart & Winston.

Middleton, J. and Edwards, D. (1990) *Collective remembering*. London: Sage.

Milbury-Steen, S.L. (1980) *European and African stereotypes in twentieth-century fiction*. London: Macmillan.

Miller, N. (1928) *The child in primitive society*. London: Kegan Paul.

Milton, G. (1996) *The riddle of the knight*. London: Allison & Busby.

Miner, E. (1972) The wild man through the looking glass. In E. Dudley and M.E. Novak (eds) *The wild man within*. Pittsburgh, PA: University of Pittsburgh Press.

Mobley, H.W. (1970) *The Ghanaian's image of the missionary*. Leiden: Brill.

Monceaux, P. (1891) La légende des Pygmées et les nains de l'Afrique Equatoriale. *Revue Historique* 47: 1–64.

Money-Kyrle, R.E. (1932) *The development of the sexual impulse*. London: Kegan Paul, Trench, Trubner.

Monkman, L. (1981) *A native heritage: images of the Indian in English-Canadian literature*. Toronto: University of Toronto Press.

Montagu, Ashley M.F. (1962) Time, morphology and neoteny in the evolution of man. In M.F. Ashley Montagu (ed.) *Culture and the evolution of man*. New York: Oxford University Press.

Montaigne, Michel de [1580] (1995) *Four essays*. London: Penguin.

Moore, J.H. (1918) *Savage survivals*. London: Watts (Reprinted 1933 in the *Thinkers' Library*).

Moorhouse, G. (1973) *The Missionaries*. London: Eyre Methuen.

Morden, Robert (1700) *Geography rectified* (4th edn). London.

More, Hannah (1811) *Strictures on the modern system of female education* (2 vols). London: Cadell & Davies.

Morgan, Lewis H. (1877) *Ancient society*. London: Macmillan.

Morris, D. (1967) *The naked ape*. London: Cape.

Morris, R.C. (1996) Anthropology in the body shop: 'Lords of the Garden', cannibalism, and the consuming desires of televisual anthropology. *American Anthropologist* 98: 137–46.

Morss, J.R. (1990) *The biologising of childhood: developmental psychology and the Darwinian myth*. Hove and London: Lawrence Erlbaum.

Morton, Samuel George (1844) *Crania Aegyptica, or Observations on Egyptian Ethnography, derived from Anatomy, History and the Monuments*. London: Madden.

Moscovici, S. (1981) On social representations. In J.P. Forgas (ed.) *Social cognition*. London: Academic Press.

Moscovici, S. (1984) The phenomenon of social representations. In R. Farr and S. Moscovici (eds) *Social representations*. Cambridge: Cambridge University Press.

Mukhopadhyay, C.C. and Moses, Y.T. (1997) Reestablishing 'race' in anthropological discourse. *American Anthropologist* 99: 517–33.

Müller-Hill, B. (1988) *Murderous science*. Oxford: Oxford University Press.

Murphy, J. (1927) *Primitive man*. London: Oxford University Press.

Muschinske, D. (1977) The nonwhite as child: G. Stanley Hall on the education of nonwhite peoples. *Journal of the History of the Behavioral Sciences* 13: 328–36.

Nadel, S.F. (1939) The application of intelligence tests in the anthropological field. In F.C. Bartlett, M. Ginsberg, E.J. Lindgren and R.H. Thouless (eds) *The study of society*. London: Kegan Paul, Trench, Trubner.

Nash, G.B. (1972) The image of the Indian in the Southern Colonial mind. In E. Dudley and M.E. Novak (eds) *The wild man within*. Pittsburgh, PA: University of Pittsburgh Press.

Naville, P., Zazzo, R., Weil, P.G., Breid, C., Boussion-Leroy, A., Horinson, S. and Belvès, P. (1951) *Le dessin chez l'enfant*. Paris: Presses Universitaires de France.

Nott, J.C. and Gliddon, G.R. (1854) *Types of mankind* (6th edn). Philadelphia, PA: Lippincott, Grambo.

O'Gorman, E. (1941) Sobre la naturaleza bestial del Indio Americano *Filosofia y Letras Revisita* de la Facultad de Filosofia y Letras, Universidad Nacional Autonoma de Mexico 2: 305–15.

Ogilvie, J.N. (1924) *Our empire's debt to missions*. London: Hodder & Stoughton.

Ohnuki-Tierney, E. (1987) *The monkey as mirror*. Princeton: Princeton University Press.

Ombredane, A. (1952) Principes pour une étude psychologique des noirs du Congo Belge. In H. Piéron, A. Fessard and P. Fraisse (eds) *L'année psychologique*. Paris: Presses Universitaires de France.

Opie, I. and Opie, P. (1959) *The lore and language of schoolchildren*. Oxford: Clarendon Press.

Pagden, A. (1982) *The fall of natural man*. Cambridge: Cambridge University Press.

Pagden, A. (1993) *European encounters with the New World*. New Haven, CT: Yale University Press.

Parry, J.H. (1940) *The Spanish theory of empire in the seventeenth century*. Cambridge: Cambridge University Press.

Passarge, S. (1907) *Die Buschmänner der Kalahari*. Berlin: Reimer.

Paton, J. (1902) *The story of J.G. Paton*. London: Hodder & Stoughton.

Pauw, Cornelius de (1770) *Recherches philosophiques sur les Américains ou mémoires intéréssants pour servir à l'histoire de l'espèce humaine* (3 vols). Berlin.

Pearce, R.H. (1953) *The savages of America*. Baltimore, MD: The Johns Hopkins University Press.

Pearson, Karl (1924) *The life, letters and labour of Francis Galton* (3 vols), Vol. 2. Cambridge: Cambridge University Press.

Pelletier, A-M. (1994) La référence animale dans 'La Brève relation de la destruction des Indes' de Las Casas. In J-L. Chevalier, M. Colin and A. Thomson (eds) *Barbares et sauvages*. Caen: Presses Universitaires de Caen.

Pénel, J-D. (1982) *Homo caudatus*. Paris: Laboratoire de langues et civilisations.

Phillips, Thomas (n.d.) A journal of a voyage made in the Hannibal of London, Ann. 1693, 1694 to Cape Monseradoe, in Africa London. In Churchill (1746) *Collected voyages and travels* (3rd edn), 6 vols, Vol. 6. London.

Piaget, J. (1928) Logique génétique et sociologie. *Revue Philosophique* 105: 165–205.

Piaget, J. (1932) *The language and thought of the child* (2nd edn). London: Routledge & Kegan Paul.

Piaget, J. (1945) *La formation du symbole chez l'enfant*. Neuchatel: Delachaux et Niestlé.

Piaget, J. (1966) Necessité et signification des recherches comparatives en psychologie génétique. *International Journal of Psychology* 1: 3–13.

Piéron, Henri (1909) L'anthropologie psychologique – son object et sa méthode. *Revue de l'Ecole d'anthropologie de Paris* 19: 113–27.

Pieterse, J.N. (1992) *White on black*. New Haven, CT: Yale University Press.

Pline l'Ancien [?] (1980) *Histoire naturelle* (36 vols), Vol. 6, trans. J. André and J. Filliozat. Paris: Société d'Edition 'Les Belles Lettres'.

Plinius Secondus [AD 77] (1601) Historia Naturalis. Trans. Philemon Holland. London: A Islip.

Plischke, H. (1937) *Johann Friedrich Blumenbach's Einfluss auf die Entdeckungsreisenden seiner Zeit.* Höttingen: Vandenhoeck & Ruprecht.

Ploss, Hermann H. (1884) *Das Kind im Brauch und Sitte der Völker* (new edn, 2 vols). Leipzig: Grieben.

Poignant, R. (1992) Surveying the field of view: the making of the RAI photographic collection. In E Edwards (ed.) *Anthropology and photography 1860–1920.* New Haven: Yale University Press.

Poliakov, L. (1974) *The Aryan myth.* London: Chatto Heinemann for Sussex University Press.

Poliakov, L. (1975) Le fantasme des êtres hybrides et la hiérarchie des races au XVIIe et XIXe siècle. In L. Poliakov (ed.) *Hommes et bêtes: entretiens sur le racisme.* Paris: Mouton.

Poole, F.J.P. (1983) Cannibals, tricksters and witches. In P. Brown and D. Tuzin (eds) *The ethnography of cannibalism.* Washington, DC: The Society for Psychological Anthropology.

Porteus, T. (1995) A glimpse of hell. *The Spectator,* 7 October 1995, pp. 18–20.

Pottinger, G. (1983) *The Afghan connection.* Edinburgh: Scottish Academic Press.

Pouchet, Georges (1864) *The plurality of human races.* London: Longman.

Preyer, W. (1894) *Mental development in the child.* London: Edward Arnold.

Prien, H-J (1978) *Die Geschichte des Christentum's in Lateinamerika.* Göttingen: Vandenhoeck & Ruprecht.

Probst, P. (1991) Angewandte Ethnopsychologie während der Epoche des Deutschen Kolonialismus (1884–1919). *Psychologie und Geschichte* 3: 67–80.

Pruner, F. (1846) *Die Ueberbleibsel der altägyptischen Menschenrace.* Munich: Akademie der Wissenschaften.

Pruner-Bey (1861) Mémoire sur les Nègres. *Mémoires de la Société d'Anthropologie,* pp 293–339.

Purchas, Samuel [16??] (1906) *Purchas his Pilgrimes* (10 vols). Glasgow: Maclehose.

Quatrefages, Jean Louis Armand de (1887) *Histoire générale des races humaines.* Paris: Hennuyer.

Quinlan, M.J. (1951) *Victorian prelude.* New York: Columbia University Press.

Raynal, Guillaume Thomas Francois [1770] (1820/1) *Histoire philosophique et politique des établissements des Européens dans les deux Indes.* Paris: Amable.

Read, P.P. (1974) *Alive: the history of the Andes survivors.* Philadelphia, PA: Lippincott.

Reade, Winwood W. (1863) *Savage Africa.* London: Smith, Elder.

Reclus, Elie (1885) *Les primitifs: études d'ethnologie comparée.* Paris: Chamerot.

Rehbock, P.F. (1983) *The philosophical naturalists.* Madison: University of Wisconsin Press.

Reinders, R.C. (1968) Racialism on the left. *International Review of Social History* XIII: 1–28.

Richards, Audrey (1932) *Hunger and work in a savage tribe.* London: Routledge.

Richards, G. (1997) *Race, racism and psychology.* London: Routledge.

Richardson, M., Hanken, J., Gooneratne, M.L., Pieau, C., Raynaud, A., Selwood, L. and Wright, G.M. (1997) There is no highly conserved embryonic stage in the vertebrates: implications for current theories of evolution and development. *Anatomy and Embryology* 196: 91–106.

Richet, Charles (1919) *La sélection humaine.* Paris: Felix Alcan.

Ridley, M. (1993) *The red queen: sex and evolution in human nature.* London: Viking.

Ritchie, J. (1943) The African as suckling and adult. *Rhodes-Livingstone Institute Paper* 9.

Ritchie, J. (1944) The African as grown-up nursling. *Rhodes-Livingstone Journal* 1: 55–60.

Rivers, W.H.R. (1901) Part I. Introduction and vision. In A.C. Haddon (ed.) *Reports of the Cambridge anthropological expedition to Torres Straits,* Vol. 2. Cambridge: Cambridge University Press.

Rivers, W.H.R. (1919) Inaugural address. *The Lancet* 1: 889–892.

Robertson, P. (1976) Home as a nest: middle class childhood in nineteenth-century Europe. In L. de Mause (ed.) *The history of childhood*. London: Souvenir Press.

Robinet, Jean-Baptiste (1768) *Considérations philosophiques de la gradation naturelle*. Amsterdam.

Romanes, George J. (1880) Mental evolution. *Glasgow Science Lectures 1878–80*: Lecture 9. Glasgow: Menzies.

Romanes, George J. (1888) *Mental evolution in man*. London: Kegan Paul, Trench.

Romanes, George J. (1895) *Thoughts on religion*, (ed.) Charles Gore. London: Longmans Green.

Roome, W.J.W. (1927) *Can Africa be won?*. London: A.C. Black.

Rosa, A. (1996) Bartlett's psycho-anthropological project. *Culture and Psychology* 2: 355–78.

Rose, S., Kamin, L.J. and Lewontin, R.C. (1984) *Not in our genes*. London: Penguin.

Rosenthal, B.G. (1971) *The images of man*. New York: Basic Books.

Ross, C.A. (1995) *Satanic ritual abuse: principles of treatment*. Toronto: University of Toronto Press.

Ross, D. (1972) *G. Stanley Hall: the psychologist as prophet*. Chicago, Ill.: University of Chicago Press.

Rousseau, Jean-Jaques [1750] (1964) *Oeuvres complètes*, Vol. III. Paris: Gallimard.

Rousseau, Jean-Jaques [1762] (1992) *Emile ou de l'éducation*. Paris: Bordas.

Routledge, W.S. and Routledge, K. (1910) *With a prehistoric people*. London: Edward Arnold.

Rupp-Eisenreich, B. (1983) Des choses occultes en histoire des sciences humanines: le destin de la 'science nouvelle' de Cristoph Meiners. *L'Ethnographie* LXXIX: 131–83.

Rupp-Eisenreich, B. (1985) Christoph Meiners et Joseph-Marie de Gérando: un chapitre du comparatisme anthropologique. In D. Droixhe and P-P. Jossiaux (eds) *L'homme des Lumières et la découverte de l'autre*. Bruxelles: Université Libre de Bruxelles.

Rushton, J.P. (1989) The evolution of race differences. *Journal of Research in Personality* 23: 7–20.

Rushton, J.P. (1990) Race differences, r/K theory and a reply to Flynn. *The Psychologist* 5: 195–8.

Rushton, J.P. (1995) *Race, evolution and behavior*. New Brunswick, NJ: Transaction Publishers.

Rushton, J.P. and Bogaert, A.F. (1988) Race differences in sexual behavior: testing an evolutionary hypothesis. *Journal of Research in Personality* 21: 529–51.

Russell, Bertrand (1946) *A history of western philosophy*. London: Allen & Unwin.

Russell, P.E. (1986) White kings on black kings: Rui de Pina and the problem of black African sovereignty. In I. Michael and R.A. Cardwell (eds) *Medieval and Renaissance studies in honour of Robert Brian Tate*. Oxford. The Dolphin Book Co.

Russett, C.E. (1989) *Sexual science*. Cambridge, MA: Harvard University Press.

Sagan, E. (1974) *Cannibalism: human aggression and cultural forms*. New York: Harper Torchbooks.

Sahlins, M. (1983) Raw women, cooked men and other 'great things' of the Fiji islands. In P. Brown and D. Tuzin (eds.) *The ethnography of cannibalism*. Washington, DC: Society for Psychological Anthropology.

Said, E.W. (1978) *Orientalism*. London: Routledge & Kegan Paul.

Sanday, P.R. (1986) *Divine hunger: cannibalism as a cultural system*. Cambridge: Cambridge University Press.

Savage-Rumbaugh, E.S., Murphy, J., Sevcik, R.A., Brakke, K.E., Williams, S.L. and Rumbaugh, D.M. (1993) Language comprehension in ape and child. *Monographs of the Society for Research in Child Development*, Serial No. 233, Vol. 58.

Schiller, Friedrich [1789] (1982) *Was heisst und zu welchem Ende studiert man die Universalgeschichte?* Jena: Jenaer Reden und Schriften, Friedrich Schiller Universität.

Schneider, W. (1977) Race and empire: the rise of popular ethnography in the late nineteenth century. *Journal of Popular Culture* 11: 98–109.

Schultze, Fritz (1900) *Psychologie der Naturvölker*. Leipzig: Veit.

Schumann, A. (1868) *Die Affenmenschen Carl Vogts*. Leipzig: Engelmann.

Schweinfurth, Georg (1874) *Im Herzen von Afrika* (2 vols). Leipzig: Brockhaus.

Scribner, S. (1985) Vygotsky's uses of history. In J.V. Wertsch (ed.) *Culture, communication and cognition: Vygotskian perspectives*. Cambridge: Cambridge University Press.

Seal, G. (1996) *The outlaw legend*. Cambridge: Cambridge University Press.

Segall, M.H. (1979) *Cross-cultural psychology*. Monterey, CA: Brooks/Cole.

Sepulveda, Juan Gines de [1550] (1991) Dialogue on the just causes of war. Reprinted in C. Strosetzki (ed.) *Der Griff nach der Neuen Welt*. Frankfurt-am-Main: Fischer.

Shaffer, R.E. and Cozolino, L.J (1992) Adults who report childhood ritual abuse. *Journal of Psychology and theology* 20: 188–93.

Sherman, J.W. (1996) Development and mental representation of stereotypes. *Journal of Personality and Social Psychology* 70: 1126–41.

Shufeldt, R.W. (1907) *The negro: a menace to American civilization*. Boston, MA: Gorham Press.

Shweder, R.A. (1982) On savages and other children. *American Anthropologist* 84: 354–66.

Shweder, R.A. (1984) Anthropology's romantic rebellion against the enlightenment, or there's more to thinking than reason and evidence. In R.A. Shweder and R.A. LeVine *Culture theory*. Cambridge: Cambridge University Press.

Shweder, R.A. (1990) Cultural psychology – what is it? In J.W. Stigler, R.A. Shweder and G. Herdt (eds) *Cultural psychology*. Cambridge: Cambridge University Press.

Simar, T. (1922) *Etude critique sur la formation de la doctrine des races*. Brussels: Lamertin.

Sinclair, A. (1977) *The savage: a history of misunderstanding*. London: Weidenfeld & Nicolson.

Sixel, F.W. (1966) Die deutsche Vortellung vom Indianer in der ersten Hälfte des 16. Jahrhunderts. *Annali del Pontifico Museo Missionario Etnologico* Vol. XXX: 9–230.

Slotkin, J.S. (1965) *Readings in early anthropology*. Chicago, Ill.: Aldine.

Smellie, William (1790) *Philosophy of natural history*. Cited in Bynum (1974).

Smith, E.W. (1929) *Aggrey of Africa*. London: Student Christian Movement.

Smith, Hamilton (1848) *The natural history of the human species*. Edinburgh.

Smith, J. (1851) *Trade and travel in the Gulph of Guinea*. London: Simpkin, Marshall.

Smith, R. (1973) The uses of history. In H.V. Rappard, P.J. Van Strien, L.P. Mos and W.J. Baker (eds) *Annals of theoretical psychology*, Vol. 8. New York: Plenum Press.

Smith, William (1744) *A new voyage to Guinea*. London: Nowell.

Snowden, F.M. (1970) *Blacks in antiquity*. Cambridge, MA: Harvard University Press.

Soemmering, Samuel Thomas (1784) *Ueber die körperliche Verschiedenheit des Negers vom Europäer*. Frankfurt.

Solin, Caius Julius [?] (1847) *Polyhistor*, trans. M. Agnant. Paris: Panckoucke.

Spencer, Herbert (1876) The comparative psychology of man. *Mind* 1: 7–20.

Spencer, Herbert (1877) *Principles of Sociology* (3 vols). London: Williams & Norgate.

Spix, J.B. von and Martius, C.F. von (1823) *Reise in Brasilien* (2 vols). Munich.

Spitzer, L. (1972) Sierra Leone Creoles 1870–1900. In P.D. Curtin (ed.) *Africa and the West*. Madison: University of Wisconsin Press.

Stanley, A.P. (1846) *The life and correspondence of Thomas Arnold, DD* (6th edn). London: Fellowes.

Stanley, Henry (1878) *Through the dark continent* (2 vols). London: Sampson Low, Marston, Searle and Rivington.

Steel, T. (1975) *The life and death of St Kilda*. London: Fontana/Collins.

Steele, R. (1905) *Mediaeval lore from Bartholomew Anglicus*. London: De la More Press.

Stefansson, V. [1577] (1938) The three voyages of Martin Frobisher (2 vols). London: The Argonaut Press.

Steinen, von den, Karl (1894) *Unter den Naturvölkern Zentral-Brasiliens*. Berlin: Reimer.

Steins, M. (1972) *Das Bild des schwarzen in der europäischen Kolonialliteratur*. Frankfurt-am-Main: Thesen Verlag.

Stepan, N. (1982) *The idea of race in science: Great Britain 1800–1960*. London: Macmillan.

Stern, William (1914) *Psychologie der frühen Kindheit*. Leipzig: Quelle & Meyer.

Steward, J.H. (ed.) (1946/50) *Handbook of South American Indians* (6 vols). Washington, DC: Smithsonian Institute Bulletin 143.

Stocking, G.W. Jr. (1982) *Race, culture and evolution*. Chicago, Ill: University of Chicago Press.

Stocking, G.W. Jr. (1987) *Victorian anthropology*. New York: The Free Press.

Stocking, G.W. Jr. (1992) *The ethnographer's magic*. Madison: University of Wisconsin Press.

Stone, B. (1906) *Sir Benjamin Stone's pictures* (descriptive notes by M. McDonagh) (2 vols). London: Cassell.

Stone, H. (1994) *The nightside of Dickens: cannibalism, passion, necessity*. Columbus: Ohio State University Press.

Stone, L. (1977) *The family, sex and marriage in England 1500–1800*. London: Weidenfeld and Nicolson.

Stowe, Harriet Beecher [1853] (1968) *The key to Uncle Tom's cabin*. New York: Arno.

Strabo (1932) *The geography of Strabo*, trans. H.L. Jones. New York: Putnam.

Street, B.V. (1975) *The savage in literature*. London: Routledge & Kegan Paul.

Street, B.V. (1985) Reading the novels of empire. In D. Dabydeen (ed.) *The black presence in English literature*. Manchester: Manchester University Press.

Street, B.V. (1992) British popular anthropology: exhibiting and photographing the other. In E. Edwards *Anthropology and photography 1860–1920*. New Haven, CT: Yale University Press.

Strong, P.T. (1986) Fathoming the primitive: Australian Aborigines in four explorers' journals 1697–1845. *Ethnohistory* 33: 175–94.

Sulloway, F.J. (1980) *Freud, biologist of the mind*. London: Fontana.

Sully, James [1985] (1903) *Studies of childhood*. London: Longmans, Green.

Super, C.M. (1981) Behavioral development in infancy. In R.H. Munroe, R.L. Munroe and B.B. Whiting (eds) *Handbook of cross-cultural human development*. New York: Garland STPM Press.

Sutherland, A. (1898) *The origin and growth of the moral instinct*. London.

Szeparowicz, V. (1973) Die Ijo (Ijaw): Ein Kulturbild vom Beginn des 16. bis zum Ende des 18. Jahrhunderts. *Wiener Ethnohistorische Blätter* 7: 33–76.

Talbot, E.S. (1898) *Degeneracy: its causes, signs and results*. London: Walter Scott.

Taine, Hyppolite (1877) M. Taine on the acquisition of language by children. *Mind* II: 252–9.

Tajfel, H. (1974) Social identity and intergroup behaviour. *Social Sciences Information* 13: 65–93.

Tajfel, H., Flament, C., Billig, M.G. and Bundy, R.P. (1971) Social categorization and intergroup behaviour. *European Journal of Social Psychology* 1: 149–78.

Taussig, M. (1987) *Shamanism, colonialism, and the Wild Man*. Chicago, Ill: University of Chicago Press.

Tauxier, L. (1924) *Nègres Gouro et Gagou*. Paris: Paul Geuthner.

Tauxier, L. (1927) *La religion Bambara*. Paris: Paul Geuthner.

Thomas, Herbert (1665) *Some Years Travels into divers Parts of Africa and Asia the Great*. London.

Thomas, K. (1983) *Man and the natural world*. London: Allen Lane.

Thomsen, C.W. (1986) 'Man-eating' and the myths of the 'New World'. In In C.F. Graumann and S. Moscovici (eds) *Changing conceptions of conspiracy*. New York: Springer.

Thomson, Joseph (1881) *To the Central African Lakes and back* (2 vols). London: Sampson Low, Marston, Searl and Rivington.

Thurnwald, Richard (1928) Varianten und Frühformen des Denkens und der Gestaltung. Prae-Logik? *Zeitschrift für Völkerpsychologie und Soziologie* 4: 324–30.

Tiedemann, F. (1837) *Das Hirn des Negers mit dem des Europäers und Orang-Outans verglichen*. Heidelberg: Winter.

Tinbergen, N. (1951) *A study of instinct*. Oxford: Clarendon Press.

Tinland, F. (1968) *L'Homme sauvage*. Paris: Payot.

Todorov, T. (1982) *La conquête de l'Amérique. La question de l'autre*. Paris: Le Seuil.

Todorov, T. (1985) *Die Eroberung Amerikas*. Frankfurt-am-Main: Surkamp.

Todorov, T. (1990) Der Reisende und der Eingeborene. In Garin, E. (ed.) *Der Mensch der Renaissance*. Frankfurt-am-Main: Campus.

Todorov, T. (1993) *On human diversity*. Cambridge, MA: Harvard University Press.

Topinard, Paul (1876) *L'Anthropologie*. Paris: Bibliothèque des Sciences Contemporaines, pp. 541–2.

Topinard, Paul (1885a) *Eléments d'anthropologie générale*. Paris: Delahaye et Lecrosnier.

Topinard, Paul (1885b) Présentation de trois Australiens vivants. Séance du 19 Novembre 1885. *Bulletin de la Société d'Anthropologie de Paris*. Série 3: 683–99.

Treffert, D.A. (1990) *Extraordinary people*. London: Black Swan.

Triandis, H.C. (1994) *Culture and social behavior*. New York: McGraw-Hill.

Trombetta, C. (1982) *Inediti psicologici* (Edouard Claparède). Rome: Bulzoni.

Tulviste, P. (1987) L. Lévy-Bruhl and problems of the historical development of thought. *Soviet Psychology* 25: 3–21.

Tuohy, F. (1931) *Occupied 1918–30. A postscript to the Western Front*. London: Thornton Butterworth.

Turnbull, C. (1976) *The forest people*. London: Pan Books.

Turner, J.C., Brown, R.J. and Tajfel, H. (1979) Social comparison and group interest in ingroup favouritism. *European Journal of Social Psychology* 9: 187–204.

Turner, J.C. (1996) Henry Tajfel: an introduction. In W.P. Robinson (ed.) *Social groups and identities*. London: Butterworth Heinemann.

Tylor, Edward (1865) *Researches into the early history of mankind and the development of civilization*. London: John Murray.

Tylor, Edward B. [1871] (1958) *The origins of culture* (Part 1 of *Primitive culture*). New York: Harper and Row.

Tylor, Edward B. [1881] (1930) *Anthropology* (2 vols). London: Watts.

Tyson, Edward (1699) *Orang-Outang, sive Homo Sylvestris: or the Anatomy of a Pygmie compared with that of a Monkey, an Ape and a Man*. London.

Veer, R. van der and Valsiner, J. (1991) *Understanding Vygotsky: a quest for synthesis*. Oxford: Blackwell.

Velden, F. von den (1906/07) Zur Psychologie der Negerrasse. *Politisch-anthropologische Revue* iv: 111–12.

Victoria Nyanza Mission, the (1878). London: Church Missionary House.

Vidal, F. (1994) La place de la psychologie dans l'ordre des sciences. *Revue de Synthèse* IV: 327–49.

Viénot, J. (1932) *Georges Cuvier*. Paris: Fischbacher.

Virey, Jules J. (1801) *Histoire naturelle du genre humain* (2 vols). Paris.

Virey, Jules J. (1824) *Histoire naturelle du genre humain* (3 vols). Brussels: Wahlen.

Virey, Jules J. (1834) *Histoire naturelle du genre humain* (3 vols). Brussels: Hauman.

Visser, R. (1990) Die Rezeption der Anthropologie Petrus Campers. In G. Mann and F. Dumont (eds) *Die Natur des Menschen*. Stuttgart: Fischer.

Voget, F.W. (1967) Progress, science, history and evolution in eighteenth- and nineteenth-century anthropology. *Journal of the History of Behavioral Sciences* 3: 132–55.

Vogt, Carl (1864) *Lectures on man*. London: Longman.

Volhard, E. (1939) *Kannibalismus*. Stuttgart: Strecker & Schröder.

Voltaire, Francois Marie Arouet de [1734] (1937) *Traité de métaphysique*. Manchester: Manchester University Press.

Voltaire, Francois Marie Arouet de [1756] (1963) *Essai sur les moeurs*. Paris: Garnier Frères.

Vygotsky, L.S (1929) The problem of the cultural development of the child. *Journal of Genetic Psychology* 36: 415–34.

Vygotsky, L.S. [1934] (1962) *Thought and language*. New York: Wiley.

Waitz, Theodor (1860) *Anthropologie der Naturvölker*, Part two: Die Negervölker und ihre Verwandten. Leipzig: Fleischer.

Waitz, Theodor (1863) *Introduction to anthropology*. London: Longmans, Green.

Wallace, Alfred Russell (1869) *The Malay Archipelago: the land of the orang-utan and the bird of paradise* (2 vols). London: Macmillan.

Wallon, H. (1928) La mentalité primitive et celle de l'enfant. *Revue Philosophique* 105: 81–105.

Walvin, J. (1973) *Black and white*. London: Allen Lane.

Walvin, J. (1992) *Black ivory*. London: HarperCollins.

Walzer, J.F. (1976) A period of ambivalence: eighteenth-century American childhood. In L. de Mause (ed.) *The history of childhood*. London: Souvenir Press.

Washburn, W.E. (ed.) (1988) History of Indian–White relations. Vol. 4 of W.C. Sturtevant, (ed.) *Handbook of North American indians* (20 vols). Washington, DC: Smithsonian Institution.

Werner, Heinz (1926) *Einführung in die Entwicklungspsychologie*. Leipzig: Barth.

Werner, Heinz [1940, rev. edn 1948] (1957) *Comparative psychology of mental development*. New York: International Universities Press.

Werner, M.R. (1923) *Barnum*. New York: Harcourt Brace.

Wertsch, J.V. (1991) *Voices of the mind*. London: Harvester/Wheatsheaf.

Wesaw, M.J. (1995) Finders keepers? Adulteration of Native American cultures in the name of profit. *Cultural Survival Quarterly* winter issue, pp. 8–10.

Wesley, John (1825) *Sermons on several occasions* (2 vols). London: Kershaw.

Weule, Karl (1926) Ostafrikanische Eingeborenen Zeichnungen. Psychologische Einblicke in die Künstlerseele des Negers. *Jahrbuch für Prähistorische und Ethnographische Kunst* 1. Halbband: 87–127.

White, Charles (1799) *An account of the Regular Gradation in Man*. London: Dilly.

White, H. (1978) *Tropics of discourse*. Baltimore: The Johns Hopkins University Press.

Willis, R. (1974) *Man and beast*. London: Hart-Davis, MacGibbon.

Wilson, Daniel (1873) *Caliban: the missing link*. London.

Wilson, E.A. (1978) *On human nature*. Cambridge, MA: Harvard University Press.

Wilson, L.G. (ed.) (1970) *Sir Charles Lyell's scientific journals on the species question*. New Haven, CT: Yale University Press.

Winterbottom, Thomas (1803) *Account of the native Africans in the neighbourhood of Sierra Leone* (2 vols). London: Hatchard.

Wittkower, R. (1942) Marvels of the East. *Journal of the Warburg and Courtauld Institutes* 5: 159–97.

Wokler, R. (1980) The ape debates in Enlightenment anthropology. *Transactions of the Fifth International Congress on the Enlightenment*. Oxford: The Voltaire Foundation.

Wolpert, L. (1992) *The unnatural nature of science*. London: Faber.

Woltmann, L. (1906/7) Die Ursachen der geistigen Minderwertigkeit der Negerrasse. *Politisch-anthropologische Revue* iv: 112–13.

Wundt, Wilhelm (1862) *Beiträge zur Theorie der Sinneswahrnehmung*. Leipzig: Winter.

Wundt, Wilhelm (1863) *Vorlesungen über die Menschen- und Thierseele*. Leipzig: Voss.

Wundt, Wilhelm (1916) *Elements of folk psychology*. London: Allen & Unwin.

Young, R.J.C. (1995) *Colonial desire: hybridity in theory, culture and race*. London: Routledge.

Young, W.C., Sachs, R.G., Braun, B.G. and Watkins, R.T. (1991) Patients reporting ritual abuse in childhood. A clinical syndrome. Report of 37 cases. *Child abuse and neglect* 15: 181–9.

Young-Bruehl, E. (1996) *The anatomy of prejudice*. Cambridge, MA: Harvard University Press.

# AUTHOR INDEX

**Note: page numbers in italics refer to illustrations**

Abd-El-Hamid-Bey 114, 115; *see also* Ducouret
Acher, R. A. 167
Adam of Bremen 1
Albertus Magnus 17, 32–3, 34, 35, 59
Allier, Raoul 144, 145, 148
Allport, G. W. xiv, 231
Altick, R. D. 49, 210
Alvernia, Petrus de 34
André, J. 31
Anon 18
Antinori, Marquis d' 116
Appleton, L. E. 167, 168
Ardrey, Robert 241
Arens, William 105, 106, 123
Ariès, Philippe 140
Aristotle 7, 8, 16, 32, 186
Arnold, Thomas 141
Augustine, Saint 5, 32
Avebury, Lord: *see* Lubbock, Sir John

Bacon, Francis 19
Bacon, Roger 27
Baer, Karl Ernst von 152
Bagehot, Walter 237
Baker, J. R. 71, 94, 95, 109
Baker, Samuel White 95, 123
Baldry, H. C. 26
Baldwin, James Mark 165, 166
Balfour, Henry 171
Banton, M. 75
Barker, A. J. 45, 46, 48, 49, 55, 56, 57
Barret, P. 149
Bartholomew the English 31
Bartlett, F. C. 4, 9, 239

Bartra, R. 235, 236, 237
Bastide, R. 240
Baudrillard, Jean 125
Bauer, E. 92
Beatty, K. J. 107
Beddoe, John 227
Behn, W. F. G. 76
Bergeron, Pierre 224–5
Bernheimer, R. 6
Binet, A. 182
Birrell, Augustine 243
Bitterli, U. 10, 133
Bloch, Marc 231–2
Blumenbach, Johann Friedrich 59, 63–5, 250 Chap 6 n1, 251 Chap 6 n2
Boas, G. 139, 229
Boesch, C. 241
Bogdan, R. 213
Bolk, Louis 175, 176
Bonaparte, Marie 165
Bonnet, Charles Etienne 38
Boswell, James 197
Boswell, John 105
Bovet, Pierre 169–70
Brackenridge, H.M. 23
Brantlinger, P. 118, 199, 201
Brantlinger, P. B. 149
Bril, B. 177
Brinton, Daniel Garrison 175
Broca, Paul 74, 76, 78, 81, 86, 156, 208
Brown, R. xv
Bry, Théodor de 102, 103
Bryson, G. 40
Bucher, B. 24, 102, 103, 104

Buffon, Georges-Louis Leclerc 20, 36, 38, 40, 41, 43, 44, 75
Bühler, Karl 173
Burke, P. 232
Burmeister, Hermann 85
Burnet, James (Lord Monboddo) 38–9, 43–4, 56
Burrow, J. W. 204
Burton, Richard 117, 200
Buschan, G. 172
Busia, Kofi xi
Bynum, W. F. 41, 57

Ca' da Mosto, d'Alvise de 224
Cairns, H. A. C. 39, 142, 202
Campbell, D. T. xiv
Campbell, Joseph 23
Campe, J. H. 198
Camper, Petrus 69, 71–4, 77, 84, 251 Chap 6 n7
Carey, J. 112
Carlin, N. 106, 214
Carothers, J. C. 159
Cassian, John 26
Castelnau, Francis de 115–16, 122
Catlin, George 210
Cavalieri, P. 241
Chamberlain, A. E. 155
Champlain, Samuel 224
Churchill, A. and J. 218
Cohen, W. B. 48, 206, 228
Cohn, N. 99, 104, 108, 232
Cole, M. xi, 243
Collinson, S. 204
Comte, Auguste 139, 171, 253 Chap 10 n3
Condamine, Charles-Marie de la 99
Condillac, Etienne 42
Conrad, Joseph 123–4
Cook, James 137
Copans, J. 77
Cope, E. D. 87
Corbain, A. 214
Cozolino, L. J. 126
Crichton, M. 245
Ctesias 31
Cureau, A. 91, 158
Cureau, A. L. 149
Curtin, P. D. 46, 48, 71, 204
Curtis, L. P. Jr 227
Cust, Robert 218
Cuvier, Georges 7, 33, 54, 74, 76–9, 84

Darwin, Charles 57–8, 123, 152, 161, 178

Daubenton, M. 251 Chap 6 n6
Daumier, Honoré 228
Davenport, C. B. 81
Davidson, S. 158–9
De Luce, J. 241
De Mause, L. 140
Dean, R. F. A. 176
Debrunner, H. W. 27, 29, 209
Defoe, Daniel 97, 110, 198
Degérando, Joseph-Marie 49, 89–90, 132
Delisle de Sales, Izonard 75
Demel, W. 226
Dennis, J. S. 147
Derrida, Jacques 24, 233
Desmond, A. 162
Detienne, M. 98
Diamond, J. 47, 241
Dickason, O. P. 4
Dickens, Charles 112, 123, 207
Drummond, Henry 142, 166, 203
Duckworth 186
Ducouret, Louis 86, 114, 116; see also Abd-El-Hamid-Bey
Dudley, E. xii
Dumas, Alexandre 114–15
Dunstan, G. R. 26
Durkheim, É. 180, 182
Duval, Pierre 31

Edwards, Bryan 34–5
Edwards, D. 239
Eickstedt, E. von 68
Elfasi, M. 27
Ellis, A. B. 156
Ellis, Havelock 175, 238
Encyclopaedia Britannica 124
Eng, Hilda 173
Engels, Friedrich 237
Erasmus of Rotterdam 223
Estwick, Samuel 48
Evans-Pritchard, E. E. 121, 180, 192–3
Eysenck, H. J. 176, 177

Farrar, Frederic William 136, 229–30
Favret-Saada, J. 243
Febvre, Lucien 231–2
Fenichel, Otto 179
Ferguson, Adam 49
Fernandez-Armesto, F. 11, 28
Field, M. J. 110
Fields, B. J. 228
Figlio, K. M. 78
Filliozat, J. 31

Fischer, E. 92, 93
Fitchett, William 149
Fontenu, Abbé 250 Chap 4 n1
Forde, Darryl C. 105
Forster, Johann Georg 63, 133
Fortes, Meyer 158, 254 Chap 11 n5
Fouillée, Alfred 138
Fraessle, J. 148
Frank, Erwin 105, 106–8, 123
Franke, E. 157
Frazer, Sir James 161, 180
Freud, Sigmund 138, 164–5, 179
Friedman, J. B. 8
Frobenius, Leo 211
Frobisher, M. 18
Froude, James 29

Galen 7
Galliker, M. 239
Galton, Francis 188, 189, 221, 251–2
  Chap 7 n3
Gauch, Dr 93
Géber, M. 176
Gehlen, Arnold 176
Gellner, E. 193
Gerbi, A. 19, 20, 21, 22
Gervase of Tilbury 5
Gillispie, C. C. 75
Gilroy, P. 245
Gleisberg, P. 86, 117
Gobineau, Joseph Arthur de 205–6
Goethe, Johann Wolfgang von 32, 199
Goldmann, S. 133, 211
Goody, J. 158, 225
Gould, S. J. 79, 161, 164, 175, 175, 176,
  177
Gratiolet, P. 81, 155
Gregorio, Gil 18
Guenther, M. G. 207, 210
Gurevich, A. 223, 232
Gwenebault, J. H. 70

Haddon, Alfred 167, 171
Haeckel, Ernest 83, 87, 152–3, 166, 169,
  254 Chap 12 n1
Haining, P. 125
Halbwachs, Maurice 239–40
Hale, J. 225
Haller, J. S. 244
Hallett, R. 30
Hallowell, A. Irving 164
Hallpike, C. R. 190–1
Hamilton, D. L. 231

Hartley, David 250 Chap 4 n3
Hegel, Georg Wilhelm Friedrich 68,
  113–14
Helmuth, H. 106
Hemmens, H. C. 203
Henry, J. 147
Herbert, Thomas 25, 45
Herodotus 1, 31
Herrnstein, R. J. 240
Hinojosa 18
Hobhouse, L. T. 105, 125, 167
Hoffmann, Johann Christian 47
Homer 31
Hooton, Earnest Albert 92
Hoppe 41
Hore, A. B. 148
Hoyme, L. E. 74
Hrdlicka, A. 174
Hulme, P. 107
Humboldt, Alexander von 10, 11, 107
Humboldt, Wilhelm von 90
Hunt, James 154, 199, 203–5
Huxley, Julian 151
Huxley, Thomas Henry 86, 123
Hyam, R. 150

Iselin, Isaak 133–4

Jaensch, E.R. 189
Jahn, J. 47
Jahoda, Gustav xi, 87, 132, 172, 191
Jamin, J. 77
Janet, Pierre 182, 183–4, 190–1, 192
Janson, H. W. 7, 33, 35, 228
Jaspers, R. 54
Jefferson, Thomas 21
Jerome, Saint 229
Jodelet, D. 243
Johnson, Samuel 197–8, 207
Johnston, Harry 92
Johnston, J. 146
Johnstone 118
Jordan, W. D. 35, 45, 46, 228
Juan, Don George *21*
Jung, Carl Gustav 179, 239, 255 Chap 13
  n2

Kames, Lord 75, 132
Kant, Immanuel 21, 63
Kappeler, M. 198
Keane, Augustus Henry 156
Keay, J. 99
Kidd, Dudley 157

Kingsley, Mary 144
Kipling, Rudyard 148–9
Kirk, G. S. 98
Kluckhohn, Clyde xiii
Knox, Robert 32, 76, 204
Koch, J. 34
Koch, T. 122
Krauss, W. 50
Kuklick, H. xii

La Fontaine, J. 127
La Mettrie, Julien 42
La Peyrère, Isaac de 25
Lafitau, J.F. 133
Lambert, J. C. 201
Lamprecht, Karl 171–2
Langer, J. 189
Langness, L. L. 207
Las Casas, Bartolomé de 16
Latini, Brunetto 27
Lave, J. 191
Lawrence, Sir William 81–2, 215
Le Goff, J. 18, 232
Leach, E. R. 7
LeBon, Gustave 85, 238
Lenz, F. 92
Leo Africanus 30
Leonard, Peter 154
Léry, Jean de 15, 100
Letourneau, Charles 137–8
Letts, M. 2
LeVaillant, François 132–3
Lévi-Strauss, Claude 9, 17, 98, 101, 102, 104, 192, 233, 234, 236
Levinas, Emmanuel 233
LeVine, R. A. xiv
Levinstein, S. 172
Lévy-Bruhl, Lucien 111, 173, 177, 179, 180–2, 183, 185, 186, 187, 190, 192
Lewis, I. M. xiv, 105, 106, 107, 109, 112
Liauzu, C. 88
Lichtenstein 207
Lilienthal, G. 59
Lilla, M. 9
Linnaeus, Carl 40–1, 46, 64, 226, 250
Chap 4 n2
Little, Kenneth 108
Livingstone, David 139
Loaysa, Garcia de 18
Locke, John 38
Lombroso, Cesare 164, 238
Long, Edward 54, 54, 55–7, 59, 216, 228
Lorimer, D. A. 237

Lorreyete, B. 245
Lovejoy, A. O. 38
Lubbock, Sir John 136–7, 140
Lugard, Lord 149, 201
Luig, U. 211
Luria, A. R. 184
Lyell, Sir Charles 23, 75, 76, 86–7
Lynn, R. 94

McClintock, A. xiii, 237
MacGaffey, W. 10
McGrew, W. C. 241
Mackintosh, D. 227
McLennan, J.F. 134–5
McLynn, F. 95, 117, 200
Maillet, Benoit de 8, 38, *39*, 116
Mair, John 16
Maistre, Joseph de 54, 142
Malinowski, Bronislav 93, 107
Mandeville, Sir John 2, 15, 27, 249
Chap 1, n1
Manetta, Filippo 155
Mann, Robert 154
Mannoni, O. 127
Marshall, P. J. 23
Martin-Luther Universität 53
Martius, C. F. von 22
Mason, P. 5, 9, 24, 103, 104, 113, 233–5, 236
Matthews, John 48
Medeiros, François de 5, 26, 27
Medicus, G. 175
Meiners, Christoph 21–2, 63, 65–8, 75, 76, 132
Métraux, Alfred 100
Michiels, Alfred 8
Middleton, J. 239
Milbury-Steen, S. L. 150
Miller, N. 158
Miner, E. 197
Mivart, St George 161
Monboddo, Lord (James Burnet) 38–9, 43–4, 56
Money-Kyrle, R. E. 126
Montagu, Ashley 176
Montaigne, Michel de 20
Moore, J. 162
Moore, J. H. 137
Moorhouse, G. 201, 202
Morden, Robert 46
More, Hannah 141
Morel, Edmund 208
Morgan, Lewis 134

Morris, Desmond 241
Morris, R. C. 245
Morton, S. G. 75, 79
Moscovici, S. 9, 10
Moses, Y. T. 245
Mukhopadhyay, C. C. 245
Müller-Hill, B. 93
Murphy, J. 182
Murray, C. 240
Muschinske, D. 169

Nadel, S. F. 190
Nash, G. B. 24
Novak, M. E. xii

Ogilvie, J. N. 144
O'Gorman, E. 18
Ohnuki-Tierny, E. 7
Ombredane, A. 160
Opie, Peter and Iona 240, 248
Ortiz, Tomas 16, 99, 153, 229
Ovideo Y Valdés, Gonzalo Hernández de 10, 19, 20, 131

Pagden, A. 10, 15, 16, 18, 24, 101, 102, 104, 122
Paracelsus 25
Paris, Mathieu 27
Parry, J. H. 18
Paton, J. 202
Pauw, Cornelius de 20–1, 22, 132, 153, 157
Pearce, R. H. 18, 23
Pelletier, A.-M. 19
Pénel, J.-D. 115, 116
Perrin, M. 235
Phillips, Thomas 218–20
Piaget, Jean 43, 182, 185, 190, 192, 193, 243
Pierce, Charles 178
Piéron, Henri 33, 89, 179
Pieterse, J. N. 26, 228
Pliny the Elder 1, 4, 31, 42, 116
Plischke, H. 64
Plutarch 42
Poignant, R. 212
Poliakov, L. xii
Polo, Marco 27
Poole, F. J. P. 107
Poryphyry 98
Pottinger, G. 149
Preyer, W. 179
Prichard, James Cowles 74

Pritchard, James 75, 203
Probst, P. 88
Proyarts, Abbé 50
Pruner-Bey (Pruner, Franz) 82, 85, 155, 206
Purchas, Samuel 45

Quatrefages, Armand de 253 Chap 9 n2
Quinlan, M. J. 141

Raynal, Guillaume Thomas François 131–2
Read, P. P. 105
Reade, Winwood 205
Reclus, Eli 88
Rehbock, P. F. 32
Reinders, R. C. 207
Retzius, Anders 64
Ricci, C. 172
Richards, Audrey 93
Richet, Charles 92, 154
Ridley, M. 241
Ritchie, J. 158
Rivers, W. H. R. 62, 78, 178–9
Robertson, P. 142
Robinet, Jean Baptiste 38
Romanes, George 161, 162–3, 164, 166
Roome, W. J. W. 147
Rose, S. 241
Ross, C. A. 127
Ross, D. 166, 167
Rousseau, Jean-Jacques 11–12, 42–3, 142
Routledge, W. S. and K. 143
Rupp-Eisenreich, B. 65, 68
Rushton, J. P. 94, 95–6, 240
Russell, Bertrand 12
Russell, P. E. 28
Russett, C. E. 238

Sagan, E. 111
Sahlins, M. 111
Said, Edward W. 215
Sanday, P. R. 107, 111
Savage-Rumbaugh, E. S. 241
Schiller, Friedrich 132
Schneider, W. 210
Schultze, Fritz 88–90, 149
Schumann, A. 86
Schweinfurth, Georg 95, 114, 117–21, 199, 219
Scribner, S. 184
Sepulveda, Juan de 19, 24–5

Serres, P.M. 81, 208
Shaffer, R. E. 126
Sharp, Granville 48
Shufeldt, R. W. *91*, 92
Shweder, R. A. xi, 191
Simar, T. 75
Simon, T. 182
Simonot 116
Sinclair, A. xii
Singer, P. 241
Sixel, F. W. 100–1
Slotkin, J. S. 41
Smellie, William 57, 58
Smith, Hamilton 76
Smith, J. 221
Smith, William 220
Snowden, F. M. 26
Soemmering, Samuel Thomas 58–9, 62, 65, 67, 74
Solin, Caius Julius 30, 31
Speke, John 95
Spencer, Herbert 78, 90, 135, 139
Spenser, Edmund 5
Spitzer, L. 215
Spix, J. B. von 22
Sprat, Thomas 36
St Hilaire, Geoffroy 77, 78, 116
Staden, Hans 100
Stanley, A. P. 142
Stanley, Henry 117, 200
Stanley Hall, Granville 165–7, 168, 169, 187
Steel, T. 227
Steele, R. 31
Stefansson, V. 224
Steggerda, M. 81
Steinen, Karl von den 171
Steins, M. 206–7
Stepan, N. 75
Stern, William 179
Stocking, G. W. Jr xv, 93
Stone, Benjamin 211, *212*
Stone, H. 112
Stone, L. 140, 141
Storch 185
Stowe, Harriet Beecher 142
Strabo 30
Street, B. V. 216, 244
Strong, Josiah 164
Subbotsky, E. 243
Suchem, Ludolph de 27
Sulloway, F. J. 164
Sully, James 137, 165, 179

Super, C. M. 177
Surgy, Rousselot de 48
Sutherland, A. 88

Taine, Hyppolite 165
Tajfel, Henri xiv, 231, 247
Talbot, E. S. 238
Thevet, André 100
Thomson, Joseph 201
Thorndike, Edward L. 167
Thurnwald, Richard 180
Tiedemann, Friedrich 65, 82
Tinbergen, N. 251 Chap 7 n2
Tinland, F. xii, 38, 43, 46
Todorov, T. 17, 19, 44, 153
Topinard, Paul 78, 199, 212
Topsell, Edward 45
Triandis, H. C. 231
Turnbull, C. 109, 110
Turner, J. C. xiv
Tylor, Edward Burnett 135, 136, 154, 155, 180
Tyson, Edward 4, 36, 38, 41, 46

Ulloa, Don Antoine de *21*

Velden, F. von den 174
Vico, Giovanni Battista 9, 65, 139
Vidal, F. 178
Virey, Jules J. 45–6, 54, 68–71, 74, 75, 199, 206
Visser, R. 72, 73
Vitoria, Francisco de 18–19, 101
Voget, F. W. 135
Vogt, Carl 34, 83–6, 92, 155, 156, 178, 208
Volhard, E. 123
Voltaire, François Marie Arouet de xvi, 11–12, 25
Vygotsky, L. S. 184–5

Waitz, Theodor 87, 154
Wallace, Alfred Russell 161, 163, 170–1
Wallon, Henri 182, 192
Walvin, J. 48
Walzer, J. F. 141
Werner, Heinz 185–90
Wesley, John 141
Weule, Karl 172–3
White, Charles 59–61, 74, 85
White, H. xii, 4, 5
Wilder, H. T. 241
Williams, G. 23

Wilson, Daniel 87, 241
Wilson, Reverend 217–18
Winterbottom, Thomas 61–2
Wittkower, R. 99
Wokler, R. 53
Woltmann, L. 174
World Health Organization 159

Wundt, Wilhelm 22–3, 178

Young, Robert xiii
Young, W. C. 126
Young-Bruehl, E. 256–7 Chap 17 n2

Zimmermann, J.G. 43

# SUBJECT INDEX

**Note: page numbers in italics refer to illustrations**

abolitionism 57; *see also* anti-slavery
  movement
aborigines, Australian 92, 176, 186–7,
  211, 212
Absolute (Hegel) 114
abstract thought 90, 188, 223
*Académie des Sciences* 114, 115
adaptability 66, 67, 187
advertisements, animality 213
Aethiopians 2, 5, 27; *see also* blacks
Afghan war 149
Africa 26, 28, 113–14, 133
Africans *see* blacks
Akan people 110
alterity *see* Otherness
altruism 142
Amazons 2
America *see* New World
American Indians: attachment principle
  10; cannibalism alleged 16, 99–100;
  child-likeness 131; cruelty 67; depravity
  21–2; displayed 210; evolutionary scale
  169; food 67; genitalia size 22; hairiness
  15, 22; ill-treatment 16–17, 19;
  immaturity 20–1, 22, 131–2; language
  24–5; legal status 23; libido 15, 22;
  myths 234; as noble savages 21;
  representations *21*; skulls 67; strength
  67; as sub-human 16–17; as wild men
  of woods 15, 226; *see also* North
  American Indians; South American
  Indians
Amo, Anthony William 53
Anativolo people 202–3
anatomy, comparative 58, 66–7, 77, 81–2

anchoring 9–10
Andaman Islanders 2, 187, 226, 230
Andes air crash 105
animality 7, 249 Chap 2 n2;
  advertisements 213; blacks ix, 55,
  69–70, 205, 206, 244–5; constance
  xi–xii, 239, 244–5; Cuvier 76–9; food
  90; and humanity 6–7; images of
  savages xv, xvi, 97–8; index of 78;
  mentally ill 243; North American
  Indians 249 Chap 2, n2; sensory
  perception 89; slavery 55; *see also*
  apishness; bestiality; cannibalism
animals, souls 7, 41
Annales historians 231–2
Anthropological Society of London 199,
  203
Anthropological Society of Paris 81, 210
anthropology xiv, 180; adult thought 193;
  ambiguous categories 7; cannibalism
  xiii; English 180; ethno-anthropology
  234; German 211; physical xiii, 64,
  92–3, 211; psychological 165
anthropometric measures 211, 256 Chap
  15 n8
anthropophagi 1, 2, 30, 99, 126; *see also*
  cannibals
anthropophagy 100, 122; *see also*
  cannibalism
anti-black literature, USA 91–2
anti-racism 151, 248
anti-slavery movement 53–4, 228
antiquity *see* Greeks; Romans
apes: Albertus Magnus 32–3; and
  child-likeness 9; chimpazees 4, 36, 41,

288

241; comparative anatomy 77; DNA 241; evolutionary scale 162, 178; four-handed 83; 'good to think' 9; human-like qualities 46–7, 71; humanized 70; and humans 7–8, 162, 241; image continuity 8; imitating 8, 34; mating with women 25; Middle Ages 8–9, 215, 229; as monstrous race 38; nations 43–4; orang-utans 41, 44, 55, 56, 70, 82, 250 Chap 4 n5; penis size 250 Chap 4 n7; raping women 8, 36, 45; revalued 241–2; sexuality 8; skills 241; symbolism 8; as term 250 Chap 3 n2

apishness 215; arrested development 155; blacks 8, 27, 35, 44–9, 204, 227–8; Bushmen 207; Dinka 118; literal/metaphorical 44–9; race 216; representations of savages xv, 7–9, 227–8; science 216

aquatic origins of humans 38

Aranda people 188

Aristotlean logic 186

arm lengths 60, 85–6

arrested development doctrine 152; apishness 155; European acceptance 160, 187; infancy/childhood 159; mentally ill 182; pre-operativeness 191; puberty 153, 155, 157–8, 160; sexuality 157–8, 159, 160; social evolutionism 160, 162; sutures of skull 155, 156; weaning 158–9; Wolof people 255 Chap 14 n5; see also child-likeness

art, primitive 170–1, 198

Arunta people, Australia 182

Ashanti people 143, 144, 254 Chap 11 n2

astrology 243

attachment principle 10, 24

Australia: aborigines 92, 176, 186–7, 211, 212; Arunta people 182

Azan, Général Paul 149–50

Azande people 117, 121–2, 192, 253 Chap 9 n7; see also Niam-Niam people

Baer, Karl Ernst von (biogenetic law) 152

Bakongo people 10

BaLese people 109–10

Bambara people 146

barbarians, and savages 16, 19

Barnum and Bailey's Circus 213

beauty, race classification 65–6

behaviour, ethologists 240

Belgian Congo 144

beliefs: children 183; mentally ill 182, 183–4; Others 214; savages 183

Bemba people 158–9

Bemoim, Wolof king 28

bestiality 98, 102, 214–15, 237–8; see also animality

Betanzos, Domingo de 18

bigots 248

Bimin-Kuskusmin people 107

binary oppositions 19

biogenetic law 160–3; Bühler 173; child-likeness 131; colonialism 164; embryology 152, 160; limitations 175; mental evolution 162; organic evolution 152–3; phylogenesis/ontogenesis 192; primitives/children/mentally ill 162–3; savage children 216

biological racism 134

biology: animality xv; arm-lengths 60, 85–6; brains 58, 82, 87, 89; child-likeness of savages 152–3; and evolution xv, 83; nerve thickness 58, 82; scientific truth xvii; sensory nerves 58–9, 89; sociobiology 182, 241; taxonomy 40–1; women/children 215

birth 11, 67

black/white symbolism 26, 69

blackness 226

blacks: advertisements 213; animality xi, 55, 69–70, 205, 206, 244–5; apishness 8, 27, 35, 44–9, 204, 227–8; arm-lengths 60, 85–6; birth 11, 67; child-likeness xi, 138, 151; child-rearing 147; civilization 148–9; climate 34, 59; colonial administrators' views 148–51; comic book depictions 202; dehumanized 70; education 215; evolutionary scale 169, 178; food 67; Greeks/Romans 26; Ham 146; humanity 47, 48, 64–5, 145, 228; and idiots 156; intelligence 69, 76–7, 146; language 47, 206, 218–19; lice 61; medical profession 66–7, 244; memory 154; Middle Ages 26–7; missionaries' views 143, 144–8; morality 69, 146–7; neoteny 176–7; penis size 61, 68, 81, 85, 92; personality 145–6, 148; power relations 218–22; psychology 173–4, 221–2; rape of white women (alleged) 208, 256; reasoning 154, 191; sensory perception 61; sexuality xi, 70, 118, 120, 147, 220; as slaves 29; souls 61; toenails 92; women 56–7, 60, 118, 120,

206–7; *see also* Bushmen; Hottentots;
   Kaffirs; pygmies
blond races 174
bodily orifices 233–4
Bokassa, Jean Bedel 253 Chap 9 n10
Bongo women 118
Bororo Indians 171, 181
Bosjemen people 230
botany, plant names 11
Bougham, Lord 227
Bragmanni 1
brain, comparative anatomy 58, 82, 87,
   89
brain development 154–5, 174, 204, 205
Brazilian expedition 22
breast shapes 47, 60, 211; nipples 55, 60
British Association for the Advancement
   of Science 162, 203
brotherhood of man 145, 228
*Bulletin de la Société d'Anthropologie* 116
Bushmen 189, 207, 210, 213

Cafres *see* Kaffirs
Cape of Good Hope 24, 47
Canada, Enfranchisement Act 249 Chap
   2 n5
Canary Islands 11, 15
cannibal jokes 125
cannibalism 104–5, 125; anthropology
   xiii; Bokassa 253 Chap 9 n10; of dead
   107, 122, 256 Chap 15 n2; debate on
   94, 106–8; deconstructed 103; Dickens
   112, 123; documentary films 245;
   ethnography 103, 104, 111–12;
   Europeans as 98–9, 109, 214, 227;
   explorers' tales 200; Fiji 213; 'good to
   think' 101–4; Greek myths 98–9; image
   xv, xviii, 214; literature 125–6;
   missionaries as food 122, *124*, 125;
   monstrous races 99; New World 16,
   99–100; offspring 230; Other 97–8,
   106; photographic 'evidence' *113*;
   psychological depths 110–11; ritual
   105, 107, 108–9; satanic cults 126–7;
   savagery 127; scientific knowledge
   215–16; and sexuality 102, 127; Sierra
   Leone 252 Chap 8 n7; slave-traders
   219; for survival 104, 105; Tannese
   people 202; teeth sharpening 116, 219,
   252 Chap 9 n1; twentieth-century view
   124–6; universal notions 109–10; Wild
   Man of the Woods 5; *see also*
   anthropophagy

cannibals 1, 114–15; *see also*
   anthropophagi
caricatures 84, 246
cartoons, savages 246
Cashibo people 109
castration 100
catastrophe theory, geology 76
Catholicism, sexual conduct 225
Caucasoids 94
Celts 2, 54, 66
cephalic index 64
chain-type drawings 188
child art 170
child development: Fortes 158, 254 Chap
   11 n5; Piaget 243
child-likeness xv, xviii, 134; abstract
   concepts lacking 90; American Indians
   131, 138; apes 9; behaviour 97, 98;
   biogenetic law 131; biological
   explanations 152; colonialism 88, 216;
   comparative psychology 137–8;
   dependence 9; Enlightenment 131;
   images 214, 215; Other 192; primitives
   179, 182, 183–4, 187; relative 192–3;
   US blacks 151; *see also* social evolution
child psychology 173, 179, 182, 187
child races 144, 200
child study movement 165–70
children: beliefs 183; dependence 9, 143,
   144; developmental stages (Piaget) 190;
   European images 140, 141–2;
   games/lore 240, 248; innocence 9, 142;
   mental processes 138, 139; morality
   141–2; primitives 179, 182, 184;
   running on all fours 174–5; savage/
   European 154, 155; as savages 135;
   string activities 167; treatment of 141–2
children's literature, savages 201–2, 207
chimpanzee 4, 36, 41, 241
Chinese 83, 215, 226
Choromandae 4
Christianity 2; ape/devil 8; black/white
   symbolism 26; evangelical 203;
   evolution 203; monogenism 75;
   sexuality xvii
christianization 28, 143, 226, 254 Chap
   11 n1
civility 225, 235
civilization: blacks 148–9; and primitive
   90; and savagery 98–9, 222–3, 245–6
class, social 139, 215, 237–8
classification of humanity 40–2, 53, 60–1,
   64, 65–6, 229–30, 253 Chap 10 n3

cleanliness 90
client relationship 254 Chap 11 n8
climate: blacks 34, 59; intelligence 154;
    New World 20; race differences xvi
cognitive development 33, 180, 193, 247,
    255 Chap 14 n5
cognitive dissonance 217
collective memory 239, 240
collective representations 180
collective unconscious 236, 239
colonial administrators 143, 148–51, 160
colonial novels 206
colonialism: biogenetics 164; child image
    88, 216; France 88, 90–1; Germany
    88–90; and independence 125; justified
    239; Reclus 88; sexual exploitation
    150–1
Columbus, Christopher 15, 99
comic books, blacks 202
comparative anatomy 58, 66–7, 77, 81–2;
    brain 58, 82, 87, 89
comparative organismic theory (Werner)
    185
comparative philology 162
comparative psychology 137–8, 161, 178
concepts, and pseudoconcepts 185
Le Congo Belge en images 144
Congolese 173, 174
conquistadores 10, 16, 99
conscience 238
continuity principle 32
conversion, psychology of 144
copulation, and eating 234
craniology xiii, 53, 64, 71, 74, 76, 78, 84,
    121, 159
creations, multiple 25
Creole women, sexuality 56–7
criminality xv, 164, 179
cross-cultural psychology xi–xii, 193
cultural environment, thinking 192–3
cultural heritage, slaves 240
cultural perspective 139–40
cultural psychology xi–xii, xvii, 193
culture–epoch theory 168, 169
Cunningham, R. A. (showman) 212
Cynocephali 2, 4, 8

da Cunha, Pero Vaz 28–9
Daily Herald 208
Daily Mail and Evening News 211
Darwinian evolutionism 76, 86–7, 161,
    178, 237
deconstruction 24, 103

degenerationism xv, 20, 64, 237
dependence 9, 143–4, 216, 254 Chap 11
    n8
development stages (Haeckel) 254 Chap
    12 n1; see also child development
developmental psychology 185
Dinka people 118
disgust, lacking 179
disinterment 256 Chap 15 n2
DNA, humans/chimpanzees 241
documentary films 245, 246
drawings: chain-type 188; savages/
    children 170–3; understanding 170–1,
    254 Chap 13 n4
dreams 164, 255 Chap 13 n2

ear waggling 33, 58–9
East Indians 4
eating habits: and copulation 234; North
    American Indians 224, 225; raw food
    17–18, 230; savages 209; and sexuality
    112; Wolofs 224; see also food
education 141, 147, 245–6, 254 Chap 11 n7
ego-centrism 243
Egyptians 79
eidetic perception 188–9
Elizabethan drama, African stereotypes 31
embryology 152, 153, 160
embryonic resemblance 152
Encyclopaedia Britannica 206
Encyclopaedia of the social sciences 125
energy 78, 251–2 Chap 7 n3
Enlightenment: animal/human
    relationship xvi, 6–7; child-likeness 131;
    humans/apes xvii; noble/ignoble
    savage xvi, 6, 11; progress 49; reaction
    to 54; savages xviii, 49, 241
entertainments, savages 198, 216
Eskimos 189, 210, 224
Ethiopia 1
ethnic groups, inferiority 94
ethno-anthropology 234
ethnocentrism: alien cultures 139–40;
    Drummond 203; and ego-centrism 243;
    images 231; psychoanalytical approach
    256–7 Chap 17 n2; social identity xiv,
    247
ethnographic exhibitions 210
ethnography: art 171, 172; cannibalism
    xiii, 122; child-likeness of primitives
    192; inversion 113; Werner's use of
    187–8
Ethnological Society 154, 203–4, 229

ethnology 44–5, 88, 227
ethnopsychology 187
ethology 240
Europe 2, 24, 113–14, 140, 222–6
Europeans xi, 208, 247; and American
  Indians 10, 23–5; cannibalism 103,
  104, 111–12; as cannibals 98–9, 109,
  214, 227; children 140, 141–2;
  evolutionary scale 178; food 223; Other
  1, 10, 113, 232; and savages xii–xiii, 7,
  30, 113–14; as savages 118, 214, 227;
  sexuality xiii, xvii, 223; superiority
  assumed 10–11
evolution: and Christianity 203;
  Darwinian 76, 86–7, 161, 178, 237;
  four-handed apes 83; mental (Romanes)
  162–3, 164; natural selection 142;
  organic 152–3; psychological 178, 180,
  184; race 87
evolutionary scales 162, 169, 178
Ewe people 156
exclusion images 234
exhibitions of savages 48, 208–13
experience, learning from 33
exploration: of Africa 28; French 114–16;
  German 114, 117–21; manners 223–4;
  monstrous races 15
explorers, writing of savages 199–201
eye–ear plane 74

facial angle (Camper) 251 Chap 6 n7, 253
  Chap 9 n5; Cuvier 77; Irish 227;
  Tinbergen 251 Chap 7 n2; Virey 69,
  71–4; Vogt 84
Faerie Queene (Spenser) 5
familiarity, principle of 9–12
fiction see literature
Fiji cannibals 213
flea-picking 8
food: American Indians 67; animality 90;
  blacks 67; Europeans 223; insects as 8,
  99, 102; raw 17–18, 230; savages 229,
  230; taboos 102; see also cannibalism;
  eating habits
foot shape 238; see also toe shape
football crowds, racial abuse 244–5
fossils 75
France: cannibalism 214; childhood 142;
  class/savagery 238; colonial novels 206;
  colonial officers 149–50; racism 245;
  savages 88
freak shows 48
Frederick II of Hohenstaufen 27

French Revolution 54
Freudian approach 6, 111, 165
Fuegians 138

Garamantes 30–1
genetic psychology 185
genitalia size 22, 27, 68, 79, 81, 93, 211;
  see also penis size
geology 75, 76
Germany: anthropology 211; ethnology
  88; exploration 114, 117–21; primitive
  peoples 88–90; race 62; savages 54
Golbéry, Sylvain de 133
Gold Coast xi
Golden Age myth 11
Golden Stool, Ashanti 143, 254 Chap 11
  n2
Good Hope, Cape of 24, 47
Great Chain of Being doctrine: Albertus
  Magnus 32–6; continuity principle 32;
  Forster 63; imagery 200; middle species
  25; Others xvii; plenitude principle 32;
  pygmies 32; racialized 54; reformulated
  38; tailed people 116; Virey 68; White
  59–60
Greeks 225–6; apes 8; blacks 26;
  cannibalism 98; monkeys 7; myths 5,
  98–9; satyrs 4
group psychology 138
Guajiro people 235

hair colour 174
hairiness 15, 22
Ham 5, 146
Heart of Darkness (Conrad) 123–4
Hebrews 5, 49
Henry the Navigator 28, 29
history xv, xvii, 171, 231–2, 243
Homo ferus 41
Homo monstruosus 41
Homo sapiens 41
Homo sylvestris 4, 41
Hottentot Venus 79, 80, 81, 208, 209
Hottentots 44, 70, 132–3, 206
Household Works 207
human sacrifice 10, 100, 126–7
humanity: Absolute 114; and animals
  6–7; aquatic origins 38; blacks 47, 48,
  64–5, 145, 228; boundaries 241;
  classified 40–2, 53, 60–1, 64, 65–6,
  229–30, 253 Chap 10 n3;
  equality/inequality 205–6, 228;
  language 41, 42–3, 56;

intra-uterine development 8; potential
163, 193; unity 64–5
humanoids 1, *39*
Husi 2
hybrids 4, 5, 38, 43, 250 Chap 4 n1

identity xiv, 2, 237, 239, 247
idiots: evolutionary scale 34, 178;
intermediate between Negro/ape 156;
microcephalous 83, *84*, 86; skull sutures
156
ill-treatment of savages 16–17, 19, 48; *see
also* slavery
*Illustrated London News* 144
images xv, xvi–xviii; constancy 230–1,
243; constructed 12; deep anchored
232; diffusion 197, 199, 248, 257
Postscript n4; identity 237, 239;
and myths 233; Other 229, 233–4;
popular 197; psychological xiii–xiv,
231
imitating behaviour 8, 34, 89
immaturity 20–1, 22, 131–2
imperialism 149
impossibilities, physical/logical 186
Incas, culture 21
independence xi, 125
*Independent* 126
Indian Citizenship Act (1924) 23
Indian Mutiny 149
indigenous cultures, as endangered species
246
infancy 159; *see also* childhood
insect-eating 8, 99, 102
instinct 138
intelligence: blacks 69, 76–7, 146; external
factors 154; medieval/modern 256
Chap 16 n1; potential 163
International African Institute 158
interspecies breeding 5, 250 Chap 4 n1
interspecies sexuality 36, *37*, 38, 43, 56
inversion concept 113
Irish 84, 214, 226–7
Isabella, Queen 19, 99
Islam *see* Muslims

Japan, monkey metaphors 7
Jefferson, Thomas 8
Jews 5, 49
John II, King of Portugal 28
*Journal of Heredity* 151
Jungian collective unconscious 236, 239
juvenility *see* neoteny

Kaffirs 48, 154, 157
Kano 30
Karen people 109
Kenya 142–3
Khoisanid people 79, 93, 252 Chap 7 n4
Kikuyu, Kenya 142–3
Korowai people 245

lake habitations, Maori/Swiss 134
language: abstractions lacking 90;
American Indians 24–5; apes 241, 250
Chap 4 n5; blacks 47, 206, 218–19;
eating/copulating words 234; evolution
162, 163; humanity 41, 42–3, 56;
indigenous 181, 186–7, 188, 230;
magical thinking 184; polygenism 75;
pre-operational 192; pygmies 34; racism
136
Laplanders 210
*Larousse* encyclopaedia 206
Lévi-Straussian analysis 24
libido: hairiness 15, 22; racial differences
68; Wild Man of the Woods 6
lice 61
life stages, collective/individual 133
linguistic psychology 162
lip size 93
literature: cannibals 125–6; children's
books 201–2, 207; colonial novels 206;
comic books 202; Elizabethan drama
31; images of savagery 197–8, 206–8
logic, Aristotelian 186
*logos*, and *mythos* 235–6
London Anthropological Society 199, 203
London Ethnological Society 154, 203–4,
229
London Missionary Society 54
Long, Edward 54, 55–7

Magellan, Ferdinand 4
magical thinking 184
Makkarika people 123
Malay Archipelago 170
Mali 27–8
manners 223
Mansa Musa, ruler of Mali 27–8
Marxism 247
Matabele people 211
medical profession, racism 244
Melanesians 205–6
memory 33, 154, 188–9, 239
Mende people, Sierra Leone 108
mental differences, hair colour 174

mental evolution (Romanes) 162–3, 164
mentality 161, 180–1, 186, 232
mentally ill; animality 243; arrested
    development 182; beliefs 182, 183–4;
    degeneracy xv; as Other 243; regression
    178–9; thought modes 181–2
mermaids 38, *39*
Methodism 141
Middle Ages: apes 8–9, 215, 229; blacks
    26–7; manners 223; savages 225–6;
    Wild Man of the Woods 5, *6*, 235
miscegenation 25
missing link hypothesis 25, 49, 116
missionaries: aims 143; American Indians
    18; blacks 49–50; as cannibal fodder
    122, *124*, 125; and savages 144–8,
    217–18; tales about savages 201–3
Mongoloids 66, 93–4
monkey image 7, 244; *see also* apes
Monkey Soap 213
monogenism 25, 44, 63, 72, 74, 75
monstrous races *3*; Amazons 2;
    anthropophagi 126; apes 38;
    cannibalism 99; Cynocephali 2, 4, 8;
    Garamantes 30–1; Husi 2; hybrids 4, 5;
    Other 233; pygmies 31–2; remoteness
    1–2; *see also* Plinian races
Montezuma 10
Moors 27
morality 69, 141–2, 146–7
murder, ritual 127
museums, savages 208–9
Muslims 2, 27
*mythos,* and *logos* 235–6
myths 98–9, 233–4, 236–7, 244

Native Americans *see* North American
    Indians
natural selection, altruism 142
naturalists 7, 20, 40–2
*Nature* 62, 117, 199–200
Nazis 49, 65, 68, 93, 240
Negritoes 187
Negroes: *see* blacks
Negroids 93–4
neoteny 153, 175–7
nerve thickness 58, 82
neuroses 165, 178
New Hebrides 217
New World: cannibalism 16, 99–100;
    climate 20; inhabitants 15–21; as young
    continent 19–20
newspapers, popular 207

Niam-Niam 114–17, 118, 120–1, 200,
    253 Chap 9 n2, n7; *see also* Azande
    people
Nimrod 5
nipple size 55, 60
noble savage xv–xvi, 6, 21, 54
North American Indians: animality 249
    Chap 2 n2; arrested development 153;
    child-likeness 138; civil rights 249 Chap
    2 n5; consumerism 249 Chap 2 n6;
    eating habits 224, 225; Janet 182;
    perception/reality 23, 24
noun-stereotypes 231
Nubians 118
Nuer people 95

*Observer Magazine* 125
obsessional neuroses 165, 232
ontogenesis, and phylogenesis 160, 165,
    172
orang-utans 41, 44, 55, 56, 70, 82, 250
    Chap 4 n5
organic evolution 152–3
organization, syncretic/diffuse 188
Other: beliefs 214; cannibalism 97–8, 106;
    as child-like 192; Europeans 1, 10, 113,
    232; images 229, 233–4; mentally ill
    243; as object of pity/scorn 213;
    sexuality 232
Otherness xiii, xiv, xvii, 9

paedomorphism *see* neoteny
pagans 2
pain, sensitivity 238
Papua New Guinea 107, 170
Paris Anthropological Society 81, 210
paternalism 149, 216, 254 Chap 11 n7
patronizing attitudes 169
Paul III, Pope 16
penis size: apes 250 Chap 4 n7; blacks 61,
    68, 81, 85, 92; pygmies 31–2
personality 145–6, 148, 159
phallus, size 6; *see also* penis size
Philippines 4
Phillips, Thomas (slave-trader) 218–20
philology 136, 162; *see also* language
philosophy 65–8
phrenology 53
phylogenesis, and ontogenesis 160, 165,
    172
phylogenetic principle *see* biogenetic law
physical anthropology xiii, 64, 92–3
physiognomic perception 187

*Pickwick Papers* (Dickens) 112
Pigafetta, explorer 4
plants, naming of 11
plenitude principle 32
Plinian races 1, 2, 6, 15, 99, 234; *see also* monstrous races
poison oracle, Azande people 192
police, racism 245
politics and race 151, 245, 247
polygamy 143
polygenism 25, 63, 69, 75, 76, 83
Polynesians 138
Pongo people 48
pop ethologists 240
porno-tropics xiii
Portuguese, slaves 29–30, 226
Portuguese kings, Lords of Guinea 28
post-colonialism xi
post-structuralism 233
pragmatism 178
precocity 176–7
prehensile foot 82, 83, 238
prejudice xi, xiii–xiv, xv, 247
pre-logicality 180, 192
pre-operativeness 190–1
primitives xii, 143; art 170–1, 189; as child-ancestors 132–4; child-likeness 179, 182, 183–4, 187; children 179, 182, 184; civilization 90; evolutionary scale 178; German studies 88–90; inferiority 169; mentality 180–1, 186; and mentally ill 181; pre-operative 190–1; psychology of 87–8, 181; syncretism 188; Werner 185–6; *see also* savages
prognathism 34–5, 60, 78, 82, 251 Chap 6 n7
progress 49
Protestantism 225
psychic development 179
psychoanalysis xiii, 232
psychological anthropology 165
psychological evolution (Vygotsky) 184
psychology: blacks 173–4, 221–2; child/genetic 185; comparative 137–8, 161; conversion 144; cross-cultural xi–xii, 193; cultural xi–xii, xvii, 193; and evolutionism 178, 180; and history 231–2; images xiii–xiv, 231; primitives 87–8, 181; races 57–8, 92; social psychology xiv–xv, 85; universalism 231
psychopathology 182
psychosis 178

puberty 153, 155, 157–8, 160
Puritanism 141
pygmies 30, *40*; in Britain 211, *212*; chimpanzee dissection 4, 36; development 8; Great Chain of Being 32; Herodotus 1; language 34; lip size 93; mosaics in Pompeii 26

*r-K* scale, reproductive strategies 94
race: apishness 216; blond race 174; classification 64, 65–6, 229–30, 253 Chap 10 n3; climate xvi; evolutionism 87; four-handed 83; Germany 62; human differences 75, 93–4; libido 15, 22, 68; monogenism 44; philosophy 65–8; psychological differences 57–8, 92; skull shapes 64; slavery 228; *see also* monstrous races; Plinian races
race theories xvii–xviii, 32, 135, 136, 250 Chap 4 n10
racial caricatures 84, 246
racial determinism 79
racial prejudice xi, xiii–xiv
racial psychology 92
racism 243; biological 134; eighteenth century 53; France 245; Hunt 203–5; individual stance against 248; jealousy 247; language 136; medical profession 244; newspapers 208; police 245; scientific 205; USA 91–2
radical materialists 42
Raikes, Assistant Native Commissioner 150–1
rape allegations: ape/women 8, 36, 45; by blacks 208, 256 Chap 15 n7; Wild Man of the Woods 5
raw food 17–18, 230
reason 33, 41, 154, 191
recapitulation theory 160, 174; child psychology 179, 182; child study movement 165–70; criminology 164; Frazer 161; sexuality 169; Stanley Hall 165–70
regression 178–9
religion, cannibals 100
Renaissance, wildness 6
reproductive strategies 94
revenge, cannibalism 98, 101
reversionary individuals 92
ritual cannibalism 105, 107, 108–9
*Robinson Crusoe* (Defoe) 97, 110, 198
Romans 8, 225–6
Royal Society 36

Samoa 54
Santa Marta, Bishop of 15
satanic cults 126–7
satyrs 4, 6, 8, 42
satyrus monkey 4
savagery: cannibalism 1, 97–8, 127;
  civilization 98–9, 222–3, 245–6;
  constructed image 12; humanity in
  infancy 132–4; as mental disorder 178–9
savages 214–17, 225–8; as ancestors xviii,
  132–4, 241; apishness xv, 7–9, 227–8;
  art 170–1, 189; and barbarians 16, 19;
  beliefs 183; cartoons 246; child-likeness
  xv, xviii, 88, 90, 134, 161; class 215,
  237; conscience 238; dependence
  143–4; displayed 208–13; education
  245–6; education of children 147;
  Enlightenment xviii, 49, 241; European
  attitudes xii–xiii, 7, 54, 88, 113–14;
  Europeans as 214, 227; fictional
  depictions 206–8; as half-breeds 45–6;
  humanity 217; ill-treatment of 16–17,
  19, 48; instinct 138; intellectual
  potential 163; Jerome, St 229; Middle
  Ages 225–6; missionaries 217–18;
  noble/ignoble xv–xvi, 6, 54; past sins
  54; race classification 229–30; sexuality
  225; see also blacks; primitives
schizophrenia 179
science xvii, 203, 215–16, 244
Scotland, civilization/savagery 214, 227
Scythians 26
semiotics 233
sensationalists 42
sensori-motor organization 188
sensory nerves 58–9
sensory perception 61, 89
sex between species 36, 37, 38, 43, 56
sexual abuse, satanism 126, 127
sexual fantasies 234
sexuality: apes 8; arrested development
  157–8, 159, 160; blacks xi, 70, 118,
  120, 147, 220; brain development 174;
  cannibalism 102, 127; Catholicism 225;
  colonials xi, 150–1; and eating 112;
  Europeans xiii, xvii, 223; humans/
  animals 56; interspecies 36, 37, 38, 43,
  56; Others 232; permissiveness 146;
  recapitulation 169; savages 225
Sierra Leone: cannibalism 108, 252 Chap
  8 n7; poem 215; Winterbottom 61–2
skin colour 202, 206; Albertus Magnus 34;
  Chinese 226

skull, closing of sutures 155, 156
skull collections 64, 72, 120–1
skull measurements 77, 84, 87, 251
  Chap 6 n6
slave-traders 115, 116, 218–20
slavery: animality 55; black/white 53–4,
  226; cultural heritage 240; debates of
  197–8; Forster 63; Lawrence 82;
  Middle Ages 226; Portuguese 29–30,
  226; race 228; racists 53–4, 204–5;
  Virey 70
Slavs 66
smell, sense of 179, 206
social dynamics (Comte) 171
social evolutionism 131, 134–9; arrested
  development 160, 162; brain
  development 154; comparative method
  134; Freud 138–9; Greek myths 98;
  Lubbock 136–7; and recapitulation
  166; regression 178; Spencer 78–9, 135;
  Tylor 136
social identity xiv, 247
social psychology xiv–xv, 85
socialization 133–4
Société de Géographie 114, 115
Société Orientale 114
socio-cultural factors 182
sociology 182, 241
sodomy 102
sorcery 243
souls 7, 41, 42, 61
South American Indians 22–3, 122, 153
South Sea Islands 22, 49, 54, 133, 188
Spanish conquistadores 10, 16, 99
spirit beings 235
St Kilda 227
status, biological/theological 238
stereotypes xiv–xv, 16, 27, 28, 31, 146,
  148, 231
sutures of skull 155, 156
syncretism 188

taboo 7
tailed people 38, 40, 43, 86, 114–17,
  252–3 Chap 9 n2, n3
Taino people 10
Tannese people 202, 217
Tasmanian people 138
teeth-sharpening 116, 219, 252 Chap 9
  n1
Terrific Register 112
territoriality 241
Texaco, racism 245

theology, status 238
thinking: abstract 90, 188, 223; cultural
environment 192–3; European structure
24; logical/pre-logical 180; mentally ill
181–2
Thracians 10
Timbuktu 30
*The Times* 109, 162, 209, 210, 245
toe nails 92
toe shape 82, 88, 238
Torres Straits 170
*Totem and Taboo* (Freud) 165
traders 218–22
travel literature 197–8
travellers 24–5, 192; *see also* explorers
Trobrianders 107
troglodyte *40*, 41
Tupinamba people 100, 101, 102, *103*

ugliness 66, 68
universalism, psychology 231
USA: anti-black literature 91–2; blacks
151; cannibalism 245; race theorists
250 Chap 4 n10; racism 245

Vedda people 187

Venus, Hottentot 79, 80, 81, 208, 209
Venus of South America 209
Victoria Nyanza Mission 217
Victorians, racial attitudes 84, 227
voyeurism 211

Wagogo people 217–18
Wakhutu people 201
weaning, arrested development 158–9
'White Man's burden' 148–9
whites *see* Europeans
Wied (traveller) 122
Wild Man of the Woods 4, 5–6, 11, 226,
233, 235
Wild Peter (dumb boy) 250 Chap 4 n2,
Chap 6 n1
wildness xii, 5, 6
witch images 103, 106, 110, 232
Wolof people 28, 224, 255 Chap 14 n5
women: black/white 60; closer to
children 215; as degenerates xv;
giving birth 11, 67; mating with
apes 25; raped by apes 8, 36, 45;
sensitivity to pain 238; sexuality
56–7, 118, 120; shared 11, 31; wild
5, *6*